KU-432-617

MODERN
ENGLISH GRAMMAR

BY

J. C. NESFIELD, M.A.

REVISED (1924) IN ACCORDANCE WITH
THE VIEWS OF THE JOINT COMMITTEE
ON GRAMMATICAL TERMINOLOGY

LONDON
MACMILLAN & CO LTD
NEW YORK · ST MARTIN'S PRESS
1957

*This book is copyright in all countries which
are signatories to the Berne Convention*

—

First Edition 1912
Reprinted 1913 *(twice)*, 1918, 1919, 1920, *(Revised)*. 1924
1927, 1928, 1934, 1939, 1942, 1943, 1944, 1945, 1947, 1949
1953, 1957

MACMILLAN AND COMPANY LIMITED
London Bombay Calcutta Madras Melbourne

THE MACMILLAN COMPANY OF CANADA LIMITED
Toronto

ST MARTIN'S PRESS INC
New York

PRINTED IN GREAT BRITAIN

CONTENTS

PART I.—MODERN ENGLISH GRAMMAR.

PART I.—MODERN ENGLISH GRAMMAR.

CHAPTER I.

ANALYTICAL OUTLINE : GENERAL DEFINITIONS.

1. A Sentence.—A combination of words that makes a *complete* sense is called a **Sentence.** The sense is not complete, unless something is *said* about something else.

> A ship went out to sea.

Note.—There are *four* different kinds of sentences :—

(*a*) **Statements,** *affirming* or *denying* :

> A man's success depends chiefly on himself.   (*Affirmative.*)
> He did not get much help from others.   (*Negative.*)

(*b*) **Questions,** *the interrogative forms of statements,* in some cases mere inversions of them or differing only in tone of voice :

> Have you finished your task ?
> You are going ?

(*c*) **Desires,** including *commands, requests, entreaties, wishes* :

> Rely on your own efforts.
> Lend me a penny.
> Thy kingdom come, Thy will be done.
> May you never have cause to regret it.

(*d*) **Exclamations** are a fourth class of sentence, always distinct in meaning and intonation, and to a great extent also in form, from both statements and questions ; but they do not stand on the same level of importance as the other three kinds of sentences enumerated above :

> What a foolish fellow you have been !
> How silly !

2. Subject and Predicate.—The word or words denoting the person or thing about which something is said are called the **Subject** of the sentence.

> A *ship* went out to sea.

The word or words which say something about the person or thing denoted by the Subject, as "*went out,*" are called the **Predicate.**[1]

---

[1] The student must therefore guard against such definitions as "The subject is what we speak about" ; or "The subject is that concerning which something is asserted." In point of fact, we make no assertion con-

E

Hence no sentence can be made without a Subject and a Predicate. These two things are necessary to make a *complete* sense.

But the subject may be understood as in *go*, and in almost all other Imper. sentences. In such a sentence as " *Companion, hence !* " (Shaks.), both the verb and the subject are understood.

3. A Phrase.—A combination of words that make sense, but not a *complete* sense, is called a **Phrase.**

On the river.   Through thick and thin.   A bird in the hand.

The student will therefore understand that a phrase *cannot contain a Predicate* either expressed or understood.

4. A Clause.—A sentence which is *part of a larger sentence* is called a **Clause.**

This is the house | where we live.

Here " where we live " is a sentence, because it has a subject " we " and a predicate " live." Similarly " this is the house " is a sentence, having " this " for its subject and " is " for its predicate. But both are *parts of a larger sentence*, and hence each of them is called a clause.

5. Nouns.—If we give a name to some person or thing, such as *man, house, ship*, we call the word used for this purpose a **Noun.** Hence a noun is the *naming* word.

6. Pronouns.—If instead of mentioning or repeating a noun we use some other word which will show what noun we are referring to, we call the word so used a **Pronoun.**

A ship went to sea, and *she* had all her sails up.

Here the pronoun " she " is used instead of the noun " ship," and saves its being mentioned twice.   Hence a pronoun is a *substitute* word, and its chief use is *to save the mentioning or repetition of a noun.*

7. Adjectives.—If we wish to restrict the application of a noun by adding something to its meaning, we call the word used for this purpose an **Adjective.**   More briefly, the adjective is said to *qualify* the noun.

A fine ship went out to sea.

The word *Adjective* means " adding," and is so called because it adds something to the meaning of a noun.   In the above sentence we do not speak of any kind of ship, but only of *a fine* ship.

8. Verbs.—If we wish to *say* something about something else, we call the word used for saying it a **Verb.**

A fine ship *went out* to sea.

---

cerning the Subject, but only about the *person or thing denoted* by the Subject.   If we say, " The ox is dead," we make no assertion about the *noun* " ox "—the subject, but about the *thing* or *animal* " ox " denoted by the noun.

Here the word which predicates or says something about a ship is "went out." This is therefore a verb; and thus *the predicate of a sentence must be a verb*, or it must at least contain one.

9. Preposition with its Object.—In the phrase "to sea,' the word "to" is called a **Preposition**. This word expresses the relation in which the thing denoted by "sea" stands to the event denoted by "went out."

The noun, pronoun, or other noun-equivalent that follows the preposition is called its **Object**.

The use of a preposition, then, is *to show the relation in which the person or thing denoted by its Object stands to something else.*[1]

10. Conjunctions.—A Conjunction is a *joining* word. It joins words and phrases to one another, or one sentence to another sentence.

> (*a*) He made himself mean *and* of no reputation.
> (*b*) May he live long *and* (may he) die happily.

In (*a*) the adjective "mean" is joined to the phrase "of no reputation" by the conjunction "and."

In (*b*) the sentence "may he live long" is joined by the same conjunction to the sentence "may he die happily."

11. Adverbs.—These, like adjectives, are *qualifying* words. An adjective, as we have shown, qualifies a *noun;* an adverb qualifies *any part of speech except a noun or pronoun.*[2]

That *very* fine ship has *already* sailed *half* through the Channel.

Here "very" is an adverb qualifying the adjective "fine"; "already" is an adverb qualifying the verb "has sailed"; and "half" is an adverb qualifying the preposition "through."

12. Interjections.—If we wish to express some feeling or emotion by a single word, and without using a whole sentence for the purpose, we call the word so used an **Interjection**.

> My son, *alas!* is not industrious.

Here "alas" is a sound thrown into the sentence to express regret. Observe that the word *alas!* is not syntactically connected with the rest of the sentence, but is a mere sound thrown into it (Lat. *inter,*

---

[1] The student must guard against such a definition as "A Preposition joins a noun to a word, indicating some relation between the noun and the word thus joined with it." In point of fact, *all* Parts of Speech (excepting interjections), and not merely prepositions, indicate relations between *words*. The peculiar function of a preposition is that it indicates a relation between *things*, that is, between the things denoted by words, and not between the words themselves.

[2] An Adverb is generally defined to be a "word used to qualify verbs, adjectives, or other adverbs." The inadequacy of this definition, which excludes Prepositions and Conjunctions from the qualifying power of adverbs, is further shown in § 216.

between, *jactus,* thrown). In this respect it stands on a different footing from all other parts of speech.

13. The Parts of Speech defined.—Words are classified according to the purpose that they are used for, and every such class is called a **Part of Speech.** (Hence, in *parsing* a word, the first thing to do is to say what *part* (quae *pars*) of speech it belongs to.) The Parts of Speech can be thus defined :—

(1) A Noun is a word used for naming some person or thing.

(2) A Pronoun is a word used instead of a noun or noun-equivalent.

(3) An Adjective is a word used to qualify a noun.

(4) A Verb is a word used for saying something about some person or thing.

(5) A Preposition is a word placed before a noun or noun-equivalent to show in what relation the person or thing denoted by the noun stands to something else.

(6) A Conjunction is a word used to join words or phrases together, or one clause to another clause.

(7) An Adverb is a word used to qualify any part of speech except a noun or pronoun.

(8) An Interjection is a word or sound thrown into a sentence to express some feeling of the mind.

Note.—Observe that the Part of Speech to which a word belongs depends on *the purpose that the word is used for* in that particular context, and that the same word may be of a different Part of Speech in a different context. Thus *man* is a noun in "The *man* has come" ; but a verb in "*Man* the lifeboat."

14. The Articles.—The words "a" and "the" are called **Articles.** "The" is called the *Definite* Article, because it particularises a noun. "A" or "an" is called the *Indefinite,* because it does not particularise a noun, but generalises it.

The articles are not a distinct part of speech, but merely adjectives. "A" or "an" is an abbreviated form of the adjective "one" ; while "the" is the root form of "this," "that," "these," "those."

15. Finite Verb : Number and Person.—Any part of a verb that can be used *as the Predicate of a sentence* is called **Finite.**

The word "*finite*" means "limited." A finite verb is so called, because it is limited to the same **Person** (*First, Second,* or *Third*) and to the same **Number** (*Singular* or *Plural*) as its Subject.

(*a*) I *see* him.　　　　　(*b*) They *see* him.

In both sentences the form of the verb "see" is the same. But in (*a*) the verb is in the First person, because its Subject "I" is in the First person, and in the Singular number, because its Subject is Singular. Similarly in (b) the verb is in the Third person, because its Subject "they" is in the Third person, and plural, because its Subject is Plural.

16. Parts of a Verb not finite.—There are some parts of a verb which are not finite, that is, are not limited to any particular Number or Person, because they cannot be used with a Subject or be made the Predicates of a sentence.

Such parts are three in number :—(1) the **Infinitive** mood, as "I wish *to retire*"; (2) a **Participle,** as "a *retired* officer"; (3) a **Gerund,** as "I think of *retiring.*"

Note.—These, though they are parts of a verb, have lost what is most essential in the verb-character ; that is, they do not enable us to *say* something about something else.

17. Double Parts of Speech.—Besides the eight parts of speech shown in § 13, there are four more which must be called double, or two parts of speech combined in one :—

(1) A **Participle.**—This is a verb and adjective combined.

A *retired* officer lives next door.

The word "retired" is a verb, because it is part of the verb "retire." It is also an adjective, because it qualifies the noun "officer." Hence a participle may be called a verbal adjective.

(2) A **Gerund.**—This is a verb and noun combined.

I think of *retiring* soon from service.

Here "retiring" is a verb, because it is part of the verb "retire." It is also a noun, because it is the object to the preposition "of."

(3) An **Infinitive.**—This too is a verb and noun combined.

I wish *to return* that book.

Here to return is a verb, because it is part of the verb "return." It is also a noun, because it is object (see § 42) to the verb "wish."

(4) A **Relative Pronoun** or **Adverb.**—A Relative pronoun, such as *who, which,* etc., or a Relative adverb, such as *where, when,* etc., has the character of a pronoun or adverb combined with that of a conjunction.

This is the house *where* we live.

Here "where" is an adverb, because it qualifies the verb "live." It is also a conjunction, because it joins the two sentences. Hence, relative adverbs have been sometimes called **conjunctive** adverbs. Similarly, relative pronouns have been called **conjunctive** pronouns.

18. Apposition of Noun with Noun.—A noun is said to be in apposition with another noun, or with a pronoun, when it refers to the same person or thing :—

Noun.—Philip, *king* of Macedon, was father to Alexander the Great.
Pronoun.—I, the *man* you were looking for, am here.

A 2

19. Apposition of Sentence with Noun.—Whenever a sentence is in apposition with a noun, the sentence must be introduced by the conjunction "that."

The rumour *that you were coming* was generally believed.

20. Apposition of Noun with Sentence.—A noun can be in apposition with a sentence or with some implied noun, which (if it were expressed) would denote the action of the verb.

He killed his prisoners,—*a barbarous act.* (Here "act" is in apposition with the implied noun, the *killing* of prisoners.)

21. Forms of Subject.—The Subject to a sentence must be either a noun or a noun-equivalent. The principal forms in which a Subject can be expressed are as follows :—

(*a*) Noun : A *ship* went out to sea.
(*b*) Pronoun : *He* (some one previously named) was convicted.
(*c*) Infinitive : *To err* (= error or proneness to error) is human.
(*d*) Gerund : *Sleeping* is necessary to health.
(*e*) Phrase : *How to do this* puzzles all of us.
(*f*) Clause : *Whoever was caught* was sent to jail.

22. Verbs used Transitively : Verb and Object.—A verb is used **Transitively**, if the action or feeling denoted by the verb does not stop with itself, but is directed towards some person or thing. The word or words denoting such person or thing are called the **Object** to the verb.

That snake bit *the man.*

23. Forms of Object.—The various forms in which the Object can be expressed are the same as those in which the Subject can be expressed. See § 21.

(*a*) Noun : That snake bit *the man.*
(*b*) Pronoun : That snake bit *him.*
(*c*) Infinitive : We desire *to succeed* (=success).
(*d*) Gerund : He loves *riding.*
(*e*) Phrase : We do not know *how to do this.*
(*f*) Clause : We do not know *what he wants.*

24. Complement. — Some Transitive verbs require not only an Object (as all Transitive verbs do), but also some other word or words to make the predication complete. They are, in fact, **Transitive verbs of Incomplete predication.**

The word or words that complete the predication (that is complete what the verb left unsaid) are called the **Complement**

He put the school (object) *into good order* (complement).
That grief drove him (object) *mad* (complement).
They made him (object) *laugh* (complement).

There is no sense in saying "he put the school," "that grief drove him," "they made him"; hence each verb must have a Complement.

25. Verbs used Intransitively.—A verb is used **Intransitively**, if the action or feeling denoted by the verb stops with itself, and is not directed towards anything else.

Fish *swim*.   Rivers *flow*.   All animals *die*.

26. Intransitive Verbs with Complement.—But Intransitive verbs, though they do not require an Object, may require a Complement, as some Transitive verbs also do.

Such verbs are called **Intransitive Verbs of Incomplete Predication.**

He became *a good scholar*.   Sleep is *necessary to health*.

27. Absolute use of Verbs.—A verb is said to be used absolutely, when it is not grammatically related to the rest of the sentence :—

(*a*) **Participle** (further explained in § 284) :—

The sun having set, all went home.   (*With Noun*.)
Supposing we are late, the door will be locked. (*Without Noun*.)

(*b*) **Infinitive Mood** (further explained in § 191 and § 192):—

To think that he should have told a lie ! (*Simple*.)
I am,—*to speak* plainly,—much displeased with you. (*Gerundial*.)

(*c*) **Imperative Mood** (further explained in § 180) :—

A few men,—*say* twelve,—may be expected shortly.

28. Introductory Adverb. — When the subject to an *Intransitive* verb is placed *after* its verb, the verb is usually introduced by the adverb "*there*." In this relation "*there*" does not signify "in that place," but merely serves *to introduce the verb*. It has no signification whatever.

There are *some men* (subject) who never drink wine.
There came a *maiden* (subject) to my door.

29. Kinds of Phrases.—The following kinds of phrases should be distinguished from one another :—

(*a*) **Adverb** phrase, or one which does the work of an adverb :—

I hope you will work better *in future*.
Bind him *hand and foot*, and take him **away**.

(*b*) **Preposition** phrase, or one which does the work of a preposition. (Such phrases end in a simple preposition.)

> *In the event of* our father's death, we shall be left poor.
> He worked hard *for the sake of* a prize.

(*c*) **Conjunction** phrase, or one which does the work of a conjunction. (Such phrases end in a simple conjunction.)

> I am tired *as well as* hungry.
> He took medicine *in order that* he might recover.

(*d*) **Absolute Participle** phrase; see § 284.

> *The sun having set*, they all went home.

(*e*) **Interjection** or exclamatory phrase; see § 241.

> *Well to be sure !*   *For shame !*   *Good heavens !*

CHAPTER II.—NOUNS.

SECTION 1.—THE KINDS OF NOUNS.

30. Noun defined.—A Noun is a word used for naming some person or thing (§ 13).

31. Nouns are of five different kinds :—

1. Proper (one thing at a time).
2. Common (any number of things).
3. Collective (a group of things).
4. Material (what a thing is made of).
5. Abstract (quality, state, or action).

Proper Nouns.

32. A **Proper Noun** denotes *one particular* person or thing as distinct from every other ; as *James* (a person), *Kenilworth* (a book), *Paris* (a city), *France* (a country).

Note 1.—The writing of a Proper noun should always be commenced with a capital letter.

Note 2.—A word or phrase is sometimes added to a proper noun to prevent ambiguity of reference. Thus we say, "Alexander *the Great*," or "*St.* Paul," or "Boston *in America*," to show which Alexander, or which Paul, or which Boston is meant : for many different persons or places might be called by these names.

Note. 3.—A large number of nouns now Proper were originally Common. A common name, as Brown, Smith, Baker, Clark (clerc), Shepherd, Butcher, Parson, Mason, etc., being frequently applied to some individual by way of distinction, was eventually restricted to that individual and his family, and so the Common name becomes a Proper name. Words, such as Father, Mother, Baby, Granny, though really Common names, are in most families used as Proper names, to denote certain individuals; as when a man says to his child, "Where is Mother?" Proper names of rivers, such as *Avon* (Celtic), *Congo* (African), were once common names for "river."

Note 4.—The name Proper is from Lat. *proprius*, one's own. Hence a Proper name means *one's own individual name*, as distinct from a Common name, that can be given to a class of individuals.

Common Nouns.

33. A **Common Noun** denotes no one person or thing in particular, but is *common to any and every person or thing of the same kind;* as "man," "book," "country."

Thus, *man* does not point out any particular man, such as James, but can be used for any and every man. *Book* does not point out any particular book, such as *Kenilworth*, but can be used for any and every book. *Country* does not point out any particular country, such as *France*, but can be used for any country in any part of the world.

Note.—The name *Common* is from the Lat. *communis*, and means that which is shared by several different individuals possessing some common characteristic, in virtue of which the name can be given to any and all of them.

34. A **Proper Noun** is said to be "*used as a Common Noun*," when it denotes (*a*) some rank or office, or (*b*) some class of persons or things.

(*a*) Such words as *Cæsar, Caliph, Sultan, Khedive, Czar,* etc., are used as Common nouns, because they denote persons holding a certain rank or office : thus we can speak of "the twelve Cæsars," "the first four Caliphs," "the Sultan of Turkey," "the Czar of Russia."

(*b*) A Proper noun becomes a Common noun, when it denotes a class of persons or things and is used in a descriptive sense. "He is *the Newton* of the age,"—that is, the greatest astronomer of the age.

Collective Nouns.

35. A **Collective Noun** denotes a *group* or *collection* of *similar individuals*, considered as one complete whole.

For instance, there may be *many sheep* in a field, but only *one flock.* Here "sheep" is a Common noun, because it may stand for any and every sheep ; but "flock" is a Collective noun, because it stands for all the sheep at once, and not for any one sheep taken separately.

36. A Collective Noun may be either Common or Proper.

Thus the term "flock" may stand for many different flocks. But "parliament," "the church," stand for only one body.

37. Nouns of Multitude.—A distinction is made between a Collective Noun and a Noun of Multitude :—

(*a*) A Collective noun denotes *one undivided whole;* and hence the verb following is singular (§ 15).

The jury *consists* of twelve persons.

(*b*) A noun of Multitude denotes the *individuals* of the group ; and hence the verb is plural, although the noun is singular (§ 15).

The jury (the men on the jury) *were* divided in their opinions.

Nouns of Material.

38. A noun of **Material** denotes some particular kind of *matter* or *substance*.

Thus "sheep" is a Common noun ; but "mutton" (or the flesh of sheep) is a Material noun.

39. The same word can be a Material noun or a Common noun according to the sense.

> *Fish* live in water.   *Fish* is good for food.

In the first sentence the noun denotes individual fish or fishes, and is therefore a Common noun.   In the second it denotes the matter of which the bodies of fish are made, and is therefore a Material noun.

Abstract Nouns.

40. An **Abstract Noun** denotes some *quality*, *state*, or *action*, apart from anything possessing the quality, etc.

> *Quality*—Cleverness, height, humility, roguery, colour.
> *State*—Poverty, manhood, bondage, pleasure, youth.
> *Action*—Laughter, movement, flight, choice, revenge.

The four kinds of nouns first named all relate to *physical objects*, to anything in short that can be weighed or measured. On the other hand, **Abstract** nouns are names of *qualities*, *states*, or *actions*, that we try to think of as if they belonged to no particular objects, but existed merely as general notions formed by the mind of the observer.

For example : We know that a stone is *hard*.   We also know that iron is *hard*.   We also know that a brick is *hard*.   We can therefore speak of *hardness* apart from stone, or iron, or brick, or any other object having the same quality.   "Abstract" means "drawn off" (abstracted in thought) from the object.   Hence *hardness* is an abstract noun ; while *stone* or *brick* or *iron* is a concrete noun.

41. The same word may be an Abstract noun or a Common noun, according to the purpose for which it is used.

When an Abstract noun is "*used as a Common noun*," it may denote (*a*) the *person* possessing the quality, or (*b*) the *thing* to which the action, state, or quality belongs : [1]—

---

[1] The conversion of Abstract nouns to Common nouns is due to the fact that it is much easier to think of some person or thing than to think of an abstract quality apart from any person or thing.   Hence we are naturally disposed to transfer the name of the quality to the name of the person or thing possessing the quality.

(a) Examples of Persons.

Justice	{ 1. The quality of being just . . .	Abstract
	{ 2. A judge, or one who administers justice	Common
Beauty	{ 1. The quality or state of being beautiful	Abstract
	{ 2. A person possessing beauty . .	Common
Authority	{ 1. The power or right to command . .	Abstract
	{ 2. A person possessing authority . .	Common
Nobility	{ 1. The quality of being noble. . .	Abstract
	{ 2. Those who are of the class of nobles .	Common
Witness	{ 1. Evidence or testimony . . .	Abstract
	{ 2. One who gives the evidence . .	Common

(b) Examples of Things.

Judgment	{ 1. The act or quality of judging . .	Abstract
	{ 2. The verdict given by the judge . .	Common
Sight	{ 1. The art or faculty of seeing . .	Abstract
	{ 2. The thing seen: "a fine sight". .	Common
Speech	{ 1. The faculty of speaking . . .	Abstract
	{ 2. The speech delivered: the word spoken	Common
Wonder	{ 1. The feeling of wonder or surprise .	Abstract
	{ 2. The wonderful event or object . .	Common
Kindness	{ 1. The quality of being kind . . .	Abstract
	{ 2. The kind thing done . . .	Common

42. The Gerunds and the Simple Infinitives of verbs (§ 188) are in fact, though not in form, kinds of Abstract nouns. The following sentences all mean the same thing :—

> *Service* is better than idleness. (*Abstract Noun.*)
> *Serving* is better than idleness. (*Gerund.*)
> *To serve* is better than idleness. (*Infinitive Mood.*)

43. An Abstract noun is used as a Proper noun, when it is **personified**,—that is, when it is spoken of as an individual person. It must then be commenced with a capital letter, as Proper nouns are.

> He is the favoured child of *Fortune*.
> Let not *Ambition* mock their useful toil.

44. There are two ways in which a Proper, Material, or Abstract noun can be used as (or changed into) a Common noun :—(a) by putting an article ("a" or "the") before it ; (b) by putting it into the plural number.

Proper Noun.	Common Nouns.
Daniel was a learned Jew.	{ *A Daniel* come to judgment.
	{ There are more *Daniels* than one.
Material Noun.	
Pear is my favourite fruit.	{ Give me *the pear* in your hand.
	{ Give me one of your *pears*.
Abstract Noun.	
Justice is a noble quality.	{ He is *a justice* of the peace.
	{ There are four *justices* present.

Point out the kind or use of each of the nouns occurring below :—

Alexander the Great, king of Macedon, was conqueror of Persia. A man ignorant of the arts of reading, writing, and ciphering is, in point of knowledge, more like a child than a man. The proper study of mankind is man. Cows are as fond of grass as men are of milk, or bears of honey. Health is one of the greatest blessings that a man or woman can hope to enjoy in this bodily existence. The Czar of Russia, although he was lord of the eastern half of Europe and the northern half of Asia, besides being master of a huge army and a large fleet, could not live in peace and safety with his own subjects, and could not leave his own palace without fear.

Section 2.—Substitutes for a Noun.

45. The following kinds of words or combinations of words can be used as substitutes for a Noun ; see §§ 21, 23 :—

(a) A Pronoun :—

> Your horse is white ; mine is a black *one* (= horse).

(b) An Adjective used as a Noun or with some noun understood :—

> *The blind* (= blind men) receive their sight.
> *The just* (= justice) is higher than *the expedient* (= expediency).

(c) A Verb in the Infinitive mood :—

> He desires *to succeed* (= success).

(d) A Gerund :—

> He was fond of *sleeping* (= sleep).

(e) A Phrase :—

> No one knew *how to do this* (= the method of doing this).

(f) A Noun-clause ; that is, a clause which does the work of a noun ; (for the definition of "clause" see § 4).

> *Who steals my purse* (= the stealer of my purse) steals trash.

Section 3.—Gender.

46. Gender.—In the grammar of Modern English, difference of Gender coincides with difference of sex or with the absence of sex :[1]—

(1) **Masculine** : *male* animals : bull, horse, hog.
(2) **Feminine** : *female* animals : cow, mare, sow.
(3) **Common** : animals of *either* sex : parent, child.

---

[1] In the proper sense of the word, this is not gender at all, since it is not based on *the form of the word.* "Gender" appears only in *he, she, it.*

(4) **Neuter** : things of *neither* sex, that is, things without life : *box, flock, pain.*

Note.—We often take no account of the sex of young children or of lower animals ; so in speaking of them we use Neuter pronouns:—

> The *child* is asleep ; let *it* sleep on.
> Have you a *horse?* will you let me ride *it?*

47. Modes of denoting Gender.—There are three different ways in which the gender or sex of living beings is indicated.—

I. By a change of word ; as *bull, cow.*

II. By adding a word ; as *he-goat, she-goat.*

III. By adding *ess* to the Masculine ; as *priest, priestess.*

I. *By a change of word :*

Masculine.	Feminine.	Masculine.	Feminine.
Bachelor	maid (or spinster)	Horse(or stallion)	mare
Boar	sow	Husband	wife
Boy	girl	King	queen
Brother	sister	Lord	lady
Buck	doe	Man	woman
Bull (or ox)	cow	Milter (fish)	spawner
Bullock(or steer)	heifer	Nephew	niece
Cock	hen	Papa	mamma
Colt	filly	Ram (or wether)	ewe
Dog	bitch (or slut)	Sir	madam (or dame)
Drake	duck	Sire	dam
Drone	bee	(father of colt)	(mother of colt)
Earl	countess	Sloven	slut
Father	mother	Son	daughter
Friar (or monk)	nun	Stag	hind
Gander	goose	Swain	nymph
Gentleman	lady	Uncle	aunt
Hart	roe	Wizard	witch

Note.—There are some Feminine nouns which have no corresponding Masculine :—*blonde, brunette, coquette, dowager, dowdy, drab, jilt, prude, shrew, siren, termagant, virago.*

II. *By adding a word :*

Masculine.	Feminine.	Masculine.	Feminine.
Billy-goat	nanny-goat	Grand-father	grand-mother
Buck-rabbit	doe-rabbit	Tom-cat	tib-cat
Cock-sparrow	hen-sparrow	Land-lord	land-lady
He-goat	she-goat	Pea-cock	pea-hen
Jack-ass	she-ass	Bull-calf	cow-calf
Man-servant	maid-servant	Washer-man	washer-woman

Note.—The Masculine "roe-buck" has no corresponding Feminine ; and the Feminine "ewe-lamb" has no corresponding Masculine.

III. *By adding* ess *to the Masculine:*

(a) By adding *ess* to the Masculine without any change in the form of the Masculine :—

Masculine.	Feminine.	Masculine.	Feminine.
Author	author-ess	Patron	patron-ess
Baron	baron-ess	Peer	peer-ess
Count	count-ess	Poet	poet-ess
Giant	giant-ess	Priest	priest-ess
God	godd-ess	Prince	princ-ess
Heir	heir-ess	Prior	prior-ess
Host	host-ess	Prophet	prophet-ess
Jew	Jew-ess	Shepherd	shepherd-ess
Lion	lion-ess	Viscount	viscount-ess

(b) By adding *ess*, and omitting the vowel of the last syllable of the Masculine :—

Masculine.	Feminine.	Masculine.	Feminine.
Actor	actr-ess	Negro	negr-ess
Benefactor	benefactr-ess	Porter	portr-ess
Conductor	conductr-ess	Songster	songstr-ess
Director	directr-ess	Tempter	temptr-ess
Enchanter	enchantr-ess	Tiger	tigr-ess
Hunter	huntr-ess	Traitor	traitr-ess
Instructor	instructr-ess	Votary	votar-ess

(c) By adding *ess* to the Masculine in a less regular way :—

Masculine.	Feminine.	Masculine.	Feminine.
Abbot	abbess	Master (boy)	miss (girl)
Duke	duchess	Mr.	Mrs.
Emperor	empress	Marquis ⎫ Marquess ⎭	marchioness
Governor	governess		
Lad	lass	Murderer	murderess
Master (teacher, etc.)	mistress	Sorcerer	sorceress

48. The following modes of distinction between Masculine and Feminine are exceptional :—

Masculine.	Feminine.	Masculine.	Feminine.
Bridegroom	bride	Fox	vixen
Widower	widow		

49. Foreign Feminines :—

Masculine.	Feminine.	Masculine.	Feminine.
Administrator	administratrix	Hero	heroine
Beau	belle	Prosecutor	prosecutrix
Czar	czarina	Signor	signora
Don	donna	Sultan	sultana
Executor	executrix	Testator	testatrix

50. Double Feminines.—The two examples of this are *songstress* and *seamstress* (sometimes spelt as *sempstress*).

Originally *ster* was a Feminine suffix, as it still is in "spinster." But the Feminine force of *ster* in "songster" and "seamster" has been lost, and so the Feminine form is now shown by changing *er* into *ress*.

51. The following are examples of Nouns in the **Common** gender :—

Parent—father or mother.
Relation—male or female.
Friend—enemy—male or female.
Cousin—male or female cousin.
Bird—cock or hen.
Peafowl—peacock or peahen.
Flirt—man or maid.
Fowl—cock or hen.
Child—son or daughter.
Deer—stag or hind.
Fallow-deer—buck or doe.
Baby—male or female.
Servant—man or maid.
Monarch—king or queen.

Person—man or woman.
Pupil—boy or girl.
Orphan—male or female.
Pig—boar or sow.
Sheep—ram or ewe.
Elephant—male or female.
Cat—male or female.
Rat—male or female.
Mouse—male or female.
Spouse—husband or wife.
Foal—colt or filly.
Calf—bullock or heifer.

Note.—Some Masculine nouns, as *colt*, *dog*, *horse*, and some Feminine nouns, as *duck*, *bee*, *goose*, are used to denote either sex, provided that no question arises as to whether the animal named is a male or a female.

> That is a fine little *colt*.
> That *horse* of yours is a splendid stepper.
> A *goose* is a much bigger bird than a *duck*.

52. Gender of Personified Things.—Things without life, when they are personified, are regarded as male or female ; and so, in speaking of them, we use Masculine or Feminine pronouns.

Masculines.—The stronger forces and more striking objects in nature (Winds, Rivers, Mountains, the Ocean, Storm, Thunder, the Sun, Summer, Autumn, Winter) ; the violent passions (Love, Fear, Anger, Despair, etc.) ; violent actions (Murder, War, etc.) ; Time, Day, Sleep, Death, the Grave.

Feminines.—The gentler forces and objects (as the Moon) ; whatever implies fertility or claims attachment (the Church, Nature, the Earth, the Mother-country, Countries, Universities, Ships, Cities, the season of Spring) ; the gentler feelings (Hope, Concord, Justice, Mercy, Charity, Faith, Humility, Modesty, etc.) ; the inferior passions (Jealousy, Pride, Anger, Revenge) ; the Arts and Sciences ; Fame, Liberty, Victory, Religion, Philosophy, Adversity, Prosperity, Fortune, Night, Morning.

A ship is always spoken of as *she*. There is a tendency to use *she* in speaking of a train, a motor car, or any familiar piece of machinery. We also speak of a *sister* ship, a *sister* institution, a *sister* gun.

Section 4.—Case.

53. Case defined.—The *relation* in which a noun stands to some other word, or the *change of form* (if any) by which this relation is indicated, is called its **Case.**[1]

54. There are five Cases in modern English,—*Nominative, Vocative, Accusative, Genitive, Dative.*

But the Genitive is the only case that is *now* indicated by a case-ending or *change of form.* The other cases have lost their case-endings, and are indicated only by grammatical relation.

55. When a noun is used as the *subject* to a verb it is said to be in the **Nominative** case.

Rain falls.   (*Nominative of Subject.*)

55a. When a noun is used for the sake of address it is said to be in the **Vocative** case.

Are you coming, my *friend* ?   (*Vocative.*)

56. When a noun is the *direct object* to a verb or to a preposition, it is said to be in the **Accusative** case.

The man killed a *rat.*   (*Object to Verb.*)

The earth is moistened by *rain.* (*Obj. to Prep.*)

When a noun is the *indirect object* to a verb it is said to be in the **Dative** case.

I gave the *boy* a penny.

57. The **Genitive** case usually denotes the *possessor* or owner. It is formed by adding *'s* (which is called *apostrophe s*) to the noun ; as—

Singular—man's. | *Plural*—men's.

N.B.—The old inflection for the Genitive case was *es.* When the *e* was omitted, as it now always is, the absence of the *e* was indicated by the comma or apostrophe ; as *moon, moones, moon's.*

58. Omission of "s."—There are three kinds of instances in which the *s,* but not the apostrophe, is omitted.

(*a*) After all Plural nouns ending in *s* ; as—

Horses' tails ; the *birds'* nests ; the *dogs'* kennels.

(*b*) Whenever the last syllable of a Singular noun begins and ends with *s* ; as—

Moses' laws.   (But we must say *Venus's* beauty ; *James's* hat, etc.)

(*c*) Whenever the last syllable of a Singular noun ends with *s* or *ce,* and the noun is followed by "sake" ; as—

Conscience' sake ; for *goodness'* sake.   (But if the noun is of one syllable, the *s* must not be omitted :—for *Ross's* sake ; *Ross's* secret.)

---

[1] *Case* lit. means "falling" (Lat. *cas-us*). The Nom. was considered the upright or perpendicular, and the other cases were said to fall off to one side of it, and were hence called *oblique* or slanting. Since English nouns have lost every case-ending but one (the Genitive), the term "case" is etymologically inappropriate. We retain it, however, to denote grammatical relation as well as change of form.

Note.—In poetry the omission of apostrophe *s* is common in words ending with *s*. Poets are guided simply by the metre :—

> As thick as *Ajax'* seven-fold shield.—BUTLER.

In prose we should say and write *Ajax's*.

59. Rare use of Genitive.—The Genitive case was once used with any kind of noun ; but it is now restricted to such examples as those shown below :—

(1) Nouns denoting *persons ;* as—

Henry's book ; a *man's* foot. (But we cannot say "a library's book," "the stocking's foot," since "library" and "stocking" are inanimate objects.)

(2) Nouns denoting any kind of *living* thing other than man ; as—

> A *cat's* tail ; a *horse's* head ; a *bird's* feathers.

(3) Nouns denoting *personified* things ; as—

> *Fortune's* favourite ; *Sorrow's* tears ; *England's* heroes.

(4) Nouns denoting time, space, or weight ; as—

Time.—A *day's* journey ; a *month's* holiday ; three *weeks'* leave ; a *year's* absence ; at six *months'* sight ; three *days'* grace.
Space.—A *boat's* length ; a *hand's* breadth ; a *hair's* breadth ; a *razor's* edge ; a *stone's* throw ; a *needle's* point.
Weight.—A *pound's* weight ; a *ton's* weight.

(5) Nouns signifying certain dignified objects ; as—

The *court's* decree ; the *sun's* rays ; the *moon's* crescent ; *nature's* works ; the *earth's* axis ; the *soul's* delight ; *heaven's* will ; the *law's* delays ; *truth's* triumph ; the *mind's* eye ; the *ocean's* roar ; *duty's* call ; the *country's* good.

> Let all the ends thou aim'st at be thy *country's*,
> Thy *God's*, and *truth's*.—*Hen. VIII.* iii. 2.

Note.—The Genitive is also used in a few familiar phrases, in which it has been retained for the sake of shortness—

Out of *harm's* way ; at his *wit's* end ; for *mercy's* sake ; he did it to his *heart's* content ; the *ship's* passengers ; at his *fingers'* ends ; he got to his *journey's* end ; the *boat's* crew.

60. Genitive Case in Apposition.—When one Genitive case is in Apposition with another (§ 18), the apostrophe *s* is added either to the first or to the last, not usually to both.

> Herod married his *brother* Philip's wife.

It is not wrong, however, and has now become more usual, to say "He called at Smith's, the grocer's."

61. Genitive Case in Phrases.—The *'s* may be added to

the last word of a phrase, when the phrase is regarded as a Compound noun and denotes some person or persons.

My son-in-law's house.
The Duke of Sutherland's death.

Section 5.—Number.

62. The form assumed by a noun to show whether it denotes one thing or more than one is called its Number.

When *one* thing is spoken of, the noun is *Singular ;* when *two* or *more* things are spoken of, the noun is *Plural.*

The only kinds of nouns that (strictly speaking) admit of being pluralised are Common and Collective nouns.

But Proper, Material, and Abstract nouns can also be put in the Plural number, when they are used as Common nouns (§ 44).

63. The general rule for forming the Plural number of a noun is by adding *s* to the Singular ; as—

Singular.	*Plural.*	*Singular.*	*Plural.*
Hand	hands	House	houses

But if the noun ends in *s, x, z, sh,* or *ch,* the Plural is formed by adding *es* to the Singular ; as—

Singular.	*Plural.*	*Singular.*	*Plural.*
Glass	glass-es	Brush	brush-es
Box	box-es	Bench	bench-es

64. If the noun ends in *y* and the *y* is preceded by a *consonant,* the Plural takes the form of *-ies.* (In proper names, however, we simply add the *s* to the Singular, as *Mary, Marys.*)

Singular.	*Plural.*	*Singular.*	*Plural.*
Duty	duties	Army	armies
Fly	flies	Lady	ladies

Note.—In older English, however, the Singular was spelt as *dutie.* Hence the Plural is really formed according to the rule given in § 63, and it is the Singular that has changed.

But if the final *y* is preceded by a *vowel,* the Plural is formed by simply adding *s* to the Singular :—

Singular.	*Plural.*	*Singular.*	*Plural.*
Day	days	Monkey	monkeys
Play	plays	Toy	toys
Key	keys	Boy	boys

Note.—Nouns ending in *quy* form the Plural in *ies,* because in such words the *u* does not make a diphthong with *y,* but the *qu* (= *kw*) is regarded as a double consonant ; as, *colloquy, colloquies.*

65. If the noun ends in *o,* and the *o* is preceded by a *consonant,* the Plural is generally formed by adding *es :*—

Singular.	Plural.	Singular.	Plural.
Cargo	cargoes	Mango	mangoes
Hero	heroes	Potato	potatoes
Buffalo	buffaloes	Echo	echoes
Motto	mottoes	Tornado	tornadoes
Negro	negroes	Volcano	volcanoes

But all nouns ending in *o* preceded by a vowel, and some ending in *o* preceded by a consonant, form the Plural in *s*, and not in *es* :—

Singular.	Plural.	Singular.	Plural.
Bamboo	bamboos	Grotto	grottos
Cuckoo	cuckoos	Halo	halos
Portfolio	portfolios	Memento	mementos
Embryo	embryos	Proviso	provisos
Cameo	cameos	Tiro	tiros
Seraglio	seraglios	Piano	pianos
Hindoo	Hindoos	Canto	cantos
Curio	curios	Solo	solos

There are a few nouns ending in *o*, which form the Plural both in *s* and *es* :—

Singular.	Plural.
Calico	calicos or calicoes
Mosquito	mosquitos or mosquitoes
Portico	porticos or porticoes

66. If the noun ends in *f* or *fe*, the Plural is generally formed by changing *f* or *fe* into *ves* :—

Singular.	Plural.	Singular.	Plural.
Wife	wives	Calf	calves
Knife	knives	Half	halves
Life	lives	Myself	ourselves
Sheaf	sheaves	Shelf	shelves
Leaf	leaves	Wolf	wolves
Thief	thieves	Beef	beeves

But there are some nouns ending in *f* which form the Plural by simply adding *s* (in accordance with the general rule given in § 63) :—

Singular.	Plural.	Singular.	Plural.
Reef	reefs	Wharf	wharfs (or wharves)
Chief	chiefs	Dwarf	dwarfs
Roof	roofs	Turf	turfs (or turves)
Hoof	hoofs (or hooves)	Gulf	gulfs
Proof	proofs	Cliff	cliffs
Scarf	scarfs (or scarves)	Grief	griefs

There are at least three nouns ending in *fe* which form the Plural by simply adding *s* :—

Safe—safes ; strife—strifes ; fife—fifes.

67. There are eight nouns which form the Plural by a change of the inside vowel. (These are called Mutation-plurals.)

Singular	Plural	Singular	Plural
Man	men	Tooth	teeth
Woman	women	Louse	lice
Foot	feet	Mouse	mice
Goose	geese	Dormouse	dormice

Note.—The plural of "mongoose," however awkward it may sound, is "mongooses," since the word is not compounded with "goose."

There are four nouns which form the Plural in *en* or *ne* :—

Ox	oxen	Brother	brethren (see § 73)
Child	children	Cow	kine (or cows) (see § 73)

68. A compound noun forms the Plural by adding *s* to the principal word :—

Singular.	Plural.	Singular.	Plural.
Father-in-law	fathers-in-law	Maid-servant	maid-servants
Son-in-law	sons-in-law	Foot-man	foot-men
Mother-in-law	mothers-in-law	Washer-man	washer-men
Daughter-in-law	daughters-in-law	Knight-errant	knights-errant
Step-son	step-sons	Coat-of-mail	coats-of-mail
Step-daughter	step-daughters	Court-martial	courts-martial
Hanger-on	hangers-on	Commander-in-	commanders-in-
Looker-on	lookers-on	chief	chief
Passer-by	passers-by		

In the above examples the distinguishing word or phrase is sometimes placed first, as in *step-son*, and sometimes last as in *father-in-law*. In either case it is not the distinguishing word or phrase that receives the suffix *s*, but the noun qualified by it. This rule applies to all of the above examples.

Note.—*Castaway* and nouns like *handful* are rather peculiar. *Castaway* is a compound participle used as a noun, which therefore takes the *s* at the end of the word, as *castaways*. *Handful*, though originally "a hand full," or enough to fill a hand, has become a compound noun, which forms its plural as *handfuls*.

There are four compound nouns which take a double Plural:—

Singular.	Plural.	Singular.	Plural.
Man-servant	men-servants	Lord-justice	lords-justices
Woman-servant	women-servants	Knight-Templar	Knights-Templars

Here two nouns are in apposition, the distinguishing noun being placed first to qualify or restrict the second. The second noun is the only one that could *claim* the plural suffix ; cf. *maid-servants, washermen*. The first noun is pluralised by attraction.

In a phrase like "Miss Brown" two different forms are used for the plural. We may either say "the Miss Browns" or "the Misses Brown." The latter is the more correct, but it is considered pedantic.

69. Foreign Plurals.—These are some Plurals which have been borrowed direct from foreign nouns :—

Singular.	Plural.	Singular.	Plural.
(Latin)		(Greek)	
Agendum	agenda	Analysis	analyses
Addendum	addenda	Basis	bases
Datum	data	Crisis	crises
Dictum	dicta	Hypothesis	hypotheses
Effluvium	effluvia	Oasis	oases
Ovum	ova	Parenthesis	parentheses
Erratum	errata	Thesis	theses
Memorandum	memoranda	Phenomenon	phenomena
Medium	media	Criterion	criteria
Stratum	strata		
Alumnus	alumni	(Italian)	
Focus	foci (or focuses)	Bandit	banditti (or bandits)
Fungus	fungi		
Genius	genii (or geniuses)	Virtuoso	virtuosi
Radius	radii	Dilettante	dilettanti
Terminus	termini (or terminuses)	(French)	
Formula	formulæ (or formulas)	Beau	beaux
Genus	genera	Bureau	bureaux
Stamen	stamina (or stamens) (see § 73)	Monsieur	messieurs
		Madam	mesdames
Axis	axes		
Index	indices (or indexes) (see § 73)	(Hebrew)	
		Cherub	cherubim (or cherubs) (see § 73)
Appendix	appendices		
Series	series	Seraph	seraphim (or seraphs)
Species	species		
Apparatus	apparatus		

70. Some nouns, Sing. in *form*, are used only in a Plural sense. These are nouns of Multitude (§ 37).

> *Poultry.*—The poultry are doing well.
> *Cattle.*—These cattle are mine.
> *Vermin.*—These vermin do much harm.
> *People.*—These people have returned home.
> *Gentry.*—These gentry are expected to-day.

Note.—When " people " is used in the sense of " nation," the Plural is " peoples."

71. Some nouns have the same form in both numbers.

Living beings.—Deer, sheep, fish (rarely fishes), swine, grouse, salmon, trout, cod, heathen.

Collective numerals.—Yoke (of oxen), brace (of birds), dozen, score, gross.

Measure of weight.—Stone, hundredweight.

This deer, these *deer*. That sheep, those *sheep*. That fish, those *fish* (rarely *fishes*). Those *heathen*. Nine *brace* of birds. Four *yoke* of oxen. Ten *dozen* books. He weighs ten *stone* and a half. That box weighs three *hundredweight*. Four *swine*. Ten *gross* of pens.

72. Some nouns, which take the Plural form at ordinary times, use the Singular instead of the Plural to express some specific quantity or number.

> A twelve-*month* rule. A three-*foot* rule. An eight-*day* clock. A six-*year*-old horse. A fort-*night* (which is a contraction of "fourteen nights"). Forty *head* of cattle. Twelve *pound* weight. Ten *sail* of the line. Five *fathom* deep. A six-*penny* piece.

73. There are some nouns which have two forms in the Plural,—each form with a separate meaning of its own.

Brother	{ Brothers,	*usually for sons of the same parents.*
	Brethren,	*usually for members of the same society.*
Cherub	{ Cherubim,	*angels of a certain rank.*
	Cherubs,	*images or models of a cherub.*
Cloth	{ Cloths,	*kinds or pieces of cloth* (Distributive).
	Clothes,	*articles of dress* (Collective).
Cow	{ Cows,	*individual cows* (Distributive).
	Kine,	*cattle* (Collective).
Die	{ Dies,	*stamps for coining* (Distributive).
	Dice,	*small cubes used in games* (Collective).
Genius	{ Geniuses,	*men of genius or talent.*
	Genii,	*fabulous spirits of the air.*
Index	{ Indexes,	*tables of contents.*
	Indices,	*signs used in algebra.*
Pea	{ Peas,	(Distributive).
	Pease,	(Collective).
Penny	{ Pennies,	=*penny-pieces* (Distributive).
	Pence,	(sometimes Collective).[1]
Staff	{ Staves,	*sticks or poles.*
	Staffs,	*departments in the army.*
Stamen	{ Stamens,	*male organs of flowers* (Distributive).
	Stamina,	*endurance, vigour,* lit. *threads* (Collective).
Shot	{ Shot,	*little balls discharged from a gun.*
	Shots,	*discharges; as,* "*he had two shots.*"

74. Nouns which have one meaning in the Singular and another in the Plural:--

Singular.	*Plural.*
Advice, counsel.	*Advices,* information.
Air, atmosphere.	*Airs,* demeanour.
Ban, a curse (under a *ban*).	*Banns,* announcement (*banns* of marriage).
Beef, flesh of ox.	*Beeves,* cattle, bulls and cows.
Compass, range or extent.	*Compasses,* an instrument.
Copper, a metal.	*Coppers,* pennies.
Domino, a kind of mask.	*Dominoes,* the game so-called.

---

[1] Hence *six-pence* has a Collective sense, denoting a single coin, which makes the noun appear to be Singular, so that we say *a sixpence* (Singular), *sixpences* (Plural).

Singular.	*Plural.*
Force, strength or energy	*Forces*, army.
Good, benefit.	*Goods*, movable property.
Iron, a metal.	*Irons*, fetters or instruments made of iron.
Physic, medicine.	*Physics*, natural science.
Return, coming back.	*Returns*, statistics.
Salt, seasoning substance.	*Salts*, smelling salts.
Sand, a kind of matter.	*Sands*, a tract of sandy land.
Vapour, invisible steam.	*Vapours*, dejection.
Vesper, evening.	*Vespers*, evening prayers.
Water, the element.	*Waters*, springs.

75. Nouns which have two meanings in the Plural against one in the Singular :—

	Singular.		*Plural.*
Colour,	hue, tint.	*Colours*	1. Kinds of colour. 2. Flag of regiment.
Custom,	habit.	*Customs*	1. Habits. 2. *Toll or tax.*
Element,	simple substance.	*Elements*	1. Simple substances. 2. Conditions of the air.
Effect,	result.	*Effects*	1. Results. 2. *Goods and chattels.*
Letter,	1. Of alphabet. 2. Epistle.	*Letters*	1. Of alphabet. 2. Epistles. 3. *Learning.*
Manner,	mode or way.	*Manners*	1. Modes, ways. 2. *Behaviour.*
Number,	as in counting.	*Numbers*	1. As in counting. 2. *Poetry.*
Pain.	suffering.	*Pains*	1. Sufferings. 2. *Trouble, care.*
Part.	portion.	*Parts*	1. Portions. 2. *Abilities.*
Premise,	a statement or proposition.	*Premises*	1. Propositions. 2. *Buildings.*
Quarter.	a fourth part.	*Quarters*	1. Fourth parts. 2. *Lodgings.*
Spectacle.	anything seen.	*Spectacles*	1. Things seen. 2. *Eye-glasses.*

76. Nouns which have two meanings in the Singular against one in the Plural :—

	Singular.		*Plural.*
Abuse	1. Wrong use. 2. Reproaches.	*Abuses*,	wrong uses.
Foot	1. Part of body. 2. Infantry.	*Feet*,	parts of body.
Horse	1. A quadruped. 2. Cavalry.	*Horses*,	quadrupeds.

	Singular.		Plural.
Issue	{ 1. Result. { 2. Offspring.	*Issues,*	results.
Light	{ 1. A lamp. { 2. Radiance.	*Lights,*	lamps.
People	{ 1. A nation. { 2. Persons.	*Peoples,*	nations.
Powder	{ 1. A medicinal mixture. { 2. Gunpowder.	*Powders,*	medicinal mixtures.
Practice	{ 1. Habitual act. { 2. Professional connection.	*Practices,*	habitual acts.
Stone	{ 1. A piece of rock. { 2. Fourteen pounds.	*Stones,*	pieces of rock.
Wood	{ 1. A forest. { 2. Timber.	*Woods,*	forests.

77. True Singulars used as Plurals. — By a "True Singular" we mean that the final *s* is part of the original Singular noun, and not a sign of the Plural.

Such nouns, though Singular by etymology, are liable to be considered Plural on account of the final *s*; and all except the first of these named below are now always used as if they were Plural.

> *Summons* (Fr. *semonce*).—This noun is still correctly used as a Singular; as "I received *a* summons to attend"; "*This* summons reached me to-day." The plural form is *summonses*.
>
> *Alms* (A.S. *ælmesse*).—"He asked *an alms*" (New Testament). But now the word is generally used as if it were Plural; as, "I gave alms to the beggar, and for *these* he thanked me."
>
> *Eaves* (A.S. *efese*).—The edge or lower borders of the roof of a house. The word is now always used as a Plural; as, "The eaves *are* not yet finished."
>
> *Riches* (Fr. *richesse*).—This too is really a Singular; as, "In one hour is so great riches come to naught" (New Testament); but now, on account of the final *s*, this noun is always used as a Plural; as, "Riches *do* not last for ever."

78. True Plurals used as Singulars.—In such nouns the final *s* is really a sign of the Plural.

> *Amends.*—This is sometimes used as a Singular and sometimes as a Plural; as, "*An* honourable amends" (Addison).
>
> *Means.*—This is now almost always used as a Singular; as, "By *this* means."
>
> *News.*—This is now almost always used as a Singular; as, "Ill news *runs* apace."
>
> *Innings.*—This is a word used in cricket to denote the turn for going in and using the bat. It is *always* used as a Singular; as, "We have not yet had *an* innings"; "Our eleven beat the other by *an* innings and ten runs."
>
> *Gallows.*—The frame-work from which criminals are hanged. This noun is used as a Singular; as, "They fixed up *a* gallows."

79. Of the following nouns some seldom, others never, take a Singular. These are for the most part names of things, which imply plurality or consist of more parts than one :—

(a) Instruments or tools :—*arms* (weapons), *bellows, fetters, pincers, scissors, tongs, shears, snuffers, tweezers.*

(b) Articles of dress :—*breeks* or *breeches, drawers, pantaloons, trappings, trousers.*

(c) Kinds of disease :—*measles, mumps, staggers, small-pox* (originally spelt as *small-pocks*).

(d) Parts of the body :—*bowels, entrails, intestines, giblets.*

(e) The names of sciences or subjects ending in *ics;* such as *physics, optics, acoustics, phonetics, politics, ethics, metaphysics,* etc.

(These nouns are Plural, because the corresponding Greek words, from which they have come, are Plural.)

(f) Miscellaneous words ; such as *ashes, annals, antics, cates, gallows, dregs, embers, chattels, lees, nuptials, obsequies, shambles, statistics, victuals, hustings, proceeds, thanks, tidings, downs, suds, wages, chaps, auspices, billiards, thews,* etc.

Note.—The phrases "a living *wage*," "a mere *chattel*," "a glowing *ember*," "cigar *ash*," can be freely used.

CHAPTER III.—ADJECTIVES.

Section 1.—The Kinds of Adjectives.

80. Adjective defined.—An adjective is a word used to qualify a noun (§ 13).

In parsing an adjective this is the definition invariably used, and it is therefore convenient to retain it. But it needs explanation. An adjective, as we know, denotes a property of some kind or other. When we say that it qualifies or modifies a noun, we mean that it *restricts* the application of the noun to such persons or things as possess the property denoted by the adjective.

Every adjective, therefore, has a *restrictive* force ; and it might be defined as "*a word used to restrict the application of a noun by adding something to its meaning.*"[1]

81. There are altogether eight different kinds of Adjectives :[2]—

---

[1] This is an abridged form of the definition given by Mason, who, in *English Grammar*, p. 37, § 88, defines an adjective thus :—" An adjective is a word which may limit (= restrict) the application of a noun to that which has the quality, the quantity, or the relation which the adjective denotes."

[2] In Mason's *English Grammar*, p. 38, § 89, Adjectives are arranged in three classes,—Qualitative or Descriptive, Quantitative (which includes Numeral), and Demonstrative. This arrangement omits Proper and Distributive.

(1) **Proper** : describing a thing by some *Proper noun.*

(2) **Descriptive** : showing *of what quality* or *in what state* a thing is.

(3) **Quantitative** : showing *how much of* a thing is meant.

(4) **Numeral** : showing *how many* things or *in what order.*

(5) **Demonstrative** : showing *which* or *what* thing is meant.

(6) **Interrogative** : asking *which* or *what* thing is meant.

(7) **Distributive** : showing that things are taken *separately* or *in separate lots.*

(8) **Possessive:** *my, thy, his, her, its, our, your, their.* See § 109.

Proper Adjectives.

82. Proper Adjectives restrict the application of a noun to such persons or things as are included within the scope of some Proper name. (A Proper adjective must begin with a capital letter.)

> A *Portuguese* sailor = a sailor from Portugal.
> The *Turkish* empire = the empire of the Turks.
> The *Gangetic* plain = the plain watered by the Ganges.
> The *English* language = the language of England.

Note.—Proper adjectives, like Proper nouns, may be used in a descriptive sense ; as, *French* leave ; *British* pluck (pluck like that of a Briton).

Descriptive Adjectives :—Quality or State.

83. Descriptive Adjectives restrict the application of a noun to such persons or things as possess the *quality* or *state* denoted by the adjective.

> A *brave* boy ; a *sick* lion ; a *tame* cat ; a *large* field ; a *black* horse ; an *industrious* student ; a *careful* workman.

Quantitative Adjectives :—Quantity or Degree.

84. Quantitative Adjectives restrict the application of a noun to such things as are of the *quantity* or *degree* denoted by the adjective.

The chief adjectives of this class are—*Much, little ; no ; some, any ; enough* or *sufficient ; all* or *whole, half.*

> He ate *much* (a large quantity of) bread.
> He ate *little* (a small quantity of) bread.
> A *half* loaf is better than *no* bread.
> He ate *some* (a certain quantity of) bread.
> He did not eat *any* (any quantity of) bread.
> He ate *enough* or *sufficient* bread.
> He ate *all* the (the *whole* quantity of) bread.

Note.—"No" is always followed by a noun, and is therefore an adjective. "None" is never followed by a noun, and is therefore a pronoun. It is a negative pronoun ; see § 117.

85. Adjectives of Quantity are always followed by a *Singular* noun ; and this noun must always be either a noun of *Material* or an *Abstract* noun ; as "much bread" (noun of Material) ; "much pain" (a high degree of pain, Abstract noun).

Note.—It is idiomatic to speak of a *quantity* of matter (Material noun), and a *degree* of some quality (Abstract noun). Hence adjectives of Quantity have also been called adjectives of Degree.

Numeral Adjectives.

86. Numeral Adjectives restrict the application of a noun to such persons or things as are of the *number* or *serial order* denoted by the adjective.

Numeral Adjectives are subdivided into two main classes :—

I. Definite.   II. Indefinite.

87. Definite numerals denote some *exact* number.

Those which show *how many* things there are (as one, two, three, four, etc.) are called **Cardinals.**

Those which show the *serial order* in which a thing stands (as first, second, third, etc.) are called **Ordinals.**

Those which show *how often* a thing is *repeated* are called **Multiplicative.**

Cardinals.	Ordinals.	Multiplicatives.
One	first	one only, single, simple
Two	second	twofold, double
Three	third	threefold, treble, triple
Four	fourth	fourfold, quadruple (four times one)
Six	sixth	sixfold (six times one)
Seven	seventh	sevenfold (seven times one)

88. Indefinite numerals denote number of some kind without saying precisely what the number is :—

All, some, enough, no ; many, few ; several, sundry.

All men are mortal.	*Some* men die young.
No men were present.	Ten men will be *enough.*
Many men are poor.	*Few* men are rich.
Several men came.	*Sundry* men went away.

A Definite numeral can be made Indefinite by placing the word *some* or *about* before it :—

Some twenty men (=*about* twenty men, twenty men *more or less*) were present.

89. The words "some," "enough," "all," "no," are adjectives of *Number* or adjectives of *Quantity*, according to the sense.

If the noun qualified by such words is a Material or Abstract noun, the adjective belongs to the class of Quantity, as has been explained in § 85.   But if the noun is a Common noun (or one used as a Common noun), and capable therefore of being in the Plural number, the adjective belongs to the class of Numeral :—

Quantitatives.	*Numerals.*
Much ; he had much bread.	*Many ;* he had many loaves.
Little ; he had little bread.	*Few ;* he had few loaves.
Enough ; he had enough bread.	*Enough ;* he had loaves enough.
Some ; he had some bread.	*Some ;* he had some loaves.
No ; he had no bread.	*No ;* he had no loaves.
All ; he had all the bread.	*All ;* he had all the loaves.
Any ; have you had any bread ?	*Any ;* did you bring any loaves ?

Demonstrative Adjectives.

90. Demonstrative Adjectives restrict the application of a noun to those persons or things that are intended to be *pointed out* by the adjective.

The word *Demonstrative* means " pointing out."

91. Adjectives of this kind are subdivided (as Numeral adjectives are) into two main classes :—

I. Definite.   II. Indefinite.

When a person or thing is pointed out *exactly*, as " this man," the adjective is called a **Definite** Demonstrative.

When it is pointed out in a certain sense, but *not exactly*, it is called an **Indefinite** Demonstrative.

Definite.		*Indefinite.*	
Singular.	*Plural.*	*Singular.*	*Plural.*
The	the	A, an	*nil.*
This	these	One, any	any
That, yon, yonder	those, yon, yonder	A certain	certain
Such	such	Such	such
The same, or self-same	the same, or self-same	Some	some
The other	the other	Another, any other	other, any other

Demonstrative adjectives are few in number, and all of them are given in the above list.

92. The adjective *" the "* is sometimes called the **Definite Article**, and *" a "* or *" an "* is called the **Indefinite Article**.

An is used before the sound of an open vowel or silent *h ;* as—

An apple ; *an h*eir ; *an h*our ; *an h*onest man.

A is used before a consonant, before *u* or *ew* or *eu* sounded as *yoo*, and before *o* sounded as *wu :*—

A kite ; *a* cart ; *a* bottle ; *a u*seful thing ; *a* one-eyed man ; *a* European ; *a* ewer ; *an u*nusual, but *a u*nique case.

We say "*a* his'-to-ry," because here the accent is on the *first* syllable "*his*," and the *h* is distinctly sounded; but we say "*an* his-tor'-i-cal account," because here the accent is on the *second* syllable "*tor*," and the *h* is practically silent.[1]

Interrogative Adjectives.

92a. Interrogative Adjectives restrict the application of a noun by asking a question :—

> *What* book is that ?   *Which* book do you like best ?

Note.—"What" has a general sense, "which" a selective one. "What" can also be used in an exclamatory sense, as "*What* folly !".

Distributive Adjectives.

93. Distributive Adjectives restrict the application of a noun by showing that the persons or things denoted by the noun are taken *singly*, or *in separate lots*.

94. There are four Adjectives of this class :—*each, every, either, neither.*

(*a*) **Each.**—This means one of *two* things or one of any number *exceeding two :*—

> The *two* men had *each* (man) a gun.
> The *twenty* men had *each* (man) a gun.

(*b*) **Every.**—This is never used for one of two, but always for some number *exceeding two :*—

> *Every* man (out of the *twenty present*) had a gun.

Note.—"Every" is a stronger word than "each," and means "*each without exception*" :—"*all* the individuals of a group, taken *singly*."

"**Every six hours**" and similar expressions.—This means every *period or space of six hours*, six hours being taken collectively as *one* period of time :—

> He came *every five hours* (=at the close of every space of five hours).

"**Every other.**"—This means *every second* or *each alternate ;* as—

> He was attacked with fever *every other day* (=on every second day).

(*c*) **Either.**—This has two meanings—(1) *one of two*, or (2) *each of two*,—that is, *both*.

> (1) You can take *either* side ; that is, one side or the other.
> (2) The river overflowed on *either* side ; that is, on both sides.

(*d*) **Neither.**—This is the negative of "either," and signifies "neither the one nor the other" :—

> "You should take *neither* side"; that is, neither this side nor that, neither the one side nor the other.

Section 2.—The Two Uses of Adjectives.

95. There are two different ways in which an Adjective can be used—(*a*) the Epithet, and (*b*) the Predicative.

---

[1] The student will see from the above that the only purpose for which the *n* is required is to separate the vowel *a* from the initial vowel-sound

(*a*) *Epithet use.*—An adjective is used as an epithet, when it qualifies its noun *directly*, so as to make a kind of compound noun :—

A *lame* horse.   A *noble* character.

All true adjectives can be used as epithets.   But we cannot say "an asleep man," because "asleep" and similar words are not adjectives, but adverbs.

(*b*) *Predicative use.*—An adjective is used predicatively, when it qualifies its noun *indirectly*—through the verb or predicate going before.

That horse went *lame*.   His character is *noble*.

An adjective so used is a form of *Complement* to the verb going before (§ 24), because it *completes* what the verb left unsaid.

Section 3.—Substitutes for Adjectives.

96. Words that restrict a noun in the same way as an adjective would restrict it, are substitutes for an adjective :—

(1) A Participle (or Verbal adjective, § 17) :—

A *fading* flower.   A *fallen* tree.

(2) An Adverb with some participle understood :—

The *then* (reigning) king.   The *down* (going) train.

(3) A Noun or Gerund used as an Adjective :—

A *river* fish (=a fish living in rivers).
A *bathing* place (=a place used for bathing).

(4) A Noun in the Genitive case or a Possessive Adjective :—

My book.   *Their* friendship.   My *son's* teacher.

(5) A Verb in the Infinitive mood :—

A chair *to sit on*.   Water *to drink*.   A house *to let*.

(6) A Preposition with its object :—

A bird *in the hand* (=a bird *caught*).

(7) An Adjective clause ; (see clause defined in § 4).

The book *that you lent me* will not be lost.

Section 4.—Comparison of Adjectives.

97. Most adjectives of Quality, two adjectives of Quantity, viz. *much* and *little*, and two adjectives of Number, viz. *many* and *few*, have degrees of comparison.

---

of the word following.   Sometimes the *n* of the article has glued itself to the word following : thus *an ewt* has become *a newt ; an eke-name* has become *a nick-name ; an ingot* has become *a ningot* or *a nugget.*   The converse process is seen in *an adder* from *a nadder, an apron* from *a napron, an auger* from *a nauger, an orange* from *a naring* or *a norange.*

Adjectives which cannot be compared may be classified thus :—

(1) Quantitative, all except *much*, *little*.
(2) Numeral, all except *many*, *few*.
(3) Proper, as *English*, *African*, etc.
(4) Demonstrative, as *this*, *that*, *other*, etc.
(5) Distributive, as *either*, *every*, etc.
(6) Descriptive, when they denote qualities which from the nature of their meaning cannot be more or less.

    (*a*) Shape, as *round*, *square*, *oblong*, *triangular*, *four-footed*, etc.

    (*b*) Material, as *golden*, *milky*, *vegetable*, etc.

    (*c*) Time, as *weekly*, *monthly*, *annual*, etc.

    (*d*) Place, as *Kentish*, *American*, *insular*, etc.

    (*e*) Natural objects, as *solar*, *lunar*, *sidereal*, etc.

    (*f*) Qualities in the highest degree, as *eternal*, *perpetual*, *perfect*, etc.

    Qualities in a moderate degree, as *pal-ish*, *redd-ish*.

Such a phrase as "more perfect" is a short, but inaccurate, way of saying "more nearly approaching perfection."

98. The degrees of comparison are three in number,—the Positive, the Comparative, and the Superlative.

The **Positive** denotes the simple quality ; as, "a *beautiful* horse."

The **Comparative** denotes a higher degree of the quality ; as, "a *more beautiful* horse." This is used when *two* things are compared with reference to some quality. Comparatives are followed by "than."

The **Superlative** denotes the highest degree of the quality ; as, "the *most beautiful* horse." This is used when *one* thing is compared with *all other* things of the same kind. "Superlative" means "lifting above."

99. In all adjectives of *more than two syllables*, and in most adjectives of two syllables, the Comparative is formed by adding "*more*" and the Superlative by adding "*most*," as in the examples already given.[1]

100. But adjectives of one syllable and some adjectives of two syllables can also form the Comparative by adding *er* or *r*, and the Superlative by adding *est* or *st*.

(*a*) If the Positive ends in *two consonants*, or in *a single consonant preceded by two vowels*, *er* and *est* are added :—

Small	smaller	smallest
Thick	thicker	thickest
Great	greater	greatest
Deep	deeper	deepest

(*b*) If the Positive ends in *one* consonant, and the consonant

---

[1] This is called the *Analytical* mode of comparing adjectives, as distinct from the *Synthetical* or *flexional* mode, which consists in adding the suffixes *-er* and *-est* to the root.

is preceded by a *short vowel*, the final consonant is doubled when *er* and *est* are added :—

Thin	thinner	thinnest
Fat	fatter	fattest
Hot	hotter	hottest
Wet	wetter	wettest

(c) If the Positive ends in *e*, only *r* and *st* are added, and not *er* and *est* :—

Brave	braver	bravest
Wise	wiser	wisest
True	truer	truest

(d) If the Positive ends in *y*, and the *y* is preceded by a *consonant*, the *y* is changed into *i*, when *er* and *est* are added :—

| Happy | happier | happiest |
| Dry | drier | driest |

(e) If the *y* is preceded by a *vowel*, the *y* is not changed into *i* :—

| Gay | gayer | gayest |
| Grey | greyer | greyest |

Note.—We cannot use the forms -*er*, -*est* with adjectives ending in such suffixes as -*al*, -*ed*, -*ful*, -*ic*, -*ile*, -*ine*, -*ose*, -*ous*, and others. Thus we cannot say, *frug-al-er*, *learn-ed-er*, *cheer-ful-er*, *com-ic-er*, *puer-il-er*, *furt-iv-er*, *verb-os-er*, *fam-ous-er*. We add *more* or *most* to such adjectives, to show that what we are comparing is the quality implied by the stem of the word, and not the suffix added to the stem.

101. Irregular Comparisons.—The Positives marked below with an asterisk have borrowed their comparatives and superlatives from other roots. Such Positives are therefore *defective*, because they have no Comp. or Superl. of their own. The Comp. and Superl. are also defective, because they have no Positive of their own. In all the other examples the Comp. and Superl. are *irregular*, but formed from the same root as the Positive.

Bad, ill, evil*	worse*	worst*
Fore	former	foremost, first
Good*	better*	best*
Hind	hinder	hindmost
Late	later, latter	latest, last
Little*	less*	least*
Much (quantity)*	more*	most*
Many (number)*	more*	most*
Nigh	nigher	nighest, next
Old	older, elder	oldest, eldest

102. There are five words which are adverbs in the Positive degree, but adjectives in the Comparative and Superlative :—

Far	farther	farthest
In	inner	innermost, inmost
Out	outer, utter	uttermost, utmost
Be-neath	nether	nethermost
Up	upper	uppermost

103. Latin Comparatives.—All of these end in *or*, and not in *er;* and all are followed by *to* instead of *than.*

His strength	is	*superior to*	(greater than) mine.
His strength	is	*inferior to*	(less than) mine.
This event	is	*anterior to* ⎫	(earlier than) that.
This event	is	*prior to* ⎭	
This event	is	*posterior to*	(later than) that.
This man	is	*senior to*	(older than) that.
This man	is	*junior to*	(younger than) that.

CHAPTER IV.—PRONOUNS.

104. Pronoun defined.—A Pronoun is a word used instead of a noun or noun-equivalent (§ 6).

A pronoun is a *substitute* word. If instead of mentioning or repeating a noun we use some other word, which will show what noun (expressed or understood) we are referring to, that word is a pronoun. Thus if some one says, "*I* am here," the word "I" is a substitute for the speaker's name, which otherwise would have to be mentioned. If we say, "*He* is here," the word *he* is a substitute for the name of some person mentioned already.

Hence it has been well said :—"Pronouns denote persons or things without being names for them." This is a suitable definition.

The usefulness of pronouns is best seen by trying to do without them :—

John saw a snake in the garden, *this snake John* thought would hurt *John,* unless *John* killed *the snake* with a stick, *this stick John* had in his hand.

The nouns in italics can all be replaced by pronouns, and the sentence can be much better expressed as follows :—

John saw a snake in the garden, *which he* thought would hurt *him,* unless *he* killed *it* with a stick *which he* had in his hand.

105. Two facts follow from the above definition :—

(*a*) Since a pronoun is used instead of a noun, it must itself be of the nature of a noun, and not of an adjective.

(*b*) Since a pronoun is used instead of a noun, it must be of the same number, gender, and person as the noun it stands for.

106. There are five different kinds of Pronouns : [1]—

(1) **Personal** ; as, *I, thou, he, she,* etc.

(2) **Demonstrative** ; as, *this, that, such, one,* etc.

(3) **Relative** ; as, *which, who, that, as,* etc.

(4) **Interrogative** ; as, *who? which? what?*

(5) **Possessive** ; as, *mine, thine, his, yours,* etc.

This classification excludes all words that are *adjectives,* and all words that are not *substitutes for nouns.* It is explained below in § 113 that *this, that, such* are not here adjectives, but substitutes for nouns.

SECTION 1.—PERSONAL PRONOUNS.

107. The **Personal Pronouns** are so called, because they stand for the three persons, and have a different form for each.

(*a*) The First, which denotes the person *speaking ;* as *I, we, myself :*—

I (*the person now speaking*) will do all I can to win a prize at the end of the year.

(*b*) The Second, which denotes the person *spoken to ;* as, *thou, you, thyself :*—

You (*the person now spoken to*) should leave off this habit of idleness.

(*c*) The Third, which denotes the person or thing *spoken of ;* as, *he, she, it, himself, herself, itself :*—

He (*the person already mentioned*) did a good day's work with his tutor.

108. Forms of Personal Pronouns.—Personal Pronouns have the same differences of gender, number, and case that nouns have :—

---

[1] A different and more elaborate classification of Pronouns is given in Mason's *English Grammar.* After giving eight classes of Pronouns, he subdivides each class, wherever this is possible, into two columns, one for Substantive pronouns, and the other for Adjective pronouns. Under Adjective pronouns he includes Distributive and Demonstrative adjectives, which in this book have already been disposed of in the chapter on Adjectives. It is difficult to see how such adjectives as "every," "each," "some," "other," "any," etc., or, in fact, any adjective, can be correctly called a Pronoun. A Pronoun is a *substitute* word,—a word used *for* another word. But "every," "each," "some," "other," "any" are simply *qualifying* words. They are not *substitute* words. There are no other words for which they are used as substitutes, and therefore they are not pronouns. The same author has a class of pronouns which he calls **Indefinite,** and subdivides into Substantives (*one, aught, naught*) and Adjectives (*any, other, some, no*). We have already shown that the last four are not pronouns at all. *Aught* and *naught* are not pronouns either, because they are not *substitutes* for any other words. *One* is a pronoun in certain contexts, as shown below in §§ 117, 119.

I. *The First Person, Masculine or Feminine.*

Case.	Singular.	Plural.
Nominative . .	I	We
Acc. and Dat. .	Me	Us
Genitive . . .	Mine	Ours

II. *The Second Person, Masculine or Feminine.*

Case.	Singular.	Plural.
Nominative . .	Thou	Ye or you
Acc. and Dat. .	Thee	You
Genitive . . .	Thine	Yours

III. *The Third Person, of all Genders.*

Case.	Singular.			Plural.
	Masculine.	Feminine.	Neuter.	All Genders.
Nominative .	He	She	It	They
Acc. and Dat.	Him	Her	It	Them
Genitive .	His	Hers	Its	Theirs

109. Possessive Pronouns and Possessive Adjectives were formerly Genitives, but are now classed as separate parts of speech :—

	Singular.			Plural.		
Poss. Adj. .	My	Thy	Her	Our	Your	Their
Poss. Pron. .	Mine	Thine	Hers	Ours	Yours	Theirs

Possessive adjectives are used *before* nouns, and qualify them like adjectives.

This is my book.   That is their house.

Possessive pronouns are used—(*a*) when separated from the qualified noun by a verb coming between ; (*b*) when the qualified noun is not expressed ; (*c*) when preceded by " of " :—

(*a*) This book is *mine*. That house is *theirs*.

(*b*) My horse and *yours* (your horse) are both tired.

(*c*) That horse *of yours* is tired.

Note 1.—"Hers," "ours," "yours," "theirs" are in fact **Double Genitives**, the "*r*" being one sign of the Genitive and the "*s*" another. The meaning of "*of*" in such a phrase as "of yours" is discussed below in § 304.

Note 2.—In poetry "mine" and "thine" are sometimes used for "my" and "thy," when the noun following begins with a vowel. This is done to separate the sounds of the two vowels :—

> Look through *mine eyes* with thine.—Tennyson.

Note 3.—In poetry "mine" can be placed after its noun; as "mother mine" instead of "my mother."

Note 4.—*Mine* and *thine* are the older forms. *My* and *thy* are merely contractions of these.

110. Reflexive and Emphasizing Personal Pronouns.—These are formed by adding "self" or "own" to a Personal pronoun.[1]

I. *The First Person.*

	Singular.	Plural.
Nom., Acc., Dat. .	Myself	Ourselves
Poss. Adj. or Pron. .	My or mine own	Our own

II. *The Second Person.*

	Singular.	Plural.
Nom., Acc., Dat. .	Thyself	Yourselves
Poss. Adj. or Pron. .	Thy or thine own	Your own

III. *The Third Person.*

	Singular.			Plural.
	Masculine.	Feminine.	Neuter.	All Genders.
Nom., Acc., Dat. .	Himself	Herself	Itself	Themselves
Poss. Adj. or Pron.	His own	Her own	Its own	Their own

[1] The student will afterwards find the origin of *self* and *own* discussed in § 311.

111. Uses of Reflexive Forms.—The Reflexive forms of Personal pronouns are used for two purposes—(*a*) to show that the person (or thing) does something to himself (or itself); (*b*) to make the pronouns more emphatic.

Examples of (a).

Singular.	*Plural.*
I hid myself.	We hid ourselves.
I hit my own head.	We hit our own heads.
Thou lovest thine own work.	You love your own work.

Examples of (b).

Singular.	*Plural.*
I myself saw the horse.	We ourselves saw it.
He himself (or she herself) saw it.	They themselves saw it.
The wall itself fell.	The walls themselves fell.

Note.—An emphasizing personal pronoun can never by itself be the subject of a verb. We cannot say, "myself saw it," "himself saw it." But we can say, "*I* myself, or *He* himself saw it."

Section 2.—Demonstrative Pronouns.

112. A **Demonstrative Pronoun** is one that *points to* some noun going before, and is used instead of it. This noun is called the Antecedent.

113. The chief pronouns of this class are :—*this, that, these, those; one, ones, none; such.*

The student will observe that some of these words have appeared already in the list of Demonstrative *Adjectives.* Where, then, is the difference?

When they **qualify** *some noun expressed or understood, they are* **Adjectives.**

When they are **substitutes** *for some noun expressed or understood, they are* **Pronouns.**

(*a*) He came to my house *one* day.

Here *one* is an adjective (Indefinite Demonstrative) qualifying its noun "day."

(*b*) Your coat is black ; mine is a white *one*.

Here *one* is a pronoun, which is used as a substitute for the previously-mentioned noun "coat," and is qualified by the adjective "white."

114. He, she, it, they.—The simplest forms of Demonstrative pronouns are *he, she, it, they.*

These have been hitherto called "Personal pronouns," partly because they exemplify the Third person as distinct from the First and Second, and partly because "he" and "she," and sometimes "they," do actually relate to *persons.* and not to things.

Yet it is equally correct to call them Demonstrative pronouns, since they *point to* some noun going before, and are *substituted* for it.

They might well be called "**Demonstrative pronouns of the Third person.**"

(1) My father has gone ; we saw *him* start a short time ago. (Here *him* is a Demonstrative pronoun used as a substitute for its Antecedent noun "father.")

(2) My mother came yesterday ; we were glad to see *her*. (Here *her* is a Demonstrative pronoun used as a substitute for its Antecedent noun "mother.")

(3) The sun has risen ; *it* shines brightly. (Here *it* is a Demonstrative pronoun used as a substitute for the noun "sun.")

(4) The travellers fell asleep as soon as *they* arrived. (Here *they* is a Demonstrative pronoun substituted for the noun "travellers.")

115. It.—This pronoun has three distinct modes of reference :—

(*a*) To a *noun* going before. In this sense it is merely a Demonstrative pronoun used in the ordinary way :—

The sun has risen ; *it* (= the sun) shines brightly.

(*b*) To a *clause* going before :—

I have treated him as he deserved ; and he knows *it*. (Here "it" points to the clause "I have treated him as he deserved.")

(*c*) To a *phrase* or *clause* coming after :—

$\begin{cases} It \text{ is sad } to \text{ hear such bad news. } (Phrase.) \\ \text{It—viz. "to hear such bad news"—is sad.} \end{cases}$

$\begin{cases} It \text{ is probable } that \text{ it will rain to-day. } (Clause.) \\ \text{It—viz. "that it will rain to-day"—is probable.} \end{cases}$

116. This, that, these, those.—The uses of these words as **pronouns**, and not as *adjectives*, are as follows :—

(*a*) When two nouns have been mentioned in a previous sentence or clause, "**this**" has reference to the *latter* and "**that**" to the *former :*—

(1) Work and play are both necessary to health ; *this* (= play) gives us rest, and *that* (= work) gives us energy.

(2) Dogs are more faithful animals than cats ; *these* (= cats) attach themselves to places, and *those* (= dogs) to persons.

Observe that in the first of these sentences "*this*" does not specify *which* or *what* play is meant, and therefore it is not a Demonstrative Adjective. It is simply put as a *substitute* for the noun "play," and therefore it is a Demonstrative Pronoun.

A similar explanation holds good for the other example.

(*b*) The word "**that**," together with its plural form "**those**," is used as substitute for a single noun previously mentioned :—

(1) The air of hills is cooler than *that* (= the air) of plains.

(2) The houses of the rich are larger than *those* (= the houses) of the poor.

Observe the word "that" in the first example does not qualify the noun "air" by saying *which* air or *what* air, and therefore it is not an Adjective. It stands for "air" in general, and is a *substitute* for the noun "air"; and therefore it is a Pronoun.

(*c*) The words "**this**" or "**that**" can be used as substitutes for a *clause* or *sentence* previously mentioned :—

(1) I studied Greek and Latin when I was young, and *that* (= I studied Greek and Latin) at Oxford.

Here by using the pronoun "*that*" as a substitute for the sentence "I studied Greek and Latin," we not only avoid repeating this sentence a second time, but we give some emphasis to the words "at Oxford."

(2) Make the best use of your time at school ; *that*'s a wise boy.

Here "*that*" = "one who makes the best use of his time at school." All this repetition is avoided by using the pronoun "*that*" as a substitute for the implied sentence.

(3) You paid your debts ; and *this* (= the payment of your debts) is quite sufficient to prove your honesty.

117. One, ones, none.—When the antecedent noun is in the Singular number, we use "*one*"; but when the antecedent noun is Plural, we use "*ones.*"

(1) He gained a prize last year ; but he did not gain *one* (= a prize) this term. (*Singular.*)
(2) There were six lazy boys and four industrious *ones* (= boys) in our class. (*Plural.*)

None is properly a contraction of *no-one*, and was originally used only as a Singular. It was so used by Dryden :—

None but the brave *deserves* the fair.

But "none" was also used in the sense of *not any*, and in this sense could have a Plural meaning. In fact, the plural sense is now equally or more common :—

Bring me some *pence ;* I have *none.*
None have gone away yet.

118. Such, so.—"Such" can be substituted for a noun in either number :—

(1) He is the judge appointed to hear this case, and as *such* (= as the appointed judge) he must not be spoken to before the trial. (*Singular.*)
(2) Kings are constituted *such* (= kings) by law, and should be obeyed. (*Plural.*)

"So" is sometimes used predicatively in place of "such"; but "so" is a Demonstrative *Adverb*, and not of the same part of speech as *such*. (On the predicative use of adverbs, see § 226).

My business is urgent ; you will find it *so* (= of such a character). Is he an enemy ? He is *so* (= of such a character).

Examples for Practice.

Show whether the words printed in italics are Demonstrative **Adjectives** *or Demonstrative* **Pronouns** :—

This horse is stronger than *that.*

Health is of more value than money ; *this* cannot give such true happiness as *that.*

I prefer a white horse to a black *one.*

You will repent of this *one* day, when it is too late.

You have kept your promise ; *this* was all that I asked for.

The faithfulness of a dog is greater than *that* of a cat.

One Mr. B. helped his friend in need ; *that* was a true friend.

Return to your work, and *that* immediately.

Bring me *that* book, and leave *this* where it is.

The step you have taken is *one* of much risk.

Such a book as yours deserves to be well read.

Prosperous men are much exposed to flattery ; for *such* alone can be made to pay for it.

Prosperous men are not always more happy than unlucky *ones.*

A pale light, like *that* of the rising moon, begins to fringe the horizon.

Will you ride *this* horse or *that ?*

A stranger could not be received twice as *such* in the same house.

The plan you have chosen does not seem to me to be a wise *one.*

One man says *this*, another *that ;* whom should I believe ?

119. Indefinite Demonstrative Pronouns. — Sometimes Demonstrative Pronouns are used *indefinitely ;* that is, they are not used as substitutes for some noun previously mentioned, but for some noun understood or implied.

All Indefinite pronouns are in the Third person. *I* and *you* cannot be indefinite, because we cannot help knowing who is speaking or who is spoken to.

(*a*) **They.** — This pronoun is sometimes used for *men in general*, or some person whose name is purposely concealed :—

(1) *They* say (=men in general say) that truth and honesty is the best policy.

(2) *They* told me (=some person or persons, whom I do not wish to name, told me) that you were guilty of theft.

Note.—In such examples the Indef. Demons. pronoun is really equivalent to a noun signifying "person." Compare the following :—

What is *he* (=the man) at the gate ?—SHAKSPEARE.

He (=the being) of the bottomless pit.—MILTON.

(*b*) **One.**—This pronoun is often used in the sense of *any person* or *every person :*—

One should take care of *one's* health.

=*A man* (any and every man) should take care of *his* health.

Note.—Whenever "one" is the subject to a verb, it must be followed by "one" and not by "he." Thus we cannot say, "*one* must take care of *his* health."

(c) **It.**—The indefinite use of this pronoun is against all rules of number, person, and gender.

Who is *it?* *It* is I.   Is *it* you?   No; *it* is he.

In such phrases as those shown below, "*it*" gives **emphasis** to the noun or pronoun following :—

It was I who told you that.   *It* is the men who work hardest, not the women.   *It* was the queen who died yesterday.   *It* is little things that chiefly disturb the mind.

Sometimes the noun, for which the word "*it*" is used, can be understood from the context :—

It is raining = rain is raining or falling.
It is blowing hard = the wind is blowing hard.
It is fine to-day = the weather is fine to-day.
It is hot = the air is hot.   *It* is cold = the air is cold.
It is still early = the hour is still early.
It is two miles from here = the distance is two miles.
It was autumn = the season of the year was autumn.

Sometimes the word "*it*" is used instead of some Personal pronoun to express endearment or contempt :—

What a pretty little girl *it* is (=she is)!   (*Endearment.*)
What an ass *it* is (=that man is)!   (*Contempt.*)

SECTION 3.—RELATIVE OR CONJUNCTIVE PRONOUNS.

120. A **Relative Pronoun** differs (1) from a Personal pronoun, because it has the same form (*who, whose, whom*) for all three persons, while there is a separate form of Personal pronoun for each person, § 107 ; (2) from a Demonstrative pronoun, because with the help of its Antecedent it joins sentences, while a Demonstrative pronoun joins nothing. In this capacity, therefore, it might be fitly called a **Conjunctive** pronoun, § 17.

This is a good house ; I live in *it*.   (*Demonstrative pronoun.*)
The house in *which* I live is a good one.   (*Relative pronoun.*)

121. Who, which. — These are declined as follows for Singular and Plural alike :—

Nom.   Who,   . . . which.
Acc., Dat. Whom,   . . . which.
Gen.   Whose,   . . . (of which).

The forms *who, whom* are used for persons only. The form *which* is now used for things without life and for any kinds of animal except men and women.

In poetry, and occasionally in prose, *whose* can be used as the Genitive form of *which* :—

The tree, under *whose* shade we are sitting.

122. Forms of Antecedent.—The antecedent may take the form of a noun, or any kind of noun-equivalent (§ 45).

You have paid your debts, which (= the fact that you have paid your debts) is a clear proof of your honesty. (*Clause.*)

123. Antecedent understood. — When the antecedent is understood, the neuter Relative takes the form of "**what,**" while the Masculine and Feminine retain the form of "**who.**"

(*a*) *Who* = *he who,* or *she who,* or *they who.*

Who (= he who) steals my purse, steals trash.—SHAKSPEARE.
Whom (= those persons whom) the gods love, die young.—*Proverb.*

(*b*) *What* = *the thing which,* or *the things which.*

I cannot tell you now *what* (= the thing which) then happened.
The laws are *what* (= the things which) you say they are.

(*c*) *So, ever,* or *soever* added to the Relative pronoun or to Relative adverbs gives the meaning of totality :—

Whosoever (= any and every person who) breaks this law will be punished, *wherever* (in any and every place where) he may live.

Note 1.—"**What**" has been called a "Compound Relative," because the antecedent is said to be contained in it. But this is not correct ; for the antecedent is sometimes expressed, either (*a*) in a subsequent clause, or (*b*) immediately after the Relative itself :—

(*a*) *What* I tell you in darkness, *that* speak ye in the light.

(*b*) Take *what* (or *whatever*) *help* you can get.

Note 2.—Whenever the antecedent is placed after the Relative, as in example (*b*), the relative is not a *substitute* word, and therefore not a true pronoun, but an adjective.

Take *whichever book* (= that book of all books which) you prefer.

124. That.—The word "*that*" is often used for "who," "whom," or "which," but never for "whose" :—

This is the house *that* (= which) Jack built.

The man *that* (= whom) we were looking for has come.

Note.—Whenever "that" is the object to a preposition, the preposition is invariably placed after the verb of its sentence, and never before its own object :—

The house *that* we live *in.*

125. As.—The word "as" can be used for a Relative pronoun, provided it is preceded by "such," or "as," or "the same." It may be in the Nominative or Acc. or Dat. case, but not in the Genitive.

This is not *such* a good book *as* I expected.
As many men *as* came were caught.
Yours is not *the same* book *as* mine (is).

After "such" and "as" the word "as" is always used. But after "the same" it is not less common to use "that."

> This is *the same* story *that* (= which) I heard ten years ago.
> This is *the same* man *that* (= whom) I saw yesterday.

Note.—The use of "*that*" or "*as*" after "the same" is guided by the following rules :—(1) When a verb is *expressed* after it, we generally use "*that*" ; (2) When the verb is *understood*, we always use "*as*" :—

> (1) This is the same man *that* came yesterday. (*Verb expressed.*)
> (2) This is not the same book *as* mine (is). (*Verb understood.*)

126. But.—The conjunction "but," *when some Demonstrative pronoun is understood after it*, is used in the sense of "who not" or "which not."

> There was no one present, *but* saw (= but *he* saw = *who* did *not* see) the deed.
> There is no vice so simple, *but* may (= but *it* may = *which* may *not*) become serious in time.

Note.—The student must avoid the common mistake of saying that *but* is a "negative relative." It is not a pronoun, but a conjunction with some Demonstrative pronoun understood after it. This pronoun is sometimes expressed, as in the common saying—

> It never rains, *but it* pours.

The uses of Who and Which.

127. Restrictive, Continuative.—These words denote two distinct uses of "who" or "which" :—

> (*a*) *Restrict.*—The man *who lived there* died yesterday.
> (*b*) *Contin.*—I have seen my friend, *who recognised* me at once.

In (*a*) the Relative clause does the work of an *adjective* to the noun "man," because it *restricts* the application of this noun to that particular man who is said to have "lived there."

In (*b*) the Relative clause "who recognised me at once" has no restrictive force on the noun "friend." It simply *continues* what was said in the previous clause :—"I have seen my friend, *and he* (= who) recognised me at once."

Note.—Besides the Restrictive and the Continuative, there are two more senses of "who" and "which,"—one implying a **Cause,** and the other a **Purpose** :—

> (*c*) *Cause.* { Balbus, *who* had been found guilty, was hanged.
> { = Balbus, *because he* had been found guilty, was hanged.

> (*d*) *Purpose.* { Envoys were sent, *who* should sue for peace.
> { = Envoys were sent, *that they* might sue for peace.

In (*c*) and (*d*) the Relative clause is neither Restrictive nor Continuative, since (*c*) implies the *cause* of something already done, and (*d*) the *purpose* for which something is going to be done.

128. Who, that.—"Who" and "which" are the only Relatives that are ever used in the sense of Continuation, Cause, or Purpose. The other, viz. "that," is invariably used in a Restrictive sense, and much more commonly so than "who" or "which."

"That" is strictly the *defining, limiting,* or *distinguishing* Relative. Hence if its antecedent has been defined already by some other word, we do not use *that* after it. Thus we do not say, "*My* father, *that,*" etc.; but only, "My father, *who* or *whom,*" because the antecedent *father* is already defined by the Possessive Adj. *my.*

SECTION 4.—INTERROGATIVE PRONOUNS.

129. An **Interrogative Pronoun** is one that asks a question.

An Interrogative pronoun has been well described as a Relative in search of an antecedent, and hence in English, as in many other languages, there has been a resemblance of form between Interrogatives and Relatives :—

> *Who* gained the prize? *John.*
> It was *John who* gained the prize.

130. Forms of Interrogatives.—The Interrogative pronoun has five different forms.

> *Who* spoke? (Nominative to the verb.)
> Of *whom* did he speak? (Accusative after preposition.)
> *What* did he say? (Accusative after verb "say.")
> *Whose* book is that? (Genitive case.)
> *Which* of these boys will win the prize? (Selective.)

131. Which, what, who.—(*a*) "Which" is used in a *selective* sense; (*b*) "who" or "what" is used in a *general* sense :—

> (*a*) *Which* of these books do you prefer?
> (*b*) *What* is the name of that book? *Who* wrote it?
> (*c*) *What* book is that? *Which* book do you like best?

In the examples in (*c*) "*what*" and "*which*," since they are followed by nouns, are Interrogative adjectives, in the same way as a Demonstrative can be either an adjective or a pronoun (see § 113) according to the context.

Similarly, if we use *what* in an exclamatory sense, as, "What folly!" *what* is not a substitute word, but an adjective qualifying "folly."

132. The student should observe the different meanings of the Interrogatives used in the following sentences :—

> (*a*) *Who* is he?
> (*b*) *What* is he?
> (*c*) *Which* is he?

In (*a*) the "who" inquires about the name or parentage of some person that has been named.

In (*b*) the "what" inquires about his calling or social status. "What is he?" A tailor.

In (c) the "which" inquires about some particular person out of a definite group of persons. "The man who stole my purse is among the prisoners here present : which is he ? Point him out."

133. Whether.—The word "*whether*," when it signifies one of two persons or things, is now almost obsolete.

> *Whether* of them twain (=*which* of these two men) did the will of his father ?—*New Testament*.

CHAPTER V.—VERBS.

Section 1.—The Kinds of Verbs.

134. Verb defined.—A Verb is a word used for *saying* something about some person or thing [1] (§ 13).

The most important item in this definition is "*saying*." "Verb" is the English rendering of Lat. *verbum*, which signifies merely "word." "Verb" has thus acquired the dignity of being pre-eminently *the word*. Why is this ? Because of all Parts of Speech it holds the highest rank, higher even than a noun. It is the *saying* something about something else which makes a *sentence*, and this cannot be done without a verb.

135. The Kinds of Verbs.—Verbs are subdivided into three main classes :—

I. Verbs used Transitively.   II. Verbs used Intransitively.
III. Auxiliary.

Note 1.—Verbs which are not used in all the moods and tenses are called "Defective." But the student must not suppose from this that "Defective" constitutes a separate or fourth class of verb. This is not at all the case. *Quoth*, for example, is a Defective verb, but also Intransitive. Again "wit" is a Defective verb, but also Transitive. Again, "may" is a Defective verb, but also Auxiliary.

Note 2.—Verbs are distinguished into Strong and Weak according to *conjugation* ; see below, § 210.

136. *A verb is used* **Transitively,** *if the action does not stop with the agent, but passes from the agent to something else.* (The word "Transitive" means "passing over.")

> (1) The man killed *a snake*.
> (2) I do not know *whether he has come*.

---

[1] The definition given in several current books is: "A verb makes an assertion." This is of questionable accuracy, because a verb cannot make an assertion without its subject. It is the sentence as a whole, and not merely the verb of the sentence, that makes an assertion. We guard against this error (as Mason does) by defining a verb to be "a word used for saying something about something else." Here, of course, "say" is meant to include all the Finite moods,—Indicative, Imperative, and Subjunctive,—and to exclude the Infinitive, Participle, and Gerund, which, though formed from verbs, have lost their verb-character and become equivalent to nouns or adjectives.

The word or words denoting that person or thing, to which the action of the verb is directed, are called the **Object** to the verb.

Note.—A shorter, and yet more suitable definition of Transitive is this :—**A verb that requires an object.** This is more suitable because it covers the ground of such Transitive verbs as *know, hold, possess, own, have, retain, inherit,* etc., in which no *action* is implied, but rather some state or condition.

137. *A verb is used* **Intransitively,** *when the action stops with the agent, and does not pass from the agent to anything else.*

Men sleep to preserve life.

Sleep what ? This is nonsense. No word or words can be placed as object to such a verb as "sleep."

Note.—Here, as in the case of Transitive, the verb may denote state or condition, and not merely action ; and hence verbs which denote the former have been sometimes called by the distinctive name of Neuter. Thus "he runs" implies action ; "he sleeps" implies condition.

138. An **Auxiliary** verb is one which (*a*) *helps* to form a tense, or a mood, of some other verb, and (*b*) *forgoes its signification as a Principal verb* for that purpose.

A merchant buys that he *may* sell.

Here *may* is not used either in its early sense of "power" or in its present sense of "permission."

I *have* come from home to-day.

Here *have* forgoes its proper signification—"possession," and helps the verb "come" to form a Present Perfect tense.

The verb that is helped by the Auxiliary is called the **Principal** verb. Thus "sell" (in the first of the above examples) is the Principal verb, and "may" is the Auxiliary.

SECTION 2.—VERBS USED TRANSITIVELY.

139. Forms of the Object.—Most Transitive verbs take a *single* object. The object to a verb may be expressed in various different forms, the chief of which are the following (§ 23):—

    (*a*) **Noun** :—The man killed a *snake* with his stick.
    (*b*) **Pronoun** :—The man lifted *me* up out of the water.
    (*c*) **Infinitive** :—He desires *to leave* us to-morrow.
    (*d*) **Gerund** :—He disliked *sleeping* in the daytime.
    (*e*) **Phrase** :—No one knew *how to make a beginning.*
    (*f*) **Clause** :—We do not know *who has come.*

140. Position of the Object.—A noun denoting the object to a verb is usually placed *after* the verb to which it belongs. But when the object is a Relative or Interrogative pronoun, **or**

when the emphasis is thrown on the noun used as object, the object is placed not after, but before the verb.

> **Relative.**—The man *whom* I saw yesterday has come back to-day.
> **Interrogative.**—*What* did you say? *Whom* were you looking for?
> **Emphasis.**—*Silver and gold* have I none; but *what* I have give I unto thee.—*New Testament.*

141. The **Double Object.**—Some Transitive verbs take two objects after them, one of which is usually the name of some *thing*, and the other of some *person or other animal.*

The *thing* named is called the **Direct** object; the *person or other animal* named is called the **Indirect.**

> I forgave him (*Indirect*) his faults (*Direct*).

Another way of distinguishing the two objects is by observing that the Indirect object always stands first. If the Indirect is placed after the Direct, it must be preceded by the preposition "*for*" or "*to*":—

> He taught Euclid (*Direct*) to his sons (*Indirect*).

This mode of showing the Indirect object suggests what is the fact, that the noun or pronoun denoting the Indirect object was originally in the *Dative* case,—a name that is still retained.

142. Complement.—Some Transitive verbs take *one* object only, but still require some word or words to make the predication *complete*. The additional word or words by which the predication is made complete are called the **Complement.**

143. Forms of the Complement.—A Complement may be in seven different forms:—a noun, an adjective, a participle, a preposition with its object, an Infinitive, an adverb, or a noun-clause:—

	Subject.	Verb.	Object.	Complement.
Noun :—	They	made	him	king.
Adjective :—	The judge	set	the prisoner	free.
Participle :—	They	found	her	still weeping.
Prep. with Object :	This plot	filled	us all	with terror.
Infinitive :—	I	like	a rascal	to be punished.
Adverb :—	They	found	the man	asleep.
Clause :—	We	have made	him	what he is.

Note 1.—The necessity of adding a Complement to certain verbs, in order to make the predication complete, can be seen at once from the example, " I like a rascal to be punished." If you merely say, " I like a rascal," you are saying the opposite to what you intended : for you do not like a rascal, but a rascal *to be punished*, or the *punishment* of a rascal.

Note 2.—Observe that when Transitive verbs of incomplete predication are used, the Complement must be separated from the verb by the object. This is required not only by idiom or custom, but to avoid a possible ambiguity. Thus "to make public confessions" would not convey the same sense as " to make confessions public."

Note 3.—In some grammars we hear of the term *Factitive object*. Such a term cannot be used for any kind of complement but nouns ; and therefore it is better to include all kinds of complements under a name (Complement) which will apply equally well to all.

144. Omission of the Relative as Object.—This occurs in two kinds of sentences—(*a*) When the verb is Transitive ; (*b*) when the verb is Intransitive, but followed by a preposition.

This never occurs, however, when the Relative is used in a Continuative sense (see § 127).

    (*a*) The books I bought cost ten shillings.
    (*b*) The house we lived in has fallen down.

145. Transitive Verbs used Intransitively.—There are two ways in which Transitives can become Intransitive :—

(*a*) When the verb is used in such a general sense that no object or objects are thought of in connection with it :—

    Men *eat* to preserve life.
    A new-born child *sees*, but a kitten is born blind.
    He *writes* well (Intr.).   He *writes* a good letter (Trans.).

(*b*) When the Reflexive pronoun is omitted :—

    He *drew* (himself) near me.   He *made* (himself) merry.

The following are common examples of Transitive verbs which have acquired an Intransitive counterpart by omitting the Reflexive pronoun :—

Transitive Verb.	*Intransitive Counterpart.*
Get you (yourself) gone.	*Get* out of my way.
Give him a penny.	The shoe *gives*.
He *obtained* a place.	This doctrine *obtained* (maintained itself) for a long time.
The fire *burnt* up the house.	He *burned* with rage.
Do not *stop* me.	Let us *stop* here a little.
They *open* the doors at nine.	School *opens* at ten o'clock.
A man *breaks* stones with a hammer.	The day *breaks* at six.
The ox *drew* this cart.	He *drew* near to me.
Move away this stone.	*Move* on a little faster.
He *broke up* the meeting.	School *broke up* at three.
The mouse *steals* food.	The mouse *steals* into its hole.

Transitive Verb.	*Intransitive Counterpart.*
They *bathed* the child.	Let us *bathe* here.
He *rolls* a ball down the hill.	The ball *rolls* down the hill.
He *burst* the door open.	The monsoon has *burst*.
Bad men *hide* their faults.	Bats *hide* during the day.
He *turned* me out of the room.	He *turned* to me and spoke.
They *drop* the boat into the water.	Rain *drops* from the sky.
They *keep* the boat on the left bank.	The boat *keeps* on the left bank.
He *sets* the books in order.	The sun *sets* at six P.M.
Lift the box.	The fog has *lifted*.
He *feeds* the horse on grain.	Many men *feed* on rice.
He *rested* his horse.	The horse *rested* in the stable.
He *lengthened* his journey.	The days begin to *lengthen*.
He *spread* his garment.	The mist *spreads* over the earth.
The shepherd *gathered* the sheep.	The sheep *gathered* round their shepherd.
The wind *dispersed* the clouds.	The clouds *have dispersed* from the sky.
He *closed* the business.	The meeting *closed* at six P.M.
The sun *melts* the snow.	The snow *melts* in the sun.
He *dashed* down the cup.	He *dashed* out of the room.

SECTION 3.—VERBS USED INTRANSITIVELY.

146. Intransitive Verbs of Complete Predication.—This is the name given to any Intransitive verb which makes a complete sense by itself, and does not require any word or words to be added to it for this purpose :—

Rivers *flow*. Winds *blow*. Horses *run*, or *walk*, or *graze*, or *lie down*. Birds *fly*. All animals *sleep*. All animals *die*.

147. Intransitive Verbs of Incomplete Predication.—This is the name given to those Intransitive verbs which do not make a complete sense by themselves, but require a **Complement** to supply what the verb left unsaid (§ 26).

The Complement to Intransitive verbs may be in the same kinds of form as the Complement to Transitive verbs :—

	Subject.	*Verb.*	*Complement.*
Noun	A horse	is	a four-legged animal.
	That beggar	turned out	a thief.
Adjective	The man	has fallen	sick.
	The dog	went	mad.
Participle	The man	appears	pleased.
	The stag	continued	running and jumping.
Prep. with	Your coat	is	of many colours.
Object	That book	proved	of no use.

	Subject.	Verb.	Complement.
Infinitive {	The flower	seems	to be fading.
	You	appear	to have forgotten me.
Adverb .	The man	has fallen	asleep.
Clause .	The results	are	what we expected.

Note 1.—When the Complement comes after an Intransitive verb, it is called a **Subjective Complement**, because it relates to the Subject.

But when it comes after a Transitive verb in the *Active* voice, it is called an **Objective Complement**, because it relates to the Object.

Note 2.—The Complement usually stands *after* its verb, but for the sake of emphasis it may be placed *before* it :—

> *Strait* is the gate, and *narrow* is the way that leadeth unto life, and *few* there be that find it.—*New Testament*.

Note 3.—The same verb, whether Transitive or Intransitive, may in different connections be used either as complete or incomplete predicates :—

{ The world *is* (exists)	. . .	(*Comp.*)
{ The world *is* round .	. . .	(*Incomp.*)
{ They *made* a snow-man	. .	(*Comp.*)
{ They *made* him *king* .	. .	(*Incomp.*)
{ The tree *is growing* .	. .	(*Comp.*)
{ He *is growing strong*.	. .	(*Incomp.*)
{ The water *filled* the pipe .	.	(*Comp.*)
{ They *filled* the pipe *with water* .		(*Incomp.*)

148. The Cognate Object.—An Intransitive verb, though it is never followed by a noun denoting an *outside* or foreign object, may sometimes be followed by a noun *already implied more or less in the verb itself*.

Thus we can say " he has lived a sad *life*," where the noun *life* is implied already in the verb " lived," and is in fact part of its meaning. Such objects are called **cognate** or "kindred," because the noun denoting them is of kindred meaning to that of the verb itself.

There are five different forms of Cognate object :—

(a) *Cognate noun formed directly from the verb.*

He laughed a hearty *laugh*.	He slept a sound *sleep*.
He died a sad *death*.	He prayed an earnest *prayer*.
He lived a long *life*.	He sighed a deep *sigh*.
He fought a good *fight*.	He sang a fine *song*.

(b) *Cognate noun of similar meaning.*

He went a long *way*.	He ran his own *course*.
He fought a hard *battle*.	It blows a brisk *gale*.
He struck a deadly *blow*.	The bells ring a merry *peal*.

(c) *A noun descriptive of the Cognate noun understood.*

They shouted *applause* = they shouted a *shout* of applause.
He served his *apprenticeship* = he served his *service* as an apprentice.
He ran a great *risk* = he ran a *course* of great risk.

He played *the fool*= he played the *part* of a fool.

He looked *daggers* at me = he looked me a *look* of daggers.

(d) *An adjective qualifying the Cognate noun understood.*

He shouted his loudest (shout). He ran his fastest (run or pace). He fought his best (fight). She sang her sweetest (song). He breathed his last (breath). He tried his hardest (trial or attempt).

(e) *Cognate noun expressed by "it."*

We must fight *it* (=the fight) out to the end.

We have no horse; so we must foot *it* (that is, go the distance on foot).

Lord Angelo dukes *it* (= acts the part of a duke) well.—SHAKSPEARE.

149. The Reflexive Object.—In older English, Intransitive verbs were often followed by a Personal pronoun, either reflexive or used reflexively.

A few such examples still occur :—

Hie *thee* home. Fare *thee* well. Haste *thee* away. They sat *them* down. He over-ate *himself*. To over-sleep *oneself*. Vaulting ambition which o'erleaps *itself*.—SHAKSPEARE.

In § 306 it is explained that what we here for convenience' sake called a Reflexive object was in reality a pronoun in the Dative case, like the Indirect object described in § 141.

150. Intransitive Verbs in a Causal sense.—If an Intransitive verb is used in the sense of causing a thing to be done, it becomes Transitive. Of these there are only a few examples in English :—

Intransitive.	*Causal.*
The horse trotted out.	They trotted out the horse (= caused it to trot out).
Water boils.	He boils the water.
The prisoners walk out.	He walks out the prisoners.
A thorn ran into his hand.	He ran a thorn into his hand.
That horse will starve.	Do not starve the horse.
Drinking freely.	Drinking himself drunk (=making himself drunk by drinking).—1 *Kings* 16, 9.
The bell rang twice.	Ring the bell.
The kite flew into the air.	He flew the kite.
The soldiers march out.	He marches out the soldiers.
Wheat grows in the field.	He grows wheat in the field.
The boat floated.	He floated the boat.
He talks hoarsely.	He talks himself hoarse (= he makes himself hoarse by talking).

151. There are a few Intransitive verbs, in which the causal sense is indicated by *some change of vowel.*

Intransitive.	*Transitive or Causal.*
The tree *falls.*	He *fells* the tree with an axe.
The sun will *rise* at six.	I cannot *raise* this box.
The cow *lies* on the grass.	The man *lays* down his coat.
We must not *sit* here.	He *set* the books in order.
He will *fare* well.	He will *ferry* me over.
The enemy *quails.*	He *quells* the enemy.

152. Prepositional Verbs.—An Intransitive verb can be made Transitive by having a preposition added to it.

Such verbs may be considered to be real Transitives, provided they can be used in the Passive voice.

$$\begin{cases} \text{We } act\ on \text{ this rule.} & (Active.) \\ \text{This rule is } acted\ on \text{ by us.} & (Passive.) \end{cases}$$
$$\begin{cases} \text{No one } relies\ on \text{ his word.} & (Active.) \\ \text{His word cannot be } relied\ on.[1] & (Passive.) \end{cases}$$

Observe that when the verb is in the Passive voice, the *on* cannot be parsed as a preposition, since there is no object to it. It must therefore be parsed as part of the verb itself.

Note 1.—In prepositional verbs, the preposition is almost always placed after the verb ; but "*with*" and "*over*" are often placed before it :—

He *withstood* (stood against, endured) the attack.

He was *overcome* (defeated) by the enemy.

The banks were *overflowed* (inundated) with water.

The field is *overgrown* (covered) with weeds.

The boundary has been *overstepped* (transgressed).

All these verbs, when they are used apart from the preposition, are Intransitive.   It is the *preposition which makes them Transitive.*

Note 2.—It sometimes happens that the preposition after the Intransitive verb is not expressed, but the verb is none the less followed by an object :—

They *laughed* (at) *him* to scorn.

He *looked* (at) *me* in the face.

Leonidas *fought* (against) *the Persians* at Thermopylæ.

I cannot *sit* (on) that horse.

I cannot *stand* (with-stand) the strain.

153. Summary.—There are thus two ways in which an Intransitive verb can become Transitive—(1) when it is used in a Causal sense (§ 150) ; (2) when it is connected with a preposition so closely that the verb, compounded with the preposition, can be made Passive (§ 152).

Similarly, there are two kinds of objects that can come after an Intransitive verb, although the verb itself continues to be Intransitive—(1) the Cognate object (§ 148) ; (2) the Reflexive or Personal object (§ 149).

---

[1] But we say *reliable*, not *reliable on* ; *laughable*, not *laughable at*.   In the adjective-forms the final preposition is dropped.

SECTION 4.—AUXILIARY VERBS.

154. Auxiliary and Notional Verbs.—Verbs have usually been subdivided into *two* classes, Transitive and Intransitive, and not, as is done in this book, into *three*, the third of which is Auxiliary. The last is an entirely distinct class.

A Notional verb (Transitive or Intransitive) is one used as a Principal verb to express a full meaning of its own :—

(1) He *has* ten horses.

Here *has* is a Transitive verb, and is used to express the notion of " possession." Now look at the following :—

(2) He *has* been ill to-day.

Here *has* is neither Transitive nor Intransitive, but merely a *tense-forming*, that is, an Auxiliary verb. It has, for the time being, *discarded its proper sense* of " possession," in order to *help* the verb " be " to form a Present Perfect tense. It is not notional, but merely modifies the notion expressed by " be."

The classification of verbs might therefore be restated as follows :—

Notional or ⎰used Transitively .   .   Class I.
Principal ⎱used Intransitively   .   Class II.
Auxiliary   .   .   .   .   Class III.

155. Uses of Auxiliary Verbs classified.—The uses of Auxiliary verbs may be classified under two separate headings : (*a*) Tense-forming ; (*b*) Mood-forming. It should be understood, however, that the same verb may be used for different auxiliary purposes at different times, just as the same verb may be used Transitively at one time and Intransitively at another.

(*a*) *Tense-forming.*—" *Shall* " and " *will* " are used for forming the **Future** tenses ; as " I *shall* go," " he *will* go." " *Be* " is used for forming the **Continuous** (or Imperfect) tenses ; as " I *am* going," " I *was* going." " *Have* " is used for forming the **Perfect** tenses ; as " I *have* gone," " I *had* gone." " *Have* " and " *be* " together are used for forming the **Perfect Continuous** tenses ; as " I *have been* going," " I *had been* going." " *Do* " and " *did* " are used for forming a special kind of **Present** and **Past** tense ; as " I *do* not go," " I *did* not go."

(*b*) *Mood-forming.*—" *Do* " is used for forming the **Imperative** mood, when the sentence is negative, as " *do* not come." (Out of this has grown the emphatic affirmative form " *do* come," used colloquially.) " *May* " and " *might*," " *should*," " *would*," are used for making certain **Subjunctive** equivalents ;

as "that he *may* go," "he *should* go," "he *would* go." "*Shall*," "*will*," "*have*," "*be*," "*do*," as has been shown under (*a*), are used for forming various tenses of the **Indicative** mood.

The verb "*be*," assisted by "*have*," "*shall*," "*will*," "*may*," is used for forming the tenses and moods of the *Passive* voice.

Note.—From the above it will be seen that Auxiliary verbs not only help Principal verbs, but also help one another. Thus in the Perfect Continuous (Active voice), "I *have been* going," we have two Auxiliaries helping each other to form a single tense. In the Future Perfect Continuous, "I *shall have been* going," we have three Auxiliaries helping one another to form a single tense.

156. List of Auxiliary Verbs.—The Auxiliary verbs make up a very small class. If our definition of Auxiliary (viz. a verb that (1) *helps* a Principal verb to form some tense, mood, or voice ; and (2) *forgoes its own sense as a Principal verb* for that purpose) is adhered to, the following list is exhaustive :—*have, be, shall, will, may, do,*—only six, all told.

But the smallness of their number is amply compensated by the frequency of their use ; for no Transitive or Intransitive verb can be conjugated without them, except in two tenses, the Present and Past Indefinite. In Old as in Mod. English the Present and Past are the only two tenses that are formed by inflexion.

Note.—*Can* and *must*, though Defective, are Principal verbs. They are not Auxiliary—(*a*) because they do not help to form any tense, mood, or voice ; and (*b*) because they do not discard their meanings as Principal verbs for auxiliary purposes. They are merely Principal verbs very defective in form.

157.—Auxiliary and Principal.—The same verb may be an Auxiliary at one time and a Principal at another. This is implied already in the definition, according to which an Auxiliary verb is one that "forgoes its proper sense as a Notional or Principal verb for the purpose of becoming Auxiliary."

To make this point perfectly clear, we will take each of the six verbs named above *seriatim* :—

Have	I *had* a fine horse	(*Principal.*)
	I *had* gone away	(*Auxiliary.*)
Be	The earth *is* (exists). A horse *is* a quadruped	(*Principal.*)
	He *was* going. He *is* loved . . .	(*Auxiliary.*)
Shall	You *shall* leave the house (Command, Authority)	(*Principal.*)
	I *shall* leave the house (Simple Futurity) .	(*Auxiliary.*)
Will	I *will* go to-day (Determination) . .	(*Principal.*)
	You *will* go to-day (Simple Futurity) . .	(*Auxiliary.*)
May	I *may* go (=am permitted to go) . .	(*Principal.*)
	He works that he *may* live (Purpose) . .	(*Auxiliary.*)

Do { You *did* that work well . . . . *(Principal.)*
{ You *did* indeed work hard . . . . *(Auxiliary.)*

SECTION 5.—ACTIVE AND PASSIVE VOICES.

158. A *Transitive* verb has two voices, the **Active** and the **Passive**.

In the Active voice the person or thing denoted by the Subject is said to *do something to* something else :—

Tom *kills* a snake. (Here the person denoted by the Subject, namely Tom, *does something to* a snake.)

In the Passive voice the person or thing is said to *suffer something from* something else :—

A snake *is killed* by Tom. (Here the thing denoted by the Subject, namely a snake, *suffers something from* Tom.)

Hence Voice may be defined as that form of a Transitive verb which shows whether the agent *does* something to something else, or *suffers* something from something else.

159. An *Intransitive* verb is not used in the Passive voice, unless it takes a Cognate object in the Active :—

I have fought the good fight. *(Active.)*
The good fight has been fought by me. *(Passive.)*

Here the subject "fight" does not really *suffer* anything. Hence an Intransitive verb, when it takes a Passive form, is merely aping the Passive voice.

160. When a sentence is changed from the Active form to the Passive, the object to the Active verb becomes the subject to the Passive verb.

Object to Active Verb.	*Subject to Passive Verb.*
Brutes cannot make *tools.*	*Tools* cannot be made by brutes.
Brutes do not possess *hands.*	*Hands* are not possessed by brutes.

161. Retained Object.—Verbs that take *two* objects after them in the Active voice (§ 141) can still retain *one* in the Passive. This object may be either—

(*a*) The Indirect object of the Active verb ; as—

Active Verb.	*Passive Verb.*
I forgave *him* his fault.	The fault was forgiven *him* by me.
We allowed *him* two pounds.	Two pounds were allowed *him* by us.

Or (*b*) the Direct object of the Active verb ; as—

Active Verb.	*Passive Verb.*
I forgave him *his fault.*	He was forgiven *his fault* by me.
We allowed him *two pounds.*	He was allowed *two pounds* by us.

Note.—It has now been shown that there are five different kinds of objects which can be used with verbs :—

(1) **Direct** (with Trans. verbs).—He taught *Euclid* (§ 141).
(2) **Indirect** (with Trans. verbs).—He taught *his sons* Euclid (§ 141).
(3) **Retained** (with Pass. verbs).—His sons were taught *Euclid* (§ 161).
(4) **Cognate** (with Intrans. verbs).—The fever must run its *course* (§ 148).
(5) **Reflexive** (with Intrans. verbs).—He sat *himself* down (§ 149).

Note.—Among these observe that (1) and (4) are Direct objects ; (2) and (5) are Indirect ; (3) is Direct or Indirect, according as the noun or pronoun was Direct or Indirect with the Active verb. "He sat himself down," when grammatically analysed, means "He sat down *for himself.*" Avoid the mistake of considering that *sat* is used in a Causal sense—"He *caused himself* to sit down." In Old Eng. the Indirect object was in the Dative case, the Direct in the Accusative.

162. Whenever a verb which takes an Object and a Complement is changed from the Active voice to the Passive, the Objective Complement becomes a Subjective one.

Active voice : Complement to Object.	*Passive voice : Complement to Subject.*
They proclaimed him *king*.	He was proclaimed *king* by them.
They did not crown him *king*.	He was not crowned *king* by them.

163. Verbs Active in form, but Passive in sense.—Transitive verbs are sometimes used in a Passive sense without being put into the Passive voice :—

(*a*) Verbs with a Complement :—

> The stone *feels* rough (is rough when it is felt).
> Honey *tastes* sweet (is sweet when it is tasted).
> The milk *smells* sour (is sour when it is smelt).
> Your blame *counts* for nothing (is worth nothing when it is counted).
> Your composition *reads* well (sounds well when it is read).
> The house *does* not *let* (is not taken when it is meant to be let).
> The horse *does* not *sell* (is not taken when it is meant to be sold).
> That cloth will *wear* thin (will become thin when it is worn).

(*b*) Verbs without a Complement :—

> The house *is building* (= is in a state of being built).
> The trumpets *are sounding* (= are being sounded).
> The cannons *are firing* (= are being fired).
> The drums *are beating* (= are being beaten).
> The house *is finishing* (= is being finished).
> The book *is printing* (= is being printed).
> The cows *are milking* (= are being milked).

Note.—The generally received and best supported opinion regarding this construction is that what looks like a present participle is, in reality, a gerund, with the preposition *on* or *in* omitted.

This house was three years in *building* (= being built).

Others, however, think that it is a real Active participle used in a Passive sense, like the verbs in examples (*a*).[1]

SECTION 6.—MOOD, TENSE, NUMBER, AND PERSON.

164. Mood defined.—Mood is the form assumed by a verb (either by inflection or with the help of Auxiliaries) for indicating the *mode* or manner in which the action or state denoted by the verb is conceived by the mind.

165. Names of the Moods.—There are four Moods, three Finite and one Infinitive :—

(*a*) Three Finite moods :—

  1. Indicative, or the mood of **Fact**.
  2. Imperative, or the mood of **Volition**.
  3. Subjunctive, or the mood of **Supposition**.

(*b*) Infinitive mood.

166. Characters of the Moods.—In the Indicative mood we *assert* or *inquire* about something as a *fact* ; as, " he comes," " he came," " he will come," " will he come ?"

In the Imperative mood we *command* or *advise* an action ; as, " come thou," or " come."

In the Subjunctive mood we *suppose* an action ; as, " if he come or should come."

The Infinitive mood expresses some action or state without reference to number or person ; as, " to come."

" Infinitive " means unlimited,—not limited by number or person.

167. Number and Person.—The number and person of a Finite verb depend upon the nature of its Subject.

Number {
If the subject is Singular, the verb must be Singular ; as, Rain *is* falling.
If the subject is Plural, the verb must be Plural ; as, Raindrops *are* falling.
}

Person {
If the subject is in the First person, the verb must be in the First person ; as, I love. We come.
If the subject is in the Second person, the verb must be in the Second person ; as, Thou lovest. You come.
If the subject is in the Third person, the verb must be in the Third person ; as, He loves. The teacher *has* come.
}

---

[1] The word ending in -*ing* must certainly be a participle in such colloquialisms as " I want a button *sewing on*." In such a sentence as " The wall is rapidly building," *building* must certainly be parsed as a participle, as otherwise the adverb *rapidly* could not be parsed.

Hence arises the following rule :—*A Finite verb must be in the same number and person as its Subject.*

Note.—All nouns and noun-equivalents take verbs in the Third person. All pronouns excepting the First Personal and the Second Personal take verbs in the Third person.

168. Tense defined.—Tense is the form assumed by a verb (either by inflection or with the help of Auxiliary verbs) for indicating either (*a*) the *time* to which an event is referred, or (*b*) the *degree of completeness* ascribed to an event at the time of its occurrence.

The verb may tell you :—

(1) That an action *is done* at the **Present** time ; as, " he sees a star."

(2) That an action *was done* in the **Past** time ; as, " he saw a star."

(3) That an action *will be done* in the **Future** time ; as, " he will see a star."

(4) That an action was at some *past* time viewed as *future*. **(Future in the Past.)** " He would see a star."

A verb, then, has four main times or tenses, viz. the Present, the Past, the Future. and the Future in the Past.

169. To each tense there are four different forms :—

I. **Indefinite** ; which denotes Present, Past, or Future time in its simplest form, nothing being said as to the degree of completeness attaching to the action or state ; as, " I love," " I loved," " I shall love."

II. **Continuous** ; which denotes that the event (in Present, Past, or Future time) is still *continuing*, and is not yet completed ; as, " I am loving," " I was loving," " I shall be loving."

Note.—This tense is sometimes called the **Imperfect**, because it denotes an event which is imperfect or not completed.

III. **Perfect** ; which denotes that the event (in Present, Past, or Future time) is in a completed or *perfect* state ; as, " I have loved," " I had loved," " I shall have loved."

IV. **Perfect Continuous** ; which combines the meanings of the two preceding forms ; as " I have been loving," " I had been loving," " I shall have been loving."

SECTION 7.—INDICATIVE MOOD.

Forms of the Tenses, Indicative Mood.

170. The four Tenses and sixteen forms of a verb in the Indicative Mood are shown in the following table :—

I.—Active Voice.

Form.	Present Tense.	Past Tense.	Future Tense.	Future in the Past.
Ind.	I love	I loved	I shall love	I should love
Cont.	I am loving	I was loving	I shall be loving	I should be loving
Perf.	I have loved	I had loved	I shall have loved	I should have loved
Perf. Cont.	I have been loving	I had been loving	I shall have been loving	I should have been loving

II.—Passive Voice.

Form.	Present Tense.	Past Tense.	Future Tense.	Future in the Past.
Ind.	I am loved	I was loved	I shall be loved	I should be loved
Cont.	I am being loved	I was being loved	(Wanting)	(Wanting)
Perf.	I have been loved	I had been loved	I shall have been loved	I should have been loved
Perf. Cont.	(Wanting)	(Wanting)	(Wanting)	(Wanting)

171. The Present, Past, and Future tenses (Indefinite) are declined in the following form, for all numbers and persons :—

I.—Active Voice.

Present Tense.

	Singular.	Plural.
1st Person	I love	We love
2nd ,,	Thou lovest	Ye or you love
3rd ,,	He loves or loveth	They love

Past Tense.

	Singular.	Plural.
1st Person	I loved	We loved
2nd ,,	Thou lovedst	Ye or you loved
3rd ,,	He loved	They loved

Future Tense.

	Singular.	Plural.
1st Person	I shall love	We shall love
2nd ,,	Thou wilt love	Ye or you will love
3rd ,,	He will love	They will love

N.B.—(1) The Singular forms of the Second person (thou lovest, thou lovedst, thou wilt love) are now seldom used except in poetry. They have been superseded by the Plural forms (you love, you loved, and you will love), which, though Plural in fact, are used in a Singular sense as well as in a Plural sense ; as, "Have you come, my son ?" "Have you," being addressed to "son," is used in a Singular sense, and may be parsed as Singular.

(2) The form "he loveth" is now seldom used except in poetry.

II.—Passive Voice.

Present Tense.

	Singular.	Plural.
1st Person	I am loved	We are loved
2nd ,,	Thou art loved	Ye or you are loved
3rd ,,	He is loved	They are loved

Past Tense.

	Singular.	*Plural.*
1st *Person*	I was loved	We were loved
2nd ,,	Thou wast loved	Ye or you were loved
3rd ,,	He was loved	They were loved

Future Tense.

	Singular.	*Plural.*
1st *Person*	I shall be loved	We shall be loved
2nd ,,	Thou wilt be loved	Ye or you will be loved
3rd ,,	He will be loved	They will be loved

172. Do and **Did.**—The Present Indefinite in the Active voice can also be formed by "*do*," and the Past by "*did.*"

Present Tense.

	Singular.	*Plural.*
1st *Person*	I do love	We do love
2nd ,,	Thou dost love	Ye or you do love
3rd ,,	He does love	They do love

Past Tense.

	Singular.	*Plural.*
1st *Person*	I did love	We did love
2nd ,,	Thou didst love	Ye or you did love
3rd ,,	He did love	They did love

This form is used for three different purposes :—

(*a*) For the sake of emphasis ; as, "I *do* love," "I *did* love."

(*b*) For the sake of bringing in the word "not"; as "I *do not* love" (which is better than saying "I love not"), "I *did not* love" (which is better than saying "I loved not").

(*c*) For the sake of asking a question ; as, "*Does* he love?" "Why *did* he love?"   "*Did* he not love?"

173. Has come, is come.—These two forms appear to be merely different, and at the same time equivalent, ways of expressing a Present Perfect tense. But they are not quite equivalent in sense. In the former *the time of the action* is prominent; in the latter *the state of the agent*. The former alone gives a Present Perfect tense.

"The flower *is* faded."[1] In what state is the flower ? Faded. No prominence is given to *the time of the fading*. The verb "is" is here not an Auxiliary, but an Intransitive verb of Incomplete Predication, to which the participle "faded" is complement.

"The flower *has* faded." By what time was the fading of the flower completed ? By the present time.[1] The verb "has"

---

[1] It is therefore incorrect to say (as is commonly done) that "has come" and "is come" are equivalent, and that the use of "is" and "was" for "has" and "had" is limited to verbs of motion. In the Tudor period

is here an Auxiliary, which with the word "faded" helps to form the Present Perfect tense of the verb "to fade."

174. Shall and Will.—These (as the student has learnt already) are the two Auxiliary verbs by means of which the Future tense is formed in both voices.

One of the puzzles in English to a beginner is to know when to use "*shall*" and when to use "*will*."

With a view to clearing up this matter it should be understood that there are *three* senses in which the future tense can be used :—

(*a*) To express *merely future time*, and nothing more.
(*b*) To combine future time with an implied *command*.
(*c*) To combine future time with an implied *intention*.

(*a*) *Merely future time.*

When nothing but future time is intended—*mere futurity*, without any idea of command or intention being mixed up with it—*shall* must be used for the *First* person, and *will* for the *Second* and *Third* persons, as below :—

		Singular.	*Plural.*
1*st Person*		I *shall* go	We *shall* go
2*nd*	,,	Thou *wilt* go	You *will* go
3*rd*	,,	He *will* go	They *will* go

In these persons *shall* and *will* are strictly *tense-forming*, that is, Auxiliary verbs (see §§ 155, 157).

(*b*) *An Implied Command, Promise, or Threat.*

Whenever we desire to express, not merely future time, but some *command*, or *promise*, or *threat* in addition, *shall* is put for *will* in the Second and Third persons ; [1] as—

You *shall* be hanged (by some one's command).
You *shall* receive your prize to-morrow (promise).
If you do this, you *shall* be hanged (threat).

In these examples, the *shall* is not a tense-forming or Auxiliary verb, but a Principal one (see §§ 155, 157).

(*c*) *An Implied Intention.*

When the speaker wishes to express some intention of his own, then *will* is put for *shall* in the First person :—

I *will* call on you to-day, and I *shall* then say good-bye.

---

the use of the verb *to be* with Past participles was much more common than it is now. Shakspeare has such phrases as—"Is stolen away," "are marched forth," "are rid," "is entered into."

[1] In Old Eng. *sceal* (shall) means "I must," "I owe," "I am liable for"; and this sense is maintained, wherever this verb is used in the Second and Third persons. *Will* in Old Eng. means to intend or desire; and this sense is maintained, whenever this verb is used in the First person. But these senses are not maintained, when *shall* is used in the First person, and *will* in the Second and Third. The verbs have then become Auxiliary, that is, they have discarded their original meanings in order to help other verbs to express future time.

Here *will* denotes the *intention* of calling, while *shall* denotes *merely future time.* Therefore *will* is a Principal verb, and *shall* is an Auxiliary.

SECTION 8.—IMPERATIVE MOOD.

175. The **Imperative** mood is used only in the Present tense, and only in the Second person :—

Singular.	*Plural.*
Speak, or speak thou.	Speak, or speak you, or speak ye.

176. To express an order or prohibition in the *First* or *Third* person we either (*a*) use the Transitive verb *let*, which is itself the Second person (Singular or Plural) of the Imperative mood of the verb "to let," or (*b*) we employ the Subjunctive mood :—

	Singular.	*Plural.*
(*a*) 1st Person	Let me speak	Let us speak
3rd „	Let him speak	Let them speak.

(*b*) Every soldier *kill* his prisoners.—SHAKSPEARE.
　　Thither our path lies ; *wind we* up the height.—BROWNING.

The Third person of the Subjunctive occurs in the common phrase *suffice it*, which means "let it suffice," "let it be sufficient" :—

　　Suffice it to say that all the prisoners were acquitted.

177. The chief uses of the Imperative mood are to express (*a*) *command*, (*b*) *precept*, or (*c*) *entreaty :*—

　　(*a*) *Command :*—
　　　　Speak,—or I fire.
　　　　Awake, arise, or *be* for ever fallen.—MILTON.

　　(*b*) *Precept* or *Invitation :*—
　　　　Go to the ant, thou sluggard ; *consider* her ways and *be* wise.
　　　　　　—*Old Testament.*

　　(*c*) *Entreaty* or *Prayer :*—
　　　　Give us this day our daily bread, and *forgive* us our trespasses,
　　　　　　as we forgive them that trespass against us.—*Lord's Prayer.*

178. When the verb is negative, that is, prohibitive, the Imperative is now formed by the Auxiliary " *do.*"

Older Form.	*Present Form.*
Fear not.	*Do* not fear.
Taste not that food.	*Do* not taste that food.

Note.—Sometimes, even when the verb is affirmative, the Imperative is formed by " do," in order to give more emphasis to an entreaty. This, however, occurs only in colloquial English.

　　　　Do leave off making that noise.
　　　　Do help me to lift this box.

179. The Imperative mood is sometimes used to express a **Supposition** :—

Take care of the pence, and the pounds will take care of themselves (= If you take care of the pence, the pounds will, etc.).
Resist the devil, and he will flee from you (= If you resist the devil, he will flee, etc.).

180. Sometimes, but very rarely, the Imperative mood is used **absolutely** ; see § 27 (*c*).

A large number of men, *say* a hundred, are working on the railroad.
Behold, this dreamer cometh.—*Old Testament.*

SECTION 9.—SUBJUNCTIVE MOOD.

181. The **Subjunctive** mood is so called, because it is generally *subjoined* to some other sentence, and seldom stands alone.

Note.—It stands alone, only when it expresses a *wish* ; see below, § 186 (2). It cannot be used either to assert a fact or to inquire about one ; that is, it cannot take the place of the Indicative mood. The Indicative, however (according to the idiom now in force), can, and frequently does, take the place of the Subjunctive. In fact, the tendency of Modern English is to get rid of the Subjunctive.

182. The Present and Past tenses are declined as follows in the Active voice :—

Present Tense.

	Singular.	*Plural.*
1st *Person*	If I love	If we love
2nd ,,	If thou love (*rare*)	If you love
3rd ,,	If he love (*rare*)	If they love

Past Tense.

	Singular.	*Plural.*
1st *Person*	If I loved	If we loved
2nd ,,	If thou lovedst	If you loved
3rd ,,	If he loved	If they loved

Note.—We call the second of these the Past tense, because it is past in *form*. But in the Subjunctive mood this past form has reference not to past, but to present or future contingencies, as is shown in § 186 (3).

183. The verb "*to be*" takes the following forms in the Subjunctive mood ; but the Present tense is now rarely used :—

Present Tense.

	Singular.	*Plural.*
1*st Person*	If I be	If we be
2*nd* ,,	If thou be	If ye or you be
3*rd* ,,	If he be	If they be

Past Tense.

	Singular.	*Plural.*
1*st Person*	If I were	If we were
2*nd* ,,	If thou wert	If ye or you were
3*rd* ,,	If he were	If they were

Note.—What has been said about the Past tense in Note to § 182 applies also to "were." The form is *Past*, but the reference is either Present or Future. See § 186 (3).

184. The forms for the Continuous and Perfect tenses in the Active voice are shown below :—

	Continuous.	*Perfect.*
Present	If I be loving	If I have loved
Past	If I were loving	If I had loved

185. In the Passive voice the Indefinite and the Perfect are the only forms of the Subjunctive mood which are in ordinary use :—

	Indefinite.	*Perfect.*
Present	If I be loved	If I have been loved
Past	If I were loved	If I had been loved

The Uses of the Subjunctive Mood.

186. The Indicative states *a fact* and sometimes a condition ; the Imperative expresses *an order* ; the Subjunctive *a purpose, a wish, a condition,* or *a doubt,* anything rather than a fact.

(1) *A Purpose.*

In this case the verb in the Subjunctive mood is preceded by the conjunction *that* or *lest* (lest = that not). The Auxiliary verbs "*may*" and "*might*" are used after "*that*," and "*should*" after "*lest*."

Indicative.	*Subjunctive : Purpose.*
Present or *Future* { I give you a prize, . .	that you *may work* well again.
I shall keep your book, .	{ lest you *lose* it. { that you *may* not *lose* it.
Past { I gave you a prize, . .	that you *might work* well again
I kept your book, . .	{ lest you *should lose* it. { that you *might* not *lose* it.

Note.—In the Tudor period, and somewhat beyond it, the Subjunctive was commonly expressed without the help of an Auxiliary:—

Love not sleep, lest thou *come* to poverty.—*Old Testament.*
See that all *be* present, when he comes.
Buy us a little food, that we *die* not.—*Old Testament.*
Speak to my brother, that he *divide* the inheritance with me.—*New Testament.*

(2) *A Wish or Order.*

Thy kingdom *come*, thy will *be* done.
May he live long and see not the grave !
I wish that he *were* as clever as his sister.
God *save* the queen. Long *live* the king.
Far *be* it from me to say anything false.
My sentence is that the prisoner *be* hanged.

(3) *Condition and its Consequence.*

A Present or Future *condition* can be expressed in four different ways, all equivalent. The verb in the *consequence* is expressed by *shall* or *should* in the first person, and by *will* or *would* in the second and third.

First Sentence : Condition.	*Second Sentence : Consequence.*
Present or *Future* { If I *meet* him, If I *met* him, If I *should meet* him, If I *were* to *meet* him, }	I *shall* know him at once. I *should* know him at once.
Past { If he *had met* me, If I *had been* in his place,	he *would have known* me. I *should have paid* the money.

The *if*, when followed by an Auxiliary, can be left out. In this case the *should, had,* or *were* must be placed before its subject :—

Present or *Future* { Should he *meet* me, Were I in his place,	he *would know* me at once. I *should pay* the money.
Past { Had he *met* me, Had I *been* in his place,	he *would have known* me. I *should have paid* the money.

Sometimes the Conditional sentence is left out or understood, and only the Consequent sentence is expressed :—

He *would* never agree to that ("if you asked him," understood).

(4) *A Doubt or Supposition.*

A verb in the Subjunctive mood, preceded by some conjunction or conjunctive pronoun, implies some *doubt* or *supposition.*

I will not let thee go, except thou *bless* me.—*Old Test.*
Murder, *though* it *have* no tongue, will speak.
When I ask her if she *love* me.—TENNYSON.
Blow till thou *burst* thy wind.—SHAKSPEARE.
Whether he *allow* me or not, I will go to him.
Provided he *confess* his fault, I will pardon him.
Unless he *consent*, we can do nothing.
Whoever he *be*, he shall not go unpunished.

Note.—The Subjunctive mood is not always preceded by a conjunction to express a doubt :—

> " *Come* weal, *come* woe, by Bruce's side,"
> Replied the chief, " will Donald bide."

SECTION 10.—INFINITIVE MOOD.

187. Infinitive defined.—The Infinitive is that part of a verb which names the action, without reference to any doer, and is therefore not limited by person or by number.

It is called Infinitive or Infinite, because it is not finite, that is, not limited by person or number. It cannot be attached to a subject, so as to make an assertion or sentence.

It is a mistake, however, to say that the Infinitive is "unlimited by time"; for it has separate forms for denoting past and present :—

(1) *Present* or *Indefinite.*—He seems *to work* hard.
(2) *Past* or *Perfect.*—He seems *to have worked* hard.

188. The use of " to."—In Old English there were two separate forms :—

The Simple or Noun-Infinitive—*drinc-an.*

The Dative or Gerundial Infinitive—*tó drinc-enne.*

As time went on, both the suffixes (-*an* and -*enne*) dropped off, and the " to" (a prep. followed by a Dative), which originally belonged only to the Gerundial Infinitive, was given to the Simple also. So we have now one form for both uses :—

Simple or Noun-Infinitive—*to drink.*
Gerundial Infinitive—*to drink.*

189. Infinitive without " to."—The preposition " to" is not an essential part of the Infinitive ; for in Old English the Noun-Infinitive was formed without it. Nor is " to" even now a necessary sign of the Infinitive ; for it is not used in the following contexts :—

(*a*) After verbs denoting some kind of perception :—*hear, see, feel, know, watch, behold, observe, perceive :—*

I heard him *speak.* I saw him *come.* I felt his hand *touch* me. I have known him *laugh.* I watched him *go.* I beheld, or observed, or perceived the fish *rise.*

(*b*) After the verbs *do, may, shall, will,* when they are used as Auxiliaries :—

He did not *go.* He works that he may *live.* I shall *go.* He will *go.* Do not *go* away.

(*c*) After the verbs *may, shall, will,* when they are used as

Principal verbs, and after the Principal verbs—*can, must, let, dare, need, make, bid* :—

> You may *go.* He shall *be* punished. I will *see* you once more. You can *go.* You must *go.* He bids me *come.* He let me *go.* I dare not *go.* You need not *go.* He made me *laugh.*

Note.—The "to" is expressed after *dare,* when the sentence is affirmative : "He dares to disobey me."

(*d*) The "to" can be left out after the adjective "better" :—

> Better *be* with the dead.—SHAKSPEARE.
> (= *To be* with the dead (would be) better.)
> Better *dwell* in the midst of alarms.—COWPER.

(*e*) The "to" is also left out after the verb "had," in such phrases as "had better," "had rather," "had sooner," "had as soon . . . as."

> You had better not *remain* here.
> I had rather *take* this than that.
> I had sooner *run* than *walk.*
> I had as soon *run* as *walk.*

Note.—"Had" is here used in a Subjunctive sense=should have. "I had better not remain here," means "I should have (it) better not to remain here" ; that is, "It would be better for me not to remain."

(*f*) The "to" is left out after the conjunction "than," especially when it can be supplied from another clause :—

> He is better able *to walk* than *run.*

(*g*) The "to" is left out after the prepositions "but" and "than," [1] provided it is preceded by the verb "do" :—

> He *did* nothing but *laugh* (=to laugh).
> He *did* nothing else than *laugh.*

The two kinds of Infinitive.

190. There are, as we have shown in § 188, two kinds of Infinitive, the forms of which are identical, though their uses are so different as to represent different parts of speech :—

I. The Noun-Infinitive (sometimes called the Simple).

II. The Gerundial or Qualifying Infinitive.

Note.—If we look only to the *form* of the Infinitive, the name "Simple" is limited to those Infinitives which are not preceded by "*to.*" But if we look to the *syntactical value,* the name "Simple" must be extended to all Infinitives, whether preceded by "*to*" or not, that do the work of a *noun ;* and the name "Gerundial" must be given only to those that do the work of an Adjective or Adverb.

191. The Noun-Infinitive may be used for any purpose for which an ordinary noun is used, viz. (*a*) as Subject to a verb ;

---

[1] The prepositional character of *than* is shown below in § 231.

(b) as Object to a verb; (c) as Complement to a verb; (d) as Object to certain prepositions (rare); or (e) as a form of exclamation. It has hence been called, though not very commonly, "the Substantive Mood."

(a) Subject to a verb :—

To err (=error) is human ; *to forgive* (=forgiveness) is divine.

(b) Object to a verb :—

They expect *to succeed* (=success).
A good man does not fear *to die* (=death).

(c) Complement to a verb :—

He appears *to be* a wise man.   (*Intransitive.*)
They ordered him *to be punished*.   (*Trans. of Incomplete Pred.*)

Note.—Most grammarians hold that such a verb as *ordered* is of incomplete predication, and *to be punished* its Complement. Some, however, have thought it better to say that *ordered* is merely Transitive, having *to be punished* as its Direct object and *him* as the Indirect. The sentence thus parsed would be, "They ordered punishment for him." But this explanation seems less satisfactory.

(d) Object to the prepositions named below :—

He was *about* (=near) *to die* (=death).
They came *for to see* (=for seeing) the sport.
They desired nothing *except* or *but to succeed* (=success).
He did nothing else *than laugh*.

Note.—Such a phrase as "for to see" is now obsolete, though it occurs in the New Testament. The "for" is now always omitted, and the Noun-Infinitive then becomes the Gerundial.[1]

(e) As a form of exclamation :—

Foolish fellow ! *to suppose* that he could be pardoned !

Note.—In this construction the Infinitive is absolute (§ 27, *b*).

192. The Dative or Gerundial Infinitive can be used (a) to qualify a verb, (b) to qualify a noun, (c) to qualify an adjective, (d) to introduce a parenthesis :—

(a) To qualify a verb, in the sense of *purpose, cause, occasion,* or *result* :—

He came *to see* (for the purpose of seeing) the sport.   (*Purpose.*)
He wept *to see* (because of seeing) that sight.   (*Cause.*)
I shall be interested *to hear* what is decided.   (*Occasion.*)
He worked hard only *to be* (with the result of being) defeated at last.   (*Result.*)

Note.—This Infinitive is also used in the sense of purpose for forming a periphrastic future with the help of the verb *go.*

I am *going to have* my dinner=I *shall* now *have* my dinner.

---

[1] The phrase "for to see" came into use during the Middle period of English, in imitation of the French idiom "pour" (=for), followed by an Infinitive.

(b) To qualify a noun, in the sense of *purpose*, or *simple futurity* :—

Purpose :—

{ A house *to let*.   (*Epithet use*.   See § 95.)
{ This house is *to let*.   This house (is) *to let*.   (*Predicative use*.)
{ Give him a chair *to sit on*.   (*Epithet use*.)
{ Your condition is *to be pitied*.   (*Predicative use*.).

Note.—Whenever the verb is Intransitive, as "*sit*," it must always be followed by a preposition. We cannot say "a chair *to sit*." In the phrase "a chair to sit on" the pronoun *it* is understood after *on* as its object. "A chair to sit on it." "A chair on which to sit."

Simple futurity :—

He will be rewarded in the world *to come*.
Those days have passed, never *to return*.
This house is *to be let* from Monday next.
This house is *to let* from Monday next.

Note.—The Passive form, such as *to be let*, is the more modern of the two. The original Gerundial Infinitive had one form only,—the Active ; and this described the action independently of Voice.

(c) To qualify an adjective, in the sense of *respect* or *purpose* :—

Quick *to hear* and slow *to speak*.

'Quick" in what respect or for what purpose ? To hear. "Slow" in what respect or for what purpose ? To speak.

(d) To introduce a **Parenthesis ;** that is, a phrase thrust into the middle of a sentence by way of comment on something said :—

I am,—*to tell* you the truth,—quite tired of this work.
They were thunderstruck,—so *to speak*,—on hearing this news.

Note.—In (a) and (c) the Gerundial Infinitive does the work of an adverb. In (b) it does the work of an adjective. In (d) it is absolute (see § 27, b).

SECTION 11.—PARTICIPLES.

193. The forms of the different Participles are as shown below :—

Transitive Verbs.

	Active Voice.	Passive Voice.
Present or Continuous	Loving	Being loved
Past . . .	(*Wanting*)	Loved
Perfect . .	Having loved	Having been loved

Intransitive Verbs.

Present or Continuous	. .	Fading
Past .	. . .	Faded
Perfect .	. . .	Having faded

Note 1.—The form *loving* stands for both Present and Continuous participles. These are not the same in meaning :—

(a) *Hearing* this he was much surprised.   (*Pres*.)
(b) He went away *sorrowing*.   (*Cont*.)

In (*a*) the action is completed, not continuous.   In (*b*) it is continuous.

Note 2.—There is no Future Participle in English. Futurity can be expressed by the Gerundial Infinitive, as "the world *to come*" (see § 192, *b*), or by a periphrasis, as "about (*prep.*) to fall" (*Noun Infin.*), "going to see" (*Gerund. Infin.*), "going to be beaten" (*Ger. Infin.*).

194. Double Character of Participles.—A Participle has two distinct functions, and can be defined as that part of a verb which may be used either (*a*) for helping to form a tense, or (*b*) as an adjective for qualifying some noun or noun-equivalent.

I. *As part of a tense.*

195. The student will have seen already that many of the tenses of English verbs are formed with the help of the Past or Present Participle.

Thus all the tenses of the Passive voice are formed out of the verb "to be" followed by the Past Participle ; as, "I am loved," "I was loved," "I shall be loved."

Again, all the Continuous tenses in the Active voice are formed out of the verb "to be," followed by the Present Participle ; as, "I am loving," "I was loving," "I shall be loving."

Again, the Perfect tenses in the Active voice are formed out of the verb "to have," followed by the Past Participle ; as, "I have loved," "I had loved," "I shall have loved."

II. *As an Adjective.*[1]

196. A Participle, when it is an adjective, belongs to the class of Descriptive (§ 83). Like other such adjectives, it can (*a*) qualify a noun, (*b*) be qualified by an adverb, (*c*) admit of degrees of comparison, (*d*) be used as a noun :—

> (*a*) *Being tired* of work, *the men* went home.
> (*b*) The man was picked up in an *almost dying* state.
> (*c*) This flower is *more faded* than that.
> (*d*) { I am much pleased with my *surroundings*.
> { None are so soon forgotten as *the dead*.

197. Since a Participle is a verb as well as an adjective, it can take an Object, which may be of five kinds (§ 161) :—

---

[1] To show how completely a Participle can assume the function of an adjective, there are instances in which it forgoes its verb-character altogether.

Astonishing to any one. *Disturbing* to any one. *Surprising* to any one.

When the words italicised are used as verbs, they are Transitive, and do not allow the prep. *to* to come between them and their object. We could not say, "This astonishes *to* me, or disturbs *to* me, or surprises *to* me."

Having shot *the tiger*, he returned home. (*Direct Obj.*)
He is busy teaching *his sons* Greek. (*Indirect Obj.*)
Having been taught *Greek*, he was a good scholar. (*Retained Obj.*)
We saw him fighting a hard *battle*. (*Cognate Obj.*)
Having sat *himself* down, he began to eat. (*Reflexive Obj.*)

198. Past Indefinite.—The use of such participles depends upon whether the verb is Transitive or Intransitive :—

(*a*) If the verb is *Transitive*, the Past Participle is never used in the Active voice, but only in the Passive :—

This much-*praised* man proved to be a rogue.
Gold is a metal *dug* out of the earth.

(*b*) If the verb is *Intransitive*, the Past Participle is not used at all in most verbs. But whenever it is used—(a matter depending entirely on custom), it must *precede* its noun, and not follow it :—

The *faded* rose. A *failed* candidate. A *retired* officer. The *returned* soldier. The *fallen* city. The *risen* sun. A *withered* flower. A *departed* guest.

If the speaker or writer desires to place the Past Participle of an Intransitive verb *after* its noun, he must insert the Relative pronoun and change the participle into a Finite verb ; as—

The house of Mr. A., *gone* to America, is for sale. (This is wrong. The sentence should be—"The house of Mr. A., *who has gone* to America, is for sale.")

But the Past Participle of an Intransitive verb is sometimes put *after* its noun *in poetry*.

A Daniel *come* to judgment.—SHAKSPEARE.
With Atë by his side *come* hot from hell.—SHAKSPEARE.
Mourn for the brave—the brave that are no more,
All *sunk* beneath the wave, fast by their native shore.—COWPER.

Even in prose the Past Participle of an Intransitive verb is sometimes, *but very rarely*, placed after its noun :—

In times *past*=in times which have passed.
He is a man *descended* from a high family.

199. The Past Participle of verbs is sometimes used to express some *permanent habit, state*, or *character* :—

A well-*read* man=a man who has read much and read well.
A well-*behaved* man=a man whose habitual behaviour is good.
An out-*spoken* man=a man who habitually speaks out his mind.
A *retired* man=a man who has given up business.
A *mistaken* man=one who errs by habit or in some specific case.

From this use of the Past Participle has arisen a large class of Adjectives, which are formed from nouns by adding " *ed* " to the end of the noun.

An evil-*heart*-ed man. A *talent*-ed man. A *land*-ed proprietor. A long-*tail*-ed ape. A smooth-*skin*-ned cat. His *saint*-ed mother. A red-*colour*-ed rose. A rough-*face*-d youth. A *hood*-ed snake. A long-*leg*-ged spider. A purple-*crest*-ed helmet. A many-*page*-d book. A long-*arm*-ed monkey. A thickly *wood*-ed hill. A noble-*mind*-ed man. A warm-*blood*-ed animal

200. Meanings implied in Participles.—Participles must be parsed as Verbal Adjectives qualifying their nouns. But sometimes there is a further *meaning* implied in them, which can be more fully expressed by changing the participial phrase into a clause.

The implied meanings are (*a*) Time, (*b*) Cause or Reason, (*c*) Condition, (*d*) Concession or Contrast.

(*a*) Time.

Walking along the street (=*while* I was walking), I met a friend. *Having met* my friend (=*after* I had met my friend), I went back with him to his house.

(*b*) Cause or Reason.

Being tired with the toil (=*because* he was tired), he sat down to rest. The letter, *having been addressed* (=*because* it was addressed) to the wrong house, never reached me.

(*c*) Condition.

Turning to the left (=*if* you turn to the left), you will find the place you want.

(*d*) Concession or Contrast (rare).

Admitting (=though I admit) what you say, I still think that you made a mistake.
He *being* dead (=although he is dead), yet speaketh.—*New Testament.*

SECTION 12.—GERUNDS.

201. A **Gerund** has four forms—two for the Active voice and two for the Passive.

	Active.	*Passive.*
Present or Continuous	Loving	Being loved
Perfect . . .	Having loved	Having been loved

202. The *forms* of a Gerund, then, are the same as those of a Participle, and both are parts of a verb. What, then, is the difference ? A Gerund is a kind of *Noun ;* but a Participle is a kind of *Adjective.* So in spite of the resemblance in *form*, they are quite distinct in *nature.*[1]

---

[1] In some books the Gerund is called a Participial noun. This name should be avoided, since a Noun is one part of speech and a Participle is another.

The reason of the resemblance in form is a matter of history. In Old English the *forms* of the Verbal Adjective and Verbal Noun were quite distinct. The suffix *-ing* originally belonged to the latter only.

Participle .   .   *Writ-ende*, or *-inde*, or *-and*.
Verbal noun   .   *Writ-ung*, or *writ-ing*.

In later English the suffix *-inde* took the form of *-ing*, while *-ende* and *-and* died out ; and *-ung* became obsolete. Hence we have now only one form instead of two for the two parts of speech.

Participle .   .   .   .   .   *Writing*.
Verbal noun   .   .   .   .   .   *Writing*.

203. Gerund defined.—A Gerund is that part of a verb which, if the verb is Intransitive, has the function of a noun only, but if the verb is Transitive, retains the function of a verb also, and can be followed by an object in the same way as if it were a Finite verb :—

Fond of *sleeping* .   .   .   (*Noun-function only.*)
Fond of *hunting* foxes .   .   (*Noun- and verb-function combined.*)

In point of *function* there is no difference between a Gerund and an Infinitive. Either may be correctly defined as "that part of a verb which names the action, without naming the doer." Both are Abstract nouns. The difference between them is not in function, but in *form ;* observe the suffix *-ing*. They differ also in syntactical usage ; for a Gerund can be preceded, as it often is, by any kind of preposition, and it can be preceded by an Art. *a* or *the ;* the same cannot be said of Infinitives. The Old Eng. Infinitive ended in *-an* or *-en*, not in *-ing.*

Subsequently the other forms of Gerund, such as *being loved, having loved, having been loved*, were developed in modern English, on the analogy of corresponding participles.

204. Gerund as Noun.—Since a Gerund is a *kind of noun*, it must be the subject to some verb (Transitive or Intransitive) ; or the object to some verb (Transitive) ; or the complement to some verb (Intransitive or Transitive) ; or the object to some preposition ; as—

Subject to a verb.—*Sleeping* is necessary to life.
Object to a verb.—He enjoyed *sleeping* in the open air.
Complement to a verb.—His almost constant habit was *sleeping*.
Object to a preposition.—He was fond of *sleeping*.

In the following sentences say whether the words noted below are Gerunds or Participles :—

The rice will grow well in the *coming* rains. We heard of his *coming* back to-day. Did you hear of his *having won* a prize ? The boy *having won* a prize was much praised. She was fond of *being admired. Being admired* by all she was much pleased. The cow *having been killed* by a tiger yesterday could not be found. The boy was ashamed of *having been beaten* in class by his sister. I am tired of *doing* this work. *Doing* this work every day you will soon improve.

Spelling is more difficult than *writing*. He was in the habit of *boasting* of his cleverness. A *boasting* man is much despised.

Note.—In such phrases as "a hunting whip," "a drinking fountain," the words *hunting* and *drinking* are Gerunds, not participles ; "a whip for hunting," "a fountain for drinking." The Gerund or noun is here used as a substitute for an adjective ; see § 96 (3).

205. Gerund as a Verb.—Since the Gerund of a Transitive verb retains its verb-character (§ 203), the object by which it is followed may be of any of the five kinds shown in § 161, *Note.*

Direct (with Trans.).—He is clever at teaching *Euclid.*
Indirect (with Trans.).—He is clever at teaching *his sons* Euclid.
Retained (with Passive).—He is pleased at being taught *Euclid.*
Cognate (with Intrans.).—He is proud of having fought a good *fight.*
Reflexive (with Intrans.).—He is in the habit of oversleeping *himself.*

206. Gerund with Genitives.—A noun or pronoun, provided it denotes a person or other animal, is usually in the Genitive case when it is placed before a Gerund :—

> I was pleased at *his* coming to-day.
> He was displeased at the *barber's* not coming.

Note 1.—The following use of a Gerund preceded by a Possessive adj. or a noun in the Genitive case sometimes occurs :—

> This was a work *of my doing* (=done by me).

Note 2.—Sometimes the letter "*a*" (an abbreviation of "*on*") is placed before a Gerund in a prepositional sense :—

> This set him *a* (=on) *thinking.*

Note 3.—The Possessive "*its,*" even though its antecedent denotes an *inanimate* object, should be used with a Gerund.

> The *wall* fell ; I am vexed at *its* having fallen.

207. Gerundive use of Participles.—Such participles are not Gerunds, but participles used in a Gerundive sense :—

> I depend on the wall *being built* immediately.

How are we to parse "being built" in such a connection ? It is not enough to say that it is an ordinary participle ; for it does more than qualify the noun "wall." The sentence does not mean "I depend on the wall that was being built," or "the wall when it was being built" ; but "I depend on the *wall-being-built* immediately," that is, "on the immediate *building of* the wall." There is therefore a gerund or verbal noun implied in the participle "being built," and hence such participles can be called Gerundive Participles. The subject is more fully dealt with in chap. xx. (79).

208. Verbal Noun.—This is the same at bottom as a Gerund, but a distinction is sometimes drawn between them.

A Verbal noun is preceded by one of the articles and followed by the preposition "*of*" ; whereas a Gerund has no article preceding it and no preposition following it :—

(a) I am engaged in *the* reading *of* a book.   (*Verbal Noun.*)
(b) I am engaged in reading a book.   (*Gerund.*)

In (a) the word "reading" is a *single* part of speech,—a noun and nothing more.   In (b) "reading" is a *double* part of speech,—a noun and verb combined.

It is better, however, to keep to the term Gerund for both uses.

Section 13.—The Conjugation of Verbs.

209. To "conjugate" a verb is to show its chief parts.

Note.—The term "conjugation" is sometimes used in a wider sense to denote *all* the inflexions and combinations that are employed to indicate Voice, Mood, Tense, Number, and Person.   The word lit. means a yoking together (Lat. *con*, together, and *jug-are, jugat-*um, to yoke).

The chief parts of a verb in English are the Present tense, the Past tense, and the Past Participle : all the other parts, Active and Passive, can be easily formed from these three.

210. There are two main kinds of Conjugation : [1]—

I. The *Strong*, which forms the Past tense by changing *the inside vowel* of the Present, and without adding the suffix *-d*, or *-t*, or *-ed* for this purpose ; as, *rise, rose.*

II. The *Weak*, which forms the Past tense and Past Participle by adding *-d*, or *-t*, or *-ed* to the stem of the Present, with or without a change of inside vowel ; as, *love, loved ; buy, bought.*

---

[1] Some grammarians distinguish verbs into Regular and Irregular.   The Regular answer to the Weak, and the Irregular to the Strong.   But these names are misleading ; for in point of fact the Strong conjugation is, in its own way, not less regular than the Weak.   (It would be more appropriate to apply the term *Irregular* to such a verb as *can* or *dare*, which leaves out the *s* in the Third pers. Sing., or to such a tense as *could*, which has admitted an *l* against rule, or to such a tense as *had*, which has discarded the *v* of the present.)

The Strong conjugation contains no verbs but such as are of the primary Anglo-Saxon stock.   All the verbs belonging to this conjugation (except a few that have had a prefix added to them) are monosyllabic.

Perhaps the reason why the Weak conjugation is so called is because it has no inherent strength for forming its Past tense, but requires the help of a suffix.

The Weak conjugation, however, is the *living* one.   The Strong has long been dead, and now numbers only about 110, all told ; even this total includes several verbs which have lost either a Strong past tense or a Strong past participle.   All borrowed verbs are Weak, and all newly coined ones.   The modern verb *to boycott* has *boycott-ed* for its Past tense   Borrowed or coined verbs did not originally possess, and were never able to acquire, the power of changing the inside vowel ; and that is why the Weak conjugation is the living one.

The student will therefore observe that vowel-change in the Past tense is not the decisive mark of the Strong conjugation, but the absence of a suffix to form the Past tense. Even this mark (the adding or not adding of a suffix to form the Past tense) is not always conclusive in modern English, because in Weak verbs ending in *d* or *t*, the addition of *d* or *t* is latent, and must be understood ; see examples in § 215.

The Strong Conjugation.

211. The Strong verbs are conjugated by internal changes, the nature of which is too various to be reduced to a single rule.

The most general process consists in (1) changing the inside vowel for the Past tense, and (2) adding *en, n*, or *ne* for the Past Participle, with or without change of inside vowel.

212. Formerly *all* verbs of the Strong Conjugation formed the Past Participle by adding *en, n, ne ;* but many of them have now laid aside this suffix.

Hence the Strong verbs, as they now exist, fall into two main groups :—

(1) Those which have retained ⎱ the *en, n*, or *ne* in the
(2) Those which have lost ⎰ Past Participle.

Besides these there is a third group, consisting of *Mixed* verbs, that have become Weak either in the Past tense or the Past Participle, but not in both. These are, however, classed among Strong verbs, because they have retained at least one mark of the Strong Conjugation.

Group I. (50 verbs).

Present Tense.	Past Tense.	Past Part.	Present Tense.	Past Tense.	Past Part.
Arise	arose	arisen	Draw	drew	drawn
Bear (produce)	bore	born	Drink	drank	*drunken, drunk
Bear (carry)	bore	borne	Drive	drove, drave	driven
Beget	begot, begat	begotten, begot	Eat	ate	eaten
			Fall	fell	fallen
Bid	bade, bid	bidden, bid	Fly	flew	flown
Bind	bound	*bounden, bound	Forbear	forbore	forborne
			Forget	forgot	forgotten
Bite	bit	bitten, bit	Forsake	forsook	forsaken
Blow	blew	blown	Freeze	froze	frozen
Break	broke	broken	Get	got	*gotten, **got**
Chide	chid	chidden, chid	Give	gave	given
			Go, wend	went	gone
Choose	chose	chosen	Grow	grew	grown

Present Tense.	Past Tense.	Past Part.	Present Tense.	Past Tense.	Past Part.
Hide	hid	*hidden, hid	Speak	spoke	spoken
			Steal	stole	stolen
Know	knew	known	Stride	strode	stridden
Lie	lay	lain	Strike	struck	*stricken, struck
Ride	rode	ridden			
Rise	rose	risen	Strive	strove	striven
See	saw	seen	Swear	swore	sworn
Shake	shook	shaken	Take	took	taken
Shrink	shrank	*shrunken, shrunk	Tear	tore	torn
			Throw	threw	thrown
Sink	sank	*sunken, sunk	Tread	trod	trodden, trod
Slay	slew	slain	Wear	wore	worn
Slide	slid	slidden, slid	Weave	wove	woven
Smite	smote	smitten, smit	Write	wrote	written

Note.—The seven participles marked * are now chiefly used as verbal adjectives only, and not as parts of some tense :—

Verbal Adjective.	Part of some Tense.
Our *bounden* duty.	He was *bound* by his promise.
A *drunken* man.	He had *drunk* much wine.
A *sunken* ship.	The ship had *sunk* under the water.
A *stricken* deer.	The deer was *struck* with an arrow.
The *shrunken* stream.	The stream has *shrunk* in its bed.
Ill-*gotten* wealth.	He *got* his wealth by ill means.
A *hidden* meaning.	The meaning is *hid* or hidden.

Group II. (32 *verbs*).

Present Tense.	Past Tense.	Past Part.	Present Tense.	Past Tense.	Past Part.
Abide	abode	abode	Sing	sang	sung
Awake	awoke	awoke	Sit	sat	sat
Become	became	become	Sling	slung	slung
Begin	began	begun	Slink	slunk	slunk
Behold	beheld	beheld, beholden[1]	Spin	spun	spun
			Spring	sprang	sprung
Cling	clung	clung	Stand	stood	stood
Come	came	come	Stick	stuck	stuck
Dig	dug	dug	Sting	stung	stung
Fight	fought	fought	Stink	stank	stunk
Find	found	found	String	strung	strung
Fling	flung	flung	Swim	swam	swum
Grind	ground	ground	Swing	swung	swung
Hold	held	held	Win	won	won
Ring	rang	rung	Wind	wound	wound
Run	ran	run	Wring	wrung	wrung
Shine	shone	shone			

[1] "Beholden" means "indebted."

Group III.—Mixed or Strong-Weak Verbs (28 *in number*).

Present Tense.	Past Tense.	Past Participle.
Beat	beat	beaten
Cleave (split)	clave, cleft	*cloven, cleft
Climb	clomb, climbed	climbed
Crow	crew, crowed	crowed, crown (rare)
Do	did	done
Grave	graved	*graven, graved
Hang [1]	hung, hanged	hung, hanged
Hew	hewed	*hewn, hewed
Lade	laded	laden
Melt	melted	*molten, melted
Mow	mowed	mown
Prove	proved	†proven, proved
Rive	rived	riven
Rot	rotted	*rotten, rotted
Saw	sawed	sawn
Seethe	seethed	*sodden, seethed
Sew	sewed	*sewn, sewed
Shape	shaped	†shapen, shaped
Shave	shaved	shaven
Shear	sheared	*shorn, sheared
Show	showed	shown
Sow	sowed	sown
Stave	stove, staved	stove, staved
Strew	strewed	strewn or strown
Swell	swelled	swollen
Thrive	throve, thrived	thriven, thrived
Wash	washed	*washen, washed
Writhe	writhed	†writhen, writhed

Note 1.—The participles marked * are now chiefly used as Verbal adjectives, and not as parts of some tense :—

Verbal Adjective.	Part of some Tense.
A *graven* image.	The image was *engraved* with letters.
A *molten* image.	The image was *melted* with heat.
A *rotten* plank.	The plank was *rotted* by water.
The *sodden* flesh.	The flesh was *seethed* in hot water.
A well-*sewn* cloth.	I have *sewed* or *sewn* it.
Un-*washen* hands.	I have *washed* my hands.
A *shorn* lamb.	The lamb was *sheared* to-day.
A *hewn* log.	The log is *hewed* or *hewn*.

Note 2.—The participles marked † are now seldom seen except in poetry.

The Weak Conjugation.

213. The mode of adding the suffix of the Past tense is not uniform ; and the two rules given below should be observed :—

---

[1] The Intransitive verb is conjugated in the Strong form only. The Transitive verb is conjugated in both forms. *Hanged* means "killed by hanging" ; as, "The man was *hanged*." *Hung* is used in a general sense ; as "He *hung* up his coat."

(1) If the verb ends in *e*, then *d* only is added; as—

> *Live, lived* (not *liveed*).
> *Clothe, clothed* (not *clotheed*).

To this rule there is no exception.

(2) The final consonant is doubled before *ed*, provided (*a*) that the final consonant is *single*, (*b*) that it is *accented* or *monosyllabic*, (*c*) that it is preceded by a *single vowel;* as—

> *Fan, fanned* (not *faned*); *drop, dropped* (not *droped*).
> *Compel, compelled; control, controlled.*

But in a verb like *lengthen*, where the accent is not on the last syllable, the Past tense is *lengthened;* in a verb like *boil*, where the vowel is not single, the Past tense is *boiled;* and in a verb like *fold*, where the last consonant is not single, the Past tense is *folded*.

To this rule there are very few exceptions. One exception occurs in the final *l*. The final *l* is doubled, even when it is not accented; as, travel, trav*elled* (not trav*eled*). But the final *l* is not doubled, if it has two vowels going before it; as, *travail, travailed* (not *travailled*).

214. (*a*) Some verbs of the Weak Conjugation form the Past tense in " *t*," and if the vowel of the Present is a long one, they shorten it:—

Present Tense.	Past Tense.	Past Part.	Present Tense.	Past Tense.	Past Part.
Creep	crept	crept	Feel	felt	felt
Sleep	slept	slept	Kneel	knelt	knelt
Sweep	swept	swept	Smell	smelt	smelt
Keep	kept	kept	Spell	spelt	spelt
Weep	wept	wept	Lean (lēn)	lĕant or	lĕant or
Burn	burnt	burnt		leaned	leaned
Deal (dēl)	dĕalt	dĕalt	Mean (mēn)	mĕant	mĕant
Dream	drĕamt or	drĕamt or	Spill	spilt	spilt
(drēm)	dreamed	dreamed	Spoil	spoilt or	spoilt or
Dwell	dwelt	dwelt		spoiled	spoiled

Exceptional Verbs.—Make, made, made. Have, had, had. **Hear,** heard, heard. Leave, left, left. Cleave, cleft, cleft. **Lose,** lost, lost. Shoe, shod, shod. Flee, fled, fled. Say, said, **said.** Lay, laid, laid. Pay, paid, paid.

(*b*) Some Weak verbs undergo a change of inside vowel. This, however, does not make them Strong verbs. They are Weak without any doubt, because they form the Past tense with the suffix *-d* or *-t* (see § 210).

Present Tense.	Past Tense.	Past Part.	Present Tense.	Past Tense.	Past Part.
Beseech	besought	besought	Seek	sought	sought
Bring	brought	brought	Sell	sold	sold
Buy	bought	bought	Teach	taught	taught
Catch	caught	caught	Tell	told	told

Present Tense.	Past Tense.	Past Part.	Present Tense.	Past Tense.	Past Part.
Think	thought	thought	Can	Could	(*Wanting*)
Work	wrought, worked	wrought, worked	Shall	should	(*Wanting*)
			Will	would	(*Wanting*)
Owe	ought, owed	owed	May	might	(*Wanting*)
Dare	durst or dared	dared	Clothe	clothed, clad	clothed, clad

215. Verbs ending in *d* or *t* in the Present tense have discarded the suffix of the Past tense, to avoid the repetition of *d* or *t*.

(*a*) Some verbs in this group have the three forms (Present tense, Past tense, and Past Participle) all exactly alike :—

Present Tense.	Past Tense.	Past Part.	Present Tense.	Past Tense.	Past Part.
Burst	burst	burst	Slit	slit	slit
Cast	cast	cast	Spit	spit or spat	spit
Cost	cost	cost			
Cut	cut	cut	Split	split	split
Hit	hit	hit	Spread	spread	spread
Hurt	hurt	hurt	Sweat	sweat	sweat
Let	let	let	Thrust	thrust	thrust
Put	put	put	Bet	bet	bet
Rid	rid	rid	Quit	quit or quitted	quit or quitted
Set	set	set			
Shed	shed	shed	Knit	knit or knitted	knit or knitted
Shred	shred	shred			
Shut	shut	shut			

Note.—"Spit" is a Weak verb, although it has a form *spat* for the Past tense. In Anglo-Saxon the Present had two forms also.

(*b*) Other verbs in this group end in *d* in the Present tense, but form the Past tense and Past Participle by changing *d* into *t*. (There are at least nine such verbs in English.)

Present Tense.	Past Tense.	Past Part.	Present Tense.	Past Tense.	Past Part.
Bend	bent	bent	Rend	rent	rent
Build	built	built	Send	sent	sent
Gild	gilt, gilded	gilt	Spend	spent	spent
Gird	girt, girded	girt	Wend	went	(*Wanting*)
Lend	lent	lent			

Exceptions :—end-ed, mend-ed, blend-ed or blent, defend-ed.

(*c*) Other verbs of this group have the three forms all alike except that they shorten the vowel in the Past forms :—

Present Tense.	Past Tense.	Past Part.	Present Tense.	Past Tense.	Past Part.
Bleed	bled	bled	Lead	led	led
Breed	bred	bred	Read	read	read
Feed	fed	fed	Light	lit, lighted	lit, lighted
Speed	sped	sped	Shoot	shot	shot
Meet	met	met			

SECTION 14.—AUXILIARY, DEFECTIVE, AND ANOMALOUS VERBS.

(1) Be.

This verb is a patchwork of parts formed from three different roots, *es* (cf. Lat. *sum, es, est*), *béo* (cf. Lat. *fi-o*), and *wes*.

		Singular.			Plural.
		1	2	3	1 2 3
Present	{ *Indicative* .	am	art	is	are
	{ *Subjunctive* .	be	be	be	be
Past	{ *Indicative* .	was	wast[1]	was	were
	{ *Subjunctive* .	were	wert	were	were

Infinitive.	Imperative.	Present Participle.	Perfect Participle.
To be	be	being	having been

This verb has two different uses :—

(1) As a Principal verb (Intransitive) (*a*) of Complete, (*b*) of Incomplete Predication :—

    (*a*) There *are* (=exist) some who, etc.—*Complete Predication.*
    (*b*) His coat *is* of many colours.—*Incomplete Predication.*

(2) As an Auxiliary verb :—

All the tenses in Passive verbs and all the Continuous tenses in Active ones are formed by the help of the verb *to be.*

(2) Have.

		Singular.			Plural.
		1	2	3	1 2 3
Present	{ *Indicative* .	have	hast	has	have
	{ *Subjunctive* .	have	have	have	have
Past	{ *Indicative* .	had	hadst	had	had
	{ *Subjunctive* .	had	hadst	had	had

Infinitive.	Imperative.	Present Participle.	Perfect Participle.
To have	have	having	having had

---

[1] *Wert* is also found in Milton and elsewhere ; but it was inaccurate from the first, and is now obsolete.

This verb has two different uses :—

(1) As a Principal verb (Transitive), denoting possession.

We have (= we possess) four cows and twenty sheep.

(2) As an Auxiliary verb :—

All the Perfect tenses, in all the Moods, Active and Passive, are formed by the help of this verb.

(3) **Shall**.

	Singular.			Plural.
Present . .	1 shall	2 shalt	3 shall	1 2 3 shall
Past . .	should	shouldst	should	should

This verb has two different uses :—

(1) As a Principal verb (Transitive, with an Infinitive as object) in the sense (a) of command, (b) of duty :—

(a) Thou *shalt* not steal.
(b) He *should* do it at once.

Note.—In the following sentence "*should*" is used in the sense of inference, rather than in that of duty ;—

He *should* have arrived by this time.

That is, "It may be inferred, according to the ordinary course of events, that he has arrived by this time."

(2) As an Auxiliary verb (a) for the First person Future, (b) for the Future in the Past, (c) and to form Subjunctive equivalents:—

(a) I *shall* go away to-day.
(b) He worked hard lest he *should* fail.

(4) **Will**.

	Singular.			Plural.
Present . .	1 will	2 wilt	2 will	1 2 3 will
Past . .	{ would { willed	wouldst willedst	would willed	would willed

Infinitive.	Imperative.	Present Participle.	Perfect Participle.
To will	...	willing	having willed

This verb has two different uses :—

(1) As a Principal verb (*a*) Transitive (with an Infinitive as object), in the sense of intention or habit ; (*b*) Transitive, in the sense of leaving property by will or testament :—

> (*a*) I *will* not do so again.   (*Intention.*)
>   The dog *would* come every day to the door.   (*Habit.*)
> (*b*) He *willed* that all he had should go to his son.

Note.—The phrase "*would-be*" is elliptical, and is used as an adjective :—

> A would-be murderer (a man who wished or intended to be a murderer, but was prevented).

(2) As an Auxiliary verb (*a*) for the Second and Third persons Future, (*b*) for the Future in the Past, (*c*) and to form Subjunctive equivalents :—

> (*a*) He *will* return to-morrow.
> (*b*) He *would* know me, if he saw me.

(5) Do.

	Singular.			Plural.
	1	2	3	1 2 3
Present . .	do	dost	does	do
Past . .	did	didst	did	did

Infinitive.	Imperative.	Present Participle.	Perfect Participle.
To do	do	doing	having done

This verb has three different uses :—

(1) As a Principal verb (Transitive) signifying " perform " :—

> I am now *doing* what you *have done* already.

Note.—It once had the sense of "cause," as in the phrase "I *do* you to wit " = I cause you to know, I give you to understand.

(2) As an Auxiliary, only in the Present and Past tenses :—

> I *did* not speak. *Do* be quiet. How *do* you do ? (Here the second "do" is Principal, in imitation of the French *faire*.)

(3) As a Pro-verb or Substitute-verb, Trans. or Intrans. :—

> He sings well, and so *do* you.   (*Intrans.*)
> He caught a worse cold than you *did*.   (*Trans.*)

(6) **May**.

	Singular.			Plural.
	1	2	3	1 2 3
Present . .	may	mayest	may	may
Past . .	might	mightest	might	might

This verb has two different uses :—

(1) As a Principal verb, Transitive, with Infin. as object :—

It *may* be true. (*Possibility.*)
You *may* now go. (*Permission.*)

(2) As an **Auxiliary, for** forming Subjunctive equivalents :—

He works that he *may* live. (*Purpose.*)
May heaven protect thee ! (*Wish.*)

(7) **Let**.

The six verbs hitherto named are the only ones that can be used as Auxiliaries. The special use of "*let*" is to express by a periphrasis the First and Third persons Imperative, as, "*let* him go." "Let" is here the Second person Imperative of the Transitive verb *to let*, followed by a Direct object "go," and by an Indirect object "him." Its conjugation is quite regular.

(8) **Can**.

	Singular.			Plural.
	1	2	3	1 2 3
Present . .	can	canst	can	can
Past . .	could	couldst	could	could

This is a Defective verb, Transitive, followed by an Infinitive as object. (Never Auxiliary, always Principal.)

You *can* (=are permitted to) go or not, as you like.
He *cannot* (=is unable to) run as fast as you.

In Old English this verb signified "to know."

(9) **Ought**.

	Singular.			Plural.
	1	2	3	1 2 3
Present or *Past* .	ought	oughtest	ought	ought

This verb is, in its origin, the Past tense of the verb *owe;* as, "you *ought*" (= *owed*) him a thousand pounds." In modern English the form "ought" is used only in the sense of *duty.* It is a Transitive verb, followed by a Noun-Infinitive as object.

Present.—You ought *to do* this ; (it is your duty to do it).
Past.—You ought *to have done* this ; (but you did not do it).

(10) **Must.**

This verb has now no varieties of form.

It is, in its origin, the Past tense of an old verb *motan*, which is now obsolete. The Infinitive following is its object.

  (*a*) What *must* come, *must.* (*Necessity.*)
  (*b*) He *must* be dead by this time. (*Inference.*)
  (*c*) We *must* pay our debts. (*Obligation.*)

(11) **Dare.**

	Singular.			Plural.
	1	2	3	1 2 3
Present . .	dare	darest	{ dares dare	dare
Past. . .	{ durst dared	durst	durst	{ durst
		daredst	dared	{ dared

Infinitive.	Imperative.	Present Participle.	Perfect Participle.
To dare	dare	daring	having dared

This verb is used in two senses :—

(*a*) A Transitive verb in the sense of *having courage,* with Infinitive as object. In this sense the Third present Singular is "dare," and not "dares," provided it is followed by a Negative :—

He *dare* not (= has not the courage to) leave the room. (*Negative.*)
He *dares* to leave the room. (*Affirmative.*)

In the Past tense, provided it is followed by a Negative, "durst" is used, and sometimes "dared" :—

  He *durst* not (or *dared* not) leave the room.

But if the verb is affirmative, we use "dared" and not "durst." The idiom "I dare say" simply means "perhaps." The verb *dare* has here lost most of its force.

(*b*) A Transitive verb in the sense of *challenging :* declined regularly in all the moods and tenses :—

  He *dares* me (= challenges me) to fight.

(12) **Quoth.**

This verb is the Past tense of an old verb, which is now obsolete except in the compound form of *be-queath*.

It means "says" or "said," and therefore stands equally for Past and Present time. It is used only in the *First* and *Third* persons, and only in the *Singular* number. It always stands *before* its subject :—

"Let me not live," *quoth* he.—SHAKSPEARE.

(13) **Need.**

A Transitive verb, signifying "require," "want." As such it is declined regularly in all its moods and tenses.

The Third person Singular is *need*, and not *needs*, just as *dare* is used for *dares*, provided it is followed by a Negative :—

He *need* not (=is under no necessity to) do any more work.

In such a phrase as "he must *needs* do this," *needs* is really a Genitive case, with the apostrophe before the *s* omitted. So *needs* =need's= of need = of necessity = necessarily : an Adverb.

(14) **Worth.**

This verb occurs in such a phrase as "woe *worth* the day" = "woe be to the day." Here "day" is in the **Accusative case.**

Worth is here the Subjunctive mood (in the sense of wish, see § 186, 2) of an old verb signifying "to become."

(15) **Wit.**

This verb signifies "to know." Only a few of its forms have survived ; the rest have become obsolete.

(*a*) The Infinitive form *to wit*, in the sense of "namely," is much used in legal documents at the present day :—

He left me by will all his land, *to wit*, the three farms.

(*b*) The Present Participle has survived in the negative adverbial form of *unwittingly*, which means "unknowingly."

You cannot blame him for this, since he did it *unwittingly*.

(*c*) Two forms of the Indicative have survived, but are rare:—

Present.—He *wot* neither what he babbles nor what he means.— TYNDALL.

Past.—They *wist* not what had become of him.—*New Testament.*

(16) **Beware.**

This is compounded of *be* + *ware*. "Ware" is an old form of the adjective "wary," and is complement to the verb "be."

The form "*beware*" is the only one used. It can be preceded by Auxiliary verbs, or by "to," as "to beware."

(17) **Wont.**

This is the Past Participle of an obsolete verb, which signified "to continue." Hence "wont" means "accustomed."

(18) **Hight.**

The Past Participle of an obsolete verb, which signified "to call or name."

(19) **Yclept.**

The Past Participle of the obsolete verb "clepe," to call or name. The *y* prefix is from Anglo-Saxon *ge.*

(20) **Impersonal Verbs.**

Verbs are said to be **Impersonal**, or to be used impersonally, when they take "it" for their subject, and are followed by some Personal pronoun in the Accusative case, which in Personal verbs would be the Subject in the Nom. case :—

> *It* shames *me* to hear this = I am ashamed to hear this
> *It* repents *me* of my folly = I repent of my folly.
> *It* behoves *me* to do this = I ought to do this.

There are three instances in which the *it* is omitted, and the pronoun in the Dative case is placed *before* the verb instead of after it :—

> *Methinks* = it seems to me.
> *Meseems* = it seems to me.
> *Melists* = it seems to me, or it pleases me.

Note.—In Modern English there is no difference of spelling between *thinks* Impersonal and *think* Transitive. But in Old Eng. the former was *thync-an* (to seem) and the latter *thenc-an* (to think.)

The following phrase is elliptical :—

> So *please* your Majesty.—SHAKSPEARE.

This means, "If *it* so please your Majesty"; that is, "If your Majesty so please or so desire."

CHAPTER VI.—ADVERBS.

SECTION 1.—THE FUNCTIONS OF ADVERBS.

216. Adverb defined.—An Adverb is a word used to qualify any part of speech except a noun or pronoun (§ 11). (The etymology, Lat. *ad verbum*, would imply that an Adverb qualifies a verb only; and probably this was the earliest use of Adverbs.)

Note.—The definition usually given is :—"An adverb is a word used to qualify a verb, adjective, or other adverb." [1]

But this is evidently wrong, since an adverb may, and very often does, qualify Prepositions and Conjunctions :—

(*a*) **Prepositions** :—

The bird flew *exactly over* the sleeper's head.
He paid the money *quite up to* date.
This mistake was made *entirely through* your fault.
He was sitting *almost outside* the door.
He arrived *long before* the time.
He wept *partly through* sorrow and *partly through* anger.

(*b*) **Conjunctions** :—

A man is truly happy *only when* he is in sound health.
I dislike this place *simply because* the air is too hot.
I wish to know *precisely how* it happened.
They locked the door *shortly before* the thieves came.
The watch was found *long after* the thieves had been caught.
He has been ill *ever since* he left us.

It is immaterial whether we say that the adverb qualifies the *Preposition only* or *the entire phrase* introduced by the preposition. Similarly, we could say with equal truth that the adverb qualifies the *Conjunction only* or *the entire clause* that follows it.

Note.—If for an adverb proper we substitute an adverbial phrase, we find that such a phrase can qualify a preposition or a conjunction in the same way as an adverb proper does :—

Preposition.—He arrived *a few hours after* midnight.
Conjunction.—He recovered *ten days after* he had been taken ill.

217. An Adverb can qualify not merely individual words, but an entire statement (§ 1, *a*). *In this case it must stand first in the sentence.*

> *Unfortunately* the thief was not caught.
> *Evidently* you were much distressed at the news.

We could rewrite these sentences in the following form :—

> It is *unfortunate that* the thief was not caught.
> It was *evident that* you were much distressed.

218. *Adverbs do not qualify Nouns or Pronouns.* This is the work of adjectives.

The apparent exceptions to the above rule can all be explained :—
(*a*) I am *sincerely yours.* That book is *certainly mine.*

---

[1] Angus and Bain both admit that the qualifying power of adverbs is not limited to adjectives, verbs, and other adverbs ; but both have none the less adhered to the old definition. The same admission, but without any departure from the old definition, is made by Mason, who in a footnote to page 105 of his *English Grammar*, points out that "an adverb sometimes modifies a preposition." Since the old definition is admittedly wrong, it is better to put a more accurate one in its place.

Here the words "yours" and "mine" are the Possessive forms of "you" and "I," and are therefore equivalent to *adjectives.*

(*b*) A by-path ; a fore-taste ; an out-house.

Here the adverbs do not qualify the several nouns, but are *compounded* with them, so that each compound makes a *single* word.

(*c*) In the following examples the adverb that precedes the noun does not qualify the noun, but some participle or adjective understood :—

> *The then* king = the king then *reigning.*
> *The late* king = the king lately *reigning.*
> *The above* account = the account *given* above.
> *A far* country = a country far *distant.*
> *An up* mail = an up-*going* mail.

(*d*) In the following example the adverb "almost" or "quite" does not qualify the noun "drunkard," but the verb "is" :—

> He is *almost* or *quite* a drunkard.

To say, " He is an almost or a quite drunkard," would be incorrect.

Note.—In colloquial speech or writing the adverb " quite " is often made to qualify nouns :—

> *Quite a panic* (= a serious panic) was caused.
> They had *quite a run* (= a long run) of ill luck.

Very often in such sentences the word *quite* is superfluous, apart from the grammatical objection to using an adverb to qualify a noun. It is best to regard such a combination of words as an idiom (see p. 215).

SECTION 2.—THE KINDS OF ADVERBS.

219. Adverbs are subdivided into three distinct classes :—

    I. Simple.   II. Interrogative.   III. Relative.

220. Simple Adverbs.—These can be distinguished from one another according to their meaning :—

(1) **Time** :—

He did this *before*, and you have done it *since.* He will *soon* arrive. He was taken ill *yesterday.*

The chief adverbs of this class are :—*Now, then, before, since, ago, already, soon, presently, immediately, instantly, early, late, afterwards, yesterday, to-day, to-morrow.*

(2) **Place** :—

> We must rest *here*, and not *there.*

The chief adverbs of this class are :—*Here, there ; hence, thence ; hither, thither ; in, out ; within, without ; above, below ; inside, outside ; far, near, etc.*

(3) **Number** :—

> He did this *once*, but he will not do it *again.*

The chief adverbs of this class are :—*Once, twice, thrice, again, seldom, never, sometimes, always, often, firstly, secondly, thirdly, etc.*

(4) **Manner, Quality,** or **State** :—

He did his work *slowly*, but *surely*.

To this class of adverb belong :—*Thus, so, well, ill, amiss, badly, probably, certainly, conveniently, asleep* (=in sleep, in a state of sleep).

(5) **Quantity, Extent,** or **Degree** :—

He is *almost*, but not *quite*, the cleverest boy in the class.

To this class of adverb belong :—*Very, much, the, too, quite, almost, little, a little, rather, somewhat, half, partly, wholly, so,* etc.

Note.—The adverb "the" is quite distinct from the Definite article. It represents the Instrumental case (*thi*) of the Demonstrative, and is never used except before an adjective or adverb in the *Comparative* degree, as in "the more, the merrier."

(6) **Affirming** or **Denying** :—

He did *not* come after all.

Examples :—*Yes, no, not, perhaps, undoubtedly, not at all, by all means,* etc.

Substitute-Adverbs.—This is the most suitable name for the Adverbs (1) *yes* (Affirm.), and (2) *no* (Negat.).

    (1) Did he come ? Yes (=He did come). *Affirm.*
    (2) Did he come ? No (=He did not come). *Negat.*

These can be fitly called *substitute*-adverbs, because in (1) *yes* is substitute for an entire affirmative sentence, and in (2) *no* is a substitute for an entire negative sentence. They might be called **pro-sentence** adverbs. Just as pro-nouns save the repetition of a noun, so do these adverbs save the repetition of a sentence. Cf. *do* in page 83 (5), where *do* is shown to be a *pro-verb* or *substitute-verb*.

Note.—In some books a 7th class is added, viz. adverbs of Cause or Consequence :—*Therefore, then, consequently, because, for.* It appears, however, that these words do not so much modify any word or words in a sentence, but are rather conjunctions combining the sense of one sentence with that of another by way of inference. They have therefore been included amongst Conjunctions in this book. But there would be nothing illogical in regarding them as Adverbs also ; for a word may be of more than one part of speech, according to the point of view from which we look at it.

221. Interrogative Adverbs.—This is the name given to those adverbs that are used for asking questions :—

    (*a*) **Time** :—

When did he *come? How long* will he remain here ?

    (*b*) **Place** :—

Where did he stop ? *Whence* has he come ? *Whither* is he going ?

    (*c*) **Number** :—

How often did the dog bark ?

(d) **Manner, Quality,** or **State** :—

How did he do this ?   *How* (in what state of health) is he to-day ?

(e) **Quantity** or **Degree** :—

How far (to what extent) was that report true ?

(f) **Cause** or **Reason** :—

Why (for what reason) did he do this ?   *Wherefore* did she weep ?

222. The adverb "*how*" is sometimes used in an exclamatory sense :—

How kind of you to do that !
How often have you been cautioned !

"*What*," in the sense of quantity or degree, is similarly used in an exclamatory sense :—

What a foolish fellow you are !
What clever sons you have !

223. Relative Adverbs.—These are the same in *form* as Interrogative adverbs ; but instead of asking questions, they join two sentences together.   Hence a Relative adverb is a double part of speech,—an adverb and conjunction combined, as was pointed out in § 17 (4).

(a) *The antecedent understood.*

This is *where* (= the place in which) we dwell.
Let me know *when* (= the time by which) you will come.

(b) *The antecedent expressed.*

This is the place *where* we dwell.
Let me know the time *when* you will come.

Note.—A list of Relative adverbs, with examples, will be found in § 239.

SECTION 3.—COMPARISON OF ADVERBS.

224. Adverbs of Quality have degrees of comparison, which are formed in the same way as those of adjectives :—

(a) If the Adverb is a word of *one* syllable, the Comparative is formed by adding *er* and the Superlative by adding *est* :—

Fast	faster	fastest	Loud	louder	loudest
Hard	harder	hardest	Late	later	latest or last
Soon	sooner	soonest	Fore	further	furthest
Near	nearer	nearest	Far	farther	farthest
Long	longer	longest	Rathe	rather	...

Till *rathe* (= early) she rose, half cheated in the thought.—TENNYSON.

(b) Some Adverbs have had a Comparative and Superlative allotted to them from another root :—

Well	better	best	Much	more	most
Ill or badly	worse	worst	Little	less	least

(c) Adverbs ending in *ly* form the Comparative by adding *more* and the Superlative by adding *most* :—

| Wisely | more wisely | most wisely |
| Beautifully | more beautifully | most beautifully |

Note.—The adverb "*early*," however, has "*earlier*" for its Comparative.

SECTION 4.—VERBS COMPOUNDED WITH ADVERBS.

225. A Verb is said to be compounded with an Adverb, when the two words are so habitually used together, that one is considered to be a part of the other.

Such Adverbs are almost always (except in poetry) placed *after* the verb ; as "speak out," "rise up." Here the *out* should be parsed as part of the verb "speak"; and *up* as part of the verb "rise."

But in forming the corresponding noun, the adverb is put first :—

Verb.	*Noun.*
The crops will *come out* well.	The *outcome* was a good crop.
No profits will *come in.*	His *income* is small.
Cholera did not *break out.*	There was no *outbreak* of cholera.
He *set out* on his journey.	He had no trouble at the *outset.*

Similar instances are :—*Set off* (verb), *offset* (noun) ; *put out* (verb), *output* (noun) ; *fit out* (verb), *outfit* (noun) ; *shoot off* (verb), *offshoot* (noun) ; *spring off* (verb), *offspring* (noun) ; *shoot up* (verb), *upshot* (noun) ; *turn out* (verb), *outturn* (noun) ; *cast out* (verb), *outcast* (noun) ; *set on* (verb), *onset* (noun) ; *lay out* (verb), *outlay* (noun) ; *look out* (verb), *outlook* (noun) ; *draw in* (verb), *indraught* (noun) ; *let out* (verb), *outlet* (noun) ; *let in* (verb), *inlet* (noun).

Note.—"Set-off," "turn-out," and a few more are also used as nouns.

SECTION 5.—THE TWO USES OF ADVERBS.

226. There are two different ways in which Adverbs can be used, viz. (*a*) the Attributive, (*b*) the Predicative.

(*a*) *Attributive use.*—An Adverb is used attributively, when it qualifies the word associated with it in the ordinary way,—that is, when it is placed as close as possible before it or after it :—

He is *entirely wrong.* He *shouted loudly.* He *did* his work *very badly. Half through* the door. I dislike him *only because* he is lazy.

(*b*) *Predicative use.*—An Adverb is used predicatively, when it is made part of the Predicate of a sentence, or in other words, when it is used as the Complement of the verb going before it :—[1]

---

[1] We cannot endorse the statement made in Mason's *English Grammar* : "The complement may consist of any Attributive adjunct ; *but an Adverb or adverbial phrase never forms the complement of a predicate.*" The examples given in the text show how very common the predicative use of Adverbs is.

Subject.	Verb.	Complement, etc.
My son	is	*well* (in good health) to-day.
He	will be	*better* (in better health) soon.
He	was turned	*adrift* (to go where he could).
The two boys	are	much *alike* (like to each other).
The bear	was caught	*alive* (in a living state).
Those men	are	*aware* (conscious) of their faults.
The game	is	*over* (finished).
Some money	was	still *over* (remaining).
The results	are	*out* (published).
The stars	are	*out* (visible).
He	was heard	*out* (to the very end).
The bargain	is	*off* (cancelled).
The train	is	*off* (started).
He	is	*well off* (in good circumstances).
Our side	is	*in* (having their innings).
The late minister	is	*in* (holding office) again.

CHAPTER VII.—PREPOSITIONS.

227. Preposition defined.—A Preposition is a word placed before a noun or noun-equivalent to show in what relation the person or thing denoted thereby stands to something else (§ 13). The noun or noun-equivalent is called the Object.[1]

I place my hand *on* the table.

Here if the word "on" is omitted there is no sense. The hand might be placed *on* the table, or *under* the table, or *above* the table. Until some preposition has been inserted, the relation between the hand and the table is not known.

228. Kinds of Objects.—Besides nouns and pronouns, we sometimes have adverbs, Infinitives, phrases, and clauses as objects to a preposition :—

(a) *Adverbs :*—

We must be ready by *then* (=that time).   By *far* the best.
He has worked hard from *then* to *now*.
He walks about from *here* to *there*.
I have heard of worse things being done before *now*.
Until *now* it has not ceased raining.
Many strange things may happen between *now* and *then*.
You must go at *once*.   This will last for *ever*.

(b) *Infinitives ;* see § 191 (d) :—

He was about *to die*.
He desired nothing but *to succeed*.

---

[1] A preposition is so called, because it is *placed before* (*prae*, before ; *positus*, placed) a noun or noun-equivalent.

(c) *Phrases :—*

The day-spring from *on-high* hath visited us.
He has come from *beyond-the-seas.*
He did not return till *about-ten-days-afterwards.*
He did not see her till *within-a-few-weeks-of-his-death.*
These books are sold at *over-one-shilling* each.
I bought this for *under-half-its-value.*
He will not return till *after-the-holidays.*
The question of *how-to-do-this* is difficult.

(d) *Clauses :—*

This depends upon | whether-he-will-consent-or-not.
He told every one of | what-he-had-heard.
Go whenever you like except | that-you must-not-go-in-the-rain.
In | that-he-died | he died unto sin once.—*New Testament.*

229. Omission of Object.—There are two cases of this :—

Relative Pronoun.—The man (*whom* or *that*) we were looking for.
Demons. Pronoun.—A chair to sit on (*it*).   (See § 192, *b, Note.*)

230. Disguised Prepositions.—" *On* " is changed into " *a* " in such phrases as " to go *a-fishing.*"

Similarly " *of* " can be changed into " *o,*" as in " four o'clock," " Jack o' lantern," etc.

To the same class belong such phrases as the following :—

Flour sells at tenpence *a pound.*
He called to see me once *a week.*
The wallpaper cost four shillings *a piece.*

The " *a* " *looks* so much like the Indefinite Article, that by a false analogy " the " is sometimes used in its place ; as—

Flour sells at tenpence *the pound.*

231. Than.—This word has been used as a Preposition by the best English writers :—

No mightier than thyself or *me*	SHAKSPEARE.
A stone is heavy, and the sand weighty ; but a fool's wrath is heavier than *them* both . .	*Old Testament.*
She suffers hourly more than *me.* . . .	SWIFT.
You are a much greater loser than *me* . .	SWIFT.
Lined with giants deadlier than *them* all .	POPE.
For thou art a girl as much brighter than *her*	
As he was a poet sublimer than *me* . .	PRIOR.
Thou hast been wiser all the while than *me* .	SOUTHEY.

The prepositional use of *than* is common in current journalistic literature.   For instance, **we find :—**

She should look worse than *him.*

Even so far back as Caxton, the first English printer, we find *than* used as a preposition :—

For ther is nothyng more suspecte to evyl people than *them,* whom they know to be wyse and trewe.—*The Curial,* 4, 18.

But in some books on Grammar its prepositional character is denied.[1] The best course to take is to parse it as a Conjunction, whenever it is possible to do so by adding a clause after it :—

> No animal is larger than a whale.
>
> No animal is larger than a whale (is large).

But in such constructions as the following "than" must still be parsed as a Preposition, because there is no omitted clause which could make it a Conjunction :—

	Kind of Object.
I will not take less than *ten shillings* . . .	} *Noun.*
No one other than a *graduate* need apply . .	
Here is my son, than *whom* a better does not exist	*Rel. Pron.*
He did nothing else than *laugh*	*Noun-Infin.*
I will suffer myself rather than (that) *he should suffer*	} *Noun-clause.*
He got more *than* (what) he asked for . . .	
He has said so more than *once*	*Adverb* (§ 228).

232. But.—In such examples as the following "but" is a Preposition. Otherwise it is a Conjunction or an Adverb.

> All *but* (except) one fulfilled their promises.
>
> He was all *but* (=everything except) ruined. (Here "ruined" is an elliptical form of the Gerund "being ruined"; and this Gerund is the object of the preposition "but.")
>
> *But* for your help (=except on account of your help=if you had not helped me) I should have been ruined. (Here the phrase "for your help" is object to the preposition.)
>
> I cannot *but* fear (=I cannot do anything except fear) that you are ill. (Here the Noun-Infinitive "fear" is the object.)

CHAPTER VIII.—CONJUNCTIONS.

233. A **Conjunction** is a word used for *joining*, and for no other purpose.

A Conjunction is never associated with an *object*, as a preposition is.

A Conjunction never *qualifies* a word, as an adverb does.

It simply *joins* words or sentences.

Hence the same word can be an adverb in one place, a preposition in another, and a conjunction in another :—

---

[1] For example, in Mason's *English Grammar*, the statement was made that "no *syntactical* explanation can be given of the relative *whom* after *than*." The syntax, however, is very simple, if we parse *than* as a preposition. There is ample analogy for the use of "than" as a preposition, besides ample authority. "Superior *to* mine" = "better *than* mine." If *to* is a preposition, why not *than*? The Scotch say, "He is taller *be* (=*by*) onie o' thaim." If *by* is a preposition, why not *than*? We find it said in Sweet's *New English Grammar*, Part I., p. 133, that *than* sometimes "governs an objective case like a preposition."

I have seen this man *before.*   (*Adverb.*)
He stood *before* the door.   (*Preposition.*)
The rain fell *before* we reached home.   (*Conjunction.*)

234. Conjunctions are subdivided into two main classes :—

I. **Co-ordinating,** which join sentences of co-ordinate (that is, of *equal*) rank, or words that stand in the same relation to some other word in the sentence.[1]

II. **Subordinating,** which join a *subordinate* or dependent clause to a *principal* sentence (that is, to a sentence of *higher* rank).

Section 1.—Co-ordinating Conjunctions.

235. *Sentences are said to be of* **Co-ordinate** *or* **equal** *rank, when one is not dependent on the other, nor enters in any way into its construction.*

236. Sentences of equal rank can be combined together in four different ways, and this gives rise to four different kinds of Co-ordinating Conjunctions :—

(*a*) **Cumulative.**—By these one statement of fact is simply *added* to another.

(*b*) **Alternative.**—By these an alternative or *choice* is offered between one statement and another.

(*c*) **Adversative.**—By these conjunctions one statement of fact is *contrasted* with or set against another.

(*d*) **Illative.**—By these conjunctions one statement of fact is *inferred* or proved from another.

(*a*) **Cumulative** (addition).

And.—The one received a prize, *and* the other was promoted.
Both . . . and.—He was *both* degraded *and* expelled.
Also.—He is guilty, and you *also.*
Too.—He is an idler, and a gambler *too.*

---

[1] Conjunctions for the most part join sentences, not words. "The single exception," says Mason, "is the conjunction *and*, which, besides uniting one sentence to another, may unite words which stand in the same relation to some other word in the sentence, as, Two and three make five." It appears to be incorrect, however, to say that *and* is the only exception. Another example is *but* in such a sentence as the following :—"I admire the character of a poor, *but* honest, man." Here we cannot possibly split up "but honest" into a separate and independent clause. *Poor* and *honest* stand in the same relation to *man*, for they both qualify the same noun. In fact, *and* and *but* necessarily stand on the same footing ; for *but* is the disjunctive or adversative counterpart of the cumulative or conjunctive *and*. *But* unites the words *poor* and *honest*, while at the same time it disjoins or contrasts their meanings.

As well as.—He *as well as* you is guilty.
No less than.—He *no less than* you is guilty.
Not only . . . but also.—He was *not only* accused, *but also* convicted.
Now.—They preferred Barabbas to Jesus ; *now*, Barabbas was a robber.
Well.—You have done the work very skilfully ; *well*, I did not expect it of you.

(b) **Alternative** (choice).

Either . . . or.—*Either* this man sinned *or* his parents.
Neither . . . nor.—He was *neither* an idler *nor* a gambler.
Otherwise, else, or.—Leave the room, *or* you will be caught.

(c) **Adversative** (contrast).

But.—He is sad, *but* hopeful.
Still, yet.—He is very rich, *still* or *yet* he is not contented.
Nevertheless.—All men were against him ; *nevertheless* he persevered.
However.—All men were against him ; he stuck, *however*, to his point.
Whereas, while.—Wise men love truth ; *whereas* or *while* fools shun it.
Only.—Go where you like ; *only* do not stay here.

(d) **Illative** (inference).

Therefore.—He was found guilty, and *therefore* he was hanged.
Then, so, so then.—It is time to go ; *so* or *so then* let us start, or let us start *then*.
For.—He will die some day ; *for* all men are mortal.

SECTION 2.—SUBORDINATING CONJUNCTIONS.

237. One sentence is said to be *subordinate* to another, when it depends upon the other, that is, enters into its construction with the force of a noun, adjective, or adverb.

That sentence on which the subordinate sentence depends is called the **Main** sentence.

Main.	*Conj.*	*Subordinate.*
I will read that book,	if	you advise me. (*Adverb.*)
We still hope	that	you may get well. (*Noun.*)

238. The chief modes of dependence are nine in number :—

(*a*) Apposition, (*b*) Causation, (*c*) Effect, (*d*) Purpose, (*e*) Condition, (*f*) Concession or Contrast, (*g*) Comparison, (*h*) Extent or Manner, (*i*) Time.

(a) **Apposition,** or in a merely **Introductory** sense : [1]—

Main.	*Subordinate.*
He told us (the fact),	*that* rain had fallen.
He wrote to us (to the effect),	*that* he had arrived safely.
He made a promise,	*that* he would return soon.

The Dependent sentence in the above examples is in apposition with the noun in brackets, which may be either omitted or expressed.

(b) **Cause** or **Reason :—**

Main.	*Subordinate.*
He will succeed,	*because* he has worked hard.
I will do this,	*since* you desire it.
Let us go to bed,	*as* it is now late.

(c) **Effect :—**

Main.	*Subordinate.*
He talked so much,	*that* he made himself hoarse.

(d) **Purpose :—**

Main.	*Subordinate.*
Men work,	*that* they may earn a living.
He took medicine,	*in order that* he might recover.
He took medicine,	*so that* he might recover.
He walked with a cane,	*lest* he should stumble.

(e) **Condition :—**

Main.	*Subordinate.*
I will do this,	*if* I am allowed.
They threatened to beat him,	*unless* he confessed (=if he did not confess).
I agree to these terms,	*provided* or *provided that* you will sign your name.
He gave a sudden start,	*as if* he had been shot (=as he would have done, if he had been shot).
You must leave the room,	*whether* you wish it *or no* (=you must leave the room under any condition whatever).

---

[1] The word "*that*," if we look to its origin, is simply the neuter Demonstrative pronoun.

"*That*" was originally the neuter pronoun used to point to the fact stated in some previous clause or sentence. "It was good ; he saw *that*." By inverting the order of the clauses, we get : "He saw *that* (namely) it was good." The primary clause has thus become a secondary or subordinate one ; and "*that*" has become a subordinating conjunction.

Mason calls it "the Simple Conjunction of Subordination,"—a longer and less convenient name than "Apposition."

Dr. Abbott, in p. 257 of *How to Parse*, calls it the conjunction of "Apposition."

When no noun stands before it for the purpose of apposition, it might be called the *Introductory* conjunction. because it is used to introduce a noun-clause.

(f) Concession or Contrast :—

Main.	Subordinate.
He is an honest man,	*though* or *although* he is poor.
He will never succeed,	*however* much he may try.
He was not contented,	*however* rich he became.
He was not refreshed,	*notwithstanding that* he slept long.

Note.—The conjunction "however," when it is *co-ordinating*, stands alone, and is seldom placed at the beginning of its sentence. But when it is *subordinating*, it must be attached to some adverb as "much," or to some adjective as "rich," and is always placed at the beginning of its sentence :—

Subordinate.	Main.
1. *Though* he punish me,	*yet* will I trust in him.
2. Hot *as* the sun is,	we must go out.

Observe that whenever "*as*" is used in a Concessive or Contrasting sense, it is invariably *preceded* by some adjective, adverb, or participle, which stands as Complement to the verb following :—

Hot as the sun is = however hot the sun is.

Note.—Sometimes no conjunction is used :—

Be it a trifle, it ought to be done well.
Were I as rich as Crœsus, I would not buy **that.**

(g) Comparison—(i.) Of equal degrees :—

The same Quality Compared.

He is *as* clever *as* I (am).
He likes you *as much as* I (like you).
He likes you *as much as* me (he likes me).

Different Qualities Compared.

The sea is *as* deep *as* the mountains are high.
He is *as* good *as* he is wise (= He is no less good than he is wise).

(ii.) Of unequal degrees.

The same Quality Compared.

He is more (or less) clever *than* I (am).
He likes you more (or less) *than* I (like you).
He likes you more (or less) *than* me (he likes me).

Different Qualities Compared.

The sea is deeper *than* the mountains are high.
He is more wise *than* (he is) good.
He is less good *than* (he is) wise.

(h) Extent or Manner :—

Main.	Subordinate.
Men will reap	*as* (= to what extent or in what manner) they sow.
This is not true,	*so far as* I can find out.
He chose the men,	*according as* they were fit.

Subordinate.	*Main.*
As men sow,	*so* will they also reap.

(i) **Time :—**

Time simultaneous.

Main.	*Subordinate.*
He called at the house,	*as* the clock struck four.
I will leave the room,	*as soon as* you open the door.
You can hold the horse,	*while* I bring the saddle.

Time before.

Main.	*Subordinate.*
He worked very hard,	*before* he succeeded.
You have much to do,	*ere* you can gain your end.
He remained a minor,	*until* he was seventeen years old.

Time after.

Main.	*Subordinate.*
He returned home,	*after* he had done the work.
He has been very weak,	*since* he was taken sick.

Time how long.

Main.	*Subordinate.*
The sun will rise,	*while* the world lasts.
No one can harm us,	*so long as* we remain friends.

Relative and Interrogative Adverbs.

239. It was explained in § 17 that a Relative adverb is a *double* part of speech,—a conjunction and adverb combined in one.

The same is true of Interrogative adverbs, when they are used as conjunctions :—

Let me ask you *how* you did this.

There is no difference in *form* between a Relative and an Interrogative adverb. The former refers to some noun expressed or understood in the Main clause. The latter is preceded by some verb that signifies *asking* or *inquiring*.

Relative and Interrogative adverbs, so far as they join sentences, constitute a special class of Subordinating conjunctions.

Time.

Main.		*Subordinate.*
He remained silent,	*when*	(=as soon as) he heard that.
He feels sad,	*whenever*	(=at any time in which) he thinks of his lost friend.
My friend inquired	*when*	I should return.

Purpose, Cause, or Reason.

Main.		*Subordinate.*
We never understood	*why*	(=the reason for which) he acted so.

Place.

Main.		*Subordinate.*
We find flowers,	*where*	(= in a place in which) we expected only weeds.
We find flowers,	*wherever*	(= in any place in which) we wander.
He did not tell us	*whence*	(= the place from which) he had come.

Respect.

Main.		*Subordinate.*
He did not tell us	*where*	(= in what point) we were wrong.
We cannot perceive	*where*	(= in what respect) the differ-en~e lies.

Manner or Means.

Main.		*Subordinate.*
Let me ask you,	*how*	(= by what means or in what manner) you did this.

State or Condition.

Main.		*Subordinate.*
Let me ask you,	*how*	(= in what state of health) you are to-day.

Doubt.

Main.		*Subordinate.*
He wished to know	*whether*	(or if) he was ready to start.

Note.—A Relative adverb can often be substituted for a Relative pronoun, as in the following examples :—

Ten o'clock is the hour *when* we must start.
Ten o'clock is the hour *at which* we must start.
Tell me the reason *why* you left us.
Tell me the reason *for which* you left us.
This is the house *where* we once lived.
This is the house *in which* we once lived.

CHAPTER IX.—INTERJECTIONS.

240. An Interjection is not a true Part of Speech, since it does not enter into the construction of a sentence.

It is merely an *exclamatory sound*, thrown into a sentence to denote some strong feeling or emotion (see §§ 12 and 13) :—

Joy.—Hurrah ! huzza !
Grief.—Oh ! ah ! alas ! alack !
Amusement.—Ha ! ha !
Approval.—Bravo !
Weariness.—Heigh-ho !
Attention.—Lo ! hark ! hush ! hist !

Reproof.—Fie ! fie !
Contempt or *ridicule*—Stuff ! bosh ! tut-tut ! pooh ! pish ! pshaw ! tush !
To call some one.—Ho ! holloa !

Note.—*Alas* is from Lat. *ah*, and *lassus*, wearied. *Alack* is from Middle Eng. *a ! lak* (loss) !

D 2

241. There are certain **phrases** which are used like Interjections to express some strong feeling or emotion :—

Ah me, or *ay me !* *Woe is me !*
For shame (=alas, on account of shame !)
Alack-a-day (=ah, lack or loss on the day !)
Hail, all hail (=be hale or healthy !) *Welcome ! Well done !*
Good-bye (= *God be with ye !*) *Adieu* (*à Dieu,* I commend you to God !) *Farewell* (may you fare well !)
Bad luck to it ! Dear me (=costly to me, or Ital. *Dio mio,* my God.)
Good gracious ! Good heavens ! Well to be sure ! (Surprise.)
Zounds (God's wounds). *'Sdeath* (God's death). *'Snails* (God's nails). *Marry* (Mary). *Parbleu,* Fr. (for *par Dieu,* by God).
Wellaway, A.S., wá lá wá, woe ! lo ! woe ! corrupted also to *welladay.*

Note 1.—It will thus be seen that there are two different ways in which interjections may arise : (1) From sounds that naturally express the feelings, as most of the monosyllables given in § 240 ; as *heigh-ho* (which is like the sound of yawning), *ah* (which is like the sound of sighing), *ha, ha* (which resembles the sound of laughing). (2) From phrases that have been worn down to single words, the origin of which is disguised ; as *alas, zounds, 'snails, parbleu, alackaday,* etc.

Note 2.—From *a-lack-a-day* we get the adj. *lackadaisical,* and the corruption *lauk-a-daisy.*

242. There are certain moods of verbs and parts of speech which can be used for an exclamatory or Interjectional purpose :—

(a) *Noun-Infinitive.—To think* that he should have died ! (§ 191, *e.*)
(b) *Subjunctive.—Would* that I had gained that prize ! (*Wish.*)
(c) *Imperative.—Hear ! hear !* (*Applause.*)
(d) *Noun.—*Dreadful *sight !* Foolish *fellow !* *Fool ! Dunce !*
(e) *Adjective* (with some noun understood).—*Strange ! Shocking !*
(f) *Adverb.—How* very kind of you ! *How* wonderful !
(g) *Pronoun.—What* a sad thing it is !
(h) *Conjunction.—If* I could only see him once more !

243. Sometimes in a rapid or exclamatory sentence an Auxiliary verb with its subject is left out, and only the main verb is expressed :—

Why dream and wait for him longer ?—LONGFELLOW.
(= Why *dost thou* or why *do we* wait for him longer ?)

CHAPTER X.—ANALYSIS OF SENTENCES.

SECTION 1.—ANALYSIS OF SIMPLE SENTENCES.

244. A sentence which has only *one* Finite verb (expressed or understood) is called a Simple sentence ; as—

Subject.	*Finite Verb.*
Rain	falls.

The word " Simple " means *single.* The sentence is called *single* (or simple), because it has only *one* Finite verb in it.

245. A sentence that has *more than one* Finite verb expressed or understood is either Multiple or Complex.

Thus :—"If I see him to-day, I will invite him to my house." This is not a Simple sentence, because it has *two* Finite verbs, viz. "see" and "will invite."

Again :—"He was well received and (was) listened to with respect, whenever he spoke." This is not a Simple sentence, because it has *three* Finite verbs, viz. "*was*" expressed, "*was*" understood, and "*spoke*."

246. There are four distinct parts or elements of which a Simple sentence can be composed ; and the analysis of a sentence consists in *decomposing* it (that is, in analysing or breaking it up) into these several parts :—

> § 1.—The Subject.
> § 2.—Adjuncts to the Subject, *if any*.
> § 3.—The Predicate.
> § 4.—Adjuncts to the Predicate-verb, *if any*.

Of these four elements the first and third (viz. the Subject and the Predicate) are essential to the sentence,—that is, the sentence could not exist without them (see § 2). But the second and fourth (viz. the Adjuncts to the Subject or to the Predicate-verb) are not essential. They are mere additions, which may or may not be present, and could be removed without destroying the sentence.

The chief use of Analysis is that it is an aid to Syntax, by showing the relations in which words stand to one another in a sentence. In a language like English, that has very few inflexions left, the best guide we can have as to the relations of words to one another is Analysis. Another use of Analysis is that it brings into prominence the *logical* side of grammar. It shows, for example, that an entire clause can be the subject to a verb, and thus logically equivalent to a noun.

247. I. The Subject must be either a *Noun* or something that has the force of a Noun.

II. The additions or Adjuncts to the Subject (if there are any) must be either *Adjectives* or words that have the force of an Adjective. They have hence been called Epithet Adjuncts. (They are sometimes also called the Enlargement of the Subject.)

III. The Predicate must either be a *Finite verb* or it must contain one.

IV. The additions or Adjuncts to the Predicate-verb (if there are any) must be either *Adverbs* or words that have the force of an Adverb. They have hence been called Adverbial Adjuncts.

(Sometimes also they have been called the Extension of the Predicate.)

I. Subject.	II. Epithet Adjuncts (to Subject).	III. Predicate-verb.	IV. Adverbial Adjuncts (to Predicate).
A tiger The horse	fierce tired	was shot will sleep	to-day. soundly.

The Subject.

248. Forms of the Subject ; as shown below :—

		Subject.	Predicate.
(a)	{ A Noun . . .	Rain	is falling.
	{ A Noun understood	The virtuous (men)	will prosper.
(b)	A Pronoun . .	We	must go.
(c)	A Noun-Infinitive .	To work	is healthy.
(d)	A Gerund . .	Working	is healthy.
(e)	A Phrase . .	How to do this	is doubtful.

Note 1.—The above list of forms tallies with that given in § 21, except that (f) a Clause has been omitted. A clause belongs to Complex and Multiple sentences, not to simple ones.

Note 2.—When a Noun-Infinitive is used as Subject, it is sometimes placed after the Predicate, and is in apposition to the pronoun " it."

It is sad to see this = It—viz. to see this—is sad.

Epithet Adjuncts (to the Subject).

249. Forms of Epithet Adjunct ; as shown below :—

(a) *Adjective.*—A *heavy* shower fell to-day.

(b) *Participle.*—A *fertilising* shower fell to-day.

(c) *Gerundial Infinitive.*—Water *to drink* is scarce in this place.

(d) *Possessive Adj. or Noun in Genitive.*—*My son's* teacher called here to-day.

(e) *Noun used as Adjective.*—The *village* school has met.

(f) *Gerund used as Adjective.*—*Drinking* water is scarce here.

(g) *Noun in Apposition.*—Philip, *King* of Macedon, perished.

(h) *Preposition with Object.*—A man *of virtue* will not tell a lie.

(i) *Adverb with Participle understood.*—The *then* king = the then (reigning) king.

Note.—Here and elsewhere in this chapter articles have been placed in the same column with their nouns. But since articles are really adjectives, it would be more correct, though less convenient, to place them in the column of Epithet Adjuncts.

The Predicate.

250. The Predicate must be either a Finite verb or it must contain one. If the verb is of such a nature, that it cannot by itself make a *complete* sense (as required by the definition given in § 1), but must have some word or words placed after it for this purpose, any such word or words must be considered parts of the predicate. All possible forms of a Predicate are shown in the following scheme :—

Subject.	PREDICATE.		
	Finite verb.	Object with qualifying words.	Complement with qualifying words.
1. { A hog	grunts.	...	...
{ The snake	was killed.	...	...
2. { My son	became	...	a good scholar.
{ The thief	was ordered	...	to be severely punished.
3. { The gardener	killed	that poisonous snake.	...
{ The teacher	will teach	(*a*) my sons (*b*) Euclid.	...
4. They	found	the weary man	sound asleep.

In (1) we have first an Intransitive verb of Complete Predication (see § 146), and then a Transitive verb in the Passive voice. Neither of these requires either an Object or a Complement. So the verb alone makes up the Predicate.

In (2) we have first an Intransitive verb of Incomplete Predication (see § 147), and then a Transitive verb of Incomplete Predication in the Passive voice (see § 162). Each of these requires a Complement to make the predication complete.

In (3) we have first a Transitive verb with a single Object (see § 139), and then a Transitive verb with a double Object (see § 141). Each of these requires the Object (single or double) to be expressed, before the predication can be complete.

In (4) we have a Transitive verb of Incomplete Predication in the Active voice, which therefore requires both an Object and a Complement (see § 142).

Note 1.—If the Object or Complement has any qualifying words attached to it, these can be mentioned with it in the same column.

Thus in the complement "a good scholar," there is no need to make a separate column for the qualifying adjective "good."

Again, in the complement "to be severely punished," there is no need of a separate column for the qualifying adverb "severely."

Again, in stating the object "that poisonous snake," there is no need of a separate column for the qualifying adjectives "that" and "poisonous."

Note 2.—An Auxiliary verb must be put in the same column with the Principal verb. Thus in stating "will teach," we need not give one column for "will" and another for "teach." But when an Auxiliary is used as a Principal verb, it must stand by itself.

Adverbial Adjuncts (to Verb of Predicate).

251. The Forms of Adverbial Adjunct are shown below:—

(a) *Adverb.*—He sleeps *soundly.*
(b) *Adverbial Phrase.*—They walked *side by side.*
(c) *Adjective.*—He went away *sad.* He stood *alone.*
(d) *Participle.*—He went away *vexed* and *disappointed.*
(e) *Gerundial Infinitive.*—He came *to see* the horse.
(f) *Adverbial Accusative.*—He walked *all day.* He walked *ten miles.*
(g) *Preposition with Object.*—He fell *into a deep well.*
(h) *Absolute Phrase.*—We all started, *he remaining behind.*

Examples for Analysis.

1. A merchant, travelling through Tartary, having arrived at the town of Balkh, entered the king's palace by mistake, thinking it to be a public inn.
2. My father taught all his sons Euclid with much success.
3. Alexander, the King of Macedon, was surnamed the Great after his conquest of the Persian Empire.
4. The man employed for this purpose caught the thief stealing a watch.
5. The merchant, having much property to sell, caused all his goods to be conveyed on camels, there being no railway in that particular part of the country.
6. A gentleman of wealth and position, living in London, some sixty years ago, had a country seat in Kent, some forty miles from the metropolis.

These are worked out in tabular form on page 107.

Section 2.—Analysis of Double and Multiple Sentences.

252. A **Double** *sentence is one made up of two, and a* **Multiple** *sentence one made up of more than two,* **Co-ordinate** *(that is, equal or independent) clauses.*

The clauses of a Multiple sentence are joined together by any of the *Co-ordinating Conjunctions* described in § 235.

(1) The sun rose with power, *and* the fog dispersed. (*Cumulative.*)
(2) Either he must go *or* I (must go). (*Alternative.*)
(3) He called at my house, *but* I did not see him. (*Adversative.*)
(4) He came back tired ; *for* he had walked all day. (*Illative.*)

Note.—Clauses which are Co-ordinate with each other may be themselves Subordinate to some other clause :—

(a) I have just seen the man (*Main clause*),
(b) { who was injured last week, } (*Adjective clauses to* (a), *and*
      { but is now recovering   } *Co-ordinate with each other*).

253. Co-ordinate clauses can also be joined together by a Relative pronoun or adverb, provided it is used in a **Continuative** and not in a Restrictive sense (see § 127).

I. Subject.	II. Epithet Adjuncts (to Subject).	III. PREDICATE. Finite Verb.	Object with qualifying words.	Complement with qualifying words.	IV. Adverbial Adjuncts (to Verb of Predicate).
1. A merchant	(a) travelling through Tartary (b) having arrived at the town of Balkh	entered	the king's palace	...	(a) by mistake (b) thinking it to be a public inn.
2. Father	my	taught	(a) all his sons (b) Euclid	...	with much success.
3. Alexander	the King of Macedon	was sur-named	...	the Great	after his conquest of the Persian Empire.
4. The man	employed for this purpose	caught	the thief	stealing a watch.	...
5. The merchant	having much property to sell	caused	all his goods	to be conveyed on camels	there being no railway in that particular part of the country.
6. A gentleman	(a) of wealth and position (b) living in London (c) some sixty years ago	had	a country seat	...	(a) in Kent (b) some forty miles from the metropolis.

He slew all the prisoners, *which* (=and this) was a very barbarous act.

He is clever at planting young trees ; for *which* purpose (=and for this purpose) every one is glad to employ him.

He went to London, *where* (and there) he stayed ten days.

254. Contracted Sentences.—Double and Multiple sentences often appear in a contracted or shortened form, so as to avoid the needless repetition of the same word :—

(*a*) When there are *two Predicates to the same Subject* :—

(1) The sun *rose* and (the sun) *filled* the sky with light.

(2) He *called* at my house, but (he) *left* soon after.

(*b*) When there are *two Subjects to the same Predicate* :—

(1) *He* as well as *you* is guilty (= He is guilty as well as you are guilty). (*Cumulative.*)

(2) Either *this man* sinned or his *parents* (sinned). (*Alternative.*)

(3) He is poor, but (he is) honest. (*Adversative.*)

(4) He is diligent, and therefore (he is) prosperous. (*Illative.*)

Note 1.—When two nouns are joined by "*and*," they may be treated, not as separate subjects to the same verb, but as *one* double subject to the Plural verb following :—

The dog-and-its-master *are* gone.

In some instances, such as the following, the two Subjects united by "*and*" are inseparable :—

He and I are great friends.

Youth and experience seldom exist together.

Note 2.—The phrase *as well as* can be used as a Subordinating conjunction, but of course in a different sense from that belonging to it as a Co-ordinating conjunction. This is explained in § 375 (2).

Examples.

(1) His greatest enemy, as well as his best friends, repeatedly declared him to be innocent of the fault laid to his charge.

A. His greatest enemy repeatedly declared him to be innocent of the fault laid to his charge.

B. His best friends repeatedly declared him to be innocent of the fault laid to his charge.

Connective :—As well as.

(2) Either you or your son must sign his name at once on that paper.

A. You must sign your name, etc.

B. Your son must sign his name, etc.

Connectives :—Either . . . or.

(3) He, not I, is certainly the author of that plan.

A. He is certainly the author of that plan.

B. I am certainly not the author of that plan.

Connective :—(*nil*). Here no connective is required.

The Clauses.	Connective.	I. Subject.	II. Epithet Adjuncts (to Subject).	III. PREDICATE.			IV. Adverbial Adjuncts (to Verb of Predicate.)
				Finite Verb.	Object with qualifying words.	Complement with qualifying words.	
Example (1) A. His greatest enemy repeatedly declared him to be innocent of the fault, etc.	...	enemy	his greatest	declared	him	to be innocent of the fault laid to his charge	repeatedly.
Example (1) B. His best friends declared him to be innocent of the fault, etc.	as well as	friends	his best	declared	him	to be innocent of the fault, etc.	repeatedly.
Example (2) A. You must sign your name at once on that paper.	either	you	nil	must sign	your name	nil	(a) at once (b) on that paper.
Example (2) B. Your son must sign his name at once on that paper.	or	son	your	must sign	his name	nil	(a) at once (b) on that paper.
Example (3) A. He is certainly the author of that plan.	...	He	nil	is	nil	the author of that plan	certainly.
Example (3) B. I am certainly not the author of that plan.	nil	I	nil	am	nil	the author of that plan	certainly not.

Section 3.—Analysis of Complex Sentences.

255. A **Complex** *sentence consists of a Main clause with one or more* **Subordinate** *clauses.*

The clause which contains *the main verb* of the entire complex sentence is called the **Main** clause.

Note.—It has been said that the Main clause is that which contains "the principal *subject* and predicate."[1] But this is not true; for sometimes there is no principal subject, the subject itself being a Subordinate clause :—

Subject (Subord. clause).	*Predicate (Prin. verb).*
Who steals my purse	steals trash.

256. Subordinate and Co-ordinate Clauses.—A Subordinate clause is a *component part* of some other clause, in which it does the work (without possessing the form) of a Noun, Adjective, or Adverb.

A Co-ordinate clause is one that has the same grammatical function as the clause preceding it in the same sentence.

257. There are three kinds of Subordinate clauses,—the **Noun**-Clause, the **Adjective**-Clause, and the **Adverb**-Clause ; and these are defined as follows :—

I. *A Noun-Clause is one which does the work of a Noun in relation to some* **word** *in some other clause.*

II. *An Adjective-Clause is one which does the work of an Adjective in relation to some* **word** *in some other clause.*

III. *An Adverb-Clause is one which does the work of an Adverb in relation to some* **word** *in some other clause.*

Note.—The same clause may be a Noun-clause in one sentence, an Adjective-clause in another, and an Adverb-clause in another. This entirely depends on the context :—

Where Moses was buried is still unknown . .	*Noun-clause.*
No one has seen the place *where Moses was buried*	*Adj.-clause.*
They encamped *where Moses was buried* without knowing it	*Adv.-clause.*

I. *The Noun-Clause.*

258. There are three kinds of connectives, by which a Noun-Clause can be introduced :—

(1) The Conjunction " *that* " used in the sense of Apposition, or in a merely Introductory sense (see § 238, *a*) :—

We did not know *that* he would leave us so soon.

---

[1] See for example Mason's *English Grammar*, page 160.

(2) A Relative or Interrogative adverb, provided that no Antecedent is expressed :—

> *Where* he is going is not known to any one.   (*Relat.*)
> Let us inquire *whether* he will go to-day.   (*Interrog.*)

Note.—The conjunction "*if*" can be used for "*whether*" as an Interrogative adverb. But "*whether*" is much to be preferred.

> Let us inquire *if* (=*whether*) he will go to-day.

(3) A Relative or Interrogative pronoun, provided that no Antecedent is expressed :—

> *Who* steals my purse steals trash.   (*Relat.*)
> I beg to inquire *who* came here to-day.   (*Interrog.*)

259. The Noun-Clause, since it does the work of a Noun, can be—

> (*a*) The Subject to a Verb.
> (*b*) The Object to a Verb.
> (*c*) The Object to a Preposition.
> (*d*) The Complement to a Verb.
> (*e*) In Apposition to a Noun.

(*a*) **Subject to a Verb**; see § 21 (*f*) :—

> *Where he is going* is not known to any one.
> *That he will come back soon* is certain.
> *Whom the gods love* die young.—*Proverb.*

(*b*) **Object to a Verb**; see § 23 (*f*) :—

> He promised *that he would soon pay back the debt.*
> I shall be glad to know *when he will pay it.*
> Perceiving *what a mistake he had made,* he yielded.

(*c*) **Object to a Preposition**; see § 228 (*d*) :—

> My success in future depends upon *who is placed over me.*
> This book will sell for *what it is worth.*
> Except *that he speaks too fast* he is an excellent teacher.

(*d*) **Complement to a Verb**; see § 143 and § 147 :—

> This is exactly *what I expected.*
> His teachers have made him *what he is.*

(*e*) **In Apposition to a Noun**; see § 19 :—

> The news *that he intended to come* gave us much pleasure.
> The report *that he was so sad* is unknown to me.

260. The conjunction "*that*" (in the sense of apposition) is often left out after a *verb*, provided that the noun with which the clause is in apposition is not expressed :—

> It seems (that) *he is not clever.*

N.B.—The conjunction "*that*" is never left out *when the noun is expressed.* Such a sentence as the following is inadmissible :—

> The *fact* he is not clever gives us much pain.

261. A sentence consisting of the very words spoken by any one may be the Subject or Object to a verb, but is not to be considered as an example of a Noun-Clause ; it should be treated as an equivalent to a single noun :—

" I have seen this man before," was the only thing that he said.
The sleeper started up from his bed, shouting, " I am bitten."

Examples of the Noun-Clause.

Pick out the Noun-Clause and say whether it is the Subject to some Verb, or the Object to some Verb, or the Object to some Preposition, or the Complement to some Verb, or in Apposition to some noun expressed.   Supply the Conjunction " that" *wherever it has been left out :*—

1. No one knows when he will come, or whether he will come at all, or whether he is even alive.
2. How this came to pass is not known to any one.
3. What is sauce for the goose is sauce for the gander.
4. It is quite evident rain will fall to-day.
5. The Equator shows where days and nights are of equal length.
6. What is one man's meat is another man's poison.
7. You must know that the air is never quite at rest.
8. I think I shall never clearly understand this.
9. We heard the school would open in ten days' time.
10. The name "Volcano" indicates the belief of the ancient Greeks, that the burning hills of the Mediterranean were the work-shops of the divine blacksmith, Vulcan.
11. Even a feather shows which way the wind is blowing.
12. Whatever faculty man has is improved by use.
13. The fool hath said in his heart, "There is no God."
14. "Know thyself," was the advice given us by a Greek sage.
15. He did not know that his father had been shot.
16. The fact that you have not signed your name to a letter shows that you lack moral courage.
17. It will be easily understood how useful even the simplest weapons were to the first dwellers on the earth.
18. The question first occurring to the mind of a savage is how is fire to be made.
19. Common sense soon taught him that fire could be produced by rubbing two sticks together.
20. In chipping their flint weapons men must have seen that fire occasionally flashed out.
21. We learn from travellers that savages can produce fire in a few seconds.
22. He shouted out to the thief, "Leave this house."
23. We cannot rely on what he says.
24. It is quite evident you have made a mistake.
25. It was very unfortunate that you were taken ill.
26. He was a man of fine character except that he was rather timid.

II. *The Adjective-Clause.*

262. An Adjective-Clause does the work of an Adjective to some noun or noun-equivalent in some other clause.

The only kind of connective word by which an Adjective-Clause can be introduced is a Relative pronoun or Relative adverb, and then only when the Relative is used in a **Restrictive** sense (see § 127).

If the Relative is used in a **Continuative** sense, the sentence is Multiple, and not Complex (see § 253).

1. Among the men, *who came here to-day,* not one turned out to be honest.

Here the italicised clause qualifies or restricts "*men.*"

2. We found the wolf lying dead in the very place *where* (*=in which*) *it was shot.*

Here the italicised clause qualifies or restricts "*place.*"

263. The Relative pronoun, provided it would be in the Accusative case, and provided its sense is Restrictive, and not Continuative, is often left out (see § 144).

The food he needed (*=which* or *that* he needed) was not procured without a great deal of trouble.

Pick out the Adjective-Clause or Clauses in each of the following examples, and point out the noun or pronoun qualified by it in some other clause. If the Relative pronoun has been omitted anywhere, supply it :—

1. Man has the power of making instruments, which bring into view stars, whose light has taken a thousand years to reach the earth.
2. The first thing that man needed was some sharp-edged tool.
3. The exact time when the theft was committed was never found out.
4. The man by whom the theft was committed has been caught.
5. The house we lived in has fallen down.
6. This is the same story that I heard ten years ago.
7. It's an ill wind that blows no one any good.
8. This is not such a book as I should have chosen.
9. He made his living by the presents he received from the men he served.
10. All that glitters is not gold.
11. In ponds from which but a week before the wind blew clouds of dust, men now catch the re-animated fish.
12. A river is joined at places by tributaries that swell its waters.
13. Of what use is a knowledge of books to him who fails to practise virtue ?
14. Fortune selects him for her lord, who reflects before acting.
15. Springs are fed by rain, which has percolated through the rocks or soil.
16. Nuncoomar prepared to die with that quiet fortitude with

which the Bengalee, so backward, as a rule, in personal conflict, often encounters calamities for which there is no remedy.

17. I have seen the house where Shakspeare was born.
18. The plan you acted on has answered well.
19. They accepted every plan we proposed.
20. Surely the story you are telling me is not true.
21. Thrice is he armed that hath his quarrel just.
22. The night is long that never finds the day.
23. He travelled home by the way his father showed him.
24. There are times when every one feels a little sad.
25. Such men as are false to their friends should always be avoided.
26. I forgot to tell you the time when I shall return.

III. *The Adverb-Clause.*

264. An Adverb-Clause does the work of an Adverb to some verb, adjective, or adverb in some other clause.

An Adverb-Clause can be introduced by any of the *Subordinating* conjunctions, excepting the conjunction "*that*," when it is used in the sense of Apposition.

Main Clause.	*Adverb-Clause.*	*Subord. Conjunc.*
He will succeed,	*because* he works hard .	*Cause.*
He worked *so* hard,	*that* he was quite tired .	*Effect.*
He took medicine	*that* he might get well .	*Purpose.*
I will do this,	*if* I am allowed . .	*Condition.*
He is honest,	*although* he is poor . .	*Contrast.*
He likes you *more*	*than* (he likes) me . .	*Comparison.*
Men will reap	*where* they sow . . .	*Place.*
The sun will rise,	*so long as* the world lasts .	*Time.*

Note.—The Subordinating conjunctions have been described and enumerated in § 238. Besides these there is the class of Subordinating connectives, which in § 239 are enumerated under the name of Relative and Interrogative adverbs. These can be used for Noun-clauses and Adjective-clauses as well as for Adverb-clauses.

265. After the conjunctions *though, when, unless, till, if, whether . . . or,* and *while,* the Predicate-verb "**to be**" is often understood. This must be supplied in the Analysis.

{ Though much alarmed at the news, he did not lose all hope.
{ Though *he was* much alarmed, etc., he did not lose all hope.
{ He sprained his foot, while walking in the dark.
{ He sprained his foot, while *he was* walking in the dark.
{ His opinion, whether right or wrong, does not concern me.
{ His opinion, whether *it is* right or wrong, does not concern me.
This must be kept, till (*it is*) called for.

266. When an Adverb-Clause is introduced by "**than**," its Predicate-verb is not always expressed; it must therefore be borrowed from the clause on which it depends :—

He loves you better than (he loves) me.
He loves you better than I (love you).

267. The Relative "**who**" or "**which**" makes an Adverb-Clause, whenever it is substituted for a Subordinating conjunction signifying Cause or Purpose. (See § 127, *Note*.)

Cause.—They should pardon my son, *who* (=*because he*) has never committed such a fault before.

Purpose.—A man was sent, *who* should deliver (=*that he* might deliver) the message.

Note.—The student can now therefore take note that four different kinds of clauses can be introduced by the Relative "who" or "which" :—(1) A *Co-ordinate* Clause, where the Relative is used in a **Continuative** sense. This belongs to Multiple sentences. (2) A *Noun*-Clause, where no Antecedent to the Relative is expressed. This belongs to Complex sentences. (3) An *Adjective*-Clause, where the Relative is used in a **Restrictive** sense. This belongs to Complex sentences. (4) An *Adverb*-Clause, where the Relative is used in the sense of **Cause** or **Purpose**. This also belongs to Complex sentences.

Pick out the Adverb-Clause or Clauses in the following. Show what word or phrase is qualified by every such clause, and what Adverbial relation is denoted thereby :—

1. He will succeed, because he has worked hard.
2. Men engage in some work, that they may earn a living.
3. He threatened to beat him, unless he confessed.
4. He was always honest, though he was poor.
5. This is not true, so far as I can tell.
6. He likes you as much as I do.
7. He tried for a long time before he succeeded.
8. Let us go to bed, as it is now late.
9. He walked with care, lest he should stumble.
10. I agree to this, provided you sign your name.
11. Though he punish me, yet will I trust in him.
12. He returned home, after he had finished the work.
13. Prove a friend, before you trust him.
14. When the cat's away, the mice will play.
15. He persevered so steadily, that he succeeded at last.
16. I will let off this man, who has been well punished already.
17. He sees very well, considering that he is sixty years of age.
18. I gave him a prize, that he might work harder next year.
19. They deserted their former associate, who had become poor and unfortunate.
20. As the tree falls, so will it lie.
21. Ever since we left the house, it has not ceased raining.
22. I would be glad to lend you that money, if I had as much in my own pocket.
23. Murder, though it have no tongue, will yet speak.
24. Unless you leave the house at once, I will send for a policeman.
25. A jackal, while prowling about the suburbs of a town, slipped into an indigo tank ; and not being able to get out he laid himself down, so that he might be taken for dead.

26. The owner of the tank, when he beheld what seemed to be a dead jackal, carried the body into the jungle and there flung it down.

27. This one fact, if closely examined, proves the man to be guilty.

28. He is an honest man, though poor ; and industrious, though old and rather infirm.

29. Better to reign in hell than serve in heaven.—MILTON.

30. If the trunk of a tree, when young and pliable, is not made to grow straight, it cannot be straightened afterwards, when old and stiff.

31. A rabbit cannot run so swiftly as a hare ; but it is more skilful than a hare in digging the ground and boring holes under the earth.

32. The wild grey rabbit is not so large as the tame rabbit kept in a cage.

268. Multiple and Complex mixed.—We often meet with sentences which are neither entirely Multiple nor entirely Complex, but a mixture of both. The following is an example:—

He seized the hill as soon as the enemy left it, and occupied the strongest position that he could find there.

This sentence consists of two main parts, as shown below :—

A. He seized the hill as soon as the enemy left it.

B. And (he) occupied the strongest position that he could find there.

So far the sentence is Double ; for it consists of two Co-ordinate parts, A and B, which are connected by the conjunction *and*. But on looking again at the parts A and B we find that A is a Complex sentence ; for it has a main clause—

He seized the hill,

and an Adverb clause qualifying the verb "seized,"—

As soon as the enemy left it.

Similarly, if we look again at B, we find B is also a Complex sentence ; for it has a main clause—

He occupied the strongest position,

and an Adjective clause qualifying the noun "position,"—

That he could find there.

From such an example as this it is evident that a Multiple sentence might be and ought to be defined more fully than it was in § 252. The new definition will run thus :—

"A Multiple sentence is one that is made up of two or more Co-ordinate parts, any of which may be either a Simple or a Complex sentence."

The mixed sentence quoted below is worked out in tabular form on the next page :—

The governor of the town, who was present, cried out with a loud voice || and ordered Androcles to explain how a savage beast had so forgotten its innate disposition all of a sudden, that it became converted into a harmless animal, which preferred rather to spare its victim than to devour him.   One Co-ord. part is separated from the other by two vertical lines.

The Clause.	Kind of Clause.	Connective.	I. Subject.	II. Epithet Adjuncts (to Subject).	III. Predicate. Finite Verb.	Object with qualifying words.	Complement with qualifying words.	IV. Adverbial Adjuncts (to Verb of Predicate).
A. The governor of the town cried out with a loud voice,	Main Clause.	..	the governor	of the town	cried out	nil	nil	with a loud voice,
B. Who was present,	Co-ordinate to A. (§ 253).	who	who	nil	was	nil	present,	nil
C. And ordered Androcles to explain	Co-ordinate to A.	and	(the governor)	nil	ordered	Androcles	to explain, etc.	nil
D. How a savage beast had so forgotten its innate disposition all of a sudden,	Noun-Clause, object to explain in C.	how	a beast	savage	had forgotten	its innate disposition	nil	(a) all of a sudden, (b) so that, etc.
E. That it became converted into a harmless animal,	Adverb-Clause in continuation of so in D.	that	it	nil	became	nil	converted into a harmless animal, which, etc.	nil
F. Which preferred rather to spare its victim	Adject.-Clause to animal in E.	which	which	nil	preferred	to spare its victim	nil	rather than, etc.
G. Than to devour him.	Adverb-Clause in continuation of rather in F.	than	(it)	nil	(preferred)	to devour him.	nil	nil

Note on the twofold form of Analysis.

Another form of Analysis is given in the *Outline of English Grammar*. The only difference between this form and that given in the present chapter is that in the *Outline* the sentence is divided into two parts—

| I. Subject (with Adjuncts). | II. Predicate (with Adjuncts). |

instead of being divided into four parts, as is done in § 246 :—

| I. Subject. | III. Predicate. |
| II. Adjuncts of Subject. | IV. Adjuncts of Predicate. |

The form of Analysis in the twofold basis is given below; and to show how it works the following sentences are analysed :—

A man convinced against his will is of the same opinion still.

The second master of the school has been teaching my sons Euclid since Thursday last.

I. SUBJECT.		II. PREDICATE.			
Subject-Noun or Equivalent.	Epithet Adjuncts to Subject.	Predicate Verb or Finite Verb.	Object (1) Indirect (2) Direct	Complement.	Adverbial Adjuncts to Finite Verb.
A man	convinced against his will	is	*nil*	of the same opinion	still
The master	(1) second (2) of the school	has been teaching	(1) my sons (2) Euclid	*nil*	since Thursday last

CHAPTER XI.

THE SAME WORD USED AS DIFFERENT PARTS OF SPEECH

A.　　*Indef. Article.*　The sportsman shot *a* tiger.
　　　　Prep.　He has gone a hunting. See § 230.
All.　*Adj. of Quantity.*　He ate *all* the bread.
　　　　Indef. Num. Adj.　We must *all* die some day.
　　　　Adj. used as Noun.　We lost our *all* on that day.
　　　　Adv.　*All* bloodless lay the untrodden snow.
Any.　*Adj. of Quantity.*　Have you *any* bread ?
　　　　Adv. of Qu.　We must stop and rest before going *any* farther.
　　　　Indef. Num. Adjective.　Did you bring *any* loaves ?
　　　　Indef. Dem. Adjective.　Take *any* book that you like best.
As.　　(a) *Relative pronoun :*—
　　　　　　He is not such a fool *as* he looks.
　　　　　　As many men *as* came were caught.
　　　　　　Yours is not the same book *as* mine.

(b) *Relative adverb* (or Subordinating conjunction) :—

Time.   He trembled *as* (at what time) he spoke.

Manner.   Do not act *as* (in what manner) he did.

State.   He took it just *as* (in what state) it was.

Extent. { He is not as (to that extent) clever *as* (to what extent) you are.

Hot *as* (to whatever extent) the sun is (= however hot the sun is), we must go out in it.

Reason.   The air is now cool, *as* (for what reason or for the reason that) the rain has fallen.

(c) *In Elliptical Phrases :*—all of these imply "extent."

I condemn you *as* a judge (to what extent or so far as I am a judge), but *as* a man (to what extent I am a man), I pity you.

I will inquire again *as* to (to what extent the question relates to) that matter.

As regards this journey (to what extent the question regards this journey), we can now decide nothing.

Better.   *Comp. Adj.*   My book is a *better one* than yours.

Comp. Adv.   You are working *better* to-day.

Adj. used as Noun.   Do not despise your *betters.*

Both.   *Def. Num. Adj.*   *Both* the men have arrived.

Conj. Co-ord.   He is *both* a fool and a knave.

But.   *Adv.*   There is *but* (only) one man present.

Prep.   Who could have done this *but* (except) him ?

I cannot *but* believe that you are lost.   (I cannot believe anything *except* that, etc.)

Conj. Co-ord.   He is a man of common sense, *but* not learned in books.

There was no one present, *but* (he) pitied (= who did not pity) the lame horse.

Conj. Subord.   Perdition **catch my soul, *but* I do love** thee.— SHAKSPEARE.   (May perdition catch my soul, *if* I do *not* love thee.)

Either.   *Distrib. Adj.*   He is ruined in *either* case.

Conj. Co-ord.   He is *either* a fool or a knave.

Else.   *Adv.*   We could not catch any one *else.*

Conj. Co-ord.   He has some real sorrow ; *else* he would not weep as he does.

Enough.   *Adj. of Quantity.*   He has eaten *enough* bread.

Adj. of Number.   We have *enough* loaves.

Adj. used as Noun.   He had *enough* to do.

Half.   *Adj. of Quantity.*   *Half* measures do not succeed.

Adj. used as Noun.   One *half* of his task is now done.

Adv. of Quantity.   He was *half* dead with fear.

Little.   *Adj. of Quality.*   A *little* blow may give much pain.

Adj. of Quantity.   He has eaten a *little* bread.

Adv. of Quantity.   Let us wait here a *little.*

Adj. used as Noun.   Man wants but *little* here below.

More. *Adj. of Quantity.* He eats *more* bread than you.
   Adj. used as Noun. *More* is done than was expected.
   Adv. of Quantity. I like him *more* than (I like) you.
   Adj. of Number. *More* men came to-day than yesterday.
   Adv. of Number. I saw him once *more*.

Much. *Adj. of Quantity.* He has wasted *much* time.
   Adv. of Quantity. I am *much* pleased with your son.
   Adj. used as Noun. You will not get *much* from me.

Neither. *Adj. Distrib.* I agree with *neither* side.
   Conj. Co-ord. *Neither* you nor I can do that.

Near. *Adv.* Stand *near*, while I speak to you.
   Prep. There is a fine tree *near* our house.
   Adj. He is a *near* relative of mine.

Needs. *Verb.* The earth is very dry and *needs* rain.
   Adv. He must *needs* know the reason of this.
   Noun. Our *needs* or wants are few.

One. *Def. Num. Adj.* There is but *one* shilling left.
   Indef. Dem. Adj. He came here *one* day.
   Indef. Dem. Pron. *One* is apt to waste *one's* time.
   Def. Dem. Pron. Your horse is white ; mine is a black
        one.

Only. *Adj.* The *only* dog I had was stolen.
   Adv. I heard of this *only* yesterday.
   Conj. Co-ord. Do what you like ; *only* (= but whatever else
        you may do) keep silence.

Round. *Adj.* A square thing does not fit into a *round* hole.
   Prep. Draw a circle *round* a given centre.
   Adv. The flies are flying *round* and *round*.
   Verb. Gama was the first to *round* the Cape of Good Hope.
   Noun. Men must go their daily *round* of duty.

Since. *Prep.* I have not seen him *since* Monday last.
   Adv. I took this house four weeks *since*.
   Conj. Subord. We must trust you, *since* you are speaking
        in earnest

Single. *Verb.* *Single* out the best.
   Adj. He is a *single* (unmarried) man.

Such. *Def. Dem. Adj.* He is not *such* a man *as* I expected.
   Indef. Dem. Adj. He came to me on *such* a day.
   Def. Dem. Pron. You are a coward ; I am not *such*.

That. *Def. Dem. Adj.* I am no admirer of *that* book.
   Def. Dem. Pron. The light of the sun is brighter than *that*
        of the moon.
   Relat. Pron. The book *that* you gave me is lost.
   Conj. { *Effect.* He aimed *so* well *that* he hit the mark.
      { *Apposit.* He heard *that* you had come.
      { *Purpose.* We must eat *that* we may live.

Than. *Conj. Subord.* I like this more *than* (I like) that.
     { These workmen, *than* whom I have never seen men
   Prep. { more industrious, have left me.
     { He was fond of any drink other *than* wine.

Then. *Adv. of Time.* He was better *then* than he is now.
   Conj. Co-ord. I see, *then*, we ought to start at once.

The.   *Def. Article.*   *The* ass is a dull animal.
           Adv. of Quantity.   *The* more, *the* merrier.
Too.   *Adv. of Quantity.*   He is *too* fond of play.
           Conj. Co-ord.   We *too* must expect to die some day.
Well. *Adv. of Quality.*   He has done the work very *well.*
           Adv. used as Noun.   Leave *well* alone.
           Conj. Co-ord.   He has finished his work in time ; *well,* I did
                             not expect it of such a lazy man.
What. *Inter. Pron.*   *What* did you say ?   *What* house is that ?
           Rel. Pron.   I do not know *what* you mean, § 123 (*b*).
           Indef. Demons.   I tell you *what* (=something) ; see § 315.
           Adverb.   *What* with illness and *what* with losses, the poor
                       man is almost ruined (see chap. xx. 76).
While. *Noun.*   Stop a little *while.*
           Conj.   *While* the cat's away, the mice play.
Yet.   *Conj. Co-ord.*   I have called ; *yet* no one answers.
           Adv. of Time.   You may *yet* (=even now, still) find him.

CHAPTER XII.—SYNTAX.

Parsing Chart.

I. *Nouns.*

Kind of Noun.	Gender.	Number.	Case.
1. Proper 2. Common 3. Collective 4. Material 5. Abstract	Masculine Feminine Common Neuter	Singular Plural	Nominative Accusative Genitive, etc.

II. *Pronouns.*

Kind of Pronoun.	Gender.	Number.	Person.	Case.
Pers. { Simple Poss. { Reflexive Demons. { Definite { Indefinite	Masculine Feminine Common Neuter	Singular Plural	1st 2nd 3rd	Nominative Accusative Genitive, etc.
Relative Interrogative	If Relative or Demonstrative, agreeing in Gender, Number, and Person with its antecedent.			

III. *The Cases of Nouns or Pronouns.*

Nom. to Verb.	*Acc.* to Verb Direct	*Acc.* to Preposition
,, as Compl. to Verb	*Acc.* ,, Retained	,, Adverbial
,, in Apposition	,, ,, Cognate	,, after certain Adjectives
Voc. Absolute	,, ,, Reflexive	
,, of Address	,, as Compl. to Verb	,, Interjectional
Genitive	,, in Apposition	*Dat.* to Verb Indirect

IV. *Adjectives.*

The Kind of Adjective.		Degree.	Use.
Proper Descriptive Quantitative Interrogative Distributive Possessive	Numer. { Def. Indef. Demons. { Def. Indef.	Positive Comparative Superlative	Epithet Predicative

V. *Adverbs.*

Kind.	Degree.	Use.	Attributive Uses.
Simple Relative Interrogative	Positive Comparative Superlative	Attributive Predicative	To qualify Verb ,, ,, Adjective ,, ,, Adverb ,, ,, Preposition ,, ,, Conjunction ,, ,, Sentence

VI. *Finite Verbs.*

Kind of Verb.	Conjug.	Voice.	Mood.	Tense.	Form of each Tense.
Trans. Intrans. Auxil.	Strong Weak Mixed	Active Passive	Indic. Imper. Subjunc.	Present Past Future Future in Past	Indefinite Continuous Perfect Perf. Contin.

Number.	Person.	
Singular Plural	1st 2nd 3rd	Agreeing in Number and Person with its subject or subjects, expressed or understood.

VII. *Infinitive.*

Form.	(a) Use as Noun-Inf.	(b) Use as Gerundial Inf.

Present
Pres. Contin.
Perfect
Perf. Contin.
	Subject to Verb
	Object to Verb
	Complement to Verb
	Object to Preposition
	Exclamatory
		To qualify—
		  ,, a Verb
		  ,, a Noun { Attributively / Predicatively
		  ,, an Adjective
		To introduce a Parenthesis

VIII. *Participle or Verbal Adjective.*

Form.	Voice.	Kind of Verb.	Use.
Present Past Perfect	Active Passive	Transitive Intransitive	Epithet Predicative { Complement / Absolute Gerundive

IX. *Gerund.*

Form.	Voice.	Kind of Verb.
Present Perfect	Active Passive	Transitive Intransitive

X. *Conjunctions.*

Co-ordinating.	Subordinating.

Most of the following rules have been incidentally given already in different places. They are here collected and summarised; and others not given before have been added, so as to make the account more complete.

269. Nominative case.—See No. III. of Parsing Chart.

(1) As Subject to a verb (see § 55) :—

> *I* did this.   *Rain* is falling.   *You* are tired.

(2) As *Subjective* Complement to a verb (see § 147) :—

> I am *the man*.   Cæsar was declared *emperor*.

Note.—An Infinitive can come between the verb and the noun :—

> He appeared *to be* a wise man.

(3) In Apposition with a noun or pronoun in the Nominative case (see § 18) :—

> John, *the carpenter*, has succeeded well in business.

(4) In the Absolute construction (see § 27, *a*) :—

(*a*) *With Participle*, in **past** or **present** sense :—

> Off we started, he *remaining behind.*
> Off we started, he *having given* the signal.

Note.—Without altering the sense, we could substitute the clause "while he remained behind" for the phrase "he remaining behind." In the absolute construction the noun or pronoun is in the Nominative case, because (as we see from this) it is *the Subject to the Finite verb that is implied in the Participle.*

(*b*) *With Gerundial Infinitive*, in **future** sense ; § 192 (*b*).

> The caul was put up in a raffle, *the winner to pay* five shillings.— DICKENS, *David Copperfield.*
> The estate has been divided between us, *you to have* two-thirds of it, and *I* one-third.

(5) Vocative, for purposes of Address (see § 55) :—

> How art thou fallen, *O Cæsar !*

270. Genitive case.—See No. III. of Parsing Chart.   (*a*) A noun in the Genitive case or a Possessive adjective qualifies Nouns and Gerunds as an adjective would do (§ 96, 4) :—

> *My* son.   The *barber's* shop.   The *tiger's* claw.—*Noun.*
> I was displeased at *his* going away without leave. ⎱ *Gerund*
> This was a plan of *your* contriving.   ⎰ (§ 206).

(*b*) When two nouns in the Genitive are in apposition with each other, the apostrophe *s* is added either to the first or the last, but not to both (see § 60) :—

> Herod married his *brother* Philip's wife.
> For the queen's sake, his *sister.*—BYRON.

(*c*) When two nouns are connected by "*and*," the apostrophe *s* is added to both to denote *separate* possession, and to the last only to denote *joint* possession :—

> A's and B's horses were sold yesterday.
> A and B's horses were sold yesterday.

(*d*) A noun in the Genitive case or a Possessive pronoun can be the Complement to a verb ; (for Pronouns, see § 109, *a*) :—

> That book is *mine*, not *yours.*

271. Accusative and Dative cases.—See No. III. of Parsing Chart.

(1) As Object to verb (§ 161, *Note*) :—

(*a*) The master teaches *Euclid.*   (*Direct.*)
(*b*) He teaches *his sons* Euclid.   (*Indirect*, *Dative Case.*)
(*c*) His sons were taught *Euclid.*   (*Retained.*)

(d) The fever will run its *course*.   (*Cognate.*) [1]
(e) He sat *himself* down.   (*Reflexive.*)

(2) As Objective Complement to a verb (§ 147) :—

The citizens made him their *king*.

Note.—An Infinitive can come between the verb and the noun :—

The people considered him *to be* a wise man.

(3) In Apposition with a noun or pronoun in the Accusative case (§ 18) :—

The people of England beheaded Charles I., their *king*.

(4) As Object to a preposition (§ 56) :—

He fought against *me*.   A house built on *sand*.

(5) Adverbial Accusative :—So called because such phrases qualify words as an adverb would do :—

He lived ten *years* (Time).   He walked ten *miles* (Space).   This cost ten *shillings* (Price).   That box weighs ten *pounds* (Weight).   The air is a *trifle* hotter to-day (Degree).   Bind him *hand* and *foot* (Attendant circumstance).

(6) Accusative after the adjectives "like" or "unlike," "near," "next." (This has probably arisen from the omission of the preposition "*to*," which is still sometimes used after these adjectives) :—

No man could bend the bow *like him*.
The house *nearest the grove* is the one that I prefer.

(7) Accusative after Interjections or in exclamatory phrases:—

Me, poor *man !* my library
Was dukedom large enough.—*Tempest*, Act I., Scene 2.

272. The two uses of Adjectives.—See No. IV. of Parsing Chart.

(a) Epithet use (§ 95) :—

An *industrious* student will generally succeed.

(b) Predicative use (§ 95) :—

He was *industrious*, and therefore he succeeded.

273. Noun or Gerund used as an Adjective (§ 96, 3).—A noun or gerund can be used as an epithet, but not predicatively :—

---

[1] We may note that it was maintained in Mason's *English Grammar* that "the cognate accusative should more properly be classed among the Adverbial Adjuncts," that is, as an Adverbial accusative, see § 271 under (5). This we cannot admit, because when the verb of the sentence is changed from Active to Passive, as "He fought a good fight," "A good fight was fought by him," the cognate object becomes the Subject; whereas if the cognate object were adverbial, it would remain adverbial.

A *village* watchman.   *Drinking* water.
A *sea* captain.   *Marble* halls.   A *bathing* place.

274. Adjective substituted for Adverb.—An adverb qualifying a *verb* can be changed into an adjective qualifying the *subject* to the verb.   The adjective in this case does the work of an "adverbial adjunct" to the verb (§ 251, *c*) :—

> The stars are shining *bright*.
> And *furious* every charger neighed.—CAMPBELL.
> *Dark* lowers the tempest overhead.—LONGFELLOW.
> And *fearless* there the lowly sleep.—MRS. HEMANS.
> They neither toil nor spin, but *careless* grow.—THOMSON.
> *Slow* rises worth, by poverty depressed.—JOHNSON.

Note 1.—When the adverb qualifies *any part of speech except a verb*, we cannot substitute an adjective for it.   Thus we cannot say "He is *immense* clever" for "He is *immensely* clever."

Note. 2.—In poetry an adjective and adverb are sometimes coupled together by "*and*" when the adjective qualifies the subject to the verb, and the adverb qualifies the verb itself :—

> When *faint* and *wearily* he drags
> Along his noontide way.—SOUTHEY.
> Trip it *deft* and *merrily*.—SCOTT.
> Very *carefully* and *slow*.—TENNYSON.

Or it might be maintained as an alternative explanation that one *ly* is made to do duty for both adjectives, making them both adverbs.

275. Pronoun and Antecedent.—See Nos. II. and III. of Parsing Chart.

(*a*) A Pronoun must be in the same person, number, and gender as its Antecedent ; but in case it depends upon its own sentence. (This is called a Concord or Agreement.)

> After Cæsar was declared *emperor* (Nominative), they slew *him* (Accusative).
> You must return the *book* (Accusative), *which* (Nominative) was lent.

Note.—To prevent any doubt as to what word is meant to be the antecedent, the antecedent should be placed as close as possible to the relative following.

(*b*) A Relative Pronoun, if it has two Antecedents, and these are not of the same person, agrees in person with the Antecedent *nearest to it* :—

> You are the man who *is* (not *are*) chosen.

276. The two uses of Adverbs.—See No. V. of Parsing Chart.

(*a*) Attributive use (§ 226).   An adverb, used attributively, may qualify anything except a noun or pronoun :—

(1) *Adjective*.—He is *remarkably clever*.
(2) *Verb*.—Act *decisively*, if you act at all.

   (3) *Other Adverb.*—He explained his views *remarkably well.*
   (4) *Preposition.*—The sun stood *exactly over* our heads.
   (5) *Conjunction.*—You may go *only if* you promise to return.
   (6) *Sentence.*—*Fortunately,* all the thieves were caught.

  (*b*) Predicative use (§ 226). Here the adverb is Complement to the verb going before :—

   (1) *Subjective.*—The results will soon be *out* (=published).
   (2) *Objective.*—We found him *quite well* (=in perfect health).

277. Verb and Subject.—See No. VI. of Parsing Chart as to Number and Person.

A Finite Verb must be in the same number and person as its Subject (§ 167). (This is another Concord or Agreement.)

Note.—Avoid such a mistake as "The man with his dog *have* just come." Such a mistake arises from confounding "*with*" with "*and.*"

278. The Third Person of Verbs.—A verb is invariably in the Third person, except when the Subject is a Personal pronoun in the First or Second person (§ 21) :—

   (*a*) *Noun.*—A *snake* is crawling through the grass.
   (*b*) *Pronoun.*—*He* returns to us to-morrow.
   (*c*) *Infinitive.*— *To err* is human.
   (*d*) *Gerund.*—*Sleeping* gives rest to the body.
   (*e*) *Phrase.*—*How to do this* was unknown to every one.
   (*f*) *Clause.*—*That we must all die* is certain.

279. Subjects not of the same Person.—(*a*) When two or more Subjects, not of the same Person, are joined by "*and,*" the verb is in the First person rather than the Second, and in the Second rather than the Third ; and *the First person should be mentioned last :*—

       James and I *are* (=we are) great friends.

(*b*) When two Subjects are joined by "*or*" or "*nor,*" the verb agrees in person with the Subject nearest to it :—

       Either James or I *am* at the top of the class.
       Either you or James *has* done it.
       Neither James nor you *were* present.

It would be better, however, to repeat the verb for each Subject. The sentences would then be re-written as follows :—

       Either James *is* at the top of the class, or I *am.*
       Either you *have* done it, or James *has.*
       Neither James *was* present, nor *were* you.

(*c*) When two Subjects are joined by "as well as," the verb agrees in number and person with the *first* one :—

       My comrades as well as I myself *were* caught.

The reason of this rule is that "My comrades were caught" is the Principal clause, to which the other clause introduced by "as well as" is Co-ordinate.

280. Two Singular Subjects with Plural Verb.—Two or more Singular nouns, when they are joined by "*and*," require a verb in the Plural.

> A man and his wife *have* come here asking for work.
> Your horse and mine (=my horse) *are* both at the door.

To this rule there are two exceptions :—

(*a*) If the two nouns joined by "*and*" refer to the same person or thing, the verb is Singular, and not Plural ; as—

> The great scholar and poet *is* dead.

Here "scholar" and "poet" refer to the same man, and the sentence might have been written :—

> The man, who was a great scholar and a great poet, is dead.

Note.—When the article is mentioned *only once*, as in the sentence "*the* great scholar and poet," it stands for *both the nouns*. This shows that *only one* person (and not two) is intended, and that hence the verb must be singular.

But if the article is mentioned twice, as in the sentence "*the* scholar and *the* poet," then two distinct persons are intended, and the verb following must be in the plural number ; as—

> The scholar and the poet *are* dead.

(*b*) If the two nouns joined by "*and*" are regarded as denoting *a single object or notion*, the verb is Singular ; as—

> Truth and honesty *is* the best policy.   Curry and rice *was* his favourite food.   Slow and steady *wins* the race.

Here "truth and honesty" = the practice of truth and honesty, and hence the verb following is singular.   Similarly, "curry and rice" = the food consisting of curry and rice, or the mixture of curry and rice. "Slow and steady" = the plan of being slow and steady.

281. One Singular Subject with Plural Verb.—A noun of *Multitude* (as distinct from a *Collective* noun, see § 37) is followed by a Plural verb :—

> The jury (*i.e.* the individual jurors) *were* divided in *their* opinions, and could not agree as to the verdict.
> The jury (as one body) selected *its* speaker.
> The multitude (individual men and women) *rise* from *their* seats and shout applause.
> This multitude (as one body) *is* too large to be contained in so small a building.

282. The Simple or Noun-Infinitive.—See No. VII. of the Parsing Chart.

The Simple or Noun-Infinitive may be (*a*) the Subject to a verb, (*b*) the Object to a verb, (*c*) the Complement to a verb, (*d*) the Object to a preposition (although this is very uncommon), (*e*) a form of exclamation (see § 191) :—

(a) *Subj. to Verb.*—*To sleep* is necessary to health.
(b) *Obj. to Verb.*—We desire *to improve.*
(c) *Compl. to Verb.*—He appears *to be clever.*
(d) *Obj. to Prepos.*—Your cow is about (=near) *to die* (=death).
(e) *Form of Exclam.*—*To think* that he should have deceived me !

283. The Gerundial or Qualifying Infinitive.—See No. VII. of the Parsing Chart.

The Gerundial or Qualifying Infinitive may be used—(a) to qualify a verb, in which case it does the work of an adverb ; (b) to qualify a noun, in which case it does the work of an adjective ; (c) to qualify an adjective, in which case it does the work of an adverb ; (d) to introduce a parenthesis, in which case it is absolute (see § 192) :—

(a) *Verb.*—They went out *to see* the sport.
(b) *Noun* { A house *to let.*   (*Epithet.*)
            { This house is *to let.*   (*Predicative.*)
(c) *Adjective.*—Be quick *to hear* and slow *to speak.*
(d) *Parenthesis.*—He is,—*to speak* plainly,—a thief.

Note.—In qualifying a *noun*, the Infinitive is sometimes used in the Passive voice. No rule, however, can be given as to when the Active voice is the more idiomatic and when the Passive :—

A man *to be admired.*   (*Epithet.*)
That man is *to be admired.*   (*Predicative.*)

284. The three uses of Participles.—See No. VIII. of the Parsing Chart.

(a) Epithet use (see § 95 for Adjectives) :—

A *willing* horse.   A *fallen* tree.   A *withered* flower.

(b) Predicative use.—This may occur either (1) when the Participle is Complement to some verb (see § 95 again), or (2) when the Participle is used absolutely with some noun going before (see §§ 27 (a) and 269, 5) :—

(1) { We found him *sleeping.*   (*Object. Complem.*)
     { He became *alarmed.*   (*Subject. Complem.*)
(2) Our pace was slow, the horse *being tired.*   (*Absolute.*)

Note 1.—That the Participle is predicative in the Absolute construction is clear from the fact that an absolute *phrase* can be easily rewritten in the form of a *clause*, in which a Finite verb or predicate is substituted for the Participle :—

{ Our pace was slow, the horse *being tired.*
{ Our pace was slow, *because* the horse *was tired.*

Note 2.—When no noun or pronoun is expressed, the Participle is called an **Impersonal Absolute.**

Supposing this to be true, you are certainly guilty.

(*c*) Gerundive use (§ 207).—Here the Participle denotes something that could be equally well expressed by a Gerund or Verbal noun : [1]—

> { This prevented the letter *being sent ;* =
> { This prevented *the sending of* the letter.

Note on Concord and Government.

The plan adopted in some books on English Grammar is to subdivide the subject of Syntax under two main headings :—

I. Concord or Agreement. II. Government.

In a highly inflected language, such as Latin, Greek, or the Old English, a subdivision of that kind is useful, since the inflexions of words depend chiefly on their mutual concord or agreement and on the extent to which they govern or are governed by one another.

In Modern English, however, in which very few of the old inflexions have been retained, the subdivision of Syntax into rules of Concord and rules of Government is of scarcely any use ; for it leaves the greater part of the ground untouched. The only points on which these principles are seen at work are the following :—

Concord or Agreement.

(1) The verb must agree with its subject in Number and Person. (This, together with the apparent exceptions thereto, has been set forth in § 277.)

(2) The Demonstrative adjective "this" or "that" must be of the same number as the noun it qualifies. (These are the only two adjectives that have one form for the Singular and another for the Plural.)

(3) A pronoun must be of the same Number, Gender, and Person as its antecedent. (So far as inflexion is concerned, this applies only to the Demonstrative pronouns of the Third person (§ 114), and to the Relative pronoun "who" or "which" (§ 121).

(4) A noun in apposition with a pronoun or other noun must be in the same case. (This is shown in § 269 (3) and § 271 (3). The only case that is now indicated by an inflexion is the Genitive, and even this case drops its inflexion when it is in apposition with another Genitive. See § 270.)

Government.

All that we can say on this point is that certain Verbs, two or three Adjectives, and all Prepositions govern a noun or pronoun in the Accusative case. The Indirect Object is in the Dative case.

---

[1] The student will find this subject more fully dealt with in chap. **xx.** (79).

I. *Questions on Parsing.*

1. *Pick out and parse all the Accusatives and Datives in the following :—*

1. Let me die the death of the righteous, and let my last end be like his.—*Old Test.*

2.   My story done,
She gave me for my pains a world of sighs.—SHAKSPEARE.

3.   Him destroyed,
For whom all this was made, all this will soon
Follow.—MILTON.   (See § 307.)

4. That coat will last you two years at least.

5. The army of the Canaanites, nine hundred chariots strong, covered the plain of Esdraelon.—MILMAN.

6. It blew a hurricane, but the wall did not quiver an inch.

7.   I have no spur
To prick the sides of my intent, but only
Vaulting ambition, which o'erleaps itself
And falls on the other side.—SHAKSPEARE.

8. He taught my children French, and taught it well.

9. Knock me this gate, and rap me well.—SHAKSPEARE. (See § 306.)

10. I was asked a question, which I could not answer.

11. I have fought a good fight ; I have kept the faith.—*New Test.*

12. O thou invisible spirit of wine, if thou hast no name to be called by, let us call thee devil.—SHAKSPEARE.

13. They sat them down on the grassy bank of the river.

14. Poor me ! everything that I relied on has failed me.

15. That coat will cost you at least two pounds.

2. *Pick out and parse all the Nominatives in the following :—*

1. If he had continued a merchant, he would soon have become a wealthy citizen.

2. Friends, Romans, countrymen, lend me your ears.
                                        SHAKSPEARE.

3.   Then I shall be no more ;
And Adam, wedded to another Eve,
Shall live with her enjoying, I extinct.—MILTON.

4. It is an ill wind that blows no one any good.

5. This was done for the sake of Herodias, his sister.

6. The sun, having set at six o'clock, left us in the evening twilight.

7. The sun having set at six o'clock, there was scarcely time left for us to get home.

8. A contented mind is a continual feast.

9. I who speak unto thee am he.—*New Test.*

10. My Lord dies a Protestant.—MACAULAY, *Hist. Eng.* vol. i.

3. *Pick out and parse the Genitives in the following :—*

1. You are very lucky in that horse of yours.

2. Have you answered Mr. A.'s letter, the late manager of your firm?

3. I expected to hear of A. and B.'s failure.

4. I expected to hear of A.'s and B.'s failure.

5. This razor is mine, not the barber's.

4. Pick out and parse the Defective verbs in the following, and say which are Notional and which are Auxiliary :—

1. Did you hear the thunder ? 2. You did a good day's work yesterday. 3. I cannot understand you. 4. I do not understand you. 5. I should like to have a little talk with you. 6. You should not do that. 7. I shall start soon ; but you shall stop where you are. 8. You may go. 9. May good digestion wait on appetite. 10. I hope you will do me this favour. I will do it, if I can. 11. Do leave off making that noise. I was not making it. 12. He worked hard lest he should be sent away. 13. He should have arrived by now. 14. I have heard that you have been ill. 15. He would know me, if he could but meet me. 16. The raven would follow me, whenever I went out of the house. 17. What must come, must. 18. I ought to go, but will he allow me ? 19. I may have done wrong ; but I did not intend it.

5. Pick out and parse the Adverbs, the Adjectives proper, and the Adjectives used as Nouns, in the following :—

1. Much has been admitted, but more remains behind, that he is much too prudent to disclose. 2. You ought to know better than to be rude to your betters. 3. It smote my very heart to see her so very unhappy. 4. Having done less work, he is less tired than he was yesterday. 5. Man wants but little here below, Nor wants that little long. 6. A long sleep in the night will make my energy last long in the day. 7. You know best whether I have done my best or not. 8. I claim a right of way right across this field ; and I am sure that my claim is right. 9. He gave me all he had ; not all men would have done as much ; and no man could have done more. 10. Those who know most about music say it was a most beautiful melody. 11. I cannot write any longer ; have you any reason to expect me ? 12. My coat is all ragged ; in fact all my clothes are worn out. 13. He swam half across the lake, a length of one mile and a half. 14. I half think he will swim all across some day. 15. I have no book to read, and am no better off than I was before. 16. Nobody else heard it. 17. Have you had enough exercise ? Yes ; I have walked long enough to-day. 18. The good can distinguish between good and ill. 19. In a garden that is ill kept ill weeds grow apace. 20. He behaved like a hero ; we shall not see his like again. 21. He has a loud voice. 22. He talks too loud. 23. He met me on the green, near the east end of the common.

6. Pick out and parse all the Infinitives in the following :—

1. I ought to go. 2. I am sure to go. 3. They like me to go. 4. We saw the ship leave the docks. 5. I am to blame, not you. 6. I am sorry to find that you are hurt. 7. We must work while it is day ; for the night cometh when no man can work. 8. Did you see that shooting star ? 9. He is quick to forgive and slow to avenge an injury. 10. Such recompense is a thing to be hoped for in the world to come. 11. Make the horse go a little faster. 12. Boys dare not speak, when the master orders them to be silent. 13. You shall do what you are told. 14. I will not disobey you. 15. You may come again to-morrow. 16. I could not find your house. 17. I was sorry not to be able to find the house. 18. We hope to see him

back soon. 19. This house is to let. 20. It was impossible to please him. 21. I will gladly accede to your wishes. 22. Let me say a word. 23. I have a word to say to you. 24. If he cannot keep his temper, he shall be punished. 25. The reason is not far to seek.

7. *Pick out and parse the Participles and the Gerunds in the following :—*

1. I praised him for having finished the work. 2. Having finished the work, he seemed more pleased with himself than usual. 3. I am tired of warning you. 4. I do not require your warnings. 5. Deepening his voice with the deepening of the darkness, he continued humming a tune. 6. Considering the long drought, it is no wonder that every plant is beginning to fade. 7. It is of no use questioning him regarding this matter. 8. Your having failed is disappointing to all of us. 9. I am tired of swimming : I have been swimming for this last hour or more. 10. The journey was soon finished, the one walking and the other riding in turns. 11. He is inside reading some book on history. 12. The reading of history is a profitable study. 13. I thoroughly enjoy reading history. 14. The trees having cast their leaves, we are now on the verge of winter. 15. The trees, having cast their leaves, look bare. 16. The trees look bare from having cast their leaves. 17. The wall is rapidly building. 18. Deceiving others amused him ; but he disliked being deceived himself. 19. I admire the grounds and trees surrounding the house. 20. I am much pleased with my surroundings. 21. Everything depends upon the work being finished in time. 22. We all set off, the clock striking one. 23. Hunting the fox is an exciting amusement. 24. This is no laughing matter. 25. On seeing this he was much surprised. 26. Seeing this he was much surprised.

8. *Pick out the Adverbs, the Prepositions, and the Conjunctions in the following, and show the work that is done by each of them in its own sentence :—*

1. He walked about the house. 2. He is walking about, not sitting down. 3. He ran down the hill. 4. The above-named book was lost. 5. The sky is above the earth. 6. We walked along the bank of the river. 7. He is going along at a great pace. 8. We must rest before going any further. 9. Men will reap as they sow. 10. As rain has fallen, the grass will soon sprout. 11. He came after a few days. 12. He came a few days after. 13. He will go after he has dined. 14. He stood below me in the class. 15. There is a world below and a world above. 16. You are working better to-day. 17. There is but one man present. 18. Who could have done this but him ? 19. He is naturally clever, but not learned in books. 20. He has worked hard enough for anything. 21. Whom was this done by ? 22. The horse is going by. 23. Come in and take a seat. 24. You will find him in the house. 25. He must needs know the reason of this. 26. Who comes next ? 27. He stood next me in the class. 28. He fell off the saddle. 29. The thief ran off. 30. I heard of this only yesterday. 31. Take what you like ; only keep silence. 32. He is over ten years of age. 33. The holidays are over. 34. I have not seen him since Monday last. 35.

I took this house four weeks since. 36. We must trust you, since you say so. 37. Take a walk round the garden. 38. The earth turns round. 39. I will ride outside the omnibus, if you will take a seat inside.

9. *Parse and comment on the italicised words in the following:—*

1. She has more *hair* than wit, and more faults than *hairs.*—SHAKSPEARE.

2. He brought twenty *head* of *cattle* to market.

3.   I have ventured,
   Like little wanton *boys* that swim on bladders,
   This many summers in a sea of glory.—SHAKSPEARE.

4. He lives a long way from *here.*

5. *Me,* poor man, my library was dukedom large enough.—SHAKSPEARE.

6. He is a friend of my *brother's.*

7. Do not play the *fool* in this place.

8. The *just* shall live by faith.

9. The *just* is to be preferred to the *expedient.*

10. This is made of *glass.* He drank two *glasses* of wine.

11. My *elder* brother is five *years older* than *me.*—SWEET.

12. Where *is* Lysander and sweet Hermia ?—SHAKSPEARE.

13. The result was *out* by four *o'clock.*

14. Woe *betide* you, if you do such a thing again.

15. He makes me *laugh.* I would rather *laugh* than *weep.*

16. That wall has been *building* a long *time.*

10. *Parse and comment on the italicised words in the following:—*

1. O speak *good* of the Lord, all ye *works* of *his,* in all places of his dominion.—*Psalm* ciii. 22.

2. I have said that civilised man has reached this point ;—the assertion is perhaps too broad and general ; I *had* better *put* it that ethical man has attained thereto.—HUXLEY.

3. The king's *having recommended* to the Commons the consideration of proper means for *lessening* the National Debt was a prelude to the famous South *Sea* Act.—SMOLLETT.

4. I am not fond of the idea of my shrubberies *being* always *approachable.*—JANE AUSTEN.

5. Democracy loves *spending,* is devoted to dignity, and *provided* they are indirect and fall *heaviest* on the *rich,* will pay any amount of taxes.—*Quarterly Review,* No. 367, p. 84.

6. I *will* speak, and the word that I *shall* speak *shall* be performed.—*Ezek.* xii. 25.

7. *The least* said, the *soonest* mended.—*Proverb.*

8. Garrick was the *Roscius* of his age.

9. *Joy* absent, grief is present for that time.—SHAKSPEARE.

10. *All* loose her negligent *attire,*
   Hung Margaret o'er her slaughtered sire.—SCOTT.

11. Death grinned horribly a ghastly *smile.*—MILTON.

11. *Comment on the uses of* it *in the following sentences :—*

1. What a silly fellow *it* is !

2. He tried to lord *it* over his equals.

3. *It* was freezing hard all last night.

4. *It* is little things that disturb the mind most.

5. *It* gives me much pleasure to see you again.

12. *Account for the ambiguity of* (1) *and the perspicuity of* (2):—

1. I met the boatman who took me across the ferry.

2. I met the boatman that took me across the ferry.

13. *Pick out and comment on all the Transitive and all the Intransitive verbs in*—

1. He looked daggers at them.

2. The book sells well : I have sold a hundred copies to-day.

3. The enemy sank the ship : it sank in a dead calm.

4. She will sing the savageness out of a bear.—SHAKSPEARE.

5. I overslept myself last night.

6. His courage failed him in this emergency.

7. The wind blew a cold blast from the north.

8. He writes well : he has written two letters to-day.

9. His opinions were laughed at by every one.

14. *Show which relatives in the following sentences are Restrictive and which are Continuative. Parse each of them.*

1. The boatman,—who seemed to be about forty years old,—took us across the ferry. 2. Did you pay the boatman, who took us across the ferry ? 3. The thief was brought before the magistrate, who sent him to prison for a month. 4. The remark offended John, but amused Mary, who took it for a joke. 5. Several questions were put to Mr. U., who returned to the House yesterday. 6. Troubles fell thick on the unfortunate woman, whose eldest son died three weeks after his father. 7. My second son, whom I designed for trade, was educated privately at home. 8. He avoided the company of his relations, most of whom had never cared to know him. 9. On the way back I met a watchman, who told me I had missed the road. 10. That is the man whom I wished to see. 11. At school I studied Latin, which I found very useful afterwards. 12. He struck the poor dog, which was sleeping on the roadside. 13. He was fond of dogs, whom he made his playfellows. 14. I heard of it from my wife, who had heard of it from a friend. 15. Last night we arrived at Colchester, which is an old Roman town. 16. Words which are signs of complex ideas are liable to be misunderstood.

II. *Fill up the ellipses in the following sentences, and then analyse in full :—*

1. He cried out as if he had been hurt.

2. Though tired, I will still go on working.

3. He has not worked so hard as I have.

4. He does not ride as well as you.

5. He as well as you is a good rider.

6. I am not such a blockhead as to misunderstand that.

7. I would as soon die as suffer disgrace.

8. Our manners are not so good as our ancestors practised.

9. He is more a fool than a knave.

10. When in doubt, beware whom you trust.

11. He left the day I came.
12. As for me, I am quite indifferent.
13. There is no one but will stand by you.
14. Methinks the lady doth protest too much.
15. He is not so wise as witty.
16. He went away the day I arrived.
17. I am not such a fool as to say that.
18. He has worked harder than you.
19. He would have failed but for me.
20. As to your opinion I care nothing about it.
21. Wisdom is sometimes nearer when we stoop than when we soar.
22. How could you make such a mistake as to suppose that I was younger than you?
23. He was so kind as to let me off the fine.
24. He has no good points whatever.
25. I admire you as a scholar, but do not love you as a neighbour.
26. Either you or he is to blame.

III. *Parse the italicised words and analyse the sentences:*—

1. Why *rather*, *sleep*, liest thou in smoky cribs,
   Upon uneasy pallets *stretching* thee
   And hush'd with buzzing night-flies to thy slumber,
   Than in the perfumed chambers of the *great*,
   Under the canopies of costly state,
   And lull'd with sounds of sweetest melody?—SHAKSPEARE.

2. If a man *be compassionate* towards the afflictions of others, *it* shows *that* his heart is like the noble *tree that* is wounded *itself* when it gives the balm.—BACON.

3. The notice *which* you have been pleased to take of my labours, had it been *early*, *had been* kind; but it has been delayed, till I am indifferent, and cannot *enjoy* it; till I am solitary, and cannot impart it; till I am known, and do not want it.—DR. JOHNSON.

4. Belial came last, than *whom* a spirit more lewd
   Fell not from heaven, or more gross *to love*
   Vice for itself.—MILTON.

5. None of us *yet know*, for none of us *have* yet *been taught* in early youth, what *fairy* palaces we *may build* of beautiful thought,—*proof* against all adversity.—RUSKIN.

6. The judges of the Common law, *who* held their situations during the King's pleasure, were scandalously obsequious.

7. *Ere* thou *remark another's* sin,
   Bid thine own conscience *look* within.—GAY.

8. I like a rascal *to be punished*, when I am quite sure that his guilt has been proved *before* a jury, *who* had no prejudice against him *before they* began *hearing* his case, and who were unanimous in *believing* him to be guilty.

9. Ah, then what honest triumph flushed my breast,
   This *truth* once known—*To bless* is to be blest!

10. His countenance bore as *little* the marks of self-denial, *as* his habit indicated contempt of worldly splendour.—SCOTT.

11. Though the same room served for parlour and kitchen, *that* only made it *the* warmer.—GOLDSMITH.

12. *On* she came with a cloud of canvas
    Right against the wind that blew.—COLERIDGE.

13. O Solitude ! *where* are the charms
    That sages have seen in thy face ?
    Better dwell in the midst of alarms
    Than *reign* in this horrible place.—COWPER.

14. Woe *worth* the *chase*, woe worth the day,
    That cost thy *life*, my gallant *grey !*—SCOTT.

15. They parted ne'er *to meet* again,
    But *never either* found another
    To free the hollow heart from paining ;
    They stood *aloof*, the *scars remaining*,
    Like *cliffs* which had been rent asunder.—COLERIDGE.

16. *Close* by the regal chair
    Fell Thirst and Famine scowl
    A baleful *smile* upon their baffled guest.—GRAY.

17. The part of the mill she *liked best* was the topmost storey.
    where were the great heaps of grain, *which* she could sit on and glide
    down continually.—GEORGE ELIOT.

18. *Him thought* he by the brook of Cherith stood
    And saw the ravens with their horny beaks
    Food to Elijah *bring* even and *morn.*—MILTON.

19.   Take physic, *pomp ;*
    Expose thyself *to feel what* wretches feel,
    That thou *mayst* shake the superflux to them,
    And *show* the heavens *more just.*—SHAKSPEARE.

20. I proceeded towards London on a fine morning, no *way uneasy*
about to-morrow, but *cheerful as* the birds *that* carolled along the
road ; and comforted myself with *reflecting that* London was the mart
where abilities of every kind were *sure* of meeting distinction and
reward.—GOLDSMITH

21. At four o'clock we reached York, *which* is a fine old town dating
back to the time of the Romans, though they called it by a different
name that I cannot now remember.

22. Behold the wretch who wastes his life away,
    Soon swallowed in disease's sad abyss ;
    While he whom toil has braced or manly play
    Has *light* as air each limb, each thought as clear as day.
                                        THOMSON.

23.   Then burst his mighty *heart ;*
    And, in his mantle muffling *up* his face,
    Even at the base of Pompey's statua,
    Which all the *while* ran *blood*, great Cæsar fell.—SHAKSPEARE.

24. O, how *it* yearn'd my *heart* when I beheld
    In London streets that *coronation* day,
    When Bolingbroke rode on roan Barbary,—
    That horse *that* thou so often hast bestrid,
    That horse that I so carefully have dress'd !—*Ibid.*

25. An inadvertent step *may* crush the snail
    That crawls at evening in the public path ;
    But he that has humanity, *forewarned*,
    Will tread aside and let the *reptile* live.—COWPER.

26. Dost thou so hunger for my empty chair,
    That thou wilt *needs* invest thee with *mine* honours ?—SHAKS.

27. When I came to my castle, I fled into it like *one* pursued ; whether I went *over* by the ladder or went *in* at the hole which I called a door, I cannot *remember ;* no, nor could I remember the next *morning.*—DEFOE.

28. This I apprehend *to be* the explanation of that conciliatory policy of *Alexander's* towards the Jews, which was pursued steadily by the *Ptolemies.*—KINGSLEY.

29. Her nearest relations were aware that she had good sense, but seem not *to have suspected* that under her demure and bashful deportment were concealed a fertile invention and a keen *sense* of the *ridiculous.*—MACAULAY.

30.   Blest are those
    Whose blood and judgment are so well commingled,
    That they are not a pipe for fortune's finger
    To *sound* what stop she *please.*—SHAKSPEARE.

31. The principles which Erasmus urged in his "Jerome" were urged with far greater clearness and force in a work which laid the foundation of the future Reformation,—the *edition* of the Greek Testament, *whose* production was almost wholly due to the encouragement he received from English scholars.—J. R. GREEN.

32. *For who,* to dumb forgetfulness a *prey,*
       This *pleasing* anxious *being* e'er resign'd,
    Left the warm precincts of the cheerful day,
       Nor cast one longing, ling'ring look *behind ?*—GRAY.

33. The house has been *building* some fourteen *months ;* but the date by which its completion is *due* according to the contract has not yet expired.

34. *Myself,*—a prince by fortune of my birth,
    Near to the king in blood, and near in love
    Till you did make him *misinterpret* me,—
    Have stooped my neck under your injuries,
    And sigh'd my English *breath* in foreign clouds,
    Eating the bitter bread of banishment.—SHAKSPEARE.

35. But *he* once *passed,* soon after, when man fell,
    Strange alteration ! Sin and Death amain
    Following his track, such was the will of Heaven,
    Paved after time a broad and better way
    Over the dark abyss, whose boiling gulf
    Tamely endured a bridge of wondrous length.
                                    Par. Lost, ii. 1023 ff.

36. When the imagination is carried away by the detection of points of resemblance—*one* of the most pleasing of mental pursuits—it is apt to be impatient of any divergence in its *new-*found parallels, and thus may overlook or refuse to recognise *such.*—MAHAN, *Sea Power.*

37. There is not a man in the world *but* desires to be or to be thought to be a wise *man ;* and yet if he considered how little he contributes himself thereunto, he might wonder *to find* himself in any tolerable degree of understanding.

38. In gallant trim the gilded vessel goes,
    Youth at the prow, and pleasure at the helm.—GRAY.

CHAPTER XIII.

Punctuation, or the Right Use of Stops.

285. Punctuation divides one sentence or one part of a sentence from another, to help the reader's eye.

286. The names of the different points, stops, or marks used for this purpose are :—

Comma, indicated by . . ,	Note of exclamation, indicated by . . . !
Semicolon, indicated by . . ;	
Colon, indicated by . . :	Brackets, indicated by . () or []
Full stop or period, indicated by .	Dash, indicated by . . —
Note of Interrogation, indicated	Hyphen, indicated by . -
by . . . . ?	Inverted commas, indi-
Apostrophe, indicated by . '	cated by . . . " "

The Comma.

287. The comma represents the shortest pause. Its chief uses in a **simple** sentence are the following :—

(a) Between nouns or pronouns in apposition ; as—

Alexander, the *son* of Philip, *king* of Macedon.

(b) Between two or more words of the same Part of Speech :—

A dull, heavy sound was heard. (*Adjectives.*)

Greece, Italy, and Spain are the peninsulas of Southern Europe. (*Nouns.*)

We should live soberly, prudently, and industriously at all times. (*Adverbs.*)

Early to bed and early to rise
Makes a man healthy, wealthy, and wise. (*Adjectives.*)

(c) After the Vocative :—

Friends, Romans, countrymen, lend me your ears.

(d) After an absolute construction :—

The sun having set, we all went home.

(e) When words of the same class or rank go together in pairs, each pair is separated by a comma :—

By night or by day, at home or abroad, asleep or awake, he is a constant source of anxiety to his father.

(f) After an adverbial phrase at the commencement of a sentence. (Here, however, the comma can be put in or not, at the option of the writer.)

In fact, his poetry is no better than prose. At last, he has gained his point.

(g) Before and after a participial phrase, provided that the participle might be expanded into a sentence, and is not used in a merely qualifying sense (see § 200) :—

> Cæsar, having defeated the Gauls, led his army into Britain.
> (Here " having defeated " means "after he had defeated.")
> Convinced of the accuracy of his facts, he stuck to his opinion.
> (Here "convinced" means "because he was convinced.")

But when the participle qualifies the noun so as merely to *restrict* its meaning, as an adjective would do, the comma should not be used :—

> A dog lying asleep on a public road is likely to be run over.
> A man convinced against his will is of the same opinion still.

(*h*) Explanatory phrases are separated by commas :—

> The field was oblong, 60 yards in length, 40 in breadth.

(*i*) Before and after gerundial Infinitives used in an explanatory or parenthetical sense :—

> I am, to tell you the truth, thoroughly sick of work.
> To sum up, the man was convicted of three charges.

(*j*) A comma is sometimes used to introduce a sentence quoted in Direct Narration. The sentence so quoted must be commenced with a capital letter :—

> What I say unto you, I say unto all, Watch.—*New Testament.*

(*k*) A comma is sometimes inserted to mark the omission and save the repetition of a verb :—

> My regiment is bound for India ; yours, for Gibraltar.

288. (*a*) In a **multiple** sentence the co-ordinate clauses, when they are expressed at full length, are generally separated by a comma :—

> His vanity is greater than his ignorance, and what he lacks in knowledge is supplied by impudence.

But when the two sentences are not expressed at full length or are very closely allied, the comma is omitted :—

> I made haste and caught him.
> I took up a stone and threw it at the mad dog.

(*b*) When the conjunction is omitted between co-ordinate clauses, these must be separated (1) by a comma, when they are short ; or (2) by a semicolon, when they are long :—

> (1) Steam propels, elevates, lowers, pumps, drains, pulls, etc.
> (2) Between fame and true honour there is much difference ; the former is blind applause ; the latter is an internal and more silent homage.

289. In **complex** sentences the following rules regarding the use of commas should be noted :—

(a) A Noun-clause is not usually separated by a comma from the Main clause :—

> It is generally allowed that the art of teaching is difficult.
> No one knows when he will come.
> His being pardoned depends upon whether he will confess his fault or not.

But Noun-clauses must be separated from each other by commas, when they are objects or subjects to the same verb :—

> No one knows when he will come, or whether he will come at all, or whether he is even alive.
> Who he was, or why he came, or what he intends to do, will all be found out in time.

(b) An Adjective-clause is not separated from the Main clause by a comma, unless it (the Adjective-clause) is rather lengthy :—

> The man *we saw* yesterday has come again to-day.
> Fortune selects him for her lord, *who reflects before acting.*

(c) An Adverb-clause is separated by a comma from the Main clause :—

> He will succeed, because he works hard.
> I will gladly do this, if I am allowed.

The comma is never omitted, unless the Adverb-clause is either very short or expressed elliptically :—

> He likes you better than me.
> Send me word before you start.

Insert commas, where necessary, in the following sentences :—

The triple alliance consisted of Germany Austria and Italy. My son so far from being blamed for his conduct was commended and even rewarded. The roof of the house having caught fire the inmates fled and remained outside the house until the fire was put out. Towns villages and hamlets were all alike attacked with the epidemic of cholera. I shall be happy to make the attempt that you speak of if I am permitted. From morning till noon from noon to evening from evening to midnight this same grief never leaves him. Early this morning when we had just left the house we met the man that we had been looking for. He found as I expected he would that the house he had lately purchased was a bad one. What was the cause of so much grief to him was never known to any of us. I hope my friend that you will come and spend at least a week with us. He has now grown so old that he spends most of his time in sleeping taking his food or sitting in an easy-chair. I remain my dear sir yours faithfully William Matthews. I shall not leave home for business unless you set the example. Example as the proverb says is the sincerest form of precept. To tell you the plain truth I should be glad to retire from business altogether considering that I am now past sixty years of age and have a son to succeed me. The boatman shouted to a man on shore throw out the rope. A snake sleeping in the grass will bite if any one treads upon it. The prisoner having been convicted of the crime of which he was accused must make up his mind to suffer the penalty. The building is a noble structure of red brick and comprises a reading-room a library a room for writing letters and a room for refreshments. It is quite true that this fine building was erected by private subscriptions. In fact of all that was subscribed L. gave the largest amount in cash but M. was not less liberal because he gave the land on which the building was erected. A dog barking at nothing is a nuisance.

The Semicolon.

290. The **Semicolon** is used, when a greater pause is required than is indicated by the comma.

Its chief uses are as follows :—

(*a*) To separate *longer* clauses from one another. Here a greater pause is necessary to prevent the sentences from being confused together :—

> Honesty of purpose in worldly affairs has many advantages over deceit ; it is a safer way of dealing with men ; it is an easier mode of despatching business ; it inspires men with greater confidence ; it acquires more and more confidence in itself, while deceit becomes more and more diffident.

(*b*) To give greater emphasis to different clauses, so that the mind may dwell longer on each of them in succession :—

> As Cæsar loved me, I weep for him ; as he was fortunate, I rejoice at it ; as he was valiant, I honour him ; but as he was ambitious, I slew him. So there is tears for his love ; joy for his fortune ; honour for his valour ; and death for his ambition.—SHAK-SPEARE.

(*c*) To divide clauses, which are connected by some Alternative or Illative conjunction. (Here a greater pause is required, because the mind requires a little more time to perceive the alternative or the inference) :—

> I met him as he was leaving his house ; *otherwise* I should not have known where he lived.
> I refused to do what he asked me to do ; *for* I was convinced that he had been misinformed of the facts.

The Colon.

291. The **Colon** may be used at the writer's discretion, if he thinks that the pause is not sufficiently marked by a semicolon. On this point no fixed rules can be given.

The main uses of the colon are the following :—

(*a*) To introduce an additional remark in explanation or in confirmation of a previous one :—

> Strive above all things, in whatever station of life you may be, to preserve health : there is no happiness in life without it.

(*b*) To introduce a quotation. In this case it is usually followed by a dash :—

> Then Peter stood forth and said :—" Of a truth I perceive that God is no respecter of persons," etc.

(*c*) To recapitulate a series of co-ordinate clauses. Here, too, the colon must be followed by a dash :—

> The storm had passed ; the sun was shining on the green leaves of the trees ; the streams were dancing around the rocks ; the birds hopped about him, as they chirped their cheerful notes :— such were the pleasant scenes and sounds that welcomed the wanderer back to his home.

(*d*) To introduce a series of co-ordinate clauses. Here, again, the colon is followed by a dash :—

> You must now hear what I have to say about the uses of iron :—we sleep on iron ; we travel on iron ; we float on iron ; we plough the fields with iron ; we shoot with iron ; we chop down trees with iron :—in fact, there is scarcely anything that we can do without the help of this wonderful metal.

(*e*) To introduce an example of some rule. Here, again, the colon is followed by a dash :—

> The Indefinite article has sometimes the force of a Numeral adjective, signifying *one* :—as, " A stitch in time saves nine."

Insert commas, colons, or semicolons, where necessary, in the following sentences :—

1. According to an old belief if a sick man sneezes it is a sure sign of recovery but when a man is going on a journey or about to commence some business should any one about him sneeze the sneeze indicates that the object in which he is interested will not be accomplished.

2. In Rome the army was the nation no citizen could take office unless he had served in ten campaigns.

3. The drill was unremitting at all times so long as a man continued to be a soldier when the troops were in winter quarters sheds were erected in which the soldiers fenced with swords buttoned at the points or hurled javelins also buttoned at the points at one another.

4. The Carthaginian army was composed entirely of mercenary troops Africa Spain and Gaul were their recruiting grounds and these countries were an inexhaustible treasury of warriors as long as the money lasted which the recruits received as pay.

5. While I was still wondering at my sudden deliverance a man came suddenly forward and said my good sir there is nothing to be surprised at I was sent here to find you and rescue you from these

robbers well I have succeeded in finding you and so I have accomplished what I was sent for as you now see.

6. Whenever you hesitate about beginning to do something which must be done eventually remember the maxim a thing begun is half done.

The Full Stop or Period.

292. The **Full Stop** or **Period** indicates the close of a complete sentence.   The sentence following must invariably be commenced with a capital letter.

The full stop is also used after abbreviations; as, A.D. (for Anno Domini); B.L. (for Bachelor of Law); Bart. (for Baronet); the Hon. (for the Honourable).

Inverted Commas.

293. Inverted Commas are used for indicating the beginning and end of a quotation, or of the actual words used by a speaker.

The councillors stood up, and with one voice exclaimed :—" Death before dishonour."

" Wine is a mocker," said the wise king.

Campbell was the author of the following stanza :—

> " The more we live, more brief appear
> Our life's succeeding stages ;
> A week to childhood seems a year,
> A year like passing ages."

Note of Exclamation.

294. A **Note of Exclamation** is used after words or sentences which express emotion.

> How are the mighty fallen in the midst of the battle !   I am distressed for thee, my brother Jonathan !
> Nonsense !   How can you talk such rubbish ?
> What a conceited fellow you are !   Be silent.
> " Land ahead ! " shouted the delighted crew.

The Apostrophe.

295. The **Apostrophe** (') is inserted to show that some letter or letters have been omitted.

The Hon'ble (for *Honourable*); e'en (for *even*); 'tis (for *it is*); ta'en (for *taken*) ; don't (for *do not*) ; shan't (for *shall not*) ; won't (for *will not*) ; tho' (for *though*) ; an ox's head (for *oxes head*); and all other instances of the Genitive case.

Note of Interrogation.

296. A **Note of Interrogation** is used after sentences which ask questions.   The sentence following must be commenced with a capital.

> Where was he born ?   When did he die !

Insert the proper stops and capitals, where necessary, in the following sentences :—

Whats the matter Thomas ist that old pain of yours again no its not that at all said he but something a good deal better would you believe it my poor old uncle is dead and he has left me five thousand pounds that was very good of him she replied but its come too late why he inquired because she answered you are now old and broken in health what a pity it is that he did not die twenty years ago or give you the money while he was still alive.

Dashes.

297. The **Dash** has five main uses :—

(*a*) To mark a break or abrupt turn in a sentence :—

> Here lies the great—false marble, where ?
> Nothing but sordid dust lies here.

(*b*) To mark words in apposition or in explanation :—

> They plucked the seated hills with all their loads—
> Rocks, waters, woods—and by the shaggy tops
> Uplifting bore them in their hands.

(*c*) To resume a scattered subject :—

> Health, friends, position,—all are gone.

(*d*) To insert a parenthesis.   Here *two* dashes are required.

At the age of ten—such is the power of genius—he could read Greek with facility.

(*e*) To indicate a hesitating or faltering speech :—

> I—er—I—that is, I don't care.

Brackets.

298. Brackets are used like a couple of dashes in (*d*), as just explained, for inserting a parenthetical sentence in the middle of a main sentence.

At the age of ten (such is the power of genius) he could read Greek with facility.

The Hyphen.

299. A **Hyphen** is used for joining the parts of a compound word ; as " bathing-place."

Note.—A hyphen, like the dash, is formed by the horizontal line. But the line is shorter.

Insert a dash, hyphen, or brackets, wherever necessary, in the following sentences, and add any other appropriate stops :—

England and Russia the two greatest empires on the face of the earth had no real cause of enmity.   I could tell you all about my but perhaps you have heard enough by this time.   My dog such is the power of jealousy attacked its rival whenever they met.   This is

very uphill work. If you read without spectacles and I believe you
can be so good as to read out the contents of this letter. When I
took my degree and this was twelve years ago I had good prospects
before me. I will never but I need not finish my sentence for you
know already what I was going to say.

Diæresis.

300. Diæresis (separation) consists of two dots placed over
the second of two vowels, to show that they are to be sounded
separately :—

Coöperation = co-operation.

Asterisks.

301. Asterisks denote that some words or clauses have
been omitted :—

The Jews * * * * * had to pay heavy taxes to the Norman kings.

QUESTIONS ON MODERN ENGLISH GRAMMAR.

Collected, in the order of their occurrence, from London
Matriculation Papers.

1. What are the different uses of the verb *to be*? From how many
roots are the different parts of this verb taken ?

2. What are Weak verbs ? Classify *bring, sing, take, seek, teach, set,
bleed, eat* as Weak or Strong. Give reasons in each case, and call attention
to peculiarities.

3. What is meant by the Infinitive mood of a verb ? Explain as fully
as you can the Infinitive form in the phrase, " This house *to let.*"

4. What adjectives cannot properly be used in the Comparative or
Superlative degree ?

5. Write two sentences showing the same word used in one as a preposition, in the other as a conjunction ; also two sentences showing the
same word as a preposition and as an adverb.

6. Classify the pronouns. Illustrate by examples the points most worthy
of attention in the Syntax of Pronouns.

7. Explain what is meant by *tense* and *mood* of verbs. Add a few notes
on the uses of the Subjunctive.

8. Which are the English Auxiliary verbs properly so called ? and why ?
Distinguish them from every other class of verb.

9. Distinguish between Co-ordinating and Subordinating conjunctions.
What are the various uses of the word *but* in English ?

10. Give instances of *Proper* nouns used as *Common* nouns, and *vice versa*.

11. State clearly the rules of English Accidence with regard to the use of *shall* and *will* in Assertive sentences.

12. What is a verb ? What is meant by the Infinitive mood ? Tell what you know of the past and present use of *to* in the Infinitive.

13. What is an adverb ? Classify the adverbs. Tell what you can of the grammatical use of the words *yes, no.*

14. Classify the conjunctions, and point out which of them are used in forming co-ordinate sentences.

15. Explain and give examples of the difference between subordinate and co-ordinate sentences, between extension and completion of the predicate, and between a direct and an indirect object.

16. Point out and answer the chief questions that may arise as to the application of the rule that a verb should agree with its subject in number and person.

17. Enumerate the elements of flexion in the Verb. What is the use of the Subjunctive mood ?

18. What part of speech is the Infinitive ? What is meant by the Dative Infinitive and the Simple Infinitive ? Show the origin of the suffixes in " the hang*ing* crane," " the hang*ing* of the crane."

19. How is the future indefinite tense expressed in English ? Illustrate your answer by an examination of the original meaning of the Auxiliaries employed for the purpose. Explain the term " Imperfect Continuous " tense.

20. Discuss the origin and grammatical use of the Gerundial Infinitive.

21. What are the chief rules for the use, in punctuation, of the comma, the colon, and the semicolon ?

22. What is exactly meant by the phrase—*part of speech ?* What by the term *parse ?* Classify the words *pen, petition, long, that, wire.*

23. Point out the grammatical difference between *the* in such a phrase as, " He did his duty, and was *the* happier for it " ; and *the* in, " He was *the* happier of the two."

24. Explain the terms *Strong* and *Weak* as applied to verbs, also the term *conjugation.* To which conjugation do you assign *teach, fight, work, do, fly, flow, flee, tell, till, toll ?*

25. What is the force of *run* in such a phrase as " to run wild " ; of *wear* in " the day wears " ; of *give* in " the shoe gives " ; of *obtain* in " this doctrine obtained " ? Mention any noticeable uses of *to taste, ring, sit, stand.*

26. Give examples of verbs that are used both as " complete " and as " incomplete predicates," and explain these terms.

27. What is an *Indefinite pronoun ?* Write a list of the Indefinite pronouns, and exemplify their uses.

28. Write eight sentences giving four examples of the use of the same verb transitively and intransitively. Rewrite the four sentences containing transitive verbs with change of voice from Active to Passive.

29. Give the fullest subdivision of an English verb into tenses that you have met with in any grammar. Which of these are distinguished by inflexions ?

30. What are the marks of a Strong verb ? About how many of such verbs have we still in use ? To which conjugation belong *shall, buy, fight, reach, touch ?*

31. Parse all the words ending in *-ing* in this sentence :—Darkling, we went singing on our way, with our walking-sticks in our hands, weary of toiling in town.

32. Define a sentence, a phrase, and a clause, and give instances of each.

33. To which conjugation do the following verbs severally belong—*see, saw, say, sow, sew, sue, sit, seethe, sell ?* Write down the past tense and past part. of each, noticing any peculiarity.

34. Mention some nouns (i.) with two plural forms ; (ii.) with no plural form ; (iii.) with only a plural form ; (iv.) of plural form which are treated as singulars ; (v.) of singular form which are treated as plurals.

35. Explain the term *preposition*. How does a preposition differ from a conjunction ? Mention some prepositions that have become conjunctions.

36. Classify our words. Show that to some extent the form of a word indicates its class. Why only " to some extent ? " To what class or classes belong *that, ink, after, stand, parallel, good ?*

37. What is the use of the Analysis of sentences ? What shapes may the subject of a sentence assume ? and in what ways may it be extended ?

38. Analyse :—

    (*a*) I saw them run.   (*d*) Who is it ?

    (*b*) He can make it go.   (*e*) He was crowned king.

    (*c*) Let her depart.   (*f*) He was hanged,—a well-deserved punishment.

39. Write a sentence containing three extensions of the predicate, one of them a clause, and let this clause contain a subject with two extensions.

40. Write down the plural form of *wharf, colloquy, potato, Mary, Knight-Templar,* and *canto,* and state and discuss the rule you go by in each case. Mention some words in which the *s* of the stem has been mistaken for the plural flexion.

41. Illustrate our habit of using nouns as adjectives both with and without change of form, and also of using adverbs as adjectives.

42. What form of the indefinite article do you use before the words— *history, historical, European, usual, humble, ever ?* Give reasons for your answers. Can you mention any instances of the transference of the *n* of the indefinite article to the beginning of the following noun ?

43. Repeat and criticise the current definitions of a verb. Which seems to you the least unsatisfactory, and why ?

44. What are the characteristic marks of the Strong conjugation ? Make a list of some half-dozen Weak verbs that have vowel-change in the Past tense ; also of half a dozen that have no change there ; also of half a dozen that do change, but not in the way of addition.

45. Parse the italicised words and phrases :—

    (*a*) *Down* with it !

    (*b*) His *having been beaten* once only made him *the* more determined to succeed.

    (*c*) *Seeing* is *believing.*

    (*d*) The *hearing* ear and the *seeing* eye, the Lord hath made *even* both of them.

46. In what two ways may Adjectives be compared ? How do there come to be two ways ? By what terms would you denote them ? State the general rule as to their use.

47. Discuss the ordinary definition of a pronoun. What other definition has been suggested ? Distinguish between the forms *my* and *mine*. Which is the older form ? What similar pairs are there ?

48. Explain the terms *voice, mood, infinitive*. Show by what means, in English, transitive verbs are used intransitively, and *vice versa*. Mention some Causative verbs.

49. By what other names than Weak and Strong are the two conjugations known ? Which is the living one ? To which do these verbs belong—*fight, think, bare, bear, catch, teach, reach, beseech, hang, fly* ?

50. What adjectives cannot be compared ? Write down those adjectives that are defective in their comparison ?

51. What English nouns make no change in the plural, and why ?

52. Describe fully, with examples, English verbs of Incomplete Predication, and the different forms that the Complement may assume.

53. State the correct modern usage of *shall* and *will ;* and show by reference to the etymology of the words how that usage is to be accounted for.

54. Define *infinitive, gerund, present participle*, and *past participle*, giving examples of each.

55. Explain the different uses of the verbal form which terminates in *-ing*, and show in what cases it is properly a participle.

56. What principle would you adopt in classifying nouns in English ? Explain fully the basis of the classification that you adopt.

57. Frame a sentence showing by subordinate clauses the use of the comma, semicolon, and colon.

58. State what is meant by a Part of Speech ; and illustrate your statement by a sentence, in which the same word shall successively be of various Parts of Speech.

59. Classify the pronouns, giving explanations where necessary.

60. Explain the primitive meaning of each of the Auxiliary verbs, and show how that meaning has been modified in modern usage.

61. Distinguish between an *adverb* and a *relative adverb*, and give a list of the relative adverbs.

62. Define, giving examples, a simple sentence, a complex sentence, and a multiple sentence.

63. How are words grouped with reference to their grammatical usage ? In which group or groups do you place *than, but, divine, single, that, while ?*

64. Give instances of nouns that can be used as verbs, and of verbs that can be used as nouns. How is it that such transferences are so commonly possible in English ?

65. Prove that vowel-change is not the decisive mark of the Strong conjugation. To which conjugation belong these verbs—*bring, fight, read, hang, beseech, go ?*

66. Show that the Weak is our living conjugation. Why is it called the Weak ? What other names for it are suggested ?

67. In what ways are Adjectives compared ? Discuss *perfect, golden, lunar,* and *French*.

68. Discriminate, giving examples, between verbs of Incomplete Predication, Transitive verbs, Intransitive verbs, and Impersonal verbs.

69. Distinguish between the Infinitive and the Gerund in modern English ; and discuss the forms in *-ing* in the following sentence :—

John and two *fishing* friends started off early this morning, with their *fishing* rods, to the river *a-fishing* ; but the *fishing* to-day has been unsuccessful.

70. What is meant by the *case* of a noun ? How did the word come to be used in such a sense ?

71. Give instances of verbs that can be used both Transitively and Intransitively ; also of some that can be used both as complete predicates and as incomplete ; also of some that can be used both as Auxiliaries and Principals.

72. Mention some Strong verbs in which the *n* of the Past participle has dropped off ; some in which the preterite has come to be used as the Past participle ; and some which have two forms of the preterite.

73. Show from still familiar forms that *melt, show, shave, swell, grave* were once of the Strong conjugation ; and write down the past participles of *shoe, light, work, knit, speed.*

74. Show how the addition of the Plural sign *-s* altogether alters the meanings of many English nouns.

75. The Infinitive is sometimes called the Substantive mood. Explain this, and give some examples of the different parts which the Infin. may play in English sentences. What is the Gerundial Infin., and how was it distinguished in Old English ?

76. Write down the plural of *gallows, topaz, solo, who, Mary.* Mention some words about whose plural form there is variety of usage, and some that have been wrongly taken for plurals, though really singular.

77. How would you describe the number of the following words—*alms, banns, heronries, optics, poultry, pride, salmon, scissors, sheep, sixpences, thanks, wheat ?*

78. Give a list of Double plurals of English nouns, in which one form has the Collective idea, and the other the Distributive.

79. What is meant by saying that there is no future tense in our language ? Indicate how we express the ideas of simple futurity, of intention, and of compulsion. How do we express a future participle ?

80. Specify as many as you can of the shades of meaning of *one*, with an illustration of each ; and explain as far as you can how they arose.

81. Are the following words properly of the Singular or the Plural number ? —*eaves, tidings, alms, news, riches, means.* Are there any words that have only a Singular form, and any that have only a Plural ?

82. What should be meant by a " mixed conjugation " ? Is there such a thing ? Prove that such verbs as *teach, seek,* and *tell* have certainly no mixture in their conjugation.

83. Give examples of Defective verbs. Write down the Second Sing. Pret. of *am.* What other form is found ?

84. Give instances of the conversion of abstract nouns into concrete, proper into common, common into proper, and try to explain why each of these conversions should occur.

85. In what various ways may Interjections arise ?

86. Give an account of the signs of number in Modern English. Indicate and explain cases where (1) a plural sense is found without a plural inflexion ; (2) a plural inflexion without a plural sense.

87. Define a sentence. How would you deal with the following :—*go ; hence ! does it rain ? yes ; let us return.*

88. Distinguish carefully the use of the word *riding* in the following :—

(a) He is very fond of *riding.*

    (b) He is always happy when *riding*.

    (c) He has capital *riding* horses.

89. Give all the grammatical forms in use of the verbs *can, shall, will, ought, must*, showing (1) how far, if at all, each has deviated from its original meaning ; (2) how the place of the wanting forms is supplied.

90. Supply the plural to each of the following, accounting for any apparent irregularity in its formation :—*man-servant, maid-servant, man-of-all-work, passer-by, looker-on, castaway, prince-consort, lord-lieutenant, camel-driver.*

91. Defend or criticise the following sentences, suggesting where you can the *explanation* of what you think grammatically anomalous :—

    (a) With selfish people, the frequency of imposture, together with the inadequacy of present arrangements, serve as an excuse for not giving at all.

    (b) Nothing but dreary dykes, muddy and straight, guarded by the ghosts of suicidal pollards, occur to break the monotony of the landscape.

    (c) Twice one are two.

    (d) Between every stitch she would look up to see what was going on in the street.

92. Define *Infinitive, Strong verbs, Weak verbs, Present participle, Verbal noun, Auxiliary verb.* Explain carefully what is meant by (i.) Irregular, and (ii.) Defective verbs. Give examples throughout.

93. Distinguish and account for the force of the words italicised in each of the following :—

    (a) I *did* say so, though I thought I *did* not.

    (b) *Do* go.   (d) I *dare* not say he did.

    (c) *Do* not go.   (e) I *dare* say he did.

94. Illustrate and explain the different uses of (i.) the Infinitive, and (ii.) the various verbal forms in *-ing.* Tell the history of *-ing* as the ending of the present participle.

95. Classify nouns according to their meaning, and illustrate the passage of nouns from one class to another.

96. Define Mood, Voice, Auxiliary verb, Strong-Weak verb.

Correct or justify the following.[1] *Point out the error, if any.*

1. I am verily a man who am a Jew.

2. Too great a variety of studies distract the mind.

3. Who do you speak to ?

4. The river has overflown its banks.

5. Man never is, but always to be blest.

6. Neither our virtues or our vices are all our own.

7. If I were old enough to be married, I am old enough to manage my husband's house.

8. I am to blame, not you.

9. Art thou proud yet ?   Ay, that I am not thee.

10.   Whoever the king favours
      The cardinal will find employment for.

---

[1] Reprinted from London Matriculation Papers.

11. Here you may see that visions are to dread.

12. Nothing but wailings was heard.

13. Neither of them are remarkable for precision.

14. I cannot tell if it be wise or no.

15. It must be confessed that a lampoon or a satire do not carry in them robbery or murder.

16. Whose own example strengthens all his laws,
     And is himself the great sublime he draws.

17. They were both fond of one another.

18. Thersites's body is as good as Ajax, when neither are alive.

19. Thou art much older than thy looks.

20. There were no less than five persons concerned.

21. Recite the first six lines of *Paradise Lost*.

22. Neither he nor we are disengaged.

23. One of the best books that has been written on the subject.

24. I like it better than any.

25. And since I never dare to write
     As funny as I can.

26. Laying the suspicion on some one, I know not who.

27. Well is him that hath found prudence !

28. Neither he nor I have any doubt of his success.

29. One of the best treatises that has been written on the subject.

30. I am one of those who cannot describe what I do not see.

31. The country was divided into counties, and the counties placed under magistrates.

32. Nobody ever put so much of themselves into their work.

33. He hath given away above half his fortune to the Lord knows who.

34. Friendships which we once hoped and believed would never grow cold.

35. Nepos answered him, Celsus replied, and neither of them were sparing of censures on each other.

36. Such are a few of the many paradoxes one would cite from his writings, and which are now before me.

37. The largest circulation of any Liberal newspaper.

38. Injustice springs only from three causes. . . . Neither of these can be found in a being wise, powerful, and benevolent.

39. This dedication may serve almost for any book that has, is, or shall be published.

40. In the best countries a rise in rents and wages has been found to go together.

41. He belongs to one caste, and the hewers of wood and drawers of water to another.

42. The second assault was met by Buckingham by a counter attack on the Earl of Bristol, whom he knew would be the chief witness against him.

43. And many a holy text around she strews,
     That teach the rustic moralist to die.

44. This view has been maintained by one of the greatest writers that has appeared in this country.

45. The administration of so many various interests, and of districts so remote, demand no common capacity and vigour.

46. He having none but them, they having none but he.

47. Breaking a constitution by the very same errors that so many have been broke before.

48. They are not only the most charitable of any other nation, but most judicious in distinguishing the properest objects of compassion.

49. The part of this reed used by the Indians is from 10 to 11 feet long, and no tapering can be perceived, one end being as thick as another.

50. If he had writ one word by the next post, this had been just and civil.

51. Thou lovest, but ne'er knew love's sad satiety.

52. *Macbeth.* There's blood upon thy face.
    Murd. 'Tis Banquo's then.
    Macb. 'Tis better thee without than he within.

53. This is he, my master said,
    Despised the Athenian maid.

54. Luckily the monks have recently given away a couple of dogs which were returned to them, or the breed would have been lost.

55. It was the most amiable, although the least dignified, of all the party squabbles by which it had been preceded.

56. Having perceived the weakness of his poems, they now reappear to us under new titles.

57. Neither you nor I am right.

58. I am one of those who cannot describe what I feel.

59. Whom they were I really cannot specify.

60. Whom do you say that I am ?

61. His is a poem, one of the completest works that exists in any language.

62. He was shot by a secretary under notice to quit, with whom he was finding fault,—very fortunately without effect.

63. It is characteristic of them to appear but to one person, and he the most likely to be deluded.

64. I think it may assist the reader by placing them before him in chronological order.

65. Few people learn anything that is worth learning easily.

66. My resolution is to spare no expense in education ; it is a bad calculation, because it is the only advantage over which circumstances have no control.

67. Image after image, phrase after phrase, starts out vivid, harsh, and emphatic.

68. Books that we can at a glance carry off what is in them are worse than useless for discipline.

69. He preferred to know the worst than to dream the best.

70. Humanity seldom or ever shows itself in inferior minds.

71. You have already been informed of the sale of Ford's theatre, where Mr. Lincoln was assassinated, for religious purposes.

72. The Moor, seizing a bolster, full of rage and jealousy, smothers her.

73. Nor do I know any one with whom I can converse more pleasantly or I would prefer as my companion.

74. They drowned the black and white kittens.

75. The then Ministry were in favour of the bill.

76. The people is one ; they have all one language.

77. George and myself went up the mountain together.

78. The Duke of Wellington is one of those who never interfere with matters over which he has no control.

79. Her voice was ever soft, gentle, and low ; an excellent thing in woman.

80. Peter the Hermit's diet was abstemious, his prayers long and fervent.

81. I shall have great pleasure in accepting your invitation.

82. Each of the girls went to their separate rooms to rest and calm themselves.

83. Being early killed, I sent a party in search of his mangled body.

PART II.—IDIOM AND CONSTRUCTION.

CHAPTER XIV.—NOUNS AND PRONOUNS.

SECTION 1.—CASES OF NOUNS AND PRONOUNS.

302. Genitive.—The meanings denoted by this case can be distinguished into (*a*) Subjective, (*b*) Objective, (*c*) Descriptive. In one point, however, they all agree : they all have the power of an Adjective, that is, they all qualify or restrict the noun following.

(*a*) *Subjective :*—

England's power is very great. (*Possession.*)
A good son will repay his *father's* benefits. (*Origin.*)
Shakspeare's plays are excellent. (*Agency.*)
His friendship (the friendship felt by him) is sincere. (*Subject.*)

(*b*) *Objective* (now rather scarce) :—

His friendship (the friendship for him) must be given up.
My *friend's* praises were heard everywhere.
Cæsar's murderers were conquered at Philippi.

(*c*) *Descriptive,* equivalent to a Descriptive adjective, § 81 :—

I'll break your *knave's* (=knavish) pate.—SHAKSPEARE.
The *mother's* (=motherly) nature of Althæa.—LOWELL.

303. Familiar "your" and "my."—These possessive adjectives are used indefinitely, and with some implication of contempt :—

Your worm is *your* only emperor for diet ; *your* fat king and *your* lean beggar is but variable service.—*Hamlet,* iv. 3, 24.
When he entered the room, on seeing a servant coming towards him to order him out, up goes *my* grave Impudence (=the grave-faced, impudent fellow whom I was watching) to the maid, etc.—*Tatler.*
He saw more than *your* fool of a tourist generally sees.—MRS. WARD.

304. "Of" followed by Noun in the Genitive or a Possessive Adjective or Pronoun.—This occurs in such phrases as "that book *of James's*," "that handsome face *of my father's*," "that book *of yours.*"

Three explanations have been offered—all conceivable :—

(1) "Of my father's" is an ellipse for "of my father's faces." Here "faces" is the Object to "of" used in a Partitive sense. This is good grammar, but it makes nonsense, since "my father" cannot have more than one face. But it is defensible on grounds of analogy with instances where it makes sense, as in "That book of my father's (books)."

(2) "Of my father's" is a Double Genitive. This explanation is the most natural, and seems to be the right one.

(3) The "of" merely denotes apposition, as in "the continent *of* Asia," which means "the continent, *namely* Asia." Similarly, the phrase "that face *of* my father's" can mean "that face, *namely* my father's (face)." This explanation is the least satisfactory.

Note.—The ambiguity of the preposition "of" is sometimes removed by placing a Genitive noun after it. Thus, "a picture of the King" means a picture consisting of a likeness of the King. But "a picture of the *King's*" means a picture of which the King is owner.

The construction by which "of" is placed before a Genitive is not a modern idiom, but is frequently met with so far back as Chaucer, and has continued in constant use up to the present day :—

> An old felawe (fellow, partner) *of youres.*—*Pardoner's Tale.*
> A trusty frende *of Sir Tristram's.*—MALORY (15th cent.).

305. Personal Genitives.—In Old English *mine, thine, our,* and *your* (= A.S. *mín, thín, úre, eówer*) had two distinct functions—(1) as independent pronouns, where we now have to say *of me, of thee, of you, of us ;* (2) as adjectives, declined in A.S. like other adjectives, so as to be in the same number, gender, and case as the noun following.

In Mod. Eng. function (1) is obsolete ; yet some traces of it can be seen in such examples as the following :—

(1) Having heard of A.'s death, *my* mind was much disturbed.

Here *my = of me,* and the implied *me* is qualified by the participle "having heard."

(2) Poor is *our* sacrifice, whose eyes
  Are lighted from above.—NEWMAN.

Here *our = of us,* and *us* is the antecedent to "whose."

(3) Have I not *all their* letters to meet me in arms ?—1 *Hen. IV.* ii. 3, 28.

Here *all their letters* mean "letters from them all" ; and *all* qualifies the pronoun *them.*

(4) At *your only* choice (= at the choice of you only).—*Coriol.* i. 9, 36.

(5) I took *her* leave (= leave of her) at Court.—*All's Well that Ends Well,* v. 3, 79.

(6) But I have sworn to frustrate *both their* hopes (= the hopes of both of them).—MARLOWE.

(7) Tell her 'tis *all our* ways (= the ways of all of us) ; it runs in the family.—SHERIDAN.

The common phrase "*in my despite*" means "in spite of me" ; cf. the obsolete phrase "maugre myn," which in the Middle period of English meant the same thing. (*Maugre* is from Old French *maugré*, Mid. Fr. *malgré*, ill-will.)

306. Dative case.—In Old English there was a Dative case distinct from the Accusative. What we now call the Indirect Object is in the Dative case. Other examples of the Dative are given below :—

(*a*) **Dative of Interest.**—The Jew ate *me* (to my astonishment) a whole ham of bacon.—ADDISON.

"Archers," he cried, "send *me* (for my satisfaction) an arrow through yon monk's frock."—SCOTT.

Knock *me* this gate, and rap *me* well.—SHAKSPEARE.

(*b*) **Reflexive Dative** (see § 149).—Fare *thee* well (= fare well *for thyself*).

He overslept *him*self (slept too long *for himself*).

> But hear *thee*, Gratiano ;
> Thou art too wild, too rude, and bold of voice.
> > *Merchant of Venice*, ii. 2, 189.

(*c*) **With Impersonal Verbs.** — *Me*thinks ; *me*seems ; it likes *us* well.—SHAKSPEARE.

(*d*) **With the Verbs "be," "worth."**—

> Woe worth *the day*!
> Woe is *me*!

(*e*) **As Indirect object to a Transitive verb** (see § 141).—He taught *my sons* Euclid.

I hope you will do *me* this favour.

307. Dative Absolute.—In Old English the noun or pronoun in the Absolute construction was in the Dative case ; cf. the Ablative in Latin and the Genitive in Greek.

Eów slǽpendum = you sleeping. (Here *slǽp-end-um* is the Dative plural of the present participle ; and *eów* is the Dative plural of the Second Personal pronoun.)

They have stolen away the body, *us* sleeping.—*Wyclif's Bible*.

The modern substitutes for the Dative Absolute are :—

(*a*) The Nominative, common even in Chaucer's time : [1]—

And *he* continuyng ever in stourdynesse.—*Clerke's Tale*, iv. 9.

---

[1] In Milton we meet with such phrases as "*me* overthrown," "*us* dispossessed," "*him* destroyed." It would be wrong to infer from this that the Dative Absolute of Old English was lingering in use up to Milton's

(b) The use of the preposition "with" in connection with a noun or participle following :—

> Besides, *with the enemy invading* our country, it was my duty to go in the campaign.—THACKERAY.

308. Cognate Accusative.—This construction (see § 148) occurs in the oldest English, and has been in constant use ever since :—

> { Thá leof-od-on heora líf.—*Anglo-Saxon.*
> { They lived their life.
> { He had bled so mychel blood.
> { He had bled so much blood.—*Middle English.*

SECTION 2.—USES OF PRONOUNS, PAST AND PRESENT.

309. "Ye" supplanted by "you."—In Old English, and in the English Bible, *ye* (= A.S. *ge*) is a Nominative, and *you* (= A.S. *eów*) is an Accusative or Dative :—

> *Ye* have not chosen me, but I have chosen *you.*—*John* xv. 16.

But prior to the date of the first Authorised Version some confusion had already been springing up in profane literature. Hence in the Elizabethan dramatists and later, when our language was still in some respects unsettled, we find *ye* and *you* apparently used indiscriminately, as if there were no difference between them :—

> I do beseech *ye*, if *you* bear me hard.—*Julius Cæsar*, iii. 1, 157.
>
> His wrath, which one day will destroy *ye* both.—*Par. Lost*, ii. 734.

Note.—*Ye* took the place of *you* in such examples as the above, because the unaccented *you* was pronounced as *y'*,—a sound very unlike that of the accented *you*. It was written as *ye*, because this spelling, though far from suitable, made a nearer approach to the sound of *y'* than the spelling of *you* did. We still say colloquially, "I tell *yer*," though this is chiefly heard in low life.

310. "Thou" and "thee" supplanted by "you."—In the fourteenth century, and throughout the Tudor period, *you* was the more formal, distant, and respectful mode of address, and *thou* the more familiar, such as a father could use to a son, but not a son to a father : [1]—

---

time. The poet was merely adopting, or attempting to reintroduce, the Latin idiom—in which attempt he met with no followers.

We say "reintroduce" advisedly, because even in Old English the Dative absolute was not a true Teutonic idiom, but a mere imitation of the Latin Ablative absolute.

[1] This question is worked out very fully by Prof. Skeat in *William of Palerne*, preface, p. xli. The results are embodied in Abbott's *Shakspearian Grammar*, pp. 153-158.

(1) *Grat.* I have a suit to *you.*
   Bass.   *You* have obtained it.
   Grat. You must not deny me. I must go with *you* to Belmont.
   Bass. Why, then *you* must. But hear *thee,* Gratiano ;
      Thou art too wild, too rude, and bold of voice.
                             Merchant of Venice, ii. 2, 187-190.

So long as the two friends are talking to each other in a formal
way on a matter of business, they adopt the respectful and more distant *you.* But as soon as the one begins to address the other in a
more confidential and intimate tone, he at once uses the more familiar
thee and *thou.*

(2) All that Lord Cobham did was at *thy* instigation, *thou* viper !
for I *thou* thee, *thou* traitor.

This language was used at Sir Walter Raleigh's trial (A.D. 1603),
when Coke, finding that argument and evidence were wanting, insulted
the illustrious prisoner by applying to him the familiar *"thou."*

Note 1.—"Thou" is retained in poetry and in addresses to the
Deity, in both of which archaisms are suitable.

Note 2.—Quakers used to address every one as *thou,* because (it is
presumed) all men in their view were or ought to be friends and
equals. They disowned the tone of distance and superiority implied
by the more formal *you.*

311. Self, my-self, him-self, etc.

When "self" is added to a pronoun of the *First* or *Second*
person, it is preceded by a *Possessive adjective.* But when it is
added to a pronoun of the *Third* person, it is preceded by a
pronoun in the *Accusative* case. Thus we have :—

   First and Second Persons.—My-self, our-selves. Thy-self, your-
   selves.
   Third Person.—Him-self, her-self, it-self, them-selves.

How is this to be explained ? The word "self" was originally an adjective signifying "same," "actual," "identical." In
Old Eng. it was declined with the preceding pronoun :—*Ic self*
(Nom. "I self or the same"), *mín selfes* (Gen. "of me the same"),
mé selfne (Accus. "me the same"), etc.

    On these *self* (= identical) hills.—RALEIGH.
    To shoot another arrow that *self* (= same) way
    Which thou didst shoot at first.—SHAKSPEARE.
    At that *self* (= same) moment enters Palamon.—DRYDEN.
    His servant was healed in the *self-same* hour.—*Matt.* viii. 13.

But in later English "self" came to be also used as a noun,
as we still see it used in such phrases as "a man's better
self" (= the better side of his character); "she was beauty's
self" (= a personification of beauty). Here the noun "self"
is very correctly qualified by a noun in the Genitive case.
Similarly in the First and Second persons we have "*my*-self,"

"*your*-self," etc., where the noun "self" is correctly qualified by the Possessive adjectives "my" and "your." The same construction occurs in what have now become provincial phrases, "his self," "their selves," in which "self" has been pluralised as a noun on the analogy of "shelf, shelves." "Self" is commonly used as a noun with the Third Personal pronoun in the Authorised Version of 1611 :—

> Who *his* own *self* bare our sins.—1 *Peter* ii. 24.
> He may make *his-self* easy.—DICKENS.

But since the Tudor period "self" has retained its original function as an *adjective*, whenever it is compounded with the Third Personal pronoun :—

> (1) He hurt *him*-self.
> (2) He did it by *him*-self.
> (3) He *him*-self did it.
> (4) They *them*-selves did it.

In (1) and (2) there is no difficulty. In (3) and (4) we have the Accusatives *him* and *them* in what seems to be apposition with *he* and *they* respectively. But the apposition is apparent, not real. The construction is merely a survival of the Old English Dative, denoting agency. If these phrases were literally translated into Mod. Eng., they would be "*by* him-self," "*by* them-self," just as we still say sometimes, "He did it by himself," "They did it by themselves." But in Mod. Eng. the *by* is usually omitted, and the Reflexive or Emphatic pronoun is placed immediately after the subject to the verb, as if it were in apposition with it.

In the phrase "they them-*selves*," there is a confusion between "self" as a noun and "self" as an adjective; and since adjectives have now no plural forms, the phrase would be more correctly worded "they them-self." But it has been assimilated to the phrase "We our-*selves*." The latter is quite correct; for here "selves," Plural noun, is in apposition to "we," Plural pronoun, and is qualified by the Possessive adjective "our."

312. Own.—This adjective is placed after the Possessive adjectives in all persons alike :—

My own, mine own. Thy own, thine own. His own, her own, its own. Our own, your own, their own.

"Own" is never placed after *double* Genitives, like "ours," "yours," "theirs." It means literally "possessed," and was originally spelt *ágen*, the p.p. of *ág-an* (A.S.), to possess.

Sometimes we have the doubly emphatic phrases, "my own self," "your own self," etc.

313. Which.—(*a*) as Interrogative ; (*b*) as Relative :—

(*a*) According to present idiom, "which" as an Interrogative has a *selective* force, and "who or what" a general (§ 131).

In Old Eng. "what" was not used as an adjective for qualifying nouns. The selective force of "which" now current is well in keeping with its etymology (A. S. *hwylc* or *hwilc*, short for *hwi-lic*, "how like": cf. Latin *qua-lis*).

Hwylc (of what sort) is mín módor (my mother ?)—*Matt.* xii. 48.

(*b*) "Which" as a Relative is now used only for Neuter (sex-less) antecedents, or for the names of young children and lower animals, when no question of sex arises about them. This restriction, however, is of recent date; for "who" *in the Nom. case* did not come into use at all as a *Relative* pronoun till the sixteenth century. Before this the Nom. had been used exclusively as an *Interrogative*, though the other cases were used as Relatives at a much earlier date :—

Our Father, *which* art in heaven.—*New Test.*
Then Warwick disannuls great John of Gaunt,
Which did subdue the greatest part of Spain.—3 *Hen. VI.* iii. 1.

314. "The whom," "the whose," "the which," etc.—In Middle English we find the Relative particularised by the Def. article. But modern idiom is against it, even in poetry :—

The *whose* power as now is falle.—GOWER.
Your mistress, from *the whom* I see
There's no disjunction.—*Winter's Tale*, iv. 4.
'Twas a foolish quest,
The which to gain and keep he sacrificed all rest.—BYRON.

315. "Who," "what," as Indefinite Demonstratives.—The Indefinite use of "who," "what," in the sense of *some one* or *something* dates back to Old English. Though modern idiom is against it, it has survived in the common word "somewhat" = something, and in the phrase "as who should say" :—

Love is bought for litil *what*.—GOWER.
Come down and learn the little *what*
That Thomalin can sayne.—SPENSER.
With promise of his sister and *what* else.—SHAKSPEARE.
The cloudy messenger turns me his back
And hums, as *who* should say, You'll rue the time
That clogs me with this answer.—*Macbeth*, iii. 6.

316. "That" for "who" or "which."—It has been shown in § 128 that "that" is pre-eminently the *Restrictive* relative, and "who" or "which" the *Continuative*.

This use of "that" as an indeclinable Relative pronoun is

by no means modern. It occurs in its present indeclinable form in A.S., and was the Relative chiefly used in Mid. Eng. In the Tudor period and later the Relative "that" yielded to the influence of "who" and "which" (both of which during the period named could be fortified, if necessary, by the Def. art. "the"), and almost disappeared. About Addison's time it again came into fashion, and has held its ground ever since as the Restrictive Relative.

Addison, however, who was evidently not acquainted with the history of our language, protested against the change. In his "Humble Petition of 'Who' and 'Which'" he makes the petitioners say :—"We are descended of ancient families, and kept up our dignity and honour many years, till the Jack Sprat *that* supplanted us."

317. "**That**" for "**what**" or "**that which**."—This use of "that" has become archaic. It arose merely from the loss of Rel. *that* following the Demonstrative *that*. In A.S. the phrase was *that the* or *that that* (= that which) :—

> We speak *that* (what) we do know, and testify *that* we have seen.—*New Test.*
> I am possessed of *that* is mine.—SHAKSPEARE.

318. "**It**" with Impersonal verbs.—Verbs used in the *third* person only, and without having a *personal* subject, are called Impersonal.

(*a*) Impersonal verbs denoting *physical* events were used with "it" in Old English, as now, and were not less common :—

> *Hit* rínth = *it* rains.   *Hit* fréoseth = *it* freezes.

(*b*) But verbs denoting *mental feelings* have undergone an important change. The Dative of the person (§ 306, *c*) has become the Subject, in the Nominative case. The change was gradual, and Impersonal verbs were more common in Shakspeare's time than now : [1]—

> It yearns me not.—*Hen. V.* iv. 3.
> It dislikes me.—*Othel.* ii. 3, 49.
> It likes us well.—*Hamlet,* i. 2, 81.
> Where it thinks best unto your royal self. [2]—*Rich. III.* iii. 1, 63.

---

[1] "An abundance of Impersonal verbs is a mark of a very early stage in a language, denoting that a speaker has not yet arrived so far in his development as to trace his own actions and feelings to his own agency."—ABBOTT, *Shakspearian Grammar*, p. 208.

[2] "Thinks," the Impersonal verb, means "seems," and is derived from A.S. *thync- ;* but the Personal verb "think" comes from A.S. *thenc- ;* and *thenc* is allied to *thanc*, "thank," a kindly remembrance.

319. It is I.—In Old and Mid. Eng. the phrase was " it am I," out of which the Mod. Eng. " it is I " has been developed :—

Old English : " I it am."

Ic sylf hit eom ⎱
I self it am ⎰ = it is myself.—*Luke* xxiv. 39.

Mid. Eng. : "it am I."

I am thy mortel foo (=foe), and *it am I*
That loveth so hoote (=hotly) Emelye the brighte.—CHAUCER,
Knight's Tale.

Mod. Eng. : "it is I."

It is not *he* that slew the man, *hit is I.*—*Gest. Rom.*

Thus in Old and Mid. Eng. "it" is the *complement* to the verb "am"; while in Mod. Eng. it has become the *subject.* Hence any pronoun of any number or person can now be placed after "it is" as complement : "it is we," "it is you," "it is they," etc., instead of "it are we," "it are you," etc.

320. "It is," "it was," for giving emphasis.—This device is found in Old English. In Mid. Eng. it was equally common.

In the tyme bitwene Abraham and Moyses *it was* that men come verst (first) to Engelond.—ROBERT OF GLOUCESTER.

CHAPTER XV.—ADJECTIVES.

SECTION ⅰ.—USES OF THE VARIOUS KINDS OF ADJECTIVES.

Quantitative.

321. Some, any.—These are used as follows :—

(*a*) **Some** is used in *affirmative* sentences ; as—

" He has procured *some* bread."   We cannot say, " He has procured *any* bread."

(*b*) **Any** is used in *negative* sentences ; as—

" He has *not* procured *any* bread."   We cannot say, "He has not procured *some* bread."

(*c*) **Any** and **some** can both be used in *interrogative* sentences :—

Has he procured *any* bread ?
Has he procured *some* bread ?

But in such sentences "any" is more commonly used than "some," and is to be preferred to it.

322. Little, a little, the little.—Each of these expressions has a distinct meaning of its own :—

(*a*) **Little** is a *negative* adjective, and means "not much."

He had *little* money = (not much money).

(b) **A little** is an *affirmative* adjective, and means "some at least" :—a certain quantity, however little.

> He had *a little* money = (some money at least, although the amount was small).

(c) **The little** implies two statements—one *negative*, and the other *affirmative*.

> He spent *the little* (or *what little*) money he had.
>
> That is—(1) The money he had was not much. (*Negative.*)
>
> (2) He spent all the money that he had. (*Affirmative.*)

Note.—When "little" and "a little" are used as Adverbs, the same distinction holds good :—

> I *little* expected (= did not expect) such treatment.
>
> I am *a little* (rather, slightly) tired.

Numeral Adjectives.

323. Few, a few, the few.—Each of these expressions has a distinct meaning of its own :—

(a) **Few** is a *Negative* adjective, and signifies "not many."

> He read *few* books (he did *not* read *many* books).

(b) **A few** is an *Affirmative* adjective, and signifies "some at least" :—a certain number, however few.

> He read *a few* books (that is, he read *some* books *at least*, though the number was small).

(c) **The few** implies two statements, *one Negative* and *the other Affirmative*.

> He read *the few* (or *what few*) books he had.
>
> That is (1) The books he had were not many. (*Negative.*)
>
> (2) He read all the books he had. (*Affirmative.*)

324. Many a, a many.—The former phrase is followed by *Singular* nouns, and the latter by *Plural* ones :—

(a) **Many a.**—Here "a" = "one"; "many a man" means "many times one man," or "many men." Hence "many" has here the force of a Multiplicative numeral :—

> *Many a* youth and *many a* maid
> Dancing 'neath the greenwood shade.—MILTON.

It is interesting to notice that this construction is met with in our language so far back as the beginning of the thirteenth century :—

> *Moni enne* (= many a) thing.—LAYAMON.

(b) **A many.**—Here "many" has the force of a *Collective noun*, and "*of*" is understood after it :—

> They have not shed *a many tears*,
> Dear eyes, since first I knew them well.—TENNYSON.

A many of our bodies.—SHAKSPEARE, *Hen. V.* iv. 3.
A many of us were called together.—LATIMER.
This many summers on a sea of glory.—*Hen. VIII.*

In prose it is more common to put in the word "great" between *a* and *many*. "A great many men" means "a large number *of* men," the "*of*" being understood, and *many* being a Collective noun. Similarly in such a phrase as "a few books," we might regard *a few* as a Collective noun, the "*of*" being understood after it.

Note.—In Old English "menigu" was a Collective *Noun*, signifying "a multitude or large number," and "manig" was an Indefinite Numeral *Adjective*, signifying "many." In Modern English the same word "many" stands for both; for it is equivalent to "menigu" in the phrase *a many*, and to "manig" in the phrase *many a* or simply *many*.[1]

325. Definite Numeral Quantities are sometimes Collective nouns, where "*of*" must be understood after them in Mod. Eng. In Mid. Eng. the sense of *of* was expressed by the Gen. Plural. Similarly, in A.S. *twelf scéapa* means "twelve of sheep." All numerals in A.S. governed Genitives plural.

A dozen (of) sheep ; *a million* (of) apples.
A hundred (of) years ; *a thousand* (of) years.
A hundred-thousand (of) years.

Demonstrative Adjectives.

326. Definite Demonstratives are used as follows :—

(*a*) **This, these** : point to something *near :*—

This tree ; *these* trees.
These eyes (=my own eyes) saw the deed.

(*b*) **That, those, yon, yonder.**[2]—These point to something *farther off ;* as—

That tree ; *those* trees ; *yon* tree, or the tree *yonder.*

---

[1] This explanation, however, contains only half the truth. The English "many" became mixed up with the Norman *meinee* (Old Fr. *meisnee*, Late Lat. *mansionata*), which meant a household, a company. In Mid. Eng. *a gret meinee* (= "a great many" in Mod. Eng.) meant "a great company of men," and this commonly used phrase was largely instrumental in producing confusion. It occurs in the ballad of "Chevy Chase" in the sense of "household troop" :—

The Percy out of Northumberland came,
With him *a great meinee.*

Out of the noun *meinee* we get the adj. *meni-al*, pertaining to household work ; which therefore has no connection, as has been supposed, with the word "manual," pertaining to the hand (*manus*).

[2] "Yon" (A.S. *geon*) was an adjective signifying "distant." "Yonder" was an adverb formed from it. Hence the phrase *the tree yonder* means "the tree there." In Mod. Eng., however, the distinction is not always observed.

(c) **Such.**—This refers either (1) to something just mentioned, or (2) to something just going to be mentioned :—

(1) His praise of me was not sincere : I do not like *such* a man.
(2) *Such* food as we get here does not suit me.

" Such " can also be used as an *Indefinite* Demonstrative :—

He called at my house on *such a* day (= some day or other), and I gave *such and such* an answer (some answer or other) to his questions.

Note.—The adverb *so* can also be used Indefinitely :—

A week or *so* (that is, a week more or less).

327. Indefinite Demonstratives are used thus :—

(a) **One.**—This word is properly a Numeral adjective ; but it may also be used as an Indefinite Demonstrative :—

He came *one* day (on a certain day which I cannot remember) to see me.
One Mr. James (a certain man whom I do not know, but who is called Mr. James) came to see me.

Note.—This use of " one " is by no means of recent date :—

Oon Grecus that reigned there some tyme.—TREVISA.

(b) **Any.**—This is more emphatic than " a " or " an," and can be used with Plural as well as Singular nouns :—

Any man (that is, any and every man) could do that.
You may take *any* books (no books in particular, but any books) that you like best.

(c) **Some.**—This is used in two senses—(1) as showing that no person or thing in particular is specified ; (2) for making a Definite number Indefinite (see § 88).

(1) *Some* man (I do not know who he was) called here to-day.
(2) He owes me *some* 20 pounds (*about* 20 pounds).

(d) **Other than.**—This means " different from " :—

He has no books *other than* English ones.

This is better than saying, " he has no other books than English." " Than " is here a preposition. " Other " was originally a Comparative adj., and hence it takes " than " after it.

(e) **The other day.**—In spite of the Definite article, " the other " is here Indefinite,—some day a little before the present.

He came here *the other* day (a day of recent date).

Note.—An explanation of this phrase is offered in chap. xx (69).

328. Some, any.—It depends upon the sense whether these are *Demonstrative, Quantitative,* or *Numeral* :—

Some $\begin{cases} (1) \textit{ Some } \text{man called here to-day} & . & \textit{Indef. Demons.} \\ (2) \text{ Give me } \textit{some} \text{ bread} & . & . & . & ,, & \textit{Quant.} \\ (3) \text{ Give me } \textit{some} \text{ loaves of bread} & . & ,, & \textit{Number.} \end{cases}$

Any { (1) Take *any* book that you like best   *Indef. Demons.*
     (2) He has not had *any* bread .   .   ,,   *Quant.*
     (3) Did you bring *any* loaves ?   .   ,,   *Number.*

Both of these adjectives are Indefinite ; but, as may be seen from the following examples, " some " is not so Indefinite as " any " :—

Did *any* man call here to-day ? Yes ; *some* man did call.
Take *any* books that you like ; but you must take *some*.
Can you come at *some* hour to-day ? Yes, at *any* hour you like.

Distributive Adjectives and Phrases.

329. Each other, one another.—In these phrases we have a Distributive adjective (*each, one*) combined with a Demonstrative adjective (*other* or *another*). *Each* is Nom., *other* is Accusative ; cf. Latin, " alius alium."

(*a*) **"Each other"** is used for *two* persons :—

The two men struck *each other* (that is, *each* man struck the *other* man).

(*b*) **"One another"** is used for *more than two* persons :—

They all loved *one another* (that is, each man loved every other man).

330. The drift of a Distributive adjective can also be expressed in the following ways :—

  (*a*) They went out two *by* two, or *by twos* (in separate pairs).
  (*b*) They went out *two and two* (in separate pairs).
  (*c*) They went out *two at a time* (in separate pairs).
  (*d*) The twenty men had a gun *apiece* (had each a gun).
  (*e*) They went to their *respective* homes (each to his own).

Section 2.—The Uses of Articles.

331. Origin and Character of the Articles.—The articles are adjectives, and not a separate part of speech. This is proved by their origin.

In Old English the Nom. masculine and feminine singular of the demonstrative adjective (which was chiefly used as a definite article) was derived from a base *sa ;* but the Nom. neuter singular, and all the other cases, whether singular or plural, in all genders were formed from a base *tha.* Out of this base " *tha* " was formed the indeclinable A.S. relative *the*, which in course of time took the place of the A.S. def. article, and has remained the Def. article ever since.

The Indefinite article comes from A.S. *án* (one), a Numeral adjective, that was declined throughout the Singular in all genders. In the Middle period of English *án* was differentiated into a regular Indefinite article by the loss of its accent and consequent shortening of the vowel. Thus *án* becomes *an*, as in Modern English ; while the numeral *án* took the form of *ón*, which in Modern English is *one*. *A* is merely an abridgment of *an*.

Note.—It is therefore opposed to history as well as to reason to consider the Articles to be a distinct part of speech. It is opposed to reason, because whenever they are used they discharge, as their origin would imply, the function of Adjectives in limiting or defining the application of a noun. The universality of their use gives them an exceptional character, which distinguishes them from ordinary Adjectives ; but this does not make them distinct parts of speech.

332. Uses of Articles.—These are exemplified as follows :—

(*a*) If we wish to *particularise* the noun, we use the *Definite* article for either number :—

> Let us go and bathe in *the* river (that is, the river near our house, or the river where we usually bathe).
> This settles *the* matter (that is, the matter in which we are engaged).

(*b*) If we wish to *generalise* the noun, we use the *Indefinite* article for the Singular and none for the Plural :—

> *A* tiger is a fierce animal (that is, any tiger ; or tigers generally).
> Cats are not so faithful as dogs.

Note.—Since " *a* " has arisen from " *one* " it is still sometimes used in the sense of " one."

> *A* stitch (=one stitch) in time saves nine.
> Two of *a* trade (=of the same trade) should live apart.

333. An article is not used with a Proper, Material, or Abstract noun, except to make it a Common noun:—

> He is *the Nestor* (=the oldest man) of the service.—*Proper.*
> Sugar-cane is one of *the grasses* (=kinds of grass).—*Material.*
> He is *a justice* of the peace.—*Abstract.*

Note 1.—" The " may, however, be placed before an Abstract noun, to show the particular connection in which the quality named by the noun stands :—

> *The injustice* of the world.   *The shortness* of life.   *The love* of money.

Note 2.—The Definite article is placed before (1) names of rivers, as *the Thames;* (2) mountain-ranges, as *the Alps;* (3) groups of islands, as *the Hebrides.* Before other geographical Proper names the article is not used. The use of the article is a French idiom, not native English.

334. " *The* " is sometimes used to indicate a *class* or *kind.* This idiom, like the preceding, is not of native, but of French, origin.

> *The lion* is a noble beast =
> *A lion* is a noble beast =
> *Lions* are noble beasts.

335. When " *the* " is placed before a *Common* noun, it sometimes gives it the meaning of an *Abstract* noun :—

He felt *the patriot* (the patriotic spirit or feeling) rise within his breast.
He acted *the lord* (the lordly character) wherever he went.

336. Omission of Article.—There are some stock phrases
in which no article is used :—

strike root	take breath	in fact	on demand
leave school	follow suit	at school	for love
give ear	do penance	in bed	for money
send word	by land	by day	at anchor
set foot	by water	by night	at ease
shake hands	at sea	in debt	at sight
keep house	on board ship	in trouble	at interest
give battle	at home	at daybreak	at dinner
give place	under ground	at sunset	in hand
cast anchor	in jail	at fault	on earth
set sail	out of doors	in court	over head and
catch fire	by name	in demand	ears

Compare *to-day*, *in-deed*, etc., where the words are fused into one.

The article can also be omitted in such colloquialisms as " Father
has gone out," when the Common noun denotes a well-known
individual, and is used as a Proper noun.   See § 32, *Note 3.*

SECTION 3.—ADJECTIVES USED AS NOUNS.

337. The change from Adjective to Noun is complete, when
the word can be used in the Plural number or in the Genitive
case.   The change is complete, because Adjectives as such have
neither case nor number.

> *Nobles* = noble men or noblemen.
> A *noble's* house = a nobleman's house.
> I have told you many *secrets* = secret things.

Note.—In using a Proper adjective to denote some language, no
article is placed before it, and no noun is expressed:—

> The grammar of *English* is simpler than that of *Greek*.

338. Some adjectives are used as nouns in the Singular only,
some in the Plural only, and some in both :—

(a) *Singular only* :—

Our all.   The whole.   Our best.   Our worst.   Much (as, Much has
been done).   More (as, More has been done).   Little (as, Little
has been done).   Less (as, Less has been done).

But we say, " If equals be added to equals, the *wholes* are equal."

(b) *Plural only* :—

Morals.   Movables.   Eatables.   Drinkables.   Valuables.   Greens
(= green vegetables).   Sweets and bitters (= the sweet and
bitter contingencies of life).   Our betters (= men better than our-
selves).   The ancients.   The moderns.   The Commons.   The actuals.

Note.—" These presents " (that is, *present letters*, *literæ præsentes*,
the present writing) is a legal term borrowed from French.   " News "

wa3 formed on the analogy of Fr. *nouvelles*, plural of Old Fr. *novel*, adj. new. "Means" is plural of the adj. "mean" used as a noun.[1]

(c) *Singular and Plural :—*

A secret; secrets. A liquid; liquids. A solid; solids. A total; totals. A capital; capitals. An elder; elders. A senior; seniors. A junior; juniors. A native; natives. A mortal; mortals. An inferior; inferiors. A superior; superiors. A criminal; criminals. Another; others. A divine (theological teacher); divines. An equal; equals. The opposite; opposites. A particular; particulars. The contrary; contraries.

339. Participles (which, in fact, are Verbal adjectives, see § 17), are sometimes used as Plural nouns :—as, *bygones*.

In Old English, nouns, whose origin was traceable to Pres. participles, were not uncommon :—

> *Feó-nd* (=fiend): akin to Pres. part. of *feón* (to hate).
> *Freó-nd* (=friend): akin to Pres. part. of *freón* (to love).

340. There are certain phrases in which adjectives go in pairs, some noun being understood after them :—

> *From bad to worse*=from a bad state to a worse one.
> *The long and short*=the sum and substance of the matter.
> *In black and white*=written with black ink on white paper.
> *Through thick and thin*=through thick or difficult obstacles and through thin or easy ones. (This occurs in Chaucer.)
> *From first to last*=from the beginning to the end.
> *At sixes and sevens*=in a state of disorder.
> *High and low*=in high places and low ones, everywhere, up and down.
> *Right or wrong*=whether the act is right or not.
> *For better, for worse*=for any good or evil that may happen.
> *Fast and loose*=with a tight or loose hold, as he may prefer; that is, at random, recklessly.
> *Black and blue.* "He beat them black and blue" (so as to bring out black and blue marks on the skin).
> *Right and left.* "He struck out right and left" (to this side and that side).
> *Slow and steady.* "Slow and steady (patient and steady progress) wins the race."
> *For good, for good and all*=finally, permanently; for all future contingencies, good or evil.

341. Adjectives preceded by "the."—When an adjective is preceded by the Definite article, it can be used as a Noun in the three senses shown below :—

(1) As a Common noun (*Plural*) denoting *Persons* :—

---

[1] "Mean" in the sense of "intermediate" is from Anglo-French *meien*, Late Lat. *medianus*. "Mean" in the sense of "common" is from Anglo-Saxon *ge-mǽne*. The plural *means* is from the former.

None but *the brave* (=those men who are brave) deserves the fair.
To *the pure* (=those persons who are pure) all things are pure.

Note.—In earlier English this construction was common in a *Singular* sense also, and the article was sometimes omitted :—

For he nought helpeth *needful* in *his* neede.—CHAUCER.

(2) As an Abstract noun (*Singular*) :—

The good = that quality which is good, = goodness in general.
The beautiful = that quality which is beautiful, = beauty in general.
All the motions of his nature were towards *the true, the natural, the sweet, the gentle.*—DE QUINCEY.

(3) As a name for some particular part of a thing :—

The white (=the white part) of the eye.
The vitals (=the most vital parts) of the body.
The thick (=the thickest parts) of the forest.
The wilds (=the wild parts) of a country.
The interior (=the inside parts) of a house.
The exterior (=the outside parts) of a house.
The middle (=the middle part) of a river.
The small (=the smallest part) of the back.

342. In poetry, adjectives are sometimes used as nouns, without having an article placed before them :—

Fair is foul, and *foul* is fair.—SHAKSPEARE.
O'er *rough* and *smooth* she trips along.—WORDSWORTH.
And fold me in the riches of thy *fair.*—GREEN.
And sudden *pale* usurps her cheeks.—SHAKSPEARE.
Say what you can. my *false* o'erweighs your *true.*—SHAKSPEARE.
My *earthly* by his *heavenly* overpowered.—MILTON.
From *grave* to *gay*, from *lively* to *severe.*—POPE.

343. There are several adverbial phrases, made up of a preposition and an adjective, in which some noun is understood after the adjective :—

Extent.—On the whole, in the main, in general, in particular, at the full or in full, at all, not at all, at most, at large, in short, a little.

Time.—At last, at the latest, at first, at the first, to the last, at present, for the present, in the past, in future, for the future. once for all, before long, for long.

Place.—On the right (hand), on the left (hand), on high, in the open (air).

Manner.—In the right (on the true or right side of the question), in the wrong (on the wrong side of the question), in the dark, in common, on the loose.

State.—At best, for the best, at worst, on the alert.

SECTION 4.—DEGREES OF COMPARISON.

344. Positive Degree.—When two persons or things are said to be *equal* in respect of some quality, we use the *Positive*

degree with *as . . . as;* or we can use the Comparative adverb
(*less* or *more*) with "not" :—

> This boy is *as* clever *as* that.
> This boy is *no less* clever *than* that.
> That boy is *not more* clever *than* this.

345. Comparative Degree.—When *two* persons or things
are said to be *unequal* in respect of some quality, we use the
Comparative degree :—

> (*a*) This boy is more clever or cleverer *than* that.
> (*b*) This boy is *the* cleverer *of the two.*

Note 1.—Form (*a*) merely denotes *superiority.* Form (*b*) denotes the
selection of the one in preference to the other. The phrase "of the two,"
though it is implied already in the comparative, gives additional point.

Note 2.—Observe that whenever the Comparative degree is used in
the (*b*) or *selective* sense, it must be preceded by the Definite article,
as might be expected ; for the proper function of this article is to particularise or select, see § 332 (*a*).

346. Superlative Degree.—When one person or thing is
said to surpass all other persons or things of the same kind, we
use the *Superlative* degree with *the . . . of.*

> Chaucer was *the* greatest *of* all the poets of his age.

The same thing can be expressed by the Comparative degree
followed by *all others,* or *all the others :*—

> Chaucer was greater than *all the other* poets of his age.

Note 1.—Care must be taken not to omit the word *other.* To say,
"Chaucer was greater than all the poets of his age" makes nonsense :
for this can only mean that Chaucer was greater than himself.

Note 2.—Milton, by a poetical license, and in imitation of a Greek
idiom, confounds the Comp. with the Superl. in the following lines :—

> Adam, the goodliest man of men since born,
> His sons ; the fairest of her daughters, Eve.

347. Comparatives which have lost their force :—(*a*)
Latin Comparatives :—*interior, exterior, ulterior, major, minor.*
These are now never followed by "*to*" :—

> A fact of *minor* (secondary) importance.
> He had an *ulterior* (further) purpose in doing this.
> The *interior* (inside) parts of a building.

Some can be used as nouns :—

> He is a *minor* (a person under age).
> He is a *major* (in the military rank).
> The *interior* of the room was well furnished.

(*b*) English Comparatives :—*former, latter, elder, hinder, inner,
outer* or *utter, upper, nether,* and the Double Comparative *lesser.*
These are now never followed by *than :*—

The *former* and the *latter* rain.—*Old Testament.*
The *inner* meaning ; the *outer* surface.
The *upper* and the *nether* mill-stones.
He talks *utter* nonsense.

The words *elder* and *elders* can also be used as nouns, to denote some person or persons of dignified rank or age ; as "the village elders."

348. Distinctions of Meaning : between (a) *eldest* and *oldest ;* (b) *farther* and *further ;* (c) *later* and *latter ;* (d) *nearest* and *next ;* (e) *outer* and *utter ;* (f) *foremost* and *first.*

(a) { My *eldest* son died at the age of twelve.
{ He is the *oldest* of my surviving sons.

Here "eldest" means first-born, and is applied only to *persons.* "Oldest" is applied to things as well as to persons. Both denote the greatest age. "That is the *oldest* tree in the grove." In the Comparative degree the same distinction of meaning holds good ; and besides this, *older* has retained its Comparative force, while *elder* has lost it.

(b) { Liverpool is *farther* from London than Dover is.
{ The *further* end of the room. A *further* reason exists.

The word "farther" (comparative of "far") denotes a greater distance between two points. The word "further" (comparative of *fore*) has the sense of additional or more in advance.[1]

(c) { This is the *latest* news.
{ This is the *last* boy in the class.

The words "later" and "latest" denote time ; the words "latter" and "last" denote position.

(d) { This street is the *nearest* to my house.
{ This house is *next* to mine.

The word "nearest" denotes space or distance ; ("this street is at a less distance from my house than any other street"). But "next" denotes order or position ; ("no other house stands between this house and mine").

(e) The *outer* surface. An *utter* failure. An *utter* fool.

"Outer" means that which is outside ; "utter" means extreme or complete, in a bad sense.

(f) { The *first* occasion. The *first* student in the class.
{ That struck the *foremost* man in all this world.—SHAKSPEARE.

"First" is a word of much wider application than "foremost." "Foremost" means most prominent, most distinguished, most conspicuous. The quotation from Shakspeare refers to Julius Cæsar, who at the time of his murder was the most conspicuous man in the world. Both are Superlatives of "fore."

---

[1] Avoid the mistake of supposing that "further" is the Comparative of *forth.* In *far-ther* and *fur-ther* the Comparative suffix is *-ther,* as also in *o-ther.* The real Positive of "further" is *fore,* which afterwards acquired the extended form of *forth.*

CHAPTER XVI.—VERBS.

SECTION 1.—USES OF TENSES.

349. The Present (Indefinite) can be used to denote :—

(a) What is always and necessarily true :—

The sun *shines* by day and the moon by night.
Things equal to the same thing *are* equal to one another.

(b) What is habitual in life or character :—

He *keeps* his promises. He *has* good health.

(c) What is present, if this is helped by the context :—

I *understand* what you *say*.
The door *is* open : no one had shut it.

(d) What is future, if this is helped by the context :—

He *comes* (= will come) in a few days' time.
When *do* you (= will you) start for Edinburgh ?

(e) What is past, provided that the event is known to be past. (This is called the Historic or Graphic present.)

Báber *now leads* (=then led) his men through the Khyber pass, and *enters* (=entered) the plains of India.

350. The Past (Indefinite).—The special use of this tense is to state something *that was true once*, but is now past and gone. *It excludes absolutely all reference to* **present** *time*.

Vasco da Gama *was* the first man from Europe who *rounded* the Cape of Good Hope.

351. The Present Perfect.—This tense connects a *completed* event in some sense or other with *the present time*.

I *have lived* twenty years in London (that is, *I am living there still*, and I began to live there twenty years ago).
The lamp *has gone out* (that is, it has just gone out, and we are *now* left in darkness).

Note.—The Present Perfect can be used in reference to a past event, provided the state of things arising out of that event is *still present.*

The British Empire in India *has succeeded* to the Mogul.

The series of events by which the British Empire superseded the Mogul took place more than a century ago. The events are therefore long past. Yet it is quite correct to use the *Present* Perfect tense "*has* succeeded," because the state of things arising out of these past events is *still present :* the British Empire *still exists*, and pertains to *present time* no less than to past time.

352. The Past Perfect (also called the Pluperfect).—This is used whenever we wish to say that *some action had been completed before another was commenced.*

The verb expressing the *previous* action is put into the Past Perfect or Pluperfect tense. The verb expressing *the subsequent* action is put into the Past Indefinite.

(a) Previous Action.	Subsequent Action.
Past Perfect.	*Past Indefinite.*
He *had been* ill two days,	when the doctor *was sent for.*
He *had seen* many foreign cities,	before he *returned* home.

(b) Subsequent Action.	Previous Action.
Past Indefinite.	*Past Perfect.*
The boat *was sunk* by a hurricane,	which *had* suddenly sprung up.
The sheep *fled* in great haste ;	for a wolf *had entered* the field.

353. The Future Perfect.—This tense denotes the completion of some event *(a)* in *future* time, *(b)* in *past* time.[1]

(a) He *will have* reached home, before the rain sets in. (The reaching of home will be completed, before the setting in of rain commences.)

(b) You *will have* heard (must have heard in some past time) this news already ; so I need not repeat it.

354. Shall and will in Interrogative sentences :—

In Assertive sentences, *merely future time* is denoted by "shall" in the First person, and by "will" in the Second and Third ; a *command* is denoted by "shall" in the Second and Third persons ; an *intention* is denoted by "will" in the First person (see § 174).

In interrogative sentences, however, the change of situation from asserting a fact to asking a question modifies to some extent the uses of "shall" and "will." All possible meanings of "shall" and "will," when they are used interrogatively, are shown in the following examples :—

Shall I.	*(a)* *Shall I* be sixteen years old to-morrow ? (Here the "shall" merely inquires after something future.)
	(b) *Shall I* post that letter for you ? (Here the "shall" inquires about a command. Do you command or desire me to post that letter for you ?)
Will I.	(This is not used at all, because "will" in the First person would imply intention, and it would be foolish to ask another person about one's own intentions.)

---

[1] It seems like a contradiction to make a *future* tense have reference to *past* time. But the future here implies an inference regarding something which is believed to have passed rather than past time itself. "You will have heard" = I infer or believe that you have heard.

Shall you.   *Shall you* return home to-day ? (This merely inquires about something future. Here the "shall" cannot imply command, because it would be foolish to inquire of any one whether he commands himself to do so and so.)

Will you.   *Will you* do me this favour ? (Here the "will" denotes willingness or intention. Are you *willing* or do you *intend* to do me this favour ? Hence "will you" is the form used for asking a favour.)

Shall he.   *Shall he* call for the doctor ? (Here the "shall" implies a command. Do you desire or command him to call for the doctor ?)

Will he.   *Will he* be fourteen years old to-morrow ? (Here the "will" merely inquires about something future.)

Note 1.—" Will I " might be used for the moment as an answer to " will you."

Will you lend me your umbrella for a few minutes ?
Answer.—Will I? Of course I will.

Note 2.—It might be questioned whether "shall" or "will" is the more correct in the following sentences :—

> (*a*) James and I *shall* be very happy to see you.
> (*b*) James and I *will* be very happy to see you.

The "shall" is demanded by "I," and the "will" by "James." according to the rule given in § 174. Both therefore might be used, but (*b*) is the more common of the two.

All doubt could be removed by rewriting the sentences as follows:—

> James *will* be very happy to see you, and so *shall* I.
> I *shall* be very happy to see you, and so *will* James.

Rewrite the following sentences, so as to bring out the full force of " shall " and " will " :—

1. You shall not go home until you have finished your lesson. 2. Shall I send the horse at four o'clock ? 3. I will give you your pay in due course. 4. Will you assist me in this matter ? 5. Shall he carry your box for you ? 6. An idle man shall not enter my service. 7. I will not grant you a certificate. 8. Will you punish me, if I leave the room without your consent ? 9. By what time of the day shall I have your dinner ready ? 10. He shall not ride that horse, till he has acquired a better seat.

SECTION 2.—FURTHER USES OF THE INFINITIVE.

355. The two main forms {of the Infinitive are—(*a*) the Present, " to love," and (*b*) the Perfect, " to have loved."

When should the one be used, and when the other ?

356. The Present Infinitive can be used after *any and every tense* of the preceding Finite verb. In fact, the tense of the preceding verb has no effect whatever on the tense of the Infinitive following it :—

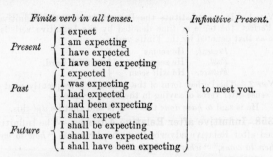

Finite verb in all tenses.   *Infinitive Present.*

Present
{ I expect
  I am expecting
  I have expected
  I have been expecting }

Past
{ I expected
  I was expecting
  I had expected
  I had been expecting }   to meet you.

Future
{ I shall expect
  I shall be expecting
  I shall have expected
  I shall have been expecting }

357. The Perfect form is used in the following ways :—

(a) After the *Past* tenses of verbs expressing wish, intention, hope, duty, etc., it shows that the wish, intention, hope, or duty *did not* (for some reason or other) *take effect :* [1]—

He wished *to have come ;*
He intended *to have come ;*   but something prevented
He hoped *to have come ;*   him from coming.
He expected *to have come ;*
He should *have come ;*   } but he neglected to do so.
He ought *to have come ;*

Note.—If we substitute the Present form of the Infinitive for the Perfect form, nothing is implied as to whether the desire. etc., was fulfilled or not :—

He wished *to come ;*
He intended *to come ;*   but whether he came or not is
He hoped *to come ;*   an open question, on which
He expected *to come ;*   the form of the Infinitive
He should *come ;*   throws no light.
He ought *to come ;*

(b) After verbs of seeming, appearing, etc., the Perfect form shows that the event denoted by the Infinitive took place at some time *previous* to that denoted by the Finite verb :—

Present. He seems
Past. He seemed   } to have worked hard (that is, at
Future. He will seem   some previous time).

---

[1] It has been represented, and this very erroneously, that the Perfect form of the Infinitive ought not to be used. But it is sanctioned by authority as well as by idiom, and was common in Elizabethan English :—
I thought thy bride-bed *to have decked,* sweet maid.—*Hamlet,* v. 1, 268.
We retain the idiom in the very common expression :—"I would (intended to) *have done* it." This construction invariably implies that the intention was not carried out. In the quotation from *Hamlet,* "thought" means "hoped," "expected."

Note 1.—If we substitute the Present form of the Infinitive for the Perfect, the tense or time denoted by the Infinitive verb is the same as that denoted by the Finite verb.

Present.	He seems	
Past.	He seemed	to work hard.
Future.	He will seem	

Note 2.—The Perfect form of the Infinitive is frequently used in a *past* sense after verbs of saying in the Passive voice :—

He is said *to have done* this = It is said that he *did* this.

358. Infinitive after Relative Adverbs.—The Infinitive is placed after Relative adverbs in such phrases as " *how to write*," " *when to come*," " *where to begin*," etc.

He did not know *how to write* (= the way to write).
He was not told *when to come* (= the time for coming).
I wish I knew *where to begin* (= the place for beginning).

Here the Relative adverb stands for the corresponding noun denoting manner, time, place, etc.

359. Infinitive after Relative Pronouns.—This occurs in such sentences as :—

(*a*) He had no money *with which to buy* food.

This is equivalent to "He had no money to buy food *with it*"; or " He had no money to buy food *with*" (§ 229).

(*b*) He is not such a fool *as to say* that.

Here the construction is elliptical. " He is not such a fool as *he would be* a fool to say (= for saying, or if he said) that."

360. For to.—At one time the Preposition " for " was often used before the Infinitive (see § 191, *d*), as in the phrase " for to see." Hence has arisen the common idiom of inserting a noun or pronoun between the preposition and the Infinitive.

There was too much noise *for any one to hear*.
The railway is the quickest way *for men or goods to be conveyed* from place to place.

SECTION 3.—SEQUENCE OF TENSES.

361. When two clauses are joined together by some Subordinating conjunction, or by some Relative (or Interrogative) pronoun or adverb, one of them is called the **Main** and the other the **Subordinate** clause (§ 234 and § 255) :—

Main.	*Subordinate.*
I will let you know	*when* I shall start.

362. There are two main rules about the Sequence of Tenses, and all special rules centre round these two.

RULE I.—*If there is a* **Past** *tense in the main clause, it must be followed by a* **Past** *tense in the subordinate clause* :—

Main Clause. (*Past Tense.*)	*Subordinate Clause.* (*Past Tense.*)
It *was* settled,	that I *should* do this.
He *would* come,	if you *wished* it.
He *was* honest,	although he *was* poor.
He *asked* me,	whether I *had seen* his dog.
He *was* informed,	that I *had been helping* him.
We never *understood*,	how or why he *did* that.
He *did* not leave off,	till he *had succeeded*.
I *was* inquiring,	what you *had heard*.
He *succeeded*,	because he *worked* hard.
He *remained* silent,	as soon as he *heard* that.
I *would* do this,	if I *were* allowed.
He *walked* so far,	that he *tired* himself.

RULE II.—*If there is a* **Present** *or* **Future** *tense in the main clause, it can be followed by* **any tense whatever** *in the subordinate clause.*

Examples of Rule II.

Present or *Future.*	that he reads a book. that he is reading. that he has read. that he has been reading.	*Any tense whatever.* The four forms of the Present tense.
I know or I shall know	that he will read. that he will be reading. that he will have read. that he will have been reading.	The four forms of the Future tense.
	that he read. that he was reading. that he had read. that he had been reading.	The four forms of the Past tense.

363. Exception to Rule I.—There is one exception to Rule I. The **Past** tense in the main clause can be followed by a **Present Indefinite** in the subordinate clause, to express some *universal* or *habitual* fact :—

Main Clause. (*Past Tense.*)	*Subordinate Clause.* (*Present Tense.*)
They *learnt* at school,	that honesty *is* the best policy.
The students *were* taught,	that the earth *moves* round the sun.
His illness *showed* him,	that all men *are* mortal.
He *was* glad to hear,	that his brother *is* industrious.
They *were* sorry to hear,	that he *has* a bad temper.

364. Conjunctions of Purpose.—When the subordinate clause is introduced by a Conjunction of *purpose* (§ 238, *d*), the two following rules must be observed :—

(*a*) If the verb in the Main clause is in the **Present** or **Future** tense, the verb in the Subordinate clause must be expressed by "may" (**Present** tense).

(*b*) If the verb in the Main clause is in the **Past** tense, the verb in the Subordinate clause must (in accordance with Rule I.) be expressed by "might" (**Past** tense).

		Main Clause.	*Subordinate Clause.*
Present	*Indef.*	He comes,	*Present tense.*
	Contin.	He is coming,	that he *may*
	Perfect	He has come,	see me.
	Perf. Cont.	He has been coming,	
Future	*Indef.*	He will come,	
	Contin.	He will be coming,	that he *may*
	Perfect	He will have come,	see me.
	Perf. Cont.	He will have been coming,	
Past	*Indef.*	He came,	*Past tense.*
	Contin.	He was coming,	that he *might*
	Perfect	He had come,	see me.
	Perf. Cont.	He had been coming,	

Note.—The word "lest" = "that not." The *only* Auxiliary verb that can be used after "lest" is *should*, whatever may be the tense of the verb in the principal sentence :—

	Main Clause.	*Subordinate Clause.*
Present . .	He goes,	lest he *should* see me.
		or that he *may* not see me.
Future . .	He will go,	lest he *should* see me.
		or that he *may* not see me.
Past . . .	He went,	lest he *should* see me.
		or that he *might* not see me.

365. Conjunctions of Comparison.—When the dependent sentence is introduced by some Conjunction of Comparison, Rule I. has no existence whatever. *Any tense can be followed by any tense.*

Main Clause.	*Subordinate Clause.*
He *likes* you better,	than he *liked* me.
He *liked* you better,	than he *likes* me.
He *will like* you better,	than he *has liked* me.
He *has liked* you better,	than he *liked* me.
He *liked* you better,	than he *is liking* me.
He *will like* you better,	than he *was liking* me, etc.

Note 1.—If the comparison is expressed by "as well as" instead of "than," the same rule holds good. Any tense may be followed by any tense, according to the sense intended by the speaker.

He *likes* you as well as he *liked* me.

He *will like* you as well as he *has liked* me, etc.

Note 2.—If no verb is expressed after "*than*" or after "*as well as,*" the tense of the verb *understood* in the subordinate clause is the same as that of the verb *expressed* in the main clause.

> He *liked* you better than (*he liked*) me.
> He *will like* you as well as (*he will like*) me.

CHAPTER XVII.—ADVERBS.

SECTION 1.—POSITION OF ADVERBS.

366. If the word to be qualified is an Adjective, or an Adverb, or a Preposition, or a Conjunction, the qualifying Adverb is placed immediately *before it*.

Adjective or *Participle*	We are *half* pleased and *half* sorry. The orange you brought was *quite* ripe. Your pay is *too* high for your work.
Adverb	A snake creeps *very* silently. He stood *far* apart from me. He seized my hand *rather* eagerly.
Preposition	He arrived *long* before the time. We sat *almost* in the shade. He stood *exactly* behind me.
Conjunction	Tell me *precisely* how it happened. I like an orange *only* when it is ripe. He did this *merely* because he was ordered.

Note.—There is one exception to the above rule. The word "enough" (when it is an Adverb and not an Adjective) is placed *after* the word it qualifies :—

> He spoke highly *enough* of what you had done.

367 (*a*). If the verb to be qualified is used *Intransitively*, the qualifying Adverb is placed immediately *after* it :—

> He lived *well* and died *happily*.
> He laughed *heartily* at that joke.
> He spoke *foolishly* about his own merits.

Note.—To this rule there are eight or nine exceptions :—

The Adverbs *always, never, scarcely ever, often, sometimes, generally, usually, rarely,* and *seldom* are usually placed *before*, and not *after*, the verb they qualify.

> He *always* laughed at a good joke.
> He *never* spoke about his own merits.
> He *often* came here to see me.
> He *sometimes* slept in my house.
> He *seldom* stayed with me for long.

But they are usually placed after the verb "to be" :—

> He is *seldom* absent.   He is *always* attentive.

(*b*) If the verb to be qualified is used *Transitively*, the qualifying Adverb must not be allowed to separate the verb and its object.

The Adverb must therefore be placed either *before the verb* or *after the object ;* but it is more commonly placed after the object :—

> He bore his losses *cheerfully.*
> He *briefly* explained his meaning.

Sometimes, however, if the object is qualified by a clause, or consists of a good many words, the adverb may come between the verb and its object :—

> He rewarded *liberally* all those who had served him well.

But this is scarcely so idiomatic as, " He liberally rewarded," etc.

368. If the tense of the verb is formed by an Auxiliary verb, the adverb is generally placed *between* the Auxiliary verb and the Principal verb : the latter may be either Trans. or Intrans. :—

> The wind has *suddenly* risen.   Your son will *soon* return.
> I have *quite* understood you.   He is *almost* dying, I fear.
> We have *not* seen him since Monday last.   (*Neg. Adverb.*)

Note.—This, however, does not justify the "split infinitive," the practice, now quite common, of inserting an adverb between "*to*" and the verb following :—

> It is my duty to *plainly* tell you, etc.

369. An Adverb is placed first in a sentence—(*a*) when it is intended to qualify *the whole sentence*, (*b*) when it is used *very emphatically*.

> (*a*) *Luckily* no one was inside, when the roof fell in.
> (*b*) *Down* went the Royal George with all her crew complete.
> COWPER.

The meaning of the two sentences given below depends entirely on the position of the adverb :—

> (1) *Happily* he did not die.
> (2) He did not die *happily.*

In (1) the adverb qualifies the entire sentence, because it stands first (as just explained). In (2) it qualifies the Intransitive verb "die," because it is placed immediately after it ; see § 367. So (1) means, " It was a happy result that he did not die " ; and (2) means, "He did not die a happy death."

370. Only.—The meaning of a sentence depends upon the position of this word, which may be either an Adj. or an Adv. :—

> (*a*) *Only* he promised to read the first chapter of that book.

Here "only" is an Adjective, qualifying the pronoun "he."

He alone, and no one else, promised to read the first chapter, etc.

> (*b*) He *only* promised to read the first chapter of that book.

Here "only" is an Adverb qualifying the verb "promised" ; and the meaning is that he merely or only promised, but did not perform the promise.

(c) He promised *only* to read the first chapter of that book.

That is, he did not promise to study, analyse, or remember, but *only to read.* Here "only" is an Adverb qualifying the word "read."

(d) He promised to read *only* the first chapter of that book.

That is, he promised to read nothing more than the *first* chapter. Here "only" is an Adverb qualifying the adjective "the first."

(e) He promised to read the first chapter of that book *only* (or, *only* of that book).

That is, he promised to read the first chapter of no book except that. Here "only" is an Adverb qualifying the phrase "of that book."

Section 2.—Adverbs qualifying Prepositions.

371. A few more examples are here given of Adverbs qualifying prepositions, as the point stated in § 216 (a) has hardly yet been sufficiently recognised by grammarians :—

A little.

We have gone *a little beyond* a mile.
The crow flew *a little above* his head.
He is *a little under* fourteen years of age.

Almost.

A sword was hanging *almost over* his head.
It fell *almost on* his head.

Along.

He *along with* his friend called on me to-day.
It was *all along of* (entirely owing to) your idleness that you were plucked. (Here the adverb "all" qualifies the prepositional phrase "along of." The phrase is colloquial and rather vulgar.)

All.

His horse sprang forward *all of* a sudden.
I have looked *all through* that book.
Your efforts were *all to* no purpose.
Such conduct is *all of* a piece (thoroughly consistent) with his character.

Altogether.

He married *altogether below* his station.

Apart.

Apart from his imprudence (without taking his imprudence into account), he has been very unfortunate.

Away.

He is never happy, *away from* home.

Close.

He is *close upon* fourteen (very nearly fourteen) years of age.
He came and sat *close beside* me.

Decidedly.

Your son's industry is *decidedly above* the average.

Distinctly.

His abilities are *distinctly above* the average.

Down.

They lived *down in* a valley.
They made him pay his debt *down to* the last farthing.

Entirely.

It was *entirely through* your neglect that we were late.
He took his hat *entirely off* his head.

Exactly.

The house stands *exactly on* the top of the hill.
Every word was copied out *exactly to* the letter.
Your quarters are *exactly under* mine.

Far.

Your work is *far below* the proper mark.
My house stands *far beyond* the river.
Far from despising that man, I greatly respect him.

Greatly.

Greatly to his credit, he came out first.

Hard.

The cottage stood *hard by* the river.

Half.

By this time we had sailed *half across* the Atlantic.

Immediately.

He went to bed *immediately after* his arrival.
Immediately on his beginning to speak, every one was silent.

Long.

He arrived *long after* twelve o'clock.

Much.

His work is *much below* the mark.
Much to his surprise he was plucked.

Out.

That was all done *out of* envy.
I am *out of* patience with that man.

Partly.

He wept *partly through* sorrow, and *partly through* anger.
The fog is *partly above* and *partly below* us.

Precisely.

It was *precisely on* that point that we differed.
He arrived *precisely at* four o'clock.

Quite.

We walked *quite through* that forest (through its entire breadth).
He held his head *quite below* the water.
I am *quite of* the same opinion as yourself.

Right.

He was leaning *right against* the wall.
The sun was *right above* our heads.

Shortly.

He reached home *shortly before* four o'clock.

Soon.

I managed to get back *soon after* six.

Up.

Your work is not *up to* date.

Well.

I am sure I am *well within* the mark.

Together.

He *together with* his accomplice has cheated me.

CHAPTER XVIII.—PREPOSITIONS.

372. Relations denoted by Prepositions.—The more important are shown in the following list :—

(1) " **Of** " **in the sense of Apposition** ; see § 304, (3). This can be traced back as far as the fifteenth century :—

He was a ryght good knight *of a yonge man.*

MALORY (15th cent.).

There was in the castell a vii score prisoners *of Frenchmen.*

BERNERS (16th cent.).

The frail sepulchre *of our flesh.*—SHAKSPEARE.

Compare the modern phrases "a fool *of a man*" ; "the two *of us*" (=we two) ; " he made an ass *of himself*" ; "he made a great success *of it*" (=made it a great success) ; "the sum *of 40 pounds.*"

The use of "*of*" in an appositional sense is common before Proper names :—

The island *of* Ceylon.   The province *of* Ulster.   The city *of* Paris. The continent *of* Asia.   The county *of* Kent.   The lake *of* Geneva.   The title *of* colonel.   The name *of* Brighton.

On the other hand, we cannot place "*of*" before the Proper names of rivers, mountains, or capes.   Thus we cannot say "the river *of* Thames" ; "the mountain *of* Blanc" ; "the Cape *of* St. Vincent."

(2) **Against** : denotes opposition of place or aim, comparison or contrast, and provision to meet some expected event :—

1. He is leaning *against* the wall   .   *Place.*
2. He is acting *against* my interests   .   *Aim.*
3. Four boys left this term *against* three last term   .   .   .   .   *Comparison.*
4. Be ready *against* the day of battle   .   *Provision for.*

The conjunctional use of *against* has become a vulgarism :—

I shall have everything ready *against* you come.

(3) **At** : denotes proximity, with actual or intended contact ; hence proximity of value, valuation ; direction, consequence, dependence :—

1. He is not *at* home just now	.	*Place.*
2. He was there *at* four o'clock	.	*Time.*
3. He is now quite *at* his ease	.	*State.*
4. *At* what price is this sold ?	.	*Valuation.*
5. He laughed *at* me. Take a shot *at* it		*Direction.*
6. He plays well *at* cricket .	.	*Action.*
7. Stand up *at* the word of command	.	*Time and consequence.*
8. He remains here *at* my pleasure	.	*Dependence.*

(4) **By** : denotes originally nearness of place ; hence time, agency, instrumentality, manner, amount, adjuration :—

1. Come and sit *by* me	.	*Proximity in place.*
2. Always get up *by* sunrise	.	*Proximity in time.*
3. ⎰ He did his duty *by* his children ⎱ ⎱ Do to others as you would be done *by* ⎰		*About, towards.*
4. He was fairly treated *by* me	.	*Agency.*
5. Seize him *by* the neck	.	*Instrumentality.*
6. Cleverer than you *by* a good deal	.	*Amount.*
7. They sell corn *by* the bushel	.	*Unit of measurement.*
8. He swore *by* heaven	.	*Adjuration.*

Note.—Such a phrase as occurs in, "He went away *by* himself," is an example of (7), and means "He went away *alone,* himself at a time." The phrase "He came *by* a large fortune" is an example of (1) : "He came into the possession of," etc.

(5) **For** : its chief uses are shown below :—

1. He will soon start *for* home	.	*Direction in space.*
2. He was imprisoned *for* life	.	*Direction in time.*
3. *For* what offence was he imprisoned ?		*Cause or reason.*
4. *For* all his learning, he has no sense		*In spite of.*
5. He sold his horse *for* a small sum	.	*Exchange.*
6. He fought hard *for* his friends	.	*On behalf of.*
7. Do not translate word *for* word	.	*Conformity.*
8. This stuff is not fit *for* food	.	*Purpose.*

(6) **Of** : its main sense is " proceeding from," or " pertaining to " ; its detailed uses are shown below :—

1. What did he die *of* ?	.	*Cause.*
2. *Of* what family is he sprung ?	.	*Source.*
3. He was despised and rejected *of* men		*Agency* (rare).
4. He was deprived *of* his appointment		*Separation.*
5. He is a man *of* strong will	.	*Quality.*
6. He sent me a box *of* books	.	*Contents.*
7. This box is made *of* leather	.	*Material.*
8. He lived in the house *of* his father	.	*Possession.*

9.	He received the sum *of* 100 rupees .	*Apposition.*
10.	What are you thinking *of* . .	*Concerning.*
11.	The horse is lame *of* one leg . .	*Point of reference.*
12.	He gave us *of* his best . . .	*Partition.*
13.	The love *of* parents (parents' love for child)	*Subject.*
14.	The love *of* parents (child's love for parents)	*Object.*
15.	He used to come here *of* an evening	*Time.*

(7) **With** : denotes " by," " near," " among "; also " against," as in Anglo-Saxon.   Its uses are enumerated below :—

1.	He lives *with* his mother . .	*Union in place.*
2.	Frogs begin to croak *with* the rainfall	*Union in time.*
3.	His views do not accord *with* mine .	*Agreement.*
4.	One king fought *with* another .	*Opposition.*
5.	I parted *with* my friend yesterday .	*Separation.*
6.	He is not popular *with* his pupils .	*Point of reference.*
7.	*With* all his wealth he is discontented	*In spite of.*
8.	He killed the snake *with* a stone .	*Instrument.*
9.	He looked upon them *with* anger .	*Manner.*

(8) **On** or **upon** : the main sense is " rest on the outside side of a thing " :—

1.	I place my hand *on* the table . .	*Place.*
2.	I came here *on* Saturday last . .	*Time.*
3.	He lives *on* his father . . .	*Dependence.*
4.	He was appointed *on* these terms .	*Condition or basis.*
5.	They made an attack *on* my house .	*Direction.*
6.	He spoke for over an hour *on* that subject	*Concerning.*

(9) **To** : literally motion towards anything ; hence purpose, limit, etc. :—

1.	He has returned *to* his father's house	*Place.*
2.	You must go back *to*-night .	*Time.*
3.	*To* all appearances he is tired .	*Adaptation.*
4.	The chances are three *to* one .	*Proportion.*
5.	They fought *to* the last man .	*Limit.*
6.	*To* their utter disgust they were beaten	*Effect.*
7.	{ They will come *to* dinner . } { He came *to* see us (Gerund. Infin.) }	*Purpose.*

Note.—The prep. " *to* " is often used as an alternative to " *of* " in such sentences as, " He is a cousin *to* me," for " He is a cousin *of* mine."

(10) **From** : literally motion or rest apart from anything :—

1.	He had gone *from* home . .	*Space.*
2.	You must begin *from* daybreak .	*Time.*
3.	He is sprung *from* noble ancestors .	*Descent.*
4.	*From* all we hear he is mad . .	*Inference.*

    5. This was done *from* spite   .   .   *Motive*.
    6. A wise man is easily known *from* a
        fool   .   .   .   .   .   *Discrimination*.

373. Prepositions compared.—The following peculiarities
should be noted :—

    (*a*) **At, in.**—"*At*" relates to a *small* extent of space or time ;
"*in*" to a *wider* extent :—

        He will start *at* six o'clock *in* the morning.
        The end is *at* hand (=very close).
        The work is *in* hand (=in a state of progress).

    (*b*) **With, by.**—"*With*" relates to the instrument employed
for doing anything ; "*by*" to the agent or doer :—

        This book was written *by* me *with* a quill pen.

    (*c*) **Between, among.**—The first (A.S. *be-twéon-um*, in pairs)
denotes "in the middle of two" ; the second (A.S. *on mang*, in a
mixture or crowd) "in the middle of more than two" :—

        Those two men quarrelled *between* themselves.
        Those three men quarrelled *among* themselves.

    (*d*) **Beside, besides.**—The former means *by the side of*, and
hence sometimes *outside of*. The latter means *in addition to* :—

    He came and sat *beside* me (=by my side).
    Your answer is *beside* (=outside of, irrelevant to) the question.
    Besides (=in addition to) advising he gave them some money.

    (*e*) **By, since, before.**—These are all used for a *point* of time,
—not for a *period* or *space* of time :—

        You must be back *by* four o'clock.
        He has been here *since* four o'clock.
        He did not get back *before* four o'clock.

    (*f*) **In, into.**—The preposition "*in*" denotes position or
rest inside anything ; while "*into*" denotes motion towards the
inside of anything :—

        The frog is *in* the well. (*Rest.*)
        The frog fell *into* the well. (*Motion.*)

    (*g*) **In, within.**—"*In*" denotes the close of some period ;
"*within*" denotes some time *short of the close* :—

        He will return *in* (=at the close of) a week's time.
        He will return *within* (=in less than) a week's time.

    (*h*) **Since, from.**—Both of these denote a *point* of time, not
a space or period. But "since" is preceded by a verb in some
Perfect tense, and "from" by a verb in some Indefinite tense.
Another difference is that "since" can be used only in reference
to *past* time, whereas "from" is used for *present* and *future*
time as well as for past :—

He *has been* ill *since* Thursday last.

{ He *begins* work *from* six o'clock daily. (*Present*.)
{ He *began* work from six o'clock in the morning. (*Past*.)
{ He *will begin* work *from* to-morrow. (*Future*.)

(*i*) **Before, for.**—"For" is used with *negative* sentences, to denote a *space* of *future* time.

"Before" is used in negative and affirmative sentences alike, to denote a *point* of *future* time.

{ The sun will *not* rise *for* an hour.
{   (We could not say "before an hour," because "before" is
{   used for a point of time, and not for a space of time.)

{ The sun will rise (*affirmative*) }
{ The sun will not rise (*negative*) } *before* six o'clock.

Insert appropriate prepositions in the places left blank :—

1. I was brought up —— Italy —— Rome. 2. The moon rose —— twelve o'clock —— the night. 3. We knew him —— a glance as soon as he came —— sight. 4. He lives —— Tonbridge —— the county of Kent. 5. The boat was tied to the shore —— a sailor —— a rope. 6. The field was ploughed up —— a peasant —— a pair of oxen. 7. The work must be done —— twelve o'clock. 8. You must be back —— a week from the present time. 9. No one has seen him —— Thursday last. 10. I have not seen him —— his last birthday. 11. He will not get home —— sunset. 12. I shall be ready to start —— two or three hours. 13. Take care to be back —— mid-day. 14. I shall not be back —— the end of the week. 15. He has been absent from home —— Friday last, and I do not think he will return —— the 30th of next month. 16. Let me see you again —— an hour's time. 17. I shall have completed my task —— to-morrow evening. 18. The train will start —— forty minutes from now. 19. I have lived —— London —— 1st March. 20. I do not expect that he will be here —— a week, and I am certain that he will not be here —— sunset to-day.

(*j*) **Participial prepositions.**—In addition to the simpler prepositions described already, there are some of participial or adjectival origin, which were once used absolutely :—

He went *past* the house (the house having been past).
All *except* two (two being excepted).
During two weeks (two weeks (en)during or continuing).
All *save* three (three being safe, saved, or reserved).
Notwithstanding his age (his age not-withstanding or not pre-
    venting).

There are other prepositions that have come from participles in the present tense used as Impersonal Absolutes ; see § 284 (*b*), Note 2.

Regarding this matter, what is your opinion ?
Considering his age, he has done well.

Compare *touching, owing to, concerning, respecting*, etc.

374. Words followed by Prepositions.—Particular words are followed by particular prepositions, although there may be several other prepositions that have the same meaning. This is purely a matter of idiom. For instance, out of the numerous prepositions or prepositional phrases signifying cause, the verb "die" has somehow or other selected "of" for denoting the illness which was the cause of death, and declines to be followed by any other. Thus we say, "He died *of* fever." We do not say, "He died *through* fever, or *by* fever, or *owing to* fever, or *on account* of fever, or *with* fever." Yet in other connections all of these prepositions may be used to denote cause.

Again, though we always say "die *of* fever," we never say "sick *of* fever," but always "sick *with* fever," where "with" and "of" are both used in the sense of cause.

(a) Nouns followed by Prepositions.

Abatement *of* the fever.
    ,,   *from* the price asked.
Admission *to* a person.
    ,,   *into* a place.
(To take) advantage *of* some one's mistake.
(To gain) an advantage *over* some one.
(To have) the advantage *of* a man.
Analogy *of* one thing *with* another.
    ,,   *between* two things.
Antidote *to* some poison.
    ,,   *against* infection.
Antipathy *to* some animal or some taste.
Arrival *at* a place.
    ,,   *in* a country.
Attendance *on* a person.
    ,,   *at* a place.
Authority *over* a person.
    ,,   *on* a subject.
    ,,   *for* saying or doing.
Aversion *to* a person or thing.

Beneficence *to* the poor.
Benevolence *towards* the poor.

Charge *of* murder (*noun*).
    ,,   *with* murder (*verb*).
Claim *on* or *against* some one.
    ,,   *to* something.
Connivance *at* any one's faults.

Contemporary (*noun*) *of* some one.
    ,,   (*adj.*) *with* some one.
(A) contrast *to* a person or thing.
(In) contrast *with* a person or thing.
Contribution *to* a fund.
    ,,   *towards* some project.

Decision *on* some case.
    ,,   *of* some dispute.
Disagreement *with* a person.
Disgust *at* meanness.
Dislike *to* or *for* a person or thing.
Distrust *of* a person or thing.
    ,,   *in* a person or thing.
Doubt *of* or *about* a thing.

Encroachment *on* one's rights.
Endeavour *after* happiness.
Envy *of* or *at* another's success.
Evasion *of* a rule.
Exception *to* a rule.
(Make) an exception *of* some person or thing.
Experience *of* a thing.
    ,,   *in* doing something.

Failure *of* a plan.
    ,,   *of* a person *in* something.

(Has) a genius *for* mathematics.
(Is) a genius *in* mathematics.
Glance *at* a person or thing.

Glance *over* a wide surface.
Gratitude *for* a thing.
　　,,　*to* a person.

Hatred *of* or *for* a person.
　,,　*of* a thing.

Imputation *of* guilt.
　　,,　*against* some one.
Influence *over* or *with* a person.
　　,,　*on* a man's action.
Innovation *upon* former practice.
Interest *in* a subject.
　　,,　*with* a person.

Jest *at* a man's bad luck.
Joy *in* his good luck.
Justification *of* or *for* crime.

Key *to* a mystery.

Libel *on* a person.
　,,　*against* his character.
Likeness *to* a person or thing.
Liking *for* a person or thing.
Longing *for* or *after* a thing.

Match *for* a person.

Need *for* assistance.
(In) need *of* assistance.
Neglect *of* duty.
　　,,　*in* doing a thing.

Offence *against* morality.
　　,,　*at* something done.

Parody *on* or *of* a poem.
Popularity *with* neighbours.
Premium *on* gold.
Pride *in* his wealth (*noun*).
Prides himself *on* his wealth (*verb*).

Proof *of* guilt.
　　,,　*against* temptation.
(In) pursuance *of* an object.

Quarrel *with* another person.
　　,,　*between* two persons.

Readiness *at* figures.
　　,,　*in* answering.
　　,,　*for* a journey.
Reflections *on* a man's honesty.
Regard *for* a man's feelings.
(In) regard *to* that matter.
Relevancy *to* a question.
Reputation *for* honesty.
(In) respect *of* some quality.
(With) respect (*to*) a matter.
Rupture *with* a friend.
　　,,　*between* two persons.

Search *for* or *after* wealth.
(In) search *of* wealth.
(A) slave *to* avarice.
(The) slave *of* avarice.
Sneer *at* good men.
Stain *on* one's character.
Subsistence *on* rice.

Taste (experience) *of* hard work.
　　,,　(liking) *for* hard work.

Umbrage *at* his behaviour.
(We have no) use *for* that.
(What is the) use *of* that?
(There is no) use *in* that.

(At) variance *with* a person.
(A) victim *to* oppression.
(The) victim *of* oppression.

Witness *of* or *to* an event.

(b) *Adjectives and Participles followed by Prepositions.*

Abhorrent *to* his feelings.
Abounding *in* or *with* fish.
Accompanied *with* his luggage.
　　,,　*by* his dog.
Accountable *to* a person.
　　,,　*for* a thing.
Adapted *to* his tastes.
　,,　*for* an occupation.

Aggravated *at* a thing.
　　,,　*with* a person.
Alien *to* his character.
Alienated *from* a friend.
Amenable *to* reason.
Amused *at* a joke.
Angry *at* a thing.
　,,　*with* a person.

Annoyed *at* a thing.
,,   *with* a person *for* saying or doing something.
Answerable *to* a person.
,,   *for* his conduct.
Anxious *for* his safety.
,,   *about* the result.
Apprised *of* a fact.
Apt (expert) *in* mathematics.
,,   *for* a purpose.

Beholden *to* a person.
Betrayed *to* the enemy.
,,   *into* the enemy's hands.
Blessed *with* good health.
,,   *in* his children.
Blind *to* his own faults.
,,   *of* or *in* one eye.
Bound *in* honour.
,,   *by* a contract.
(Ship) bound *for* England.

Careful *of* his money.
,,   *about* his dress.
Charged *to* his account.
,,   (loaded) *with* a bullet.
,,   *with* (accused of) a crime.
Clothed *in* purple.
,,   *with* shame.
Cognisant *of* a fact.
Complaisant *to* a person.
Compliant *with* one's wishes.
Concerned *at* or *about* some mishap.
,,   *for* a person's welfare.
,,   *in* some business.
Consequent *on* some cause.
Conspicuous *for* honesty.
Contingent (conditional) *on* success.
Covetous *of* other men's goods.

Deaf *to* entreaties.
Debited *with* a sum of money.
Deficient *in* energy.
Determined *on* doing a thing.
Disappointed *of* a thing not obtained.
,,   *in* a thing obtained.
,,   *with* a person.
Disgusted *with* a thing.
,,   *at* or *with* a person.
Displeased *with* a person.

Disqualified *for* a post.
,,   *from* competing.

Eager *for* distinction.
,,   *in* the pursuit of knowledge.
Easy *of* access.
Economical *of* time.
Emulous *of* fame.
Engaged *to* some person.
,,   *in* some business.

False *of* heart.
,,   *to* his friends.
Familiar *with* a language.
,,   (well known) *to* a person.
Favourable *to* his prospects.
,,   *for* action.
Fruitful *in* resources.
Fruitless *of* results.

Glad *of* his assistance.
,,   *at* a result.
Good *for* nothing.
,,   *at* cricket.

Hardened *against* pity.
,,   *to* misfortune.

Ill *with* fever.
Impatient *of* reproof.
,,   *at* an event.
,,   *for* food.
Impervious *to* water.
Indebted *to* a person.
,,   *for* some kindness.
,,   *in* a large sum.
Indignant *at* something done.
,,   *with* a person.
Indulgent *in* wine.
,,   *to* his children.
Inspired *with* hope.
Introduced *to* a person.
,,   *into* a place.
Irrespective *of* consequences.

Jealous *of* his reputation.

Lavish *of* money.
,,   *in* his expenditure.
Liable *to* error.
,,   *for* payment.

Mad *with* disappointment.
Moved *to* tears.
  ,,   *with* pity.
  ,,   *at* the sight.
  ,,   *by* entreaties.

Negligent *of* duty.
  ,,   *in* his work.

Obliged *to* a person.
  ,,   *for* some kindness.
Occupied *with* some work.
  ,,   *in* reading a book.
Offended *with* a person.
  ,,   *at* something done.

Parallel *to* or *with* anything.
Paramount *to* everything else.
Popular *with* schoolfellows.
  ,,   *for* his pluck.
Possessed *of* wealth.
  ,,   *with* a notion.
Preferable *to* something else.
Preventive *of* fever.
Profuse *of* his money.
  ,,   *in* his offers.
Provident *of* his money.
  ,,   *for* his children.
Pursuant *to* an inquiry.

Quick *of* understanding.
  ,,   *at* mathematics.

Ready *for* action.
  ,,   *at* accounts.
  ,,   *in* his answers.
Receptive *of* advice.
Reconciled *to* a position.

Reconciled *to* or *with* an opponent.
Requisite *to* happiness.
  ,,   *for* a purpose.
Resolved *into* its elements.
  ,,   *on* doing a thing.
Responsible *to* a person.
  ,,   *for* his actions.
Revenge *on* a person *for* doing
    something.

Satisfied *of* (concerning) a fact.
  ,,   *with* his income.
Secure *from* harm.
  ,,   *against* an attack.
Sensible *of* kindness.
Sick *of* waiting.
  ,, *with* fever.
Significant *of* his intentions.
Slow *of* hearing.
  ,, *in* making up his mind.
  ,, *at* accounts.
Subversive *of* discipline.
Suitable *to* his income.
  ,,   *for* his purpose.
Suited *to* the occasion.
  ,,   *for* a post.

Tired *of* doing nothing.
  ,,   *with* his exertions.

Vexed *with* a person *for* doing
    something.
  ,,   *at* a thing.

Weak *of* understanding.
  ,, *in* his head.

Zealous *for* improvement.
  ,,   *in* a cause.

(c) *Verbs followed by Prepositions.*

Abide *by* a promise.
Absolve *of* or *from* a charge.
Accord *with* or *to* a thing.
Admit *of* an excuse.
  ,,   *to* or *into* a secret.
Agree *to* a proposal.
  ,,   *with* a person.
Answer *to* a person.
  ,,   *for* conduct.
Apologise *to* a person.
  ,,   *for* rudeness.

Appeal *to* a person.
  ,,   *for* redress or help.
  ,,   *against* a sentence.
Apply *to* a person *for* a thing.
Ask *for* a thing.
  ,, *of* or *from* a person.
Aspire *after* worldly greatness.
  ,,   *to* some particular ob-
         ject.
Attend *to* a book or speaker.
  ,,   *on* a person.

Bear *with* a man's impatience.
Beat *against* the rocks (the waves).
  ,, *on* one's head (the sun).
Beg pardon *of* a person.
  ,, a person *to* do a thing.
Blush *at* one's own faults.
  ,, *for* any one who is at fault.
Borrow *of* or *from* a person.
Break *into* a house (thieves).
  ,, oneself *of* a habit.
  ,, *through* restraint.
  ,, ill news *to* a person.
  ,, (dissolve partnership) *with*
     a person.
Bring a thing *to* light.
  ,,   ,, *under* notice.
Burst *into* a rage.
  ,, *upon* (suddenly invade) a
     country.
Buy a thing *of* or *from* a person.
  ,,   ,, *from* a shop.

Call *on* a person (visit him at his
     house).
  ,, *to* (shout to) a person.
  ,, *for* (require) punishment.
Charge a man *with* a crime.
Come *across* (accidentally meet)
     any one.
  ,, *into* fashion.
  ,, *by* (obtain) a thing.
  ,, *of* (result from) something.
  ,, *to* (amount to) forty.
Communicate a thing *to* a person.
  ,, *with* a person *on* a
     subject.
Compare similars *with* similars—
     as one fruit *with* an-
     other.
  ,, things dissimilar, by way
     of illustration — as
     genius *to* a lightning
     flash.
Complain *of* some annoyance *to* a
     person.
  ,, *of* or *against* a person.
Confer (*Trans.*) a thing *on* any one.
  ,, (*Intrans.*) *with* a person
     about something.
Confide (*Trans.*) a secret *to* any
     one.
  ,, (*Intrans.*) *in* one's honour.

Conform *to* (follow) a rule.
  ,, *with* one's views.
Confront a man *with* his accusers.
Consist (made up) *of* materials.
  ,, (have its character) *in*
     hypocrisy, falsehood,
     charity.
Correspond *with* a person (write).
  ,, *to* something (agree).
Count *on* a thing (confidently
     expect).
  ,, *for* nothing.

Deal well or ill *by* a person.
  ,, *in* (trade in) cloth, tea, spices,
     etc.
  ,, *with* a person (have dealings
     in trade. etc.).
  ,, *with* a subject (write about
     it).
Descant *on* a subject.
Die *of* a disease.
  ,, *from* some cause, as overwork.
  ,, *by* violence.
Differ *with* a person *on* a subject.
  ,, *from* anything (to be un-
     like).
Divide *in* half, *into* four parts.
Draw money *on* a bank.
Drop *off* a tree.
  ,, *out of* the ranks.

Embark *on* board ship.
  ,, *in* business.
Encroach *on* one's authority.
Enter *upon* a career.
  ,, *into* one's plans.
Entrust any one *with* a thing.
  ,, a thing *to* any one.
Err *on the side of* leniency.
Exchange one thing *for* another.
  ,, *with* a person.
Excuse a person *from* coming.

Fail *in* an attempt.
  ,, *of* a purpose.
Fall *among* thieves.
  ,, *in love with* a person.
  ,, *in with* one's views.
  ,, *on* the enemy (attack).
  ,, *into* a mistake.
  ,, *under* some one's displeasure.

Feed (*Intrans.*) *on* grass.
  ,, (*Trans.*) a cow *with* grass.
Fill *with* anything.
    (*full of* something). (*Adject.*)
Fly *at* (attack) a dog.
  ,, *into* a rage.
Furnish a person *with* a thing.

Gain *on* some one in a race.
Get *at* (find out) the facts.
  ,, *over* (recover from) an illness.
  ,, *on with* a person (live or work
      smoothly with him).
  ,, *out of* debt.
  ,, *to* a journey's end.
Glance *at* an object.
  ,, *over* a letter.
Grieve *at* or *for* or *about* an event.
  ,, *for* a person.
Grow *upon* one = (a habit grows
    on, etc.).

Impose *on* (deceive) a person.
Impress an idea *on* a person.
  ,, a person *with* an idea.
Indent *on* an office *for* stamps.
Indict a person *for* a crime.
Indulge *in* wine.
  ,, oneself *with* wine.
Inquire *into* a matter.
  ,, *of* a person *about* or *con-*
      cerning some matter.
Intrude *on* one's leisure.
  ,, *into* one's house.
Intrust a person *with* a thing.
  ,, a thing *to* a person.
Invest money *in* some project.
  ,, a man *with* authority.

Jump *at* (eagerly accept) an offer.
  ,, *to* a conclusion.

Kick *against* (resist) authority.
  ,, *at* a thing (scornfully reject).

Labour *under* a misapprehension.
  , *for* the public good.
  ,, *in* a good cause.
  ,, *at* some work.
Lay facts *before* a person.
  ,, a sin *to* one's charge.
  ,, a person *under* an obligation.
Lean *against* a wall.

Lean *on* a staff.
  ,, *to* a certain opinion.
Live *for* riches or fame.
  ,, *by* honest labour.
  ,, *on* a small income.
  ,, *within* one's means.
Look *after* (watch) some business.
  ,, *at* a person or thing.
  ,, *into* (closely examine) a
      matter.
  ,, *for* something lost.
  ,, *over* (examine cursorily) an
      account.
  ,, *through* (examine carefully)
      an account.
  ,, *out of* a window.

Make *away with* (purloin) money.
  ,, *for* (conduce to) happiness.
  ,, *up to* (approach) a person.
  ,, some meaning *of* a thing.
March *with* (border on) a bound-
    ary.

Operate *on* a patient.
Originate *in* a thing or place.
  ,, *with* a person.

Pass *from* one thing *into* another.
  ,, *for* a clever man.
  ,, *over* (omit) a page.
  ,, *by* a man's door.
Perish *by* the sword.
  ,, *with* cold.
Play *at* cricket.
  ,, *upon* the guitar.
  ,, tricks (trifle) *with* one's health.
Point *at* a person.
  ,, *to* some result.
Prepare *for* the worst.
  ,, *against* disaster.
Preside *at* a meeting.
  ,, *over* a meeting.
Prevail *on* (persuade) a person to
    do something.
  ,, *against* or *over* an adver-
      sary.
  ,, *with* a person (have more
      influence than anything
      else).
Proceed *with* a business already
    commenced.

Proceed *to* a business not yet commenced.

,, *from* one point *to* another.

,, *against* (prosecute) a person.

Reckon *on* (confidently expect) something.

,, *with* (settle accounts with) a person.

Reconcile *to* a loss.

,, *to* or *with* an adversary.

Reflect credit *on* a person.

,, (*Intrans.*) *on* a man's conduct (discreditably).

Rejoice *at* the success of another.

,, *in* one's own success.

Repose (*Intrans.*) *on* a bed.

,, confidence *in* a person.

Rest *on* a couch, *on* facts, etc.

(It) rests *with* a person to do, etc.

Result *from* a cause.

,, *in* a consequence.

Run *after* (eagerly follow) new fashions.

,, *at* (attack) a cat.

,, *into* debt.

,, *over* (read rapidly)an account.

,, *through* (squander) his money.

See *about* (consider) a matter.

,, *into* (investigate) a matter.

,, *through* (understand) his meaning.

,, *to* (attend to) a matter.

Set *about* (begin working at) a business.

,, a person *over* (in charge of) a business.

,, *upon* (attack) a traveller.

Sit *over* a fire.

,, *down under* an imputation.

Smile *at* (deride) a person's threats.

,, *on* (favour) a person.

Speak *of* a subject (briefly).

,, *on* a subject (at greater length).

Speculate *in* shares.

,, *on* a possible future.

Stand *against* (resist) an enemy.

,, *by* (support) a friend.

,, *on* one's dignity.

,, *to* (maintain) one's opinion.

Stare *at* a person.

,, a person *in* the face.

Stick *at* nothing.

,, *to* his point.

Succeed *to* a property.

,, *in* an undertaking.

Supply a thing *to* a person.

,, a person *with* a thing.

Take *after* (resemble) his father.

,, a person *for* a spy.

,, *to* (commence the habit of) gambling.

,, *upon* oneself to do a thing.

Talk *of* or *about* an event.

,, *over* (discuss) a matter.

,, *to* or *with* a person.

Think *of* or *about* anything.

,, *over* (consider) a matter.

Touch *at* Gibraltar (ships).

,, *upon* (briefly allude to) a subject.

Trespass *against* rules.

,, *on* a man's time.

,, *in* a man's house.

Trust *in* a person. }

,, *to* a man's honesty. } (*Intr.*)

,, a man *with* money. (*Trans.*)

Turn verse *into* prose.

,, *to* a friend *for* help.

,, *upon* (hinge on) evidence.

Wait *at* table.

,, *for* a person or thing.

,, *on* (attend) a person.

Warn a person *of* danger.

,, ,, *against* a fault.

(d) *Adverbs followed by Prepositions.*

Note.—Adverbs are followed by the same prepositions as the corresponding adjectives.

Adversely *to* one's interests.

Agreeably *to* one's wishes.

Amenably *to* reason.

Angrily *with* a person.

Anxiously *for* one's safety.

Appropriately *to* an occasion.

Compatibly *with* reason.	Irrespectively *of* consequences.
Conditionally *on* some event.	Loyally *to* one's rulers.
Conformably *to* reason.	Obstructively *to* happiness.
Consistently *with* reason.	Offensively *to* a person.
Contentedly *with* one's lot.	Prejudicially *to* one's interests.
Effectively *for* a purpose.	Previously *to* some event.
Favourably *to* one's interests.	Profitably *to* oneself.
Fortunately *for* a person.	Proportionately *to* anything.
Independently *of* persons or things.	Simultaneously *with* some event.
	Subsequently *to* some event.
Irrelevantly *to* a question.	Sufficiently *for* the purpose.

CHAPTER XIX.—CONJUNCTIONS AND CONJUNCTIONAL PHRASES.

375. The distinction between Co-ordinating and Subordinating Conjunctions has been shown already in chapter viii. The present chapter shows how individual Conjunctions or Conjunctional phrases can be idiomatically used :—

(1) **Both . . . and.**—This is an emphatic way of expressing the union of two facts, without giving priority to either :—

He is *both* a fool *and* a knave. (He is not a fool only, not a knave only, but both at once, one as much as the other.)

Note.—If, however, one fact is more important than the other, the more important one should be mentioned last :—

He was *both* degraded from his class, *and* expelled for one year from the school.

(2) **As well as.**—This conjunctional phrase is Co-ordinating in one sense and Subordinating in another :—

(*a*) *Co-ordinating.*—In adding one co-ordinate sentence to another, it gives emphasis to the *first :*—

He as well as you is guilty = Not only you, but he also is guilty.

(*b*) *Subordinating :*—

Main.	Subordinate.
He does not write	as well as you do

= His writing is not as good as yours.

(3) **Not only . . . but** or **but also.**—In adding one sentence to another, these give emphasis to the *second* of the two :—

Not only I, *but* all other men declare this to be true.

That man was *not only* accused of the crime, *but also* convicted of it by the magistrate.

(4) **Nay.**—This has sometimes the force of "not only . . . but also": by appearing to deny the first statement, it places the second one in a stronger light :—

He was accused, *nay* convicted (accused, and what is more, convicted) of the crime by the magistrate.

(5) **Aye, yea.**—These have practically the same force as *nay*, although *nay* is the negative form of *aye*. They mean "more than this," and are used to mark the introduction of a more specific or more emphatic clause :—

> I therein do rejoice, *yea*, and will rejoice.—*Phil.* i. 18.

Sometimes they are used to introduce a clause with the sense of "indeed," "truly," "verily."

> *Aye*, call it holy ground.—MRS. HEMANS.
> *Yea*, hath God said, Ye shall not eat of every tree of the garden ?
> —*Genesis*, iii. 1.

(6) **Or rather.**—This has very much the same force as "nay." It corrects the first statement in order to place the second one in a stronger light :—

> He was injured, *or rather* ruined altogether, by the failure of that bank.

(7) **Now.**—This Conjunction (which must not be confounded with the adverb of time) introduces a new remark in *explanation* (not simply in continuation) of a previous one :—

> And Pilate said unto them, " Will ye have this man or Barabbas ? "
> They answered, " Not this man, but Barabbas." *Now* Barabbas was a robber.—*New Testament*.

(8) **Well.**—This word (when it is used as a Conjunction, that is, as a Conjunctive and not a Simple adverb) introduces a new remark implying satisfaction, regret, surprise, or any other feeling of the mind suggested by the previous remark :—

> You have finished the work that was given you ;—*well*, you have done a good deal better than you usually do, and I am much pleased with your improvement.

(9) **Or.**—This conjunction has four different meanings :—

(*a*) An alternative or exclusive sense (§ 236, *b*) :—

> Either this man sinned *or* his parents.

(*b*) An inclusive or non-alternative sense. Here the " or " is nearly equivalent to " and."

> Such trades as those of leather, *or* carpentry, *or* smith's work flourish best in large cities.

(*c*) To indicate that one word is synonymous or nearly synonymous with another :—

> The tribes *or* castes of India are very numerous.

(*d*) As an equivalent to "otherwise" (§ 236, *b*) :—

> You must work hard ; or (=otherwise=if you do not work hard) you will lose your place in the class.

(10) **If.**—This conjunction has three different uses :—

(*a*) For asking a question in the Indirect form of narration :—

I asked him *if* (= whether) he would return soon.

(*b*) For expressing a condition or supposition :—

If you return to us to-morrow (= in case you return, or in the event of your returning), we shall be glad to see you.

(*c*) For making an admission or concession. (Here the verb must be Indicative, because it concedes something as a *fact*) :—

If I *am* dull (= though I admit that I am dull), I am at least industrious. (I am dull *indeed*, *but* nevertheless industrious.)
Considering how ill I was, it is no wonder *if* (= that) I made some mistakes yesterday.

(11) **But.**—The uses of this word as a Preposition have been shown already in § 232. Its uses as a Conjunction and as an Adverb have still to be shown.

(*a*) As a Subordinating conjunction :—

(1) It never rains *but* it pours.—*Proverb.*
　　(It never rains *except that* it pours, or It never rains *without* pouring.)

(2) I found no one *but* he was true to me.—SHAKSPEARE.
　　(I found no one who was not true to me.)

(3) Perdition catch my soul, *but* I do love thee.—SHAKSPEARE.
　　(Perdition catch my soul *if* I do *not* love thee.)

(4) It cannot be *but* Nature hath some Director of infinite power.
　　　　　　　　　　　　　　　—HOOKER.
　　(It cannot be, or it is impossible, *that* Nature hath *not* a Director, etc.)

(5) No one saw that sight *but* **w**ent away shocked.
　　(No one saw that sight *except that* he went away, or *who* did *not* go away, shocked.)

Note 1.—In (5) the Demonstrative *he* is understood after "but"; see § 126.

Note 2.—The above use of "but" as a Subordinating conjunction has arisen from the omission of the conjunction "that." If "that" were expressed, "but" would retain its original character as a preposition signifying "except," and the Noun-clause following it would be its object.

(*b*) As an Adversative conjunction of the Co-ordinating class :—

He is rich, *but* discontented.

(*c*) As an Adverb in the sense of "only" :—

There is *but* (= only) a plank between us and death.
We can *but* die (nothing worse than death can befall us).

(12) **While** or **whilst.**—"While" is properly a noun signifying "time." The conjunction "while" is an abridged form

of the phrase " the while that," etc., and in this phrase the noun " while" is an Adverbial accusative (see § 271).

The Conjunction " while " has three different uses :—

(a) To denote the *simultaneity* of two events :—

You can sit down, *while* (at the same time that) I stand.

(b) To denote *indefinite duration* :—

While (so long as) the world lasts, human nature will remain what it is.

(c) To denote some kind of antithesis or contrast :—

Men of understanding seek after truth ; *while* (= whereas) fools despise knowledge.

(13) **Lest.**—This in the Tudor period was followed by the present Subjunctive :—

$$\begin{cases} \text{Take heed, } lest \text{ you } fall= \\ \text{Take heed, } that \text{ you may } not \text{ fall.} \end{cases}$$

In the later Modern English the tense and mood following this conjunction is formed by the Auxiliary verb "should" :—

$$\begin{cases} \text{He worked hard, } lest \text{ he } should \text{ fail}= \\ \text{He worked hard, } that \text{ he } might \text{ not fail.} \end{cases}$$

(14) **As.**—Since this word is a Relative adverb, it is also a Conjunction (see § 17, 4).

Its uses and meanings as a Conjunction can be seen from the following examples :—

(a) *Time* :—

He trembled *as* (= at what time, or while) he spoke.

(b) *Manner* :—

Do not act *as* (= in what manner) he did.

(c) *State* or *Condition* :—

He took it just *as* (= in what state) it was.

(d) *Extent* :—

He is not so clever *as* (to what extent) you are.

(e) *Contrast* or *Concession* resulting from the sense of extent :—

$$\begin{cases} \text{Hot } as \text{ the sun is (to whatever extent the sun is hot), we must leave} \\ \quad \text{the house}= \\ \text{However hot the sun is, we must leave the house}= \\ \text{Although the sun is ever so hot, we must leave the house.} \end{cases}$$

(f) *Cause* :—

As (from what cause or for the reason that) rain has fallen, the air is cooler.

(15) **However.**—This is a Co-ordinating conjunction, when it stands alone ; but Subordinating, when it qualifies some adjective or adverb.

(a) Co-ordinating :—

All men were against him ; he kept his courage, *however*, to the last.

(b) Subordinating :—

However poor a man is, he need not be dishonest.
However well you may work, you cannot demand more than your
    stipulated pay.

(16) **When, where.**—These conjunctions or Relative adverbs
(in the same way as the Relative pronouns "who" or "which")
can be used in two very distinct senses :—

(a) The Restrictive or qualifying (§ 127) :—

The house where (= in which) we lived has fallen down.
The hour *when* (= at which) you arrived was four P.M.

(b) The Continuative or simply connective :—

On 24th January we reached Paris, *where* (= and there) we stayed
    a fortnight.
We stayed at Paris for two weeks, *when* (= and then) I received a
    letter which compelled me to return to London.

(17) **Though, but.**—Both of these conjunctions (the first
Subordinating, the second Co-ordinating) denote concession **or**
contrast :—

(a) He is honest, *though* poor ;
(b) He is poor, *but* honest.

These two sentences mean precisely the same thing, because
in (a) "He is honest" is the *Main* clause, and in (b) the
Co-ordinate clause, "but he is honest," is more *emphatic* than
the clause preceding it ; see (3) in this chapter. Thus the Main
clause and the Emphatic clause are the same.

If, however, we rewrite the two sentences thus :—

(a) He is honest, though poor ;
(b) He is honest, but poor,

the two sentences are not equivalent. The first emphasises the
fact that he is honest in spite of his poverty. The second
emphasises the fact that he is poor in spite of his honesty.

CHAPTER XX.—MISCELLANEOUS WORDS, PHRASES,
AND CONSTRUCTIONS.

(1) **All of them, both of them** :—

All of them (= they all) consented.
Both of them (= they both) consented.

In phrases like "some of them," "one of them," "two of
them," the "*of*" has a partitive sense. Such a sense is, how-

ever, impossible where "all" or "both" are concerned. We must therefore conclude that phrases like "all of them," "both of them," have come into use by analogy.

(2) **"Am," "have," with Infinitive** :—

> I am or was to go.
> I have or had to go.

These two sentences mean much the same thing. The Infinitive in both expresses future time, combined sometimes with a sense of duty. The Infinitive is Gerundial. See § 192 (*b*), and § 269 (5), (*b*). It is interesting to note that both constructions have come down to us from Old English [1] :—

> Hé is *tó cumenne* ⎰ = Lat. Ille venturus est.
> He is to   come   ⎰   Eng. He is about-to-come.

> Thone calic the ic *tó drincenne* hæbbe⎰ = The cup that I am
> The   cup that I to   *drink*   have ⎰   about-to-drink.

From these examples it will be observed that in Old English the verb "*be*" was used when the verb following was *Intransitive*, and "*have*" when the verb following was *Transitive*. The syntactical propriety of such distinction (which has been lost in Mod. English) is obvious.

Note.—It should be observed, however, that the Perfect Infinitive cannot be used after *have*, but only after the verb *be*. We can say, "I *was* to have gone" (that is, it was settled for me to go, only something prevented me) ; but we cannot say, "I *had* to have gone," nor can we say, "I *had* to have drunk."

(3) **An if** :—this is a reduplication = if if. *An* is a contraction of *and*, which in the Northern dialect of English meant "if" :—

> But *and if* that evil servant shall say.—*Matt.* xxiv. 48.
> Now *an* thou dalliest, then I am thy foe.—BEN JONSON.

When the old meaning of *an* or *and* was forgotten, the *if* was placed after it to remove any doubt as to its meaning.

(4) **And** in Interrogative sentences :—

> And art thou cold and lowly laid ?—SCOTT.

In such sentences the "and" does not join its own sentence to a previous one, but introduces a form of exclamation :—"Can it be true that thou art cold and lowly laid ?"

(5) **And all** :—

> The soldiers had decamped, horses *and all*.
> The strawberry-runners have been planted out, soil *and all*.

"And all" appears to be a more inclusive and more emphatic

---

[1] Sweet's *Short Historical English Grammar.* ed. 1892, p. 120.

phrase than *et cetera* (= and the rest), and to have been formed on the same type. The first sentence means, "The soldiers had decamped, with their horses and everything else belonging to them." The second means, "The runners have been planted out, with their own soil."

(6) **As**, before a noun :—

    (*a*) This box will serve us *as* a table.
    (*b*) We will not have this man *as* our chief.

The ellipses can be filled up as follows :—

    (*a*) This box will serve us *as* a table (would serve us, if we had a table).
    (*b*) We will not have this man *as* (in the way in which we would have) our chief.

(7) **As**, before an adjective :—

He considered the report *as* false.

That is, "He considered the report *as* (he would consider it, if it were) false."

(8) **As**, before "*if*" and "*though*" :—

    (*a*) He clung to it *as if* his life depended on it.
    (*b*) He clung to it *as though* his life depended on it.

That is, (*a*) "He clung to it, as (he would have clung to it), if his life depended on it." (*b*) "He clung to it as (fast as he could have clung to it, for he could not have clung to it faster) though his life depended on it."

(9) **As thee, as me** :—

The nations not so blest as *thee*.—THOMSON.
Even such weak minister as *me*
May the oppressor bruise.—SCOTT.

These uses of the Accusative case, if we consider "*as*" to be here a conjunction, are grammatical blunders; for the right construction would be "not so blest as *thou* (art blest)," and "such weak minister as *I* (am weak)." But it has been suggested by one writer that "*as*" might perhaps be here regarded as a preposition of comparison followed by a pronoun in the Accusative case. In colloquial English this use of "as" is common; but careful writers avoid a phrase of such doubtful accuracy.

(10) **As to** :—

I have heard nothing more *as to* that matter.

This phrase is of French origin = *quant à*, an elliptical phrase denoting "as far as relates to," etc. It has been explained in the same way in chapter xi.

(11) **As usual** :—

He came at four o'clock, *as usual.*

"As" is here used as a Relative for "which," and the verb "*is*" is understood after it :—"He came at four o'clock, which (his coming at four) is or was usual (with him)."

(12) **At best, at its best**, or **at the best** :—

At best he is only a moderate speaker.

He was *at his best* this morning.

In Superlative phrases of very frequent occurrence, such as "at best," "at worst," "at first," "at last," "at most," "at least," no pronoun or article is placed between the preposition and the adjective, unless we wish to particularise.

But in similar phrases that are of less frequent occurrence, a pronoun or the Definite article should be inserted :—

The wind is *at its loudest* or *the loudest.* The storm is *at its fiercest.* To-day the patient is *at his weakest.* The season is now *at its loveliest.* The air is now *at its hottest.*

(13) **At ten years old, at four miles distant** :—

{ (1) My son was *ten years old* when he died.
{ (2) My son died *at ten years of age.*
{ (3) My son died *at ten years old.*
{ (1) My house is *four miles distant* from the sea.
{ (2) My house is *at four miles' distance* from the sea.
{ (3) My house is *at four miles distant* from the sea.

Sentences (1) and (2) in both sets of examples are quite correct. Sentence (3) has arisen from a confusion between the constructions in (1) and (2). This mixed construction is not grammatically correct ; and, though it is used by some writers and speakers, it is best to avoid it.

(14) **Away** (after Intrans. verbs) :—

Fight *away*, my men.

This adverb is a contraction for "on-way." It denotes continuity ("go on, continue fighting") and sometimes intensity ("fight hard"), because such action implies movement on the way, not rest or inactivity. After verbs of motion it generally means "off," as "go *away*," "send him *away*."

(15) **Bid fair to**, etc. :—

This institution *bids fair* (=makes a fair or good promise) to flourish for many years to come.

Here the adjective "fair" qualifies some noun implied in the verb "bid" : "bids a fair bidding or promise."

(16) **But he, but they.**—(Old Eng. *bútan*, by-out).

What stays (=supports) had I *but they?*—SHAKSPEARE.
And was he not the earl?   'Twas none but *he.*—WILLIAM TAYLOR.
The boy stood on the burning deck,
Whence all but *he* had fled.—MRS. HEMANS.

The Nominative after "but" appears to have arisen from a confusion between "but" as an Adversative conjunction of the Co-ordinating class and "but" as a preposition.   "Whence all had fled, *but he* had not fled,"—that is, all had fled except him.

On *but* as a preposition, see § 232 ; as a conjunction, § 375 (11).   In the curious phrase *"But* me no *buts"* (Shaks.), *but* is used as a verb in the Imperative mood, and *buts* as a noun in the Plural number.   *Me* is the Dative or indirect object.   *Buts* is the direct object.   Compare the following in Scott :—*"Woman* me no more than I *woman* you :   I have not been called Mistress to be *womaned* by you."—*Peveril of the Peak.*

(17) **But what** :—

> (*a*) I cannot say *but what* you may be right.
> (*b*) Not *but what* he did his best.

Here "what" has come into use as a substitute for "that." In both sentences "but" is a preposition, to which the following Noun-clause is the object (see § 259, *c*).

(*a*) This sentence could be reworded thus :—" I cannot say anything *against* the fact that-you-are-right,"—that is, anything to the contrary of your being right.

(*b*) This sentence is elliptical.   The ellipse could be filled up as follows :—" I do not say anything except that he did his best, or to the contrary of his having done his best."

Note.—The substitution of *"what"* for *"that"* after the preposition "but" occurs only after the verbs "say" or "believe."   It does not occur after any other verbs.

(18) **By thousands, by little, by himself**, etc. :—

> (*a*) The ants came streaming out *by thousands.*
> (*b*) The water oozes out little *by little.*
> (*c*) He went out of the room *by himself.*

From denoting cause or agency, the preposition "by" came to denote manner or number ; in which sense it often does the work of a Distributive adjective (see § 330, *a*).   In (*a*) "by thousands" means "in the manner or to the number of thousands,"—that is, "a thousand at a time," or "one thousand after another."   In (*b*) "little by little" is elliptical for "by little and by little" ; as in Pope :—

> Loth to enrich me with too quick replies,
> *By little and by little* (he) drops his lies.

In (c) the phrase "by himself," which is often used for "alone," is founded on the analogy of the above phrases :—"He went out by himself,"—that is, "he went out himself at a time," or "he went out *alone*, unaccompanied by any one else." See § 372 (4).

(19) **Came to pass, came to be considered,** etc. :—

In this construction (which is very common), the Infinitive is Gerundial, and the "to" denotes *effect* or *result*. On this use of the preposition "to" before a noun, see § 372 (9); on its use in the same sense with the Gerundial Infinitive, see § 192 (a).

(20) **Can but, cannot but** :—

> (a) We *can but* die.
> (b) We *cannot but* die.

In (a) the word "but" is an adverb : "We can *only* die,"—that is, we cannot come to anything worse than death. In (b) the word "but" retains its original character as a preposition :—"We cannot do anything *except* die." Here "die" is the Noun-Infinitive used as object to the preposition "but."

(21) **Come, go** :—

> (a) Are you *coming* to the meeting to-day ?
> (b) Are you *going* to the meeting to-day ?

In sentence (a) the use of the verb "come" implies that the questioner himself intends to be present at the meeting, and he inquires whether the person addressed will be present also. The person addressed might say in reply, "Yes, I shall be there with you" ; or "No, I shall not join you there."

In sentence (b) the use of the verb "go" is perfectly general ; and hence the person addressed might reply :—"Yes, I am going to the meeting ; are you ?" or "No, I am not going ; are you ?"

"*Come*" means motion *towards* a person or place ; "*go*" means motion *from* a person or place. Thus we say, "The sun is *coming* up," or "the sun is *going* down" ; "The plant is *coming* into *flower*," or "the plant is *going* to *seed*,"—that is, it has passed its prime, and is beginning to fade or pass away.

> He has *come* to grief.
> He has *gone* to the dogs.

These colloquial phrases mean almost the same thing. There is no saying why "come" is used in one and "go" in the other.

(22) **Dare, dares, dared, durst** :—

> (a)   For I know thou darest,
>   But this thing (Trinculo, the jester) *dare* not !—SHAKSPEARE.
> (b) Here boldly spread thy hands ; no venomed weed
>   *Dares* blister them, no slimy snail *dare* creep.
>   BEAUMONT AND FLETCHER.

(c) That man hath yet a soul, and *dare* be free.—CAMPBELL.

(d) Why then did not the ministers use their new law? Because they *durst* not.—MACAULAY.

It has been clearly proved that *dare* is one of the verbs which use an old past tense for a present, and that "he *dares*" is grammatically as bad as "he *shalls*," "he *mays*," "he *cans*." Nevertheless in the fifteenth century a practice began to spring up of using *dares* for *dare* in the Third Person Sing.; and the example quoted in (b) shows that in the Tudor period the two forms could be used promiscuously.

It is also well known that *durst* is a Weak past tense formed by adding the suffix -*te* to the stem *dors*: thus in A.S. the form is *dors-te*. Historically this is the proper past tense, as in example (d). Nevertheless a new form *dared* has also come into use.

As often happens in Modern English, when there are double forms, they are differentiated in use; cf. the double forms *is come*, *has come*, the different uses of which are described above in § 173; cf. also *elder, older; later, latter; nearest, next; outer, utter; foremost, first;* see § 348.

The following are the uses of *dare, dares, dared*, and *durst* that appear to be getting more and more established in current idiom:—

Dare is used for the Third Person Sing. whenever the sentence is negative, *or* whenever the Infin. following is unaccompanied by *to*:—

> He dare not *go*.
> He dare *be* free.   See example (c).

Dares is used, whenever the sentence is affirmative, *and* whenever the Infin. following is accompanied by *to*:—

> He dares *to* insult me.

Dares is also used, whenever the verb is followed by a personal object, in the sense of challenge:—

> He *dares* me to my face.

Dared is much used with reference to direct assertions, and *durst not* with reference to hypothetical ones:—

> He durst not do it = He would not dare to do it.

Another point of idiom is that *durst* is not used in affirmative sentences. We do not say, "He durst do it," but "He dared to do it."

(23) Dependent on, independent of:—

> I am wholly dependent *on* your help.
> I am quite independent *of* your help.

Why is the same preposition not used with both adjectives? "On" is used after "dependent," because this preposition denotes "rest," "support," as on some foundation. "Of" is used after "independent," because this preposition denotes "separation," and the same meaning is implied in the adjective "independent."

(24) **Doubt that, doubt but** :—

> (a) I do not doubt *that* he is ill.
> (b) I do not doubt *but* or *but that* he is ill.

These two sentences amount to the same thing. They might be rewritten as follows :—

> (a) I do not doubt (=question) the fact that he is ill.
> (b) I do not doubt anything *against* the fact that he is ill.

In (b) the word "but" is a preposition, and the Noun-clause "that he is ill" is its object; or if "that" is omitted after "but," the "but" is a Subordinating conjunction.

(25) **Even** (as an adverb) :—

> (a) The hearing ear and the seeing eye, the Lord hath made *even* both of them (not merely one, but both alike).
> (b) *Even* so (just in the same way) did the Gauls occupy the coast.
> (c) Thou wast a soldier *even* to Cato's wish (fully up to the level of Cato's wish).
> (d) I have debated *even* in my soul (in my very soul, to my level best).

We thus see that *even* is an intensifying adverb, signifying "so much as," "fully up to the mark."

In A.S. *efn*, the adjective, means "level." The adverbial counterpart is from A.S. *efn-e*, which has become *even*.

(26) **Excuse, excuse not** :—

> (a) I hope you will excuse my coming here to-day.
> (b) I hope you will excuse my *not* coming here to-day.

These two sentences amount to the same thing, and could be rewritten as follows :—

> (a) I hope you will excuse (=dispense with, not insist on) my coming here to-day.
> (b) I hope you will excuse (=pardon) my *not* coming (my neglect to come) here to-day.

Observe that the verb "excuse" is used in a different sense in each sentence.

Note.—Owing to the ambiguity of the verb "excuse," sentence (a) might mean "I hope you will excuse or *pardon* the fact of my having come here to-day." So it is best to avoid construction (a).

(27) **Far from, anything but** :—

> His manners are *far from* pleasant.
> His manners are *anything but* pleasant.

The phrase "far from" is equivalent to "anything but" :—
"His manners are anything *but* (= except) being pleasant."
Here "being pleasant" is the object to the preposition "but."
"The quality of being pleasant is not merely absent from his
manners, but *far distant from* them."

(28) **First importance, last importance** :—

       (*a*) This is a matter of the *first* importance.
       (*b*) This is a matter of the *last* importance.

Though "first" and "last" are usually of opposite meanings,
yet in the above phrases their meaning is the same. In (*a*)
"first" denotes "foremost,"—taking precedence of everything
else. In (*b*) "last" denotes "utmost," "greatest,"—which comes
to the same thing as "foremost."

The opposite phrase to "of the first or of the last importance" is "of the least importance" :—

This is a matter of the least importance (= of little or no import-
    ance, of less importance than anything else).

(29) **Good-looking** :—

       He is a *good-looking* (handsome) man.

This is a well-established phrase. Yet we cannot turn it
round and say "He looks good" for "He is handsome"; and if
we say "He looks *well*," this means, "He looks (or seems to be)
in good health."

(30) **Had as lief, had rather, had better, had as soon.**
etc.—These phrases, preceded by a noun or pronoun in the Nom.
and followed by a *to*-less or Simple Infinitive, are well-established idioms :—

    I had as lief not be, as live to be
    In awe of such a thing as I myself.—SHAKSPEARE.
    I had rather be a kitten, and cry mew.—SHAKSPEARE.

But the original construction was different. What is now
the subject was in the Dative case (§ 306), and some form of the
verb *be* was used where we now use *had* :—

    And *leever me is* be poure and trewe.—*Cursor Mundi*.
    (= And it is more agreeable to me to be poor and true.)

But in the transition between the old and the present con-
structions we find the Dative case used with *had* instead of the
Nominative, and the Nominative used with *be* instead of the
Dative :—

    Poor lady ! *she were better* love a dream.—SHAKSPEARE.
    You were best hang yourself.—BEAUMONT AND FLETCHER.
    Me rather had my heart might feel your love.—SHAKSPEARE.

This is the history of the construction. But in parsing such a sentence as, "I had as lief do this as that," we must now paraphrase it into, "I should have it as agreeable to me to do this as that." *Lief* is from A.S. *léof*, dear, agreeable; cf. *love*.

(31) **He to deceive me**, and similar phrases:—

> (a) *I* to be so foolish !
> (b) *He* to deceive me !

These exclamatory sentences are elliptical. (a) "Am I a person to be so foolish !" (b) "Could he be a person to deceive me !" The Infinitive is here Gerundial, and qualifies the noun or pronoun going before.[1]

(32) **How do you do ?**—

The first *do* is the Auxiliary, which is used for asking a question in the present or past (Indefinite) tense (§ 172).

The second *do* may be explained as an imitation, or rather translation, of the French *faire*, in the old French sentence: *Comment faites-vous ?* How do you make or do ?

It has been also suggested that *do* is from A.S. *dúg-an*, to avail. This is possible. But it is probably more correct to take the phrase as an adaptation from French.

(33) **I do you to wit**:—

This quaint and almost obsolete expression means "I cause you to know." In Old English the verb *dó-n* (= do) meant (amongst other things) "cause," and this was very freely used in Middle English, when our language had lost the power of forming fresh Causal verbs, like *raise* from *rise*.

(34) **That will do**:—

The explanation usually given is that this *do* is not from A.S. *do-n*, but from A.S. *dúg-an*, to avail, to be sufficient (*Intrans.*), out of which we get the Adjective *dought-y*, valiant; and that hence the sentence "That will do" is equivalent to "That will suffice." This explanation has been rejected on the ground that the modern pronunciation and spelling of *dúg* would

---

[1] The construction of a Nominative case with the Gerundial Infinitive is at least as old as the fifteenth century, and is not uncommon in Shakspeare (see Kellner's *Hist. Eng. Syntax*, p. 255):—

Thow to lye by our moder is too muche shame for us to suffre.—MALORY.
A heavier task could not have been imposed
Than *I to speak* my griefs unspeakable.—SHAKSPEARE.

In Modern English this construction is chiefly seen (*a*) in exclamatory phrases, as shown above, and (*b*) in the absolute construction, as shown in § 269 (*b*).

be *dow*, and not *do*. This, however, is not a just ground for rejection ; for the verb in similar contexts was actually spelt as *dow* (Past tense *dowed* or *dought*, hence "doughty") in Mid. English, and still appears as *dow* in Burns. It is the equivalent of Dutch *deugen*, Danish "at *due*," spelt in Mod. Eng. as "do."

(35) **I beg to**, etc. :—

> I *beg* to inquire whether I may go home.

This is a common ellipse for "I beg leave to," etc. It is more common to omit the noun "leave" than to insert it.

(36) **I take it** :—

> You will win in that case, *I take it*.

This is a common phrase for "in my opinion."

(37) **I was given to understand** :—

If this sentence is converted from the Passive form to the Active, it becomes :—"Some one gave or caused me to understand." Here "me" is the Indirect object, and "to understand" (Noun-Infinitive) is the Direct. By the rule given in § 161, a verb which has two objects in the Active voice can retain one in the Passive. Hence in the sentence "I was given to understand," the Noun-Infinitive is *Retained object* to the Passive verb "was given."

(38) **If you like** :—

> You can do this, *if you like*.

We now regard *you* as the subject to the verb *like*, to which *it* is the object understood. But originally the phrase was, "If (it) like you," *i.e.* if it is agreeable to you. Cf. what Shakspeare says in *Hamlet*, "It *likes us* well." Here *like* or *likes* is an Impersonal verb, followed by *you* or *us*, which in Old English was in the Dative case ; see above, § 306 (*c*). *Like* is, of course, the Third Person Sing. *Subjunctive*, not Indicative.

(39) **In respect of, with respect to** :—

> He is senior to me *in respect of* service.
> We must have a talk *with respect to* that subject.

These phrases are not identical in meaning. "In respect of" means "in point of" some quality, and is preceded by an adjective. "With respect to" means "concerning," and qualifies some verb or noun : we should not say, "We must have a talk in respect of that subject."

(40) **In that** :—

> *In that* he died, he died unto sin once.—*New Testament*.

The words " in that " might be called a conjunctional phrase. But strictly speaking *in* is a preposition, having as its object the noun-clause " that he died." Here *that* is the Introductory conjunction, or if we say, " In the fact that," it is the conjunction of Apposition. See § 238 (*a*).

(41) In thorough working-order :—

Here " thorough " is an adjective qualifying the compound noun " working-order " (that kind of order which is suitable for working). It does not qualify either *working* or *order*, but the compound noun made up of both.

(42) It's me, that's him :—

These phrases are condemned by grammarians, because " me " and " him " are Subjective complements to the verb " is," and such complements must be in the same case as the Subject,— that is, in the Nominative case (see § 269, 2).

Nothing can be said in defence of the vulgarism " that's him."

But the phrase " it's me " has been defended on two grounds: (1) because it is the counterpart and exact translation of the French " *c'est moi*," which is recognised as an established idiom by the best French writers ; (2) because " me " is an adopted or borrowed accusative of " I," and might be used as a complement, though not as a subject. It is best, however, not to use it.

(43) Lesser, less.—" Lesser " is a Double Comparative, which is used for euphony to balance the sound of " greater " :—

The *greater* light to rule the day, and the *lesser* light to rule the night.—*Old Testament.*

Note.—Observe " lesser " is always an adjective. But " less " may be either an adjective or an adverb.

(44) Methinks, I think :—

The two verbs, though spelt alike in Modern English, are from different roots. *Methinks* = it seems to me ; the *me* is in the Dative case (see § 306, *c*), and the *thinks* (impersonal) is from A.S. *thync-an*, to seem. The *personal* verb exemplified in " I think " is from A.S. *thenc-an.*

(45) More than, with adjectives and verbs :—

(*a*) It is *more than* probable that he will fail. (*With Adj.*)
(*b*) He *more than* hesitated to promise that. (*With Verb.*)

The construction is elliptical. The two sentences could be written at greater length as follows :—

(*a*) It is not only probable, but more than this,—it is practically certain, that, etc.

(*b*) He *did* more than *hesitate* (that is, he refused) to promise.
(Here the Noun-infinitive "hesitate" is object to "than";
§ 231.)

(46) **Mutual friend** :—

The word "mutual" implies reciprocity ; as "our friendship
is mutual,"—that is, "I love you, and you love me in return."
But the phrase "a mutual friend" has come into vogue in a sense
quite different from that of reciprocity. "I made his acquaint-
ance through a *mutual* friend,"—that is, a *common* friend, some
one who was a friend to myself as well as a friend to him. The
use of the word "mutual" in this particular phrase is anomalous,
but sanctioned by usage. We could not speak of two persons
having "mutual ancestors."

(47) **Never so, ever so** :—

(*a*) He refuseth to hear the voice of the charmer, charm he *never so*
wisely.—*Old Testament*.
(*b*) He refuseth to hear the voice of the charmer, charm he *ever so*
wisely.

These two phrases mean the same thing. In (*a*) the dependent clause written out in full would be, "although he
charm *so* wisely as he *never* charmed before." In (*b*) the clause
can be rewritten "however wisely he may charm." The phrase
"*ever so*" is the one now used; "*never so*" was used in the
sixteenth century.

Note.—The phrase *ever so* is sometimes used as follows :—

Ever so many persons called here to-day.

Here "ever so many" means a larger number than usual, or a larger
number than I care to count. Here *ever* is a mistake for "never";
and the sentence written in full would be—

Never so many persons called here before (as called here) to-day.

(48) **"No," "none,"** as adverbs :—

(*a*) He is *no* scholar.
(*b*) He is *none* the wiser for all his experience.

In (*a*) the word "no" = in no respect. In (*b*) "none" = in
no degree. "None" is used in this adverbial sense, only when
it is followed by such a phrase as "the wiser,"—that is, by "the"
and a Comparative. Similarly we can say "*all* the better,"
where "all," like "none," is used adverbially.

(49) **No more**, preceded by "do" :—

I will *do no more* than I can help.

Two different ways of explaining this construction suggest
themselves. (*a*) We might consider that the Transitive verb

"do" is here used Intransitively on the principle described in § 145 (a). Or (b) we might accept the Transitive character of "do" and suppose that some object is implied in the word "more." In either case "no" is an adverb qualifying "more." "More" cannot be itself a noun, since it is followed by *than*.

But *more* can be used as a noun when it is not followed by *than*, in the same way as *much* can; see below (70).

> Let knowledge grow from *more to more.*—TENNYSON.

(50) **None of them** :—

> None of them *were* present.

"None," when it is used as a Subject, is properly a Singular = not one, or no one. But the phrase "none of them," when it is used as a Subject, takes a Plural verb by attraction :—"they none." Or the Plural may be explained by analogy to the phrases "all of them," "some of them," etc. See above (1).

(51) **Odds and ends**, scraps, leavings. Here *odds* is for *ords*, beginnings (A.S. *ord*, beginning), not for *orts*, leavings.

(52) **One more . . . and** :—

> (a) *One more* whistle, *and* the train started.
> (b) *One more* such loss, *and* we shall be ruined.

In each of these sentences there is an ellipsis of some verb in the Principal clause. (a) "*There was* one more whistle, and the train started,"—that is, *after* one more whistle, the train started. (b) "*We must incur* one more such loss, and then we shall be ruined,"—that is, *if we incur* one more such loss, we shall be ruined. This sentence therefore expresses a condition and its consequence.

(53) **One to another, to one another, to each other** :—

> (a) They shouted *one to another.*
> (b) They shouted *to one another.*

The phrase in (a) is grammatically correct, while that in (b) is grammatically wrong, since "one" is in the Nominative case in apposition with "they" :—"They shouted—one shouted to another." Nevertheless the phrase "*to one another*" has become established by usage, and is now the more idiomatic of the two.

If we use the phrase "each other," we could not say "they shouted each to other"; but we should have to say "they shouted each to *the other*," because "each other" is used for two persons, whereas "one another" is used for more than two (see § 329). "Each to the other" is, however, an awkward phrase and far less idiomatic than "to each other."

(54) **Or, nor,** in Negative sentences :—

> He was not a clever man in books *or* in business.

The question has been raised whether " or " is correct in such sentences, or whether " nor " should be written in the place of it.

The answer is that the " or " is correct. The sentence, however, is elliptical ; and the ellipse would be filled up as follows :—

> He was not clever *either* in books *or* in business.

If " nor " is used instead of " or," the sentence must be rewritten in the following form, which, however, is awkward and cumbersome :—

> He was not clever in books, *nor* was he clever in business.

(55) **Or ere, or ever** :—

> Would I had met my dearest foe in heaven, *or ever* I had seen that day, Horatio.—SHAKSPEARE.

It is generally explained that *or* is a corruption of *ere*. Hence the phrase *or ere* is merely a reduplication. " Or ever " (= ere ever) has been compared to such compound conjunctions as *whenever, wherever, however,* etc. Some, however, think that *ever* has been confounded with *ere*, misspelt as *e'er*. In this case the phrase *or ever* would be another instance of reduplication.

(56) **Other than, other besides** :—

> (a) No person *other than* a graduate need apply.
> (b) No *other* person *besides* my friend applied.

In (a) "other than " means "different from," "except," "but ": —" No one except a graduate." The word "than " is here a preposition (not a conjunction), which compares a graduate from other men and distinguishes him from them. In (b) the phrase " other besides," though common, is not commendable. Either leave out *other* or change *besides* to *than*.

(57) **Out, out and out** :—

> (a) *Out*, brief candle !
> (b) He was quite *out* of it.
> (c) *Out* upon it !
> (d) He was beaten *out and out*.
> (e) He proved to be an *out and out* deceiver.

In (a) *out* is an adverb compounded with some verb "go " understood. In (b) *out* is an adverb qualifying the preposition *of ;* § 371. In (c) some verb is understood, as in (a), before the adverb *out*. The phrase is exclamatory, and used to express indignation. In (d) the adverb is repeated for the sake of intensifying it : the reduplicated adverb means " utterly." In (e) some participle is understood with the reduplicated adverb, which gives it the force of an adjective signifying "utter"; see § 96 (2).

(58) **Out of temper, in a temper** :—

    (*a*) He is *out of temper* (angry).

    (*b*) He is *in a temper* (angry).

These phrases mean the same thing, and written in full would be, (*a*) out of his *ordinary* or *good* temper, (*b*) in a *bad* temper.

(59) **Please**, followed by an Imperative :—

    Please write more legibly.

This is elliptical. The full sentence would be, "*If it please you*, write more legibly." It is a very polite way of making a request.

(60) **Prevent being, prevent from being** :—

    (*a*) The delay *prevented* your letter *being* sent.

    (*b*) The delay *prevented* your letter *from being* sent.

These two sentences mean the same thing, and both are correct. But in (*a*) "being sent" is a Passive Participle *used gerundively*, while in (*b*) "being sent" is not a participle at all, but a Passive gerund or noun used as object to the preposition "from."

In (*a*) the Gerundive Participle (see § 207 and § 284, *c*) contains an implied noun, and the words "prevented your letter *being sent*" are equivalent to "prevented *the sending of* your letter."

(61) **Save he, save we**, etc. :—

There was no stranger in the house save *we* two.—*Old Testament.*
No man hath seen the Father, save *he* which is of God.—*New Test.*
All the conspirators, save only *he.*—SHAKSPEARE.
None shall be mistress of it save *I* alone.—SHAKSPEARE.

This Nominative (which is now gradually going out of use) is a survival of the Nominative Absolute, which was used when "save" was still an Adjective used absolutely, and had not been changed into a Preposition. On Participial prepositions see § 373 (*j*).

(62) **Several people, several persons** :—

    Several people think that the winter is over.

The phrase "several people," though common, is not so correct as "several persons," because "several" has a distributive force and denotes individuals, while "people" is a Collective noun.

(63) **Shortly, briefly** :—

    I will write *shortly* (=in a short time).

    I will write *briefly* (=in few words).

The adverb "shortly" is used to denote shortness only of *time*, and only of *future* time. We cannot say "He went away *shortly*" (a short time ago); nor can we say "He lived there *shortly*" (for a short time). The adverb "briefly" is used only in the sense of shortness in *language*.

(64) **So and so, or so, so so, and so on** :—

   (*a*) He asked what I meant, and I told him *so and so*.
   (*b*) I shall return in a week *or so*.
   (*c*) *So so* it works : now, mistress, sit you fast.—DRYDEN.
   (*d*) He disliked dances, plays, picnics, *and so on*.

In (*a*) "so and so" is the adverbial form of the Indefinite adjective "such and such." "I told him *so and so*," might be rewritten "I gave him *such and such* an answer" (see § 326, *c*). These expressions are used, when the speaker does not think it necessary or does not desire to enter into particulars.

In (*b*) "or so" is also used Indefinitely, and the sentence might be rewritten, "I shall return in a week or such-like,"— that is, a week more or less (see § 326, *c*).

In (*c*) "so so" means "fairly well," and is used when the speaker does not wish to say anything definite. When the phrase is preceded by "but," it means something less than "well." "His leg is but *so so*" (Shakspeare),—that is, "his leg is in rather a worse state than usual."

In (*d*) the phrase "and so on" means "and such-like," or "etc." (*et cetera*). The adverb "on" means "forward,"—that is, to the end of the list :—"He disliked dances, plays, picnics, and such-like amusements to the end of the list."

(65) **So as to**, etc. :—

   I got up at six A.M. *so as to be* certain of being in time.

This construction is elliptical, and the ellipse should be filled up as follows :—"I got up at six A.M. *so* (= in such a way) *as* (= in which way I should get up) to be certain," etc. The Infinitive in such phrases is Gerundial.

(66) **So kind as to**, and similar phrases :—

   He was *so kind as to* take me into his house.

"He was so (to that extent) kind as (to which extent a man would be kind) to take me (for taking me)," etc. Here too the Infinitive is Gerundial. The sentence is equivalent to "He was kind *enough* to take me."

(67) **Somehow or other, anyhow** :—

   He managed *somehow or other* to pay off his debts.

Here "how" has been substituted for the corresponding

noun. " He managed some how or other how = in some *way* or other (way) to pay off his debts."

(68) **Thank you.**—This is merely an ellipse for " I thank you."

(69) **The other day.**—In § 327 (*e*) it has been pointed out that this phrase is Indefinite,—some day a little preceding the present, that is, a few days ago. Perhaps *the other day* meant " the second day," that is, two days from now, two or three days ago ; for in Old English " other " meant " second." Shakspeare has *this other day* as an equivalent to *the other day*. The same explanation suits this phrase equally well :—" This is the second day that has passed since such and such a thing happened."

(70) **This much, so much, so much for** :—

    (*a*) *This much* at least we can promise.
    (*b*) He is now *so much* better that we need not be alarmed.
    (*c*) *So much for* his courage ; now as to his honesty.

In (*a*) " much " is used as a noun : " this much " is equivalent to " this amount," " this quantity."

In (*b*) " much " is an adverb qualifying the adjective " better " ; and " so " is another adverb qualifying " much."

In (*c*) the first clause written out in full would be :—" As *for* (= regarding) his courage, *so much* has been or can be said." Here there is a confusion between " this much " as a noun and " so much " as an adverb. The phrase " so much " is used in this place as a noun to some verb understood. It is generally used when the speaker or writer is ridiculing something. " This is all that can be said about his courage ; now let us see what can be said about his honesty."

(71) **To be mistaken** :—

    (*a*) You will find that you *were mistaken*.
    (*b*) You will find that you *mistook it*.

The form of the verb in (*a*) is according to idiom ; and this must be adhered to. The form in (*b*) is what we should have expected from the meaning of the verb " mistake," which is " to misapprehend, or to misunderstand."

Note—The origin of this use of the word "mistaken " is explained in § 199. Past participles are sometimes used to denote state. character, or habit ; thus " grazéd ox " = the ox that grazes.

      Lik'ning his Maker to the *grazéd* ox.—MILTON.
        The *ravinéd* salt-sea shark.—SHAKESPEARE.

Where *ravinéd* means "addicted to ravening,"—that is, ravenous. If this explanation is correct, the only peculiarity about *mistaken* is that the word denotes a special act of mistaking something as well as a habit of mistaking things. "Mistaken" is often used in the sense of habit ; as, "He was a very *mistaken* man," a man who had formed many false opinions, and was accustomed to act on them.[1]

(72) **To be sure** :—

> Shall you go ? *To be sure* I shall.

Here "to be" is the Gerundial Infinitive, and the phrase "to be sure" signifies "certainly." The phrase, "Well, to be sure !" is a form of exclamation denoting astonishment.

(73) **To boot** :—

> I give you this *to boot*.

I give you this by way of an extra. "To boot" means "in addition," "over and above." "Boot" has always meant profit ; and is of the same root as the first syllable in *better*. The prep. *to* is here used in the sense of purpose ; § 372 (9).

(74) **What not** :—

When this phrase is used, it stands after a string of nouns or verbs, and denotes that many more might be added, but there is no need to mention them :—

> Steam propels, lowers, elevates, pumps, drains, pulls, and what not (what else does it not do ?).
> Persians, Copts, Tartars, Medes, Syrians, and what not (=several other nations that I need not name) were brought under the dominion of Alexander the Great.

(75) **What was, what was not** :—

> (*a*) *What was* my astonishment on seeing this !
> (*b*) *What was not* my astonishment on seeing this !

These two sentences come to the same thing, in spite of the "not." The first means "How great was my astonishment," etc. ; the second means "No astonishment could be greater than mine was," etc.

(76) **What with, somewhat** :—

The phrase "what with," repeated before two or more nouns, is sometimes used for enumerating a series of things :—

> *What with* the cunning of his methods, *what with* the flattery of his tongue, and *what with* the influence of his money, he soon became the leading man in the town.

It might be supposed that "what with" is an elliptical phrase for "what *he effected* with cunning," etc. But more probably "what" is here an Indefinite Demonstrative adjective (§ 315) used as an adverb in the sense of "partly." The com-

---

[1] The word "drunken" is used in the same way. Among the *dramatis personæ* of the *Tempest* we have "Stephano, a *drunken* butler."

pound word "somewhat" is still used sometimes as a noun signifying "something," and sometimes as an adverb signifying "to some extent" or "partly" :—"I am *somewhat* tired of this book." In colloquial English we still say, "I tell you what," which means "I tell you something," or "I have something to tell you." In Shakespeare we have :—

> I tell thee *what* (= something), Antonio.

(77) **Who**, in the phrase "*as who should say*," where *who* is used as an Indefinite demonstrative pronoun.

One example has been given from Shakspeare in § 315.

But the expression is still common :—

> "Is the present generation of young men at Oxford affected to any appreciable degree by the traditions of the place?"
> "Oh, yes," replied my host, *as who should say*, "We haven't altogether gone to the dogs."—*Quiver.*

(78) **Write you, write to you** :—

> I will *write you* a letter on this matter.
> I will *write to you* soon.

We can use the phrase "*write you*," when "you" is the Indirect object to the verb and is followed by a Direct object But if there is no Direct object and the verb "write" is used Intransitively (§ 145, *a*), we must say "*write to you*."

(79) **Gerundive use of Participles.**—In this construction a Participle is made to denote what would otherwise be expressed by a Gerund or Verbal noun. It was a common construction in Latin: "anno urbis *conditae*," in the year of the city *built, i.e.* in the year of the *building* of the city. In our own language, however, it is not older than the sixteenth century.[1]

---

[1] Mr. Kellner, however (in *Historical Syntax*, p. 262), quotes two examples of a much earlier date than the sixteenth century :—

(1) Tó-janes þo sunne risinde.—*Old. Eng. Misc.* p. 26.
(2) After the sunne goyng down.—WYCLIFF, *Gen.* xxviii. 11.

But here he appears to be mistaken. Ex. (1) is from Old Kentish Sermons, that were copied by a Norman scribe, who betrays his imperfect knowledge of English by spelling the Verbal noun at first as *-inde*, then as *-inke*, and then at last correctly as *-inge*. The misspellings of such a scribe cannot be set up as an authority for Old English. The word *risinde* is not a pres. part. but a misspelling for *risinge*, a Verbal noun, and this noun is preceded by *sunne*, the Genitive case, which originally was spelt *sunnan*, then *sunnen*, then *sunne*. So example (1) means "at the time of the *sun's* rising," where "rising" (*risinde*) is a noun, and not a pres. part. Ex. (2) is equally clear. Here *sunne*, as before, is a Genitive case coupled with the Verbal noun *goyng-down*.

We have no right to be hurt at a *girl telling* me what my faults are.
—THACKERAY.
There is always danger of this *disease appearing* in the sound eye.
—HUGH CONWAY.
Don't fear *me being* any hindrance to you.—DICKENS.
I ask where there could be pictures at Compton Green without *me
knowing* it.—BESANT AND RICE.
Would you mind *me asking* you a few questions ?—STEVENSON.

In the first of the following sentences "*being sent*" is a participle used Gerundively; in the second it is an actual Gerund :—

(1) This prevented the letter *being sent.*
(2) This prevented the letter from *being sent.*   See (60).

(80) Phrases and words suggested by French :—

(*a*) "How do you *do ?*"   See (32), where it is shown that *do*
is a translation of the French *faire.*

(*b*) "It's *me.*"   A translation of Fr. "*c'est moi*"; see (42).

(*c*) "The window *gives* upon the street."   Here *gives* is a
translation of the Fr. *donne,* which, though lit. "gives," means
looks, abuts.   Here we must parse *gives* as a Transitive verb
used Intransitively on the principle shown in § 145 (*b*).

(*d*) "That goes *without saying.*"   A translation of Fr. *sans
dire;* so evident that there is no need to mention it.

(*e*) "That subject came *upon the carpet.*"   A translation of Fr.
sur le tapis; we often say "on the *tapis,*" that is, on the tablecloth, before the meeting.   "Carpet" once meant a covering of
any kind, a tablecloth as much as a floorcloth.

(*f*) "*As to,*" followed by a noun : "I am indifferent *as to* his
success."   A translation of Fr. *quant à,* as much as relates to.   See
explanation in chap. xi.   The phrase *as to* is at least as old as Wycliff.

(*g*) "*Solidarity* of interests."   A phrase originally borrowed
from French Communists.   Entire union of interests.

(*h*) "He *affects* the latest fashion."   Translation of Fr. *affect-er,*
follows, adopts.

(*i*) "To *exploit* a new invention."   From Fr. *exploit-er,* to make
the most of for the sake of trade, to utilise to the utmost.

NOTES ON CERTAIN GRAMMATICAL TERMS.

Absolute Construction.   Any construction may be called absolute, in
which a word or phrase is independent of the rest of the sentence ; § 27.
Accidence (Lat. *accidentia,* Neut. Plur., "things which befall"): the
collective name for all those changes of form that are incidental to certain
Parts of Speech.

H

Analysis (Gr. *ana*, up ; *lysis*, loosening or breaking). Analysis means "breaking up" a whole into its component parts. Grammatically, this term admits of several applications, such as (*a*) the breaking up of a compound letter into its parts, as *x* into *ks*, or the vowel *ī* into *a*+*i* ; (*b*) the breaking up of a syllable into its letters ; (*c*) the breaking up of a word into its prefixes, stem, and suffixes ; (*d*) the breaking up of a Multiple or a Complex sentence into its component clauses ; (*e*) the breaking up of a clause into its component parts,—the subject, attributive adjuncts, predicate, and adverbial adjuncts.

Anomaly, a solitary or very uncommon deviation from accidence, syntax, or idiom : (Greek word, *anōmalia*, unevenness of ground).

Apposition (Lat. *ad*, *posit-*, placed): the placing of one noun or sentence against another for the purpose of explanation ; see §§ 18-20.

Archaism (Gr. *archai-os*, ancient) : the use of a word that was once common, but is now out of ordinary use, as *clomb* for *climbed*, *meseems* for *it seems to me*, *eyen* for *eyes*.

Assimilation (Lat. *ad*, to, *similis*, like) : the process by which a consonant is made to take the form of another consonant through the influence of contact, as in the word *as*(=*ad*)*similation*.

Defective : deficient in certain forms. This term can be applied to (1) verbs that are wanting in certain parts ; (2) adjectives that have no comparative or superlative of their own, but borrow them from other roots ; (3) nouns which have a singular but no plural, or a plural but no singular.

Dialect (Gr. *dia-lect-os*, discourse, conversation) : a local or provincial form of speech characterised by some peculiarities of accent, pronunciation, or grammatical usage, which distinguish it from the standard speech of the nation, such as the Yorkshire dialect or the Dorsetshire dialect. Until some standard has become established, the different local varieties of kindred speech are dialects of coequal rank. But when a standard speech has been formed, the dialects or local varieties fall into a lower rank and are regarded as the speech of the unlearned.

Ellipsis (Gr. *en*, in, and *leipsis*, leaving) : an omission (allowed by idiom or custom) of a word or words, which must be mentally supplied in order to make the phrase or sentence grammatical, as, "It is *more than certain* that," etc.—that is, "it is not only certain, but something more, that," etc.

Etymology (Gr. *etymos*, true, *logos*, word) : that branch of philology which traces the origin or true beginning of a word. Sometimes, however, the word is used for Accidence.

Euphony (Gr. *eu*, well, and *phon-e*, a sound) : the pleasing effect produced on the ear by pronouncing or grouping words in a particular way.

Good English. This implies five things at least : (1) the choice of suitable words—see **Impropriety** below ; (2) correct syntax and accidence : no bad grammar—see *bad grammar* below under **Grammar** ; (3) correct order of words, as, for example, that the antecedent must be placed as close as possible to its Relative—see § 275 (*a*) *Note ;* (4) correct idiom—see *phraseological idiom* under **Idiom** below ; (5) absence of verbiage—see **Verbiage** below.

Grammar (Gr. *gramma*, a letter ; Old Fr. *gramaire*): an exposition, partly practical and partly theoretical, of the various forms and methods employed in any given language for the expression of thought.

The above definition, since it makes no reference to time, is wide enough to include the forms and methods formerly used (Historical Grammar) as well as those in present use (Modern Grammar). Grammar includes Accidence and Syntax, the order of words as well as the relations of words to one another, phraseological idiom as well as the principles of more regular construction, the sounds and symbols used in word-making, the prefixes and suffixes by which words are built up, the clauses of which a compound or complex sentence consists.

The subjects of punctuation, prosody, rhetoric, poetic diction, and the derivations of words, though closely allied to Grammar, do not come within the scope of Grammar proper.

When we say that a phrase or sentence is in "bad grammar" we generally mean that it is a violation of Accidence or Syntax.

Homonym (Gr. *homos*, the same, and *onoma*, a name) : words spelt and sounded alike, but differing in sense and origin ; as *bear*, verb (A.S. *ber-an* ; Sanskrit, *bhar*), *bear*, noun (A.S. *ber-a* ; Sanskrit, *bhal-a*).

Homophone : words sounded, but not spelt, alike ; as *some*, *sum*.

Idiom (Gr. *idiom-a*, peculiarity) is used in two senses :—(*a*) Grammatical idiom, viz. whatever pertains to the structure of a language in its accidence and syntax ; (*b*) Phraseological idiom, viz. some particular combination of words that is not strictly in accordance with the general structure of a language, and therefore requires a specific explanation or exposition. The latter is the sense in which "idiom" is chiefly used.

Note.—In this book, Part I. deals chiefly with Grammatical idiom, and Part II. with Phraseological.

Impropriety (Lat. *in*, not, *proprius*, proper) : the using of a word in a sense that does not properly belong to it, as "to *perpetrate* a virtuous action." (*Perpetrate* is always used in reference to something bad, although etymologically it means simply "to perform.")

Inflexion (Lat. *in*, and *flexum*, to bend or change). "By inflexion we understand an addition to a whole class of words, expressing some grammatical function, or a meaning so general as not to constitute a new word. Thus the inflexion *s* is added to *tree* to express the meaning of plurality, this meaning being so general that we feel *trees* to be essentially the same word as the uninflected singular *tree*."—SWEET.

Neologism (Gr. *neos*, new, and *logos*, speech) : the use of a new word suitable and sanctioned by authority, but not thoroughly established in general use and therefore still rather uncommon ; as *altruism*, to denote the habit of living for others in contrast with selfishness ; *solidarity*, to denote entire union of aims, duties, and interests.

Paronym (Gr. *para*, beside, *onoma*, name) : a word pronounced in the same way as another, but differently spelt, as *hair*, *hare* ; *air*, *heir* ; *were*, *ware*, *wear* ; *mare*, *mayor* ; *one*, *won*.

Parse (Lat. quæ *pars* orationis) : to parse a word is to show (1) to what part of speech it belongs ; (2) to account for its inflexions, if it has any ; (3) to show in what relation it stands to any other word or words in the same sentence.

Philology (Gr. *philos*, friend, *logos*, word or speech) : the study of words ; but usually in the more specific sense,—the comparative study of kindred languages, such as the Teutonic group, or the still wider Aryan group.

Phonetics (Gr. *phonetica*, things pertaining to the voice) : that branch of grammar that deals with speech-sounds.

Pleonasm (Gr. *pleion*, more) : redundancy ; as "a *sole* monopoly."

Poetic license. A license or liberty allowed to poets, but not allowed to writers of prose ; such as the use of uncommon or archaic words, the use of uncommon constructions or phrases, etc.

Poets, however, are prohibited the use of solecisms (see this word defined below), that is, blunders. For instance, we cannot tolerate Byron's "There let him *lay*," but we can tolerate such a phrase as "Trip it *deft and merrily*," because the conjoining of an adverb to an adjective, though rare, admits of syntactical explanation (see § 274).

Purity (Lat. *puritas*) : the use of words sanctioned by the best modern writers. This excludes (*a*) the use of obsolete words, (*b*) the use of foreign words or phrases when suitable English ones exist, such as saying Lat. *de die in diem*, for "from day to day," or Fr. *à propos*, for "with reference to" ; (*c*) the use of slang words, as *jolly* for *very ; see **Slang**.

Slang (Sc. *sleng*) : a mode of speaking peculiar to some particular place or calling ; as stockbrokers' slang, schoolboys' slang, the slang of sailors, soldiers, the theatre, the university. Sometimes a slang word rises into general acceptance as part of the national speech, as *donkey, dunce, a jingo, to boycott, whig, tory.*

Solecism (Gr. *Soloikos*, a dweller at Soloi, a town notorious for speaking bad Greek) : this word denotes (*a*) a violation of accidence or syntax, that is, a grammatical blunder, or (*b*) a violation of idiom ; as,

(*a*) *Whom* do men say that I am (*whom* for *who*).

(*b*) He died *with* fever (*with* for *of*).

Style (Lat. *stilus*, an instrument for writing) ; such use of words in the expression of thought as distinguishes one writer or speaker from another. Thus a style may be terse or diffuse ; pithy or pointless ; obscure or perspicuous ; explicit or vague ; simple or rhetorical ; spirited or tame ; light or ponderous, etc.

Synonym (Gr. *syn*, with, *onoma*, name) : a word having the same or nearly the same meaning as another, and capable of being used in the same or nearly the same context, as *unlikely, improbable.*

Note.—We are obliged to introduce the word *nearly*, as there are few, if any, examples of *perfect* synonyms. *Unlikely* and *improbable* are as nearly perfect synonyms as any other pair of words that we could easily find. Yet we could hardly substitute "*improbable* to happen" for "*unlikely* to happen."

Syntax (Gr. *syn*, with, *taxis*, arrangement) : that part of Grammar that deals with the order of words in a sentence, and with their relations to one another in its construction.

Synthesis (Gr. *syn*, with, *thesis*, placing). Analysis means "breaking up"; synthesis means "adding on." The one is in all possible applications (see those given under **Analysis**) the converse of the other.

A language is said to be in the *Synthetic* stage, when the different parts of a word are formed by adding inflexions to the stem. A language is in the *Analytical* stage, when it has discarded most of its inflexions, and makes a very frequent use of auxiliary words.

Tautology (Gr. *to auto*, the same, *logos*, word) : employing superfluous words in the same grammatical relation ; as "safe *and secure.*"

Technology (Gr. *techne*, art or science, *logos*, word): an explanation of technical terms, as when a word has some specific meaning in connection with some art or science, different from that in general use. Thus *elbow* has one sense in architecture, another in navigation, and another in ordinary use.

Verbiage (Lat. *verbum*): a needless profusion of words. It includes pleonasm and tautology together with any other offence against brevity.

QUESTIONS ON IDIOM AND CONSTRUCTION.

Collected from London Matriculation Papers.

1. Explain the construction of *self*. What part of speech is it? Trace its history.

2. Correct or justify:
      (*a*) That's him.
      (*b*) Many a day.
      (*c*) I expected to have found him better.

3. State clearly the rules of English accidence regarding the use of *will* and *shall* in Interrogative sentences.

4. Discuss, with reference to the history of their usage, the words *ye* and *you*, *that* and *which* (as Relatives).

5. Tell what you know of the origin and present use of *a* and *the*. How would you place them among the parts of speech, and why?

6. What is a Relative pronoun? Point out and explain the different uses of *that*, *what*, *which*, *whether*.

7. What is the real power of the Genitive case? Distinguish its uses according to meaning.

8. Tell the history of the forms *a* and *an*, and discuss their grammatical use.

9. Take six of our common English prepositions, and show in what way each has been taken to represent different relations of place, time, and causality.

10. Discuss the syntax of the following:—
      (*a*) I meant to have written to you.
      (*b*) I heard of him running away.
      (*c*) It's me.

11. Explain how you would classify the words *aye*, *yea*, *yes*, *no*, *nay* among the parts of speech.

12. How do you classify pronouns? Parse the word *what* in the sentences:—
      (*a*) I will tell you *what*.
      (*b*) He was some*what* weary.
      (*c*) *What* o'clock is it?
      (*d*) *What* man is this?
      (*e*) *What* with the wind, and *what* with the rain, it was not easy to get on.

13. Explain and parse the following phrases :—*methinks ; woe is me ; I had as lief.*

14. Define the terms *inflexion, analysis, synthetic, interjection ; strong* and *weak* as applied to verbs ; *abstract* and *concrete* as applied to nouns ; *simple* and *complex* as applied to sentences.

15. What exactly is meant by a *Pronoun ?* What by a *Relative pronoun ?* Mention any differences in usage between *who* and *that.*

16. Write some short sentences to show the various meanings of the prepositions *at, with, if, from, against.* Explain :—

     (*a*) He did his duty *by* him.
     (*b*) *Under* these circumstances.
     (*c*) Ten *to* one it is not so.
     (*d*) Add ten *to* one.
     (*e*) Keep up *for* my sake.

17. Parse *after* and *out* in each of the following :—

     (*a*) *After* him then, and bring him back.
     (*b*) *After* he came, all went wrong.
     (*c*) You go first, and I will come *after.*
     (*d*) *After* that I will say no more.
     (*e*) *Out,* brief candle.
     (*f*) He was quite *out* of it.
     (*g*) *Out* upon it !
     (*h*) He was beaten *out and out.*
     (*i*) He proved an *out and out* deceiver.

18. Parse each of the four words, *But me no buts.* What other parts of speech may *but* be ? Would you say, *They all ran away but me,* or *They all ran away but I ?*

19. What is meant by an *idiom ?* Mention two or three English idioms, and try to explain them.

20. Point out what is idiomatic in these phrases :—

     (*a*) There came a letter.
     (*b*) Let me fight it out.
     (*c*) We spoke to each other.
     (*d*) Many a man would flee.
     (*e*) What an angel of a girl !
     (*f*) What with this, and what with that, I could not get on.

21. What errors have crept into these phrases :—

     (*a*) Ever so many.
     (*b*) To do no more than one can help.
     (*c*) These sort of things.

Suggest some explanation of " *of* " in such phrases as " a friend *of* mine."

22. Parse the italicised words and phrases :—

     (*a*) *Down* with it !
     (*b*) His *having been beaten* once only made him the more determined to succeed.
     (*c*) *Seeing* is *believing.*
     (*d*) The *hearing* ear and the *seeing* eye, the Lord hath made *even* both of them.

    (e) *Whatever* sceptic could inquire for,
        For every *why*, he had a *wherefore*.
    (f) *Let* knowledge grow from *more* to more.

23. Distinguish between *farther* and *further*, *gladder* and *gladlier*, *nearest* and *next*, *latest* and *last*, *peas* and *pease*, *genii* and *geniuses*.

24. Give instances of common nouns becoming proper, and of proper becoming common. How does the possessive of personal pronouns differ from the genitive ?

25. Discuss these phrases :—

    (a) He found them *fled*, horses *and all*.
    (b) Fight *away*, my men.
    (c) Get *you* gone.
    (d) I give him this *to boot*.
    (e) He overslept *himself*.
    (f) How did he come *by* such a fortune ?

26. Define the words *grammar, etymology, syntax, gender, number, case, mood,* and *tense*.

27. Correct or justify :—

    (a) Thinking of them, my pen tarries as I write.
    (b) It's me.
    (c) I intended to have written to him.

28. Give the sources of the following expressions, pointing out the objection to their use as English idioms, and showing how the meaning might in each case be properly conveyed :—

    (a) That window *gives* upon the street.
    (b) That affair came *upon the carpet*.
    (c) That goes *without saying*.
    (d) He is feeble *as to* his mind.
    (e) *Solidarity* of interests.
    (f) He *affected* the latest fashion.
    (g) To *exploit* a new invention.

29. Notice any differences in usage between the relatives, *that, who, which*.

30. Point out any grammatical errors that are common in ordinary colloquial speech. State exactly what you understand by " good English."

31. Write several sentences illustrating the correct modern usage of *shall* and *will* in Interrogative sentences, giving any explanations that appear to be necessary.

32. Why are Prepositions so called ? Discuss the use of *past* in " He went *past* the house " ; of *of* in " The island *of* Great Britain " ; of *by* in " Do your duty *by* the University."

33. What do you understand by a Pronoun ? What by a Reflexive pronoun ? Point out the inconsistency of saying *I myself*, and yet *He himself*, and account for it.

34. Give the meaning and origin of the following prepositions :—*maugre, but, between, notwithstanding, during*. And mention as many as you can of the various senses in which *by, to, with* are used.

35. Explain and illustrate the terms *inflexion, assimilation, etymology, phonetics,* and *accidence*.

36. **Discuss the verbal forms in italics :—**

(a) How *do* you *do* ?   (b) I *do* you *to wit.*
(c) Woe *worth* the day.   (d) *Seeing* is *believing.*
(e) He that hath ears to *hear*, let him *hear.*
(f) The hawthorn bush, with seats beneath the shade,
    For *talking* age and *whispering* lovers made.

37. Parse the words italicised in the following :—

(a) *Please* write clearly.   (b) *Thank* you.
(c) If you *like.*   (d) From *bad* to worse.
(e) *Get you* gone.   (f) He was accused of *having run* away.

38. **Discuss carefully these words and ways of speaking :—** *talented ; a friend of mine ; reliable ; neither he nor she are at hand ; they all hoped to have succeeded.*

39. Define and illustrate the terms : — *dialect, slang, technology, archaism, neologism, solecism.*

40. Parse *but* in the following sentences, and explain carefully its idiomatic usage in each case, with reference to its original meaning :—

(a) There is none here *but* hates me.
(b) And was not this the earl ?   'Twas none *but* he.
(c) He would have died *but* for me.
(d) He is all *but* perfect.
(e) There's not the smallest orb which thou behold'st,
    But in his motion like an angel sings.
(f) He is *but* a madman.

41. Distinguish between the comparative degree of an adjective and an adjective with comparative force.   To which class belong—*former, inferior, older, elder, outer, utter.*

42. Point out any defects in the grammar or style of the following :—

(a) Homer was not only the maker of a nation, but of a language.
(b) He is better versed in theology than any living man.
(c) Shakspeare frequently has passages in a strain quite false, and which are entirely unworthy of him.
(d) Nothing can hinder this treatise from being one of the most considerable books which has appeared for the last half-century.
(e) A statute inflicting the punishment of death may be and ought to be repealed, if it b: in any way expedient.

43. Differentiate the following as regards usage :—*further, farther ; late, latter ; older, elder ; outer, utter ; foremost, first.*

APPENDIX I.—PROSODY AND POETRY.

1. Prosody (Gr. *pros-odia*, lit. a song sung to an instrument) treats of the laws of metre. It might be called "the grammar of verse."

2. Rhythm (Gr. *rhuthmos*, measured flow or motion) is "the musical flow of language." This is produced for the most part by a well-balanced recurrence of pauses and accents.

Rhythm has been elsewhere defined "a principle of proportion introduced into language."[1] This definition is practically equivalent to our own, though perhaps it scarcely gives enough prominence to *sound*. It is only a practised reader who can perceive "the proportion of language" without reading the composition aloud.

Rhythm is not confined to verse. It is quite as necessary to an orator as to a poet ; and there is scarcely any kind of prose, of which the attractiveness is not increased by the recurrence of pauses and accents at suitable intervals.

3. Rime (A.S. *rím*, "number," misspelt as *rhyme* from a supposed connection with Gr. *rhuthmos*) is a repetition of the same sound at the *ends* of two or more lines. The effect of rime, however, is not produced, unless the lines succeed one another immediately or near enough for the resemblance of sound to strike the ear. Monosyllabic rimes are always accented.

Note 1.—A rime is usually of *one* syllable. But rimes can also be in two or more syllables, provided that the first syllable is accented and the rest are unaccented ; as, *motion, ocean; behaviour, saviour*. Double rimes are called in French, and sometimes in English, female or feminine, while a single rime is called a male. Double and treble rimes are more commonly used in comic poetry :—

> To hear them rail at honest *Sunderland*,
> And rashly blame the realm of *Blunderland.*—Pope.

Note 2.—A monosyllabic rime is *perfect* under three conditions : (1) the vowel or vowels, whatever the spelling may be, must produce precisely the same effect on the ear ; (2) if any consonant or consonants *follow* the riming vowel or vowels, these (whatever the spelling may be) must produce precisely the same effect ; (3) the consonant that *precedes* the rime must, to prevent monotony, pro-

---

[1] Abbott and Seely's *English Lessons for English People*, p. 143.

duce a *different* effect on the ear. Thus *hair* and *fair* are perfect rimes, because the three conditions just stated are all satisfied. But *bear* and *fear* are not perfect rimes, because the vowel-sounds, though not very different, are not quite the same. Again, *fare* and *af-fair* are not perfect rimes, because the riming vowel is preceded by the same consonant. Again, ap-*peased*, re-*leased* are not perfect rimes, because the final consonants in the former have the sound of *zd*, while those in the latter have the sound of *st*.

When the rime is dissyllabic or polysyllabic, every syllable except the first must begin with the same consonant; cf. *Sunderland*, *Blunderland*, un-*fortunate*, im-*portunate*.

4. Assonance (Lat. *ad* + *sonant-ia* verba).—This term is applied to words which rime in the vowel or vowels, but not in the consonant or consonants following. It is therefore a very imperfect kind of rime ; as, *slumber*, *blunder ; same*, *cane*.

5. Alliteration (Lat. *ad* + *litera*).—When two or more words begin with the same vowel, or the same consonant, or the same syllable, this is called alliteration. It is *initial* riming as distinct from *end*-riming.

Ruin seize thee, *ruthless* king !—GRAY.

Note.—All our earliest poetry was alliterative. The last great specimen of such poetry in our literature is *Piers the Plowman*, by William Langland, born in A.D. 1332. The poem is written in lines of ten to twelve syllables. The following is a specimen :—

In a *s*omer *s*eson, when *s*oft was the *s*onne,
I *s*hope me in *s*hroudës, as I a *s*hepe were.

6. Cæsura (a Latin word denoting "a cut"). In Latin prosody this meant the "cut" or division of a foot somewhere near the middle of the line, the cut being followed by a pause of the voice in reading the line aloud. In English prosody cæsura means merely the *pause* of the voice, by which lines of eight or more syllables are usually divided, when they are read aloud ; and this pause may occur either at the end or in the middle of a foot. (For the meaning of "foot" see below, § 590.) Rhythm greatly depends on the position of the cæsura.

In the following example the figure against each line shows the number of feet (with or without a half foot) preceding each cæsura. When a comma or other stop occurs in the same place as the cæsura, the rhythm of the line is helped by the sense ; but a pause or cæsura can be made independently of punctuation, if the rhythm of the line is improved thereby. Sometimes a line has no cæsura ; that is, neither the rhythm nor the sense of the line require that any pause should be made in reading or repeating the line aloud :—

3½   Of man's first disobedience ‖ and the fruit
3   Of that forbidden tree, ‖ whose mortal taste
     Brought death into the world and all our woe
2½   With loss of Eden, ‖ till one greater Man
1½   Restore us ‖ and regain the blissful seat,
2   Sing, Heavenly Muse, ‖ that on the secret top, etc.
                                   MILTON.

Observe that monotony is avoided and the rhythm of the lines enhanced by varying the place of the cæsura.

Observe also that the third line does not need any cæsura.

7. Metre (Gr. "measure") is "rhythm reduced to law." It depends on two factors :—

   (*a*) The accentuation of syllables.

   (*b*) The number of *accented* syllables to a line.

Note.—**Quantity** means the amount of time required for pronouncing a syllable distinctly. In Latin prosody syllables were subdivided by quantity into Long and Short. In English versification, however, quantity is of no importance excepting so far as it affects accentuation. It is entirely subordinated to accent.

Then tore′ | with blood′- | y tal′- | on the′ | rent plain′.—BYRON.

Here the short syllable *the* is made as long as possible for the sake of giving it an accent, and the long syllable *rent* is made as short as possible for the sake of removing its accent.

8. A specific combination of accented and unaccented syllables is called a **foot**. The number of syllables to a foot may be either two or three, but it cannot be less than two or more than three, and *one of these must be accented.*

   (*a*) An **Iambus** consists of one unaccented and one accented syllable. This is the commonest of all our feet.

            Ap-pear′, be-sides′, at-tack′, sup-ply′.

   (*b*) A **Trochee** consists of one accented and one unaccented syllable. Not so common as the Iambus.

            Ho′-ly, up′-per, grand′-eur, fail′-ing.

   (*c*) An **Anapæst** consists of two unaccented syllables followed by an accented one. Rather uncommon.

            Col-on-nade′, re-ap-pear′, on a hill′.

   (*d*) A **Dactyl** consists of one accented syllable, followed by two unaccented ones. Very rare.

            Mes′-sen-ger, mer′-ri-ly, prop′-er-ty, in′-fa-mous.

Note 1.—A fifth kind of foot is sometimes added, called an **Amphibrach**, consisting of an accented syllable between two unaccented ones ; as *re-venge′-ful, a-maz′-ing.* The following line from Campbell may be quoted as an example :—

     There came′ to | the beach′ a | poor ex′-ile | of E′-rin.

It would be easy, however, to subdivide the line into anapæsts by making the first foot an Iambus, which is common in anapæstic metre :—

> There came' | to the beach' | a poor ex'- | ile of E'-rin,

in which *Erin* is a double rime.

But the following lines contain amphibrachs, which cannot be resolved into anapæsts :—

> Most friend'-ship | is feign'-ing,
> Most lov'-ing | mere fol'-ly ;
> Then heigh'-ho | the hol'-ly,
> This life' is | most jol'-ly.—SHAKSPEARE.

Note 2.—A sixth kind of foot, long and consisting of two accented syllables, is sometimes added. In Latin prosody this foot is called a **Spondee**. But in English prosody no such foot is recognised, since theoretically there cannot be more than one accent to an English foot. Sometimes, however, two accented syllables are placed together for the artificial purpose of making the sound of the line suggestive of the sense :—

> When A'- | jax strives' | *some* rock's' | *vast* weight' | to throw',
> The line' | *too* la'- | bours and' | the words' | *move* slow'.

Note 3.—The names of all the feet are derived from Greek. *Iambus* means "aiming at," "attacking," so called because this foot was first used in Satire. *Trochee* means "running," so called because it is a rapid measure. *Dactyl* means "finger," so called because this foot, like a finger, consists of one long followed by two shorts. *Anapæst* means "thrown back," because this foot is a dactyl reversed. *Spondee* means "pertaining to libations," so called because, when libations were poured out, slow and solemn melodies were used. *Amphibrach* means "short at both sides," so called because this foot consists of one long syllable enclosed by two short ones.

9. To **scan** a line (Lat. *scan*-d-ere, to climb) is to divide it into its several feet, and say *what kind* of feet they are, and *how many* of them there are. Lines of two feet are called *dimeters ;* of three, *trimeters ;* of four, *tetrameters ;* of five, *pentameters ;* of six, *hexameters.* In Tennyson's *Locksley Hall* we have an example of *octometers* (8 feet). In scanning a line the following precautions should be noted :—

(*a*) The number of feet to a line depends on the number of *accented* syllables, not on the total number of syllables (§ 589).

(*b*) An accented monosyllable at the beginning of a line is sometimes made to do duty for an entire Iambic foot :—

> *Stay'*, | the king' | hath thrown' | his war'- | der down'.—SHAKS.
>
> (*Iambic pentameter*, 5 feet.)

(*c*) In the Trochaic and Dactylic metres, an accented monosyllable at the end of a line counts as an entire foot, though in

the former this foot is short of one unaccented syllable, and in the
latter of two :—

> Life' is | but' an | em'-pty | dream'.—LONGFELLOW.
> > (*Trochaic tetrameter*, 4 feet.)
> Com'-rades, | leave' me | here' a | lit'-tle, | while' as | yet' 'tis |
> ear'-ly | morn'.—TENNYSON (*Trochaic octometer*, 8 feet.)
> Mer'-rily, | mer'-rily | shall' I live | now',
> Un'-der the | blos'-som that | hangs' on the | bough'.—SHAKS.
> > (*Dactylic tetrameter*, 4 feet.)

(*d*) Metres are not always perfectly carried out. In an
Iambic line the first foot is sometimes a Trochee instead of an
Iambus. In the Anapæstic metre, Iambic feet are sometimes
put for Anapæsts, and this in any part of the line :—

> Daugh'-ter | of God' | and man', | ac-com'- | plished Eve'.—MILTON.
> > (*Iambic pentameter*, 5 feet.)
> Not a drum' | was heard', | not a fu'- | neral note'.
> > (*Anapæstic tetrameter*, 4 feet.)

(*e*) In scanning a line, two short syllables coming together
can be counted as one for the sake of the metre :—

> Wing''d with | red light'- | ning and' | impet'- | *uous* rage',
> The mul'- | ti-tud'- | *inous* sea' | incarn'- | adine'.

(*f*) Two open vowels belonging to different words can be
slurred, so as to be fused together and pronounced as one :—

> Impressed' | th*e e*fful'- | gence of' | his glo'- | *ry a*bides'.
> By her'- | ald's voice' | explained' ; | the hol'- | *low a*byss',
> Abom'- | ina'- | b*le, u*nut'- | tera' | b*le, a*nd worse'.
> T*o i*nsult' | the poor' | or beau'- | ty in' | distress'.
> May I' | express' | th*ee u*nblamed, | since God' | is light'.

10. Blank Verse.—" Blank " means unrimed. This is much
used in Epic and Dramatic verse, and generally in Iambic pentameters. This is the noblest of all verse. It is the most difficult
to write effectively, though it seems the easiest.

See example of Epic blank verse quoted from *Paradise Lost* in
§ 588 under **Cæsura.**

In Longfellow's *Hiawatha* we have a solitary example of
blank verse in Trochaic tetrameters:—

> > Then' the | lit'-tle | Hi'-a- | wa'-tha
> > Learned' of | ev'-ery | bird' the | lan'-guage.

Occasionally we have blank verse in Dactylic dimeters :—

> > Can'-non to | right' of them,
> > Can'-non to | left' of them,
> > Can'-non in | front' of them.—TENNYSON.

Some attempts have been made to introduce Classical (Latin

and Greek) metres into English; but they have not been success-
ful. This is a third kind of blank verse. The best examples
of Latin hexameters are Longfellow's *Evangeline* and Kingsley's
Andromeda :—

> This' is the | for'-est pri- | mev'-al, the | mur'-mu-ring | pines',
> and the | hem'-lock.—Longfellow.

Special Metres.

11. The Heroic Couplet.—In this metre lines consisting
of five Iambic feet rime together in pairs.

This is called "Heroic" because it has been much used in trans-
lating Epic or Heroic poetry ; as in Dryden's translation of Virgil, and
Pope's translation of Homer.

This metre is sometimes varied by a triplet, in which the third
line (called an Alexandrine) can have *six* Iambic feet instead of five :—

> The sacred lake of Trivia from afar,
> The Veline fountains, and sulphureous Nar,
> Shake at the baleful blast, the signal of the war.—Dryden.

12. The Sonnet.—Borrowed from Italy. It consists of
fourteen Iambic pentameters, of which the first eight lines are
called the octave, and the last six lines the sestette. The Italian
octave (followed by Milton) has two rimes, in the order of
abba, abba ; the octave in Shakspeare has *four* rimes, in the order
of *ab ab cd cd.* The sestette has either two or three rimes.

The subject of a sonnet is usually either reflective or amatory. The
word *sonnet* is derived from Ital. *sonetto.*

13. Ottava Rima.—Borrowed from Italy. Each stanza
consists of eight Iambic pentameters. The letters *a, b, c* show
the system of riming. (The word *ottava* means " octave.")

> *a* 'Tis sweet to hear the watch-dog's honest bark
> *b*   Bay deep-mouthed welcome as we near our home ;
> *a* 'Tis sweet to know there is an eye will mark
> *b*   Our coming, and look brighter when we come ;
> *a* 'Tis sweet to be awakened by the lark,
> *b*   Or lulled by falling waters ; sweet the hum
> *c* Of bees, the voice of girls, the song of birds,
> *c* The lisp of children and their earliest words.—Byron.

14. The Spenserian Stanza.—Called Spenserian from its
originator, Spenser, who used it in writing *The Faery Queen.*

> *a* Roll on', | thou deep' | and dark'- | blue O'- | cean, roll,
> *b*   Ten thou'- | sand fleets' | sweep o'- | ver thee' | in vain :
> *a* Man marks' | the earth' | with ru'- | in ; his' | control
> *b*   Stops with' | the shore' ; | upon' | the wa'- | tery main
> *b*   The wrecks' | are all' | thy deed' ; | nor doth' | remain

c A shad'- | ow of' | man's rav'- | age save' | his own,
b When for' | a mo'- | ment like' | a drop' | of rain
c He sinks' | into' | thy depths' | with bub'- | bling groan,
c Without' | a grave', | unknelled', | uncof'- | fined, and' | unknown.
                                                    BYRON.

The ninth and last line, which in this metre always consists
of six feet instead of five, is called an Alexandrine, like the third
line in heroic triplets, § 593.

15. The Metre of "In Memoriam."—This consists of a
four-line stanza in which each line contains four Iambic feet, the
fourth line riming with the first, and the third with the second.
This metre was not, as is often supposed, originated by Tennyson.
It was used by Sandys in his metrical paraphrase of the Psalms,
A.D. 1636 :—

> What profit can my blood afford,
>   When I shall to the grave descend ?
>   Can senseless dust thy praise extend ?
> Can death thy living truth record ?—*Psalm* cxxx.

(Quoted from Skeat's *Student's Pastime*, p. 347, No. 424.)

16. Stanzas (Ital. *stanza*, Old Ital. *stantia*, so called from
the stop or pause at the end of it). Almost all stanzas are in
rimed, not in blank, verse.

A stanza of three lines is called a **Triplet**, as in Tennyson's
Two Voices, in which each line consists of an Iambic tetrameter ;
the third line is not an Alexandrine.

> Whatev'- | er cra'- | zy sor'- | row saith',
> No life' | that breathes' | with hu'- | man breath'
> Has ev'- | er tru'- | ly longed' | for death'.

A stanza of four lines is called a **Quatrain** (Fr. *quatre*, Lat.
quatuor, four). Of such stanzas the most common examples are
—(1) the **Ballad** metre, as in *Chevy Chase ;* and (2) the **Elegiac**
metre, as in Gray's *Elegy*. In both of these the rimes alternate :
—in the former a tetrameter with a trimeter ; in the latter a
pentameter with a pentameter. The stanza used in *In Memoriam*
is another kind of quatrain ; see § 597.

A stanza of six lines is called a **Sextant**, in which the rimes
may occur in the following orders :—(1) *a, b, a, b, a, b ;* (2) *a, a,
b, c, c, b ;* (3) *a, b, a, b, c, c.*

A stanza of eight lines is called an **Octave ;** but it is best
known under the name of Ottava Rima (Ital. sounded as *ottàva
reema*, Lat. *octavus*, eighth) ; see § 594.

A stanza of nine lines is the Spenserian ; see § 596.

Poetic Diction.

17. Prose, Poetry.—Poetry (from Gr. *poiët-es*, an originator, is distinguished from prose (Lat. *prosa*, for *prorsa* or *pro-versa*, turned forward, rapid, unchecked) not only by the possession of metre, but by certain peculiarities of diction and of thought. The most prosaic matter may be expressed in the most prosaic language, and yet in the most perfect metre; the metre does not make either the matter or the language poetical.

> Something had happened wrong about a bill,
> Which was not drawn with sound commercial skill;
> So, to amend it, I was told to go
> And seek the firm of Clutterbuck and Co.—CRABBE.

18. Poetic Diction. — The chief peculiarities are the following :—

(1) *The use of archaic or less common words.*—Poetry pays little or no attention to changes in current speech. At the same time it likes to distinguish itself from prose. It therefore avoids common words, and retains words that were used by former poets, after they have gone out of general use :—

Nouns.—Poetry often uses *swine* for *pigs; swain* for *peasant* or *husbandman; billow* for *wave; main* for *sea* or *ocean; maid* or *damsel* for *girl; nuptials* for *marriage; vale* for *valley; steed* or *charger* for *horse; ire* for *anger; woe* for *sorrow* or *misery; thrall* for *distress*, etc.

Adjectives.—Poetry often uses *lone* or *lonesome* for *lonely; drear* for *dreary; dread* for *dreadful; intrepid* or *dauntless* for *brave; rapt* for *delighted; hallowed* for *holy; baleful* for *pernicious*, etc.

Adverbs.--Poetry often uses *scarce* for *scarcely; haply* for *perhaps; sore* for *sorely; oft* for *often; erst* or *whilom* for *formerly; of yore* or *of old* for *in ancient times; scantly* for *scantily; anon* for *at once*, etc.

Verbs.—Poetry often uses the older forms of past tenses in preference to the modern or Weak ones; as *wrought* for *worked; bade* for *bid; begat* for *begot; clove* for *cleft; crew* for *crowed; drave* for *drove; throve* for *thrived; clomb* for *climbed; stove* for *staved; clad* for *clothed*.

Conjunctions.—Poetry often uses *what though* or *albeit* for *although; ere* or *or ere* for *before; nathless* for *nevertheless; an if* for *if*.

(2) *Omission of words required by Prose.*—Two purposes are served by such omissions : the metre is preserved, and the diction is made less like that of prose:—

The brink of (the) haunted stream	} *Article.*
Creeping like (a) snail unwillingly to school	
(He) who steals my purse steals trash	} *Noun or*
Lives there (the man) who loves his pain?	*Pronoun.*
For is there aught in sleep (that) can charm the wise?	} *Relative as Subject to a Verb.*
'Tis distance (that) lends enchantment to the view	

Mean though I am, (I am) not wholly so . .	
Happy (is) the man, whose wish and care, etc. .	*Finite Verb.*
To whom thus Adam (spoke)	
Soldier, rest, thy warfare (being) o'er, etc. .	*Participle.*
My ramble (being) ended, I returned . .	
He knew himself (how) to sing	*Conjunction.*
Permit (that) I marshal thee the way . .	
He mourned (for) no recreant friend . . .	
Through the dear might of Him that walked (on)	*Preposition.*
the waves	
Despair and anguish fled (from) the struggling soul	

(3) *Change in the regular order of words.*—The same two purposes are hereby served as before.

   (*a*) Adjective placed after its noun, instead of before it :—

> Or where the gorgeous East with richest hand
> Showers on her kings *barbaric* pearl and gold.—MILTON.

   (*b*) Subject placed after its verb, and object before it :—

> No *hive* hast *thou* of hoarded sweets.

   (*c*) Preposition placed after its noun instead of before it :—

> Where echo walks steep hills *among.*

   (*d*) Infinitive placed before the finite verb, instead of after it :—

> When first thy sire *to send* on earth,
> Virtue, his darling child, designed.—GRAY.

   (*e*) Adverb placed before its verb, instead of after it :—

> *Up* springs from yonder tangled thorn
> A stag more white than mountain snow.—SCOTT.

   (*f*) Complement placed before its verb, instead of after it:—
> *Grieved* though thou art, forbear the rash design.

(4) *Use of adjectives or participles for clauses.*—One of the aims of poetry is to say as much as possible in the fewest possible words : hence an adj. or part. is made to do duty for a clause.

   (*a*) He can't combine each well-*proportioned* part.

That is, he cannot make the different parts proportionate to each other, and then combine them into a symmetrical whole.

   (*b*) From his *slack* hand the garland wreathed for me
> Down dropped, and all the faded roses shed.

Here "slack" stands for "which had become slack."

   (*c*) From *loveless* youth to *unrespected* age
> No passion gratified except her rage.

Her youth was devoid of love, the peculiar grace of youth ; and her old age was devoid of respect, the peculiar privilege of age ; all through life the one predominant passion was her evil temper.

Note.—In paraphrasing poetry into prose one of the first things to be done is to convert such adjectives or participles as those quoted above into verbs, adding such Relatives or Conjunctions as may be necessary.

(5) *Use of ornamental epithets not required by the sense :*—

> The breezy call of *incense-breathing* morn,
> The swallow twittering from its *straw-built* shed,
> The cock's shrill clarion, and the echoing horn
> No more shall rouse them from their lowly bed.—GRAY.

Note.—In paraphrasing poetry, such epithets, if they are repeated at all, should be thrown into the background, as they are out of place in prose composition, and tend to encumber the sense.

(6) *A freer use of figurative language.*—See the Figures of Speech in Appendix II.

The different kinds of Poetry.

19. Epic. From Gr. *epik-os, epos,* a word, speech, or tale. Heroic legends told in metrical language were originally recited, not written ; hence such poems were called "words."

"The epic poem treats of one great complex action, in a grand style, and with fulness of detail."—T. ARNOLD.

Lyric. From Gr. *lurik-os,* adapted to the lyre. Short rapid poems in irregular metre. Such poems are often called *Odes* (Gr. literally "songs").

Dramatic, the poetry of the stage. From Gr. *dramatik-os,* that which pertains to action or acting.

Note.—Thus in the name "Epic," the idea of recitation is prominent ; in "Lyric," the music ; and in "Dramatic," the acting.

Pastoral. From Lat. *pastor,* a shepherd. The poetry of rural life.

Didactic. From Gr. *didaktik-os,* instructive. Instruction on some technical or moral subject, set forth in verse and embellished as far as possible with poetic ornament.

Satire. From Lat. *satira,* "a dish of mixed foods." Poetry which exposes and censures the faults of persons or communities.

Added to these there is **Descriptive** poetry, such as Thomson's *Seasons ;* **Elegiac** poetry (from Gr. *elegos,* a lament), as Wolfe's *Burial of Sir John Moore ;* the poetry of **Romance** or **Legend,** as Macaulay's *Lays of Ancient Rome,* or Scott's *Lady of the Lake ;* **Ballad** poetry, as *Chevy Chase.*

APPENDIX II.—FIGURES OF RHETORIC.

A FIGURE of rhetoric is a deviation from the ordinary use of words, with a view to increasing their effect.

(1) **Simile** (Lat. *similis*, like): a formal expression of the likeness said to exist between two different objects or events :—

> Errors, *like* straws, upon the surface flow ;
> He that would search for pearls must dive below.

(2) **Metaphor** (Gr. transference): an informal or implied simile :—

> Experience is the *lamp* by which our feet are guided.

(3) **Personification**: the ascription of mind and will to inanimate things :—

> *Weary* wave and *dying* blast
> *Sob* and *moan* along the shore ;
> And all is peace at last.

(4) **Fable, Parable, Allegory**: a description of one event under the image of another. These are the same at bottom, but a parable is more serious than a fable, and an allegory is a parable carried to a greater length. The aim of all is to enforce some prudential or moral truth by a story, in which a personification or series of personifications is maintained to the end. In fables the lower animals are personified as men.

Note.—*Fable* is from Lat. *fabula*, a story. *Parable* is from Gr. *parabolé*, a comparison. *Allegory* is from Gr. *allegoria*, a description of one thing under the image of another.

(5) **Metonymy**: lit. "a change of name" (Gr. *meta*, change, *onoma*, name): to describe a thing by some *accompaniment* instead of naming the thing itself :—

> The *crown* (=king) would not yield to the *mitre* (=priest).

(6) **Syn-ec-do-ché** (Greek): "the understanding of one thing by means of another," as in the following examples :—

All *hands* (=men) at work	(part for whole).
The smiling *year* (=season)	(whole for part).
He acted *the lord* (=lordly character)	(concrete for abstract).
A *justice* (=judge) of the peace	(abstract for concrete).
The *marble* (=statue) speaks	(material for thing made).

(7) **Euphemism** (Gr. *eu*, well, *phemismos*, speaking): the describing of something disagreeable or offensive in agreeable or non-offensive terms :—

> That statement was purely an effort of imagination (*i.e.* a lie).

Note.—Euphemism must not be confounded with *Euphuism,* an affected, high-flown style assumed as a mark of good breeding (Gr. *Euphues,* "well-born," the title of a book by Lyly, a contemporary of Shakspeare, who made his hero talk in this style, and wrote in the same style himself).

(8) **Climax** (Gr. ladder) : a series of representations that succeed one another in an ascending order of impressiveness :—

> It is an *outrage* to *bind* a Roman citizen ; to *scourge* him is an *atrocious crime ;* to *put him to death* is almost a *parricide ;* but to *crucify* him, what shall I call it ?

(9) **Anticlimax** or **bathos** (Gr. depth) : a ludicrous descent from the more impressive to the less impressive :—

> Here thou, great Anna, whom three realms obey,
> Dost sometimes *counsel* take, and sometimes *tea.*—POPE.

(10) **Interrogation** : an emphatic mode of affirming or denying something by means of asking a question :—

> Who is here is so base that would be a bondman ? Who is here so rude that would not be a Roman ?—SHAKSPEARE.

(11) **Antithesis** (Gr. *anti,* against, *thesis,* placing) : placing words in contrast to each other :—

> A *friend* exaggerates a man's *virtues,* an *enemy* his *crimes.*

(12) **Epigram** (Gr. *epi,* on, *gramma,* writing) : a tersely expressed combination of ideas that might seem to be contradictory, or are rarely thought of together :—

> Art lies in concealing art (*Ars est celare artem*).—*Latin Proverb.*
> By *merit* raised to that *bad* eminence.—MILTON.
> A past that was never present.—GROTE.

(13) **Irony** (Gr. dissimulation): praise intended for blame:—

> And Brutus is an *honourable* man.—SHAKSPEARE.

(14) **Litotes** (Gr. extenuation) : the use of a negative before a noun or adjective to indicate a strong affirmative in the opposite direction :—

> He is no dullard (decidedly clever).

(15) **Apostrophé** (Gr. *apo,* away, *strophé,* turning) : addressing some absent person, as if he were present, or some inanimate thing (concrete or abstract), as if it were living :—

> O Luxury ! thou curst by heaven's decree,
> How ill exchanged are joys like these to thee !—GOLDSMITH.

(16) **Prosopopœia** (also called Vision, from Gr. *prosōpon,* face, *pœia,* making) : describing the past or future as if it were present, the imaginary as if it were real :—

> Is this a dagger that I see before me ?—SHAKSPEARE.

Note.—The Historic present (see § 349, *e*) exemplifies this figure.

(17) **Onomatopœia** (Gr. *onomat-os*, name, *pœia*, making): the use of words that suggest the sense by their sound.   See p. 224, *Note* 2 :—

> Rend with tremendous sound your ears *asunder*,
> With *gun, drum, trumpet, blunderbuss,* and *thunder.*

(18) **Circumlocution, Periphrasis** (Gr. *peri*, around = *circum; phrasis*, speaking = *locutio*) : a roundabout way of describing any-thing ;—an aid to euphemism, if such aid is wanted :—

He resembled *the animal that browses on thistles* (= an ass).
His *prominent feature* (nose) like an eagle's beak.—WORDSWORTH.

(19) **Hyperbolé** (Gr. exaggeration): not always a fault :—
They were swifter than eagles and stronger than lions.—*Old Test.*

APPENDIX III.—SYNONYMS.

FOR a definition of synonym, see p. 216.

(1) **Adoration, worship.**—The former gives prominence to the outward act ; the latter to devotional feeling.

(2) **Allude, refer.**—We *refer* to a thing that has been speci-fied, or is just going to be specified.   We can *allude* to a thing by implication, without specifying it at all.

(3) **Aid, help.**—We *aid* a man, when we add our efforts to his own, as in raising a ladder against a wall.   We *help* him, when we give him something that he requires, as by throwing him a rope to save him from drowning.

(4) **Apparent,** what seems to be ; **evident,** what is and cannot be otherwise.

(5) **Aware, conscious.**—*Aware* of something external to oneself ; *conscious* of one's own thoughts and feelings.   "He was *aware* of the enemy's designs, and *conscious* of his inability to cope with them."

(6) **Confess, admit.**—We *confess* a fault ; *admit* an error.

(7) **Couple, pair.**—Except in the phrase "a married couple," a *couple* means two things not matched : cf. "a *couple* of horses," "a *pair* of horses."

(8) **Delightful, delicious** : as "*delightful* music," "*delicious* fruit."   What pleases the lower senses is delicious ; what pleases the higher ones is delightful.

(9) **Discover, invent.**—We *discover* some fact or law that existed before, but was unknown.   We *invent* some new device or contrivance, that did not exist before.   *Discovery* belongs to science ; *invention* to art.

(10) **Distinguish, discriminate.**—We *distinguish* sounds into high and low. We *discriminate* them as being either high or low, when we hear them.

(11) **Habit, custom.**—*Habit* is the tendency of *mind*, on which custom or customary *action* depends. A *habit* of industry leads to the *custom* of keeping punctual hours.

(12) **Imagination, fancy.**—*Imagination* is the faculty by which we mentally realise effects before they are produced. *Fancy* is the more playful exercise of the same faculty ; and hence the word sometimes degenerates into the sense of whim or freak : "That is mere *fancy*."

(13) **Import, meaning.**—*Import* is the actual sense of a word ; *meaning* is the sense intended by the speaker, which might not tally with the actual sense or real import.

(14) **Liberty, freedom.**—*Liberty* implies previous restraint : "He set his slaves at *liberty*." *Freedom* implies simply the absence of restraint : "He is *free* to go where he likes."

(15) **Patient, passive.**—*Patient* means absence of anger or complaint ; *passive* means absence of resistance.

(16) **Part, portion.**—*Part* is a fraction of a whole ; *portion* is a part allotted : "The estate was divided into four *parts*, and each heir received his *portion*."

(17) **Perpetual, eternal.**—The first word is not so strong as the second.

(18) **Politician, statesman.**—The first is a self-seeker who makes a trade of politics. The second is one who in his political capacity consults the general good.

(19) **Stop, stay.**—A man may *stop* at a house and *stay* inside it for the night. The one implies arrested motion ; the other implies a halt for some period after arrested motion.

(20) **Strict, severe.**—A man may be *strict* in observing rules, and *severe* in punishing the breach of them.

(21) **Unlikely, improbable.**—*Unlikely* applies chiefly to the future ; *improbable* to the present and past. We say a thing is unlikely, but not improbable, to happen.

APPENDIX IV.—CHANGES OF MEANING.

ONE important branch in the history of a language is to trace the changes of meaning that some of its words have undergone

in the course of their literary use.[1] The changes can be classified as follows :—(*a*) Elevation of meaning; (*b*) degradation of
meaning; (*c*) narrowing of meaning; (*d*) widening of meaning;
(*e*) shifting to some side-meaning, which gradually ousts the
original, as in *x*, *xy*, *y*.

(a) *Elevation of Words.*

Amiable (Lat. *amabilis*) ; once denoted physical beauty.
   So *amiable* a prospect.—HERBERT.

Babe, baby ; once denoted a doll or puppet.
   The *baby* of a girl.—SHAKSPEARE (*Macbeth*).

Brave ; once denoted brilliant, gaudy.
   Sweet rose, whose hue angry and *brave*.—HERBERT.

Companion ; once a term of contempt ; a low fellow.
   Companion, hence !—SHAKSPEARE (*Julius Cæsar*, iv. 3).

Delicate ; once used in a bad sense ; luxurious, voluptuous.
   Haarlem is a very *delicate* town.—EVELYN.

Emulation ; once used in the sense of an evil passion,—envy.
   Such factious *emulations* shall arise.—SHAKSPEARE.

Feminine ; once in the sense of womanish ; now, womanly.
   The *feminine* son of a brave father.—HOLLAND.

Generous ; once noble only in birth ; now noble in character.
   The *generous* and gravest citizens.—SHAKSPEARE.

Liberal ; once free in a bad sense ; unscrupulous.
   A profane and *liberal* counsellor.—SHAKSPEARE.

Mountaineer ; once used in the sense of freebooter.
   No savage fierce, bandit, or *mountaineer*.—MILTON.

Prestige ; once used in the sense of illusion.
   The sophisms of infidelity and the *prestiges* of imposture.
             WARBURTON.

Popularity ; once the practice of courting popular applause.
   Indicted for *popularity* and ambition.—HOLLAND.

Spinster ; could once denote a woman of bad life.
   Many would never be indicted *spinsters*, were they spinsters
   indeed.—FULLER.

(b) *Degradation of Words :* much more numerous than (*a*).

Animosity ; once, spiritedness or courage ; now, resentment.
   A man of *animosity* and courage.—HALES.

Artificial ; could once mean artistic, with the sense of natural.
        Artificial strife
   Lives in these touches, livelier than life.—SHAKSPEARE.

Base ; once, humble, low, without being depraved.
   A peasant and *base* swain.—BACON.

---

[1] Out of the 156 illustrative sentences quoted in this Appendix nearly
all are from Webster's *English Dictionary*, a few are from the author's
own reading, and a few more, about 20 in number, from Trench's *Select
Glossary*.

Brat ; once, a child in a favourable sense.
> Oh Abraham's *brats*, oh brood of blessed seed.—GASCOIGNE.

Censure ; once, merely opinion ; now, blame.
> Take each man's *censure*, but reserve thy judgment.
>   SHAKSPEARE.

Conceit ; once, any kind of notion ; now, vanity.
> A *conceit* of somewhat ridiculous.—BACON.

Counterfeit ; once, to imitate without any sinister purpose.
> Christ doth not set forth this unrighteous steward for us to *counterfeit*.—TYNDALE.

Demure ; once modest without affectation.
> Sober, steadfast, and *demure*.—MILTON.

Doleful dumps ; once used seriously ; now, in a comic sense.
> The pensive court in *doleful dumps* did rue.—FULLER.

Egregious ; once, remarkable ; now, remarkably bad.
> Wiclif's *egregious* labours are not to be neglected.—MILTON.

Formal ; once, essential, real, pertaining to the form (essence).
> The *formality* (essence) of the vow lies in the promise made to God.—STILLINGFLEET.

Fulsome ; once, simply full ; now, full *ad nauseam*, sickening.
> His lean, pale corpse grew *fulsome*, fair, and fresh.—GOLDING.

Garble ; once, to pick out the good and reject the bad ; as " to garble spices."

Gossip ; once, a sponsor in baptism ; now, a mischief-maker.
> A lady invited to be a *gossip*.—SELDEN.

Gross ; once, great ; now, coarse.
> A *gross* body of horse under the Duke.—MILTON.

Idiot ; once, uneducated, simple-minded.
> Christ was received of *idiots* and the simple sort.—BLOUNT.

Imp ; once, a child ; now, a goblin or little fiend.
> The tender *imp* was weaned.—FAIRFAX.

Insolent ; once, unusual ; now, insulting.
> If any should accuse me of being new or *insolent*.—MILTON.

Knave ; once, merely a boy or servant ; now, a rascal.
> Fortune's *knave*, a minister of her will.—SHAKSPEARE.

Libel ; once, a bill or indictment ; now, a false charge.
> A *libel* of forsaking (a bill of divorce).—WYCLIFF.

Libertine ; once, free-thinker ; now, free-liver.
> Our modern *libertines*, deists, and atheists.—A.D. 1711.

Lust ; once, eager desire ; now, carnal or other evil passion.
> My *lust* to devotion is little.—BISHOP HALL.

Maudlin (contr. of *Magdalene*) ; once, penitent, sorrowful in a good sense.

Mere ; once, pure ; now used in a depreciatory sense.
> Our sorrows would be *mere* and unmixed.—TAYLOR.

Minion ; once, favourite ; now, an unworthy favourite.
> Brave Macbeth, like Valour's *minion*.—*Macbeth*, i. 2, 32.

Naughty ; once used of adults ; now only of children.
So shines a good deed in a *naughty* world.—SHAKSPEARE.

Obsequious ; once, obedient in a good sense ; now, servile.
Obsequious to his orders, they bear him hither.—ADDISON.

Officious ; once, helpful, dutiful ; now, meddlesome.
Yet not to earth are these bright orbs *officious*.—MILTON.

Plausible ; once, commendable ; now, specious, disingenuous.
Which made a *plausible* bishop seem to be Antichrist.—HACKET.

Portly ; once, stately ; now, bulky, corpulent.
He bears him like a *portly* gentleman.—SHAKSPEARE.

Prejudice ; once, prejudgment in a neutral sense, foresight.
Naught might hinder his quick *prejudice*.—SPENSER.

Puny ; once, younger, junior ; now, paltry, insignificant.
If *punies* or freshmen neglect Aristotle.—JACKSON.

Rascal ; once, a man of the common sort ; now, a scoundrel.
The heads of clans with their several *rascalities* (=retainers, followers).—JACKSON.

Resentment ; once, reciprocal feeling ; now, angry feeling.
They declared their *resentment* of his services.
Council Book, 1651.

Retaliation ; once, requital in a neutral sense ; now, revenge.
He sent word to the duke that his visit should be *retaliated*.—
HERBERT.

Sad ; once, serious, settled ; now, sorrowful.
Ripe and *sad* courage.—CHAUCER.

Sensual ; once, appealing to any outward sense ; now, carnal.
Pleasing and *sensual* rites and ceremonies.—BACON.

Silly ; once, timely ; then, innocent ; now, simple, foolish.
The *silly* (innocent) virgin strove him to withstand.
SPENSER.

Tawdry (*St. Awdry*) ; once, fine and showy ; now, trashy and vulgar.

Tempt ; once, to put to the test ; now, to entice to evil.
God did *tempt* Abraham.—*Old Testament*.

Tinsel ; once, a silver or gold texture ; now, paltry finery.
Under a duke, no man to wear cloth-of-gold *tinsel*.—A.D. 1551.

Umbrage ; once, a shadow ; now, offended feeling.
That opinion carries no *umbrage* of reason.—WOODWARD.

Uncouth (lit. *unknown*) ; once, rare and elegant ; now, inelegant.
Harness . . . so *uncouth* and so rich.—CHAUCER.

Varlet ; once, a groom, stripling ; now, a term of contempt.
My gentle *varlet* has come in.—MALORY.

Vassalage ; once, *valorous* service rendered by a vassal.
For all forgotten is his *vassalage*.—CHAUCER.

Vilify ; once, to hold cheap ; now, to abuse.
I do *vilify* your censure (hold your opinion cheap).—BEAU
MONT AND FLETCHER.

Wiseacre ; once, a sage or wise man ; now, always ironical.
Pythagoras became a mighty *wiseacre*.—LELAND.

Wizard ; once, a sage or wise man ; now, a sorcerer.
> The star-led *wizards* haste with odours sweet.—MILTON.

(c) Words that have narrowed their meaning.

Amuse ; once, to occupy the mind with anything, not merely mirth.
> He *amused* his followers with idle promises.—JOHNSON.

Brook ; once, to use in any way ; now, only to tolerate.
> Let us *bruik* the present hour.—*Scotch Ballad.*

Carpet ; once, any kind of covering, not only of floors.
> The subject came upon the *carpet* (table-cloth, *i.e.* it was brought before the meeting ; see p. 213 (80)).

Disease ; once, discomfort of any kind ; now, sickness.
> So all that night they passed in great *disease*.—SPENSER.

Duke ; once, captain or leader ; now, only a title.
> Theseus, *duke* of Athens.—SHAKSPEARE.

Harness ; once, equipment of any kind, as "die in *harness*."
> At least we'll die with *harness* on our back.—SHAKSPEARE.

Knuckle ; once, joint of any kind ; now, only a finger.
> She kneeled down sadly with weary *knuckles*.—GOLDING.

Manure ; once it could denote moral improvement.
> *Manure* thyself, then ; to thyself be improved.—DONNE.

Mediterranean ; once, of land as well as sea.
> Cities as well *mediterranean* as maritime.—HOLLAND.

Repeal ; once, to recall or cancel anything ; now, only a law.
> Repelling sorrows and *repealing* gladness.—SYLVESTER.

Starve ; once, to die from any cause ; now, only from hunger.
> Thus *starved* the mighty Hercules.—CHAUCER.

Vermin, worm ; once, a crawling animal of any length.
> The crocodile is a dangerous *vermin*.—HOLLAND.
> When Cerberus perceived us, the great *worm*,
> His mouth he opened and displayed his tusks.—LONGFELLOW

Voyage ; once, any kind of journey (Lat. *viaticum*).
> So steers the prudent crane
> Her annual *voyage* borne on winds.—MILTON.

Wife ; once, woman ; now, married woman.
> On the green he saw sitting a *wife*.—CHAUCER.

(d) Words that have widened their meaning.

Assure ; once, to betroth ; now, to make certain in any sense.
> To me, sad maid, he was *assured*.—SPENSER.

Chest ; once, coffin ; now, a strong box (Lat. *cista*).
> He dieth and is *chested*.—HAWES.

Harbinger ; once, one who prepared *harbour* (*herberge*, Old Norse) for another by going on first ; now, simply a forerunner.
> A gentleman expostulated with a *harbinger*, who had prepared him a very ill room.—BACON.

Help ; once, to heal ; now, to assist in any sense.
> The true calamus *helps* coughs.—GERARDE.

Institute ; once, to teach ; now, to establish in any sense.
> If children were early *instituted*.—DR. MORE.

> *Note.*—We still call an Arts School a Technical *Institute*.

Maker ; once, a poet ; now, a maker of anything.
> We Englishmen have met well with the Greeks in calling a poet
> a *maker*.—SIDNEY.

Misery ; once, avarice ; now, wretchedness of any kind.
> He will die in *misery* and niggardliness.—BROWNE.

State ; once, a republican,—now any kind of,—government.
> Well, monarchies may own religion's name,
> But *states* are atheists in their very fame.—DRYDEN.

(e) Words that have shifted their meaning.

Abandon : (1) to cast out, expel ; (2) relinquish.
> That he might *abandon* them from him.—UDALL.

Abuse : (1) to deceive, cf. *disabuse* ; (2) revile.
> Their eyes *abused* by a double object.—TAYLOR.

Allow : (1) to praise, cf. Lat. *laud*-em ; (2) permit.
> Ye *allow* the deeds of your fathers.—*Luke* xi. 48.

Angry : (1) red, ruddy ; (2) incensed.
> Sweet rose, whose hue *angry* and brave.—HERBERT.

Awkward : (1) contrary, untoward ; (2) ungainly, clumsy.
> *Awkward* wind.   *Awkward* casualties.—SHAKSPEARE.

Battle : (1) battalion ; (2) combat.
> The king divided his army into three *battles*.—BACON.

Bombast : (1) cotton-wadding ; (2) inflated diction.
> A candle with a wick of *bombast*.—LUPTON.

Boor : (1) a cultivator ; (2) a country bumpkin.
> The Dutch farmers in South Africa are still called *Boors*.

Buxom : (1) yielding, pliable ; (2) blithe and pretty.
> The joyous playmate of the *buxom* breeze.—COLERIDGE.

By-and-by : (1) immediately ; (2) some time afterwards.
> When persecution ariseth, *by-and-by* he is offended.—*Matt.* xiii. 21.

Cheer : (1) face, countenance ; (2) repast.
> Be of good *cheer*.—*New Test.*   All dreary was his *chere*.—CHAUCER.

Christendom : (1) baptism ; (2) the Christian world.
> Sins will wash off the water of *christendom*.—TYNDALE.

Churl : (1) a rustic labourer ; (2) a surly, ill-bred man.
> Let men of cloth bow to the stalwart *churls*.—EMERSON.

Copy : (1) the original to be copied ; (2) the copy itself.
> What is sent to be printed is still called the *copy*.

Danger : (1) jurisdiction ; (2) risk.
> You stand within his *danger*, do you not ?—SHAKSPEARE.

Defend : (1) to prohibit, to forbid ; (2) to protect.
> Which God *defend* that I should wring from him.—SHAKSPEARE.

Defy : (1) to renounce, discard ; (2) challenge.
> For thee I have *defied* my constant mistress.—BEAUMONT AND
> FLETCHER.

Depart : (1) to separate ; (2) to go away.
　　Till death us *depart* (now changed to *do part*).—*Prayer-Book.*

Discourse : (1) the faculty of inference ; (2) conversation.
　　Since he hath made us with such large *discourse,*
　　Looking before and after.—MILTON.

Disoblige : (1) to release from an obligation ; (2) to fail in con
ferring one.
　　　　　Disobliged from payment.—TAYLOR.

Document : (1) unwritten warning ; (2) written evidence.
　　They were stoned to death as a *document* to others.—RALEIGH.

Ebb : (1) shallow, *adj.* ; (2) the outflow of the tide.
　　Cross the stream where it is *ebbest.*—*Proverb.*

Elephant : (1) ivory ; (2) the animal.
　　Of silver, gold, and polished *elephant.*—CHAPMAN.

Feature : (1) the whole of a bodily form ; (2) a part, an aspect.
　　So scented the grim *feature,* and upturned
　　His nostril wide into the murky air.—MILTON.

Firmament : (1) foundation ; (2) sky.
　　Custom is the *firmament* of the law.—TAYLOR.

Forlorn hope : (1) vanguard (Dutch *verloren hoop,* lost band) ; (2)
a hopeless case.
　　Our *forlorn* of horse marched within a mile of the enemy.
　　　　　　　　　　　　　　　　　　　CROMWELL.

Garland : (1) a king's crown ; (2) a wreath of flowers.
Corona regis, quæ vulgariter *garlanda* dicitur.—MATTHEW OF PARIS.

Gist : (1) resting-place (Lat. *jacet*) ; (2) main point.
　　These quails have their set *gists.*—HOLLAND.

Harvest : (1) autumn ; (2) the fruits of autumn.
　　At *harvest,* when corn is ripe.—TYNDALE.

Husband : (1) rustic, ploughman ; (2) husband of wife.
　　The painful (laborious) *husband* ploughing up his ground.
　　　　　　　　　　　　　　　　　　　HAKEWILL.

Imp : (1) engrafted shoot ; (2) child in a bad sense, goblin.
　　Of feeble trees there comen wretched *imps.*—CHAUCER.

Indifferent : (1) impartial, the same to all ; (2) unconcerned.
　　Truly and *indifferently* to minister justice.—*Prayer-Book.*

Ingenuity : (1) ingenuousness, sincerity ; (2) cleverness.
　　Openness and *ingenuity* in contracts.—TAYLOR.

Kind : (1) natural, pertaining to its kind ; (2) loving.
　　It becometh sweeter and loseth the *kind* taste.—HOLLAND.

Lace : (1) a snare, noose (Lat. *laqueus*) ; (2) lace.
　　Vulcanus hath caught thee in his *lace.*—CHAUCER.

Legacy : (1) commission, appointed task ; (2) bequest.
　　My *legacy* wherefore I am sent into the world.—TYNDALE.

Livery (short for *delivery*) : (1) food allowance for horses ; (2)
dress uniform of men-servants.
　　Liverye is allowance of horse meate.—SPENSER.

Lumber: (1) a pawnshop (orig. Lombard) ; (2) goods not in use.
      They put all their plate in *lumber* (pawn).

Medley: (1) conflict ; (2) mixture, confusion.
      The *medley* was hard fought between them.—HOLLAND.

Mess: (1) a quartette ; (2) distribution of food (lit. by fours).
      Where are your *mess* of sons to back you now ?—SHAKSPEARE.

Miscreant: (1) unbeliever (Lat. *minus credent-em*) ; (2) a wicked
wretch.
      Thou oughtest to constrain *miscreants* to keep the faith.—RIVERS.

Obnoxious: (1) liable, answerable (persons) ; (2) objectionable
(things).
      Lawyers are *obnoxious* to their particular laws.—BACON.

Occupy: (1) to lay out money ; (2) to take possession of.
              Occupy till I come.—*Luke* xix. 13.

Overture: (1) an opening ; (2) a proposal.
           The cave's inmost *overture.*—CHAPMAN.

Palliate: (1) to hide a fault ; (2) to make excuses for one.
      They never hide or *palliate* their vices.—SWIFT.

Pester: (1) to crowd ; (2) to annoy.
      All rivers and pools *pestered* with fishes.—HOLLAND.

Plantation: (1) colony, settlement ; (2) plantation of tea, etc.
While these *plantations* were forming in Connecticut.—TRUMBULL.

Race: (1) root of a plant (Lat. *radic-em*) ; (2) lineage.
           A *race* of ginger.—SHAKSPEARE.

Reduce: (1) bring back, restore ; (2) bring down, lower.
      And to his brother's house *reduced* the wife.—CHAPMAN.

Restive: (1) backing (Lat. *re-stare*) ; (2) eager to go forward.
      Restive or *resty*, drawing back instead of going forwards.—
         PHILLIPS.

    Note.—Cf. the phrase "the horse turned *rusty*" (for *resty*).

Sad: (1) steadfast, serious-minded ; (2) mournful.
      Lady Catherine, a *sad* and religious woman.—BACON.

Secure: (1) without fear or anxiety ; (2) safe, without danger.
      Men may *securely* sin, but safely never.—BEN JONSON.

See: (1) seat (Lat. *sed-es*) of a king's power ; (2) of a bishop's.
      Jove laughed at Venus from his sovereign *see.*—SPENSER.

Sight: (1) a multitude ; (2) a spectacle.
         A wonderful *sight* of flowers.—GOWER.

Staple: (1) chief market-place ; (2) chief commodity.
      Alexandria was the *staple* of the Indian trade.

Suspect: (1) to respect ; (2) to regard with suspicion.
The tyrant did not *suspect* the dignity of an ambassador.—NORTH.

Symbol: (1) a contribution ; (2) a token.
      They paid their *symbol* in a war or in a plague.—TAYLOR.

Tarpaulin: (1) sailor, jack tar ; (2) tarred palling, *i.e.* tarred
canvas.
    To landsmen these *tarpaulins* seemed a strange and half-savage
    race.—MACAULAY.

Thews: (1) qualities of mind, manners ; (2) muscles.

Evil speeches destroy good *thewes.*—WYCLIFF.

Trade: (1) the path we *tread ;* (2) buying and selling.

The *trade*-winds, *i.e.* the winds of certain seasons.

Treacle: (1) antidote against venomous bites ; (2) saccharine fluid.

Christ is *treacle* to every harm.—MORE.

Tree: (1) timber as used by carpenters ; (2) living tree.

Jesus whom they slew and hanged on a *tree.*—Acts x. 39.

Union: once a pearl in which all the best qualities were united. *Onion* is so called from its likeness to such pearls.

If pearls be white, great, round, smooth, and weighty, our dainties and delicates here call them *unions.*—HOLLAND.

Vivacity: (1) longevity ; (2) sprightliness.

The *vivacity* of some of these pensioners is little less than a miracle : they live so long.—FULLER.

(f) Words once used for males as well as females.

(Cf. *flirt*, still used for both sexes.)

Coquet (masc.), *coquette* (fem.). You are *coquetting* to a maid of honour.—SWIFT.

Hag. That old *hag*, Silenus.—GOLDING.

Girl (child). A boy was called a knave-*gerl* in Mid. Eng.

Hoyden (doublet of *heathen*). Shall I argue with this *hoyden*, at *his* opportunities in the larder ?—MILTON.

Maid. Sir Gelehad is a *maid* and sinner never.—MALORY.

Man, person ; hence *wife-man*, woman.

Muse.   So may some gentle *Muse*

With lucky words favour my destined urn,

And as *he* passes turn, etc.—MILTON's *Lycidas.*

Termagant. This terrible *termagant*, this Nero.—BALL.

Witch. Thy master is a rare man ; they say he's a *witch.*—BEAUMONT AND FLETCHER.

(g) There is a large number of words sprung from the same root, but differently spelt and rather differently formed, which once had the same, but have since differentiated their meanings.

Achievement, hatchment.	Drench, drown.	Polite, polished.
Artisan, artist.	Drift, drove.	Propriety, property.
Benefice, benefit.	Fact, feat.	Prune, preen.
Caitiff, captive.	Handsome, handy.	Punctual, punctilious.
Cattle, chattels.	Heathen, hoyden.	
Chivalry, cavalry.	Ingenuousness, ingenuity.	Queen, quean.
Convince, convict.	Lively, living.	Sensual, sensuous.
Demerit, merit.	Needful, needy.	Spice, species.
Diamond, adamant.	Novelist, innovator.	Taint, tint.
		Virtuous, virtual.

APPENDIX V.—NOTE BY PROFESSOR SKEAT.

NAMES OF VOCALIC SOUNDS IN MODERN ENGLISH.

THE difficulty of understanding and explaining the vocalic sounds in Modern English is chiefly due to the unfortunate names by which we denote the symbols *a, e, i, o,* and *u.*

For example, the symbol *ā* (long *a*) was used in Latin, and in all languages (including A.S.) which employed the Latin alphabet, to denote the sound of the *a* in *path* or *father;* and nearly all foreign languages still employ this symbol for the same purpose ; and the *name* which they give to the symbol is still pronounced in such languages as it always has been ; *i.e.* the name is sounded like the modern English *ah* (*a* in *path, al* in *calm,* and even (in many parts of Southern England) as *ar* in *cart*).

But the change in the vocalic sounds of Modern English, as compared with those of Middle English, is so great, that none of the present vowel-names are at all suitable for the symbols used to represent them.   The names of the symbols *a, e, i, o, u* can only, at the best, be intelligently employed to denote the *long* vowels or diphthongs, and it is remarkable that only one out of the whole set still represents a pure long vowel, viz. *e* (*ee*).   The names of the remaining symbols, viz. *a, i, o, u,* are all so pronounced as to form diphthongs.   Even the name of the vowel *e* is misleading ; for it denotes a sound which in Latin, and in a large number of languages which employ the Latin symbols, is denoted by (long) *i.*   Indeed, we actually employ the symbol *i* ourselves, in order to represent the sound to which we now give the name of *e;* viz. in words derived from modern French, such as *unique, machine, glacis, quinine, pique,* and several others.

It follows, from the above explanation, that the vowel-names are wholly inappropriate for the symbols.   The convenience of having names which are really appropriate for them is so obvious, that it is worth while for every English child to *know* them, in order that he may be able to distinguish what sounds are being discussed.   All philologists are agreed that the only *appropriate* names for the symbols *a, e, i, o, u* (all supposed long) are the names which the Romans themselves gave them.[1]   These names are represented, respectively, by the following sounds :—

1. The symbol *a* was called *ah ; i.e.* it had the sound of E. *a* in *father,* or of *al* in *calm.*

2. The symbol *e* was called *eh ; i.e.* it had the sound of the *e* in *vein ;* for it must be particularly noted that the *ei* in *vein* is a diphthong, composed of long *e* (*eh*) followed by a slight glide (denoted by *i*) such as is heard at the end of the word *they,* in which it is denoted by the final *y.*   Or we may say that the *e* was sounded like Fr. *é* in *été.*

---

[1] The Roman names for their letters of the alphabet are given in Postgate's *New Latin Primer* as follows :—Ah, Beh, Keh (*i.e.* C), Deh, Eh, ef, Geh, Hah, ee, Kah, el, em, en, Oh, Peh, Coo (Q), er, ess, Teh, oo (U, V), ix (X), ypsīlon, Zēta.

3. The symbol *i* was called *ee; i.e.* it had the sound of E. *ee* in *seem*, or of E. *i* in *unique*.

4. The symbol *o* was called *o*, the *o* being purely pronounced, as in the German word *so*. The E. *o* in *so* is not the same sound, being in fact impure ; for it not only expresses the German *o*, but is followed by a slight after-sound, like a faint utterance of the Eng. *u* in *full*. This after-sound is expressed by *w* in the case of the word *know*, pronounced as (nou).[1] The Englishman who pronounces the German *so* as if it were spelt *zo* in English, can immediately be detected as being no German ; his *z* for *s* is right enough, but the sound which he gives to the *o* is peculiarly and unmistakably his very own.

5. The symbol *u* was called *u*, as in E. *rule*, a sound which English usually represents by *oo*, as in *doom, loose, cool, soon*.

If the reader who has mastered the above facts will now reconsider the names of the English so-called " long vowels," he will begin to realise what the English vowel-names really imply.

1. The English symbol *a* is *now* called by a name resembling the very sound of *a* in the word *name*. This sound is precisely that of the *ei* in *vein; i.e.* the E. *a* in *name* is really a diphthong, such as in French is composed of the Latin *e*, followed by a glide which may be represented by a short *i*. Hence, in phonetic writing, the sound is represented by (ei).

2. The English symbol *e* is now called by a name which is pronounced like E. *ee* in *seem*, or E. (and Fr. and foreign) *i* in *unique*. It is a pure vowel, and was denoted in Latin by *i*, which is often written *ī* by grammarians in order to express its length. Hence, in phonetic writing, the sound may be represented by (ii), the *i* being repeated to indicate length.[2]

3. The English symbol *i* is now called by a name which is pronounced somewhat like the *ai* in Is*ai*ah, but with the former element a little shorter and less distinct. It may approximately be denoted by (ai), though the symbol (əi) is perhaps better. The meaning of the symbol (ə) is given below.

4. The English symbol *o* is now called by a name which is pronounced like E. *ou* in *soul* or *ow* in *know*. It really consists of a German long *o*, followed by a slight (u), where (u) denotes the *u* in *full*. Hence its phonetic symbol is (ou) ; though this is only approximate, unless we remember that the *o* is stressed, and the *u* is slight.

5. The English symbol *u* is now called by a name which is pronounced like the word *yew*, or the *u* in *duke*. The former element is the glide or semi-vowel which we usually denote by *y*, denoted in phonetics by (j); *i.e.* the German *j* in *ja*, or by (i). The latter element is the sound of long *u* in *rule*. Hence the phonetic symbol is (juu) or (iuu) ; where the repetition of (u) denotes that the latter element is long.

---

[1] All pronunciations which are denoted by true phonetic symbols are enclosed, as here, between brackets.

[2] The latter element is apt to pass into a glide ; hence some write (ij), where the (j) represents the German *j* as in *ja*, or E. *y*. The glide is well heard in a word like *seeing* (sijing).

Recapitulating the above results, we see that, when we utter the names of the symbols *a, e, i, o, u,* we really utter sounds which, in older English, in Latin, and in most Continental languages, would rather be expressed by such symbols as (ei), (ii), (ai), (ou), and (iuu) or (iū). The accent falls on the former element in the case of the diphthongs which we denote by *a, i, o ;* and on the latter element in the case of the diphthong which we denote by *u.* Only one of the symbols, viz. *e,* denotes a pure vowel ; and even here, the sound meant is that of the *i* in *unique.*

When we apply their usual names to the short vowels, *i.e.* to the symbols *a, e, i, o, u,* as in the words *cat, bed, it, not, full,* it is obvious that, here again, the mere names are utterly inapplicable to the sounds intended. It follows that the English vowel-names are altogether useless for denoting sounds, unless in every case an example is given of the way in which the sound is written ; and for this purpose the example given must be an entire word, having an invariable pronunciation. It would, obviously, be a great help to have a *true* name for every one of the *sounds* of the English vowels and diphthongs ; and the following list may be taken as giving a *sufficient* approximation to the desired result.[1] The twenty vocalic sounds of the English language are these :—

A. Four sounds frequently denoted by the symbol *a ;* one short and three long.

(1) Short : a sound between French *a* and French *e.* Name : short *æ,* pronounced "short *æ,*" where by *æ* is meant the sound of *a* in *cat,* as heard in the South of England. In order to produce this sound, think of *cat,* and then sound the vowel *only,* omitting *c* and *t.* Phonetic symbol (æ). Sound : that of *a* in *cat* (kæt).

(2) Long. Name : long *æ,* pronounced "long *æ.*" Phonetic symbol (ae). Sound : that of *a* in *Mary* (maeri). This vowel occurs by itself only before a trilled *r* (*i.e.* an *r* followed by a vowel in the same or the next word). With an untrilled *r,* as in *care, bare,* it helps to form a diphthong, being followed by the sound numbered 18. That is, *care, bare* (before a consonant) are pronounced as (kaeə, baeə).

(3) Long. Name : diphthongal *ei,* pronounced "diphthongal *eh-ee.*" Phonetic symbol (ei). Sound : that of *a* in *mate* (meit).

(4) Long. Name : long *aa,* pronounced "long *ah.*" Phonetic symbol (aa). Sound : that of *a* in *path* (paath), *father* (faadhə). (There is no "short *ah.*" The vowel formerly so pronounced has passed into the sound numbered 18.)

E. Two sounds commonly denoted by the symbol *e ;* one short and one long.

(5) Short. Name : short *eh,* pronounced "short *eh.*" Phonetic symbol (e). Sound : that of *e* in *bed* (bed).

---

[1] In other words, we can only speak clearly, so as to be always understood, if we give *foreign* names to the symbols. Unless this be done, it is impossible to emerge from chaos. And it must be remembered, that the pronunciation here spoken of is that of Southern and Midland English, that of the higher classes in London. In the North, the *a* of *cat* is often sounded as the Italian *a* in *matto,* and the *u* of *but* as the Southern English *u* in *full.*

I

(6) Long. Name: long *e*, pronounced "long *ee*." Phonetic symbol (ii). Sound: that of *i* in *unique*, or of *e* in *mete* (miit).

I. Two sounds commonly denoted by *i*; one short and one long.

(7) Short. Name: short *e*, pronounced "short *ee*." Phonetic symbol (i). Sound: that of *i* in *bit* (bit).

(8) Long. Name: diphthongal *ai*, pronounced "diphthongal *ah-ee*." Phonetic symbol (ai). Sound: that of *i* in *bite* (bait). Also written (bəit), meaning that the (a) is indistinct.

O. Three sounds commonly denoted by *o*, with which may be associated the sound of *aw* in *hawk*, seldom written with *o*, except in a few words, such as *off*, *soft*, *frost*.

(9) Short. Name: short *au*, pronounced "short *au*." Phonetic symbol (o). Sound: that of *o* in *not* (not).

(10) The unaccented *o* in *omit* (o'mit·), the phonetic symbol for which is written as (o') by Miss Soames, to indicate that the *o*, if not sounded as No. 18, is nearly pure, the element (u) being scarcely noticeable. It is, of course, quite different from the (o) in *not*, being a close *o* instead of an open one. Name: the unaccented *o*.

(11) Long. Name: long *au*, pronounced "long *au*." Phonetic symbol (ao). Sound: that of *aw* in *hawk* (haok), or *au* in *naught* (naot), or of *o* in *frost* (fraost).

(12) Long. Name: diphthongal *o*, pronounced "diphthongal *oa*." Phonetic symbol (ou). Sound: that of *oa* in *boat*, or *o* in *note* (bout, nout); also written (ow), as (bowt, nowt). The (u) is more distinct at the end of a word.

OO. Two sounds commonly denoted by *oo*; one short and one long.

(13) Short. Name: short *oo*; pronounced "short *oo*." Phonetic symbol (u). Sound: that of *oo* in *book* (buk), or *u* in *full* (ful).

(14) Long. Name: long *oo*; pronounced "long *oo*." Phonetic symbol (uu). Sound: that of *oo* in *boot* (buut).

(15) **U.** The diphthongal sound to which we give the name of *u*. Phonetic symbol (iuu) or (juu); as in *duke* (djuuk) or (diuuk).

(16) The diphthong *oi*; pronounced *oi*; composed of Nos. 11 and 7. Phonetic symbol (oi); as in *toil* (toil).

(17) The diphthong *ow*; pronounced as *ow* in *now*; composed of Nos. 4 and 13. Symbol (au); as in *now* (nau).

Three obscure vowel-sounds, the first of which only occurs in *unaccented* syllables.

(18) Name: the unaccented obscure vowel. Phonetic symbol (ə); called "turned *eh*," or (colloquially) "turned *ee*." Example: the final *a* in *China* (chainə).

(19) Name: the long obscure vowel. Similar to the preceding in sound, but long, and mostly occurring in accented syllables. Phonetic symbol (əə); called "double turned *eh*." Example: the *ur* in *turn* (təən).

(20) Name: the unrounded *u*. Phonetic symbol (ɐ), called "turned *ah*." Example: the *u* in *cut* (kɐt).

Hence there are eight short vowels (æ, e, i, o, o', u, ə, ɐ); six long vowels (aa, ae, ii, ao, uu, əə); and six diphthongs (ei, ai, ou, iuu, oi, au).

Note.—As "turned *ah*" is rather troublesome to print, there is no *great* objection to using the same symbol as in No. 18. For though the sounds are not quite the same, the fact that No. 20 only occurs in *accented* syllables always distinguishes it, *in practice*, from No. 18, which only occurs in *unaccented* syllables. Hence we may write *cut* as (kət). Miss Soames uses the symbol (œ), but it is liable to confusion with (æ).

It has already been said that the name *a* (ei) is very inappropriate, inasmuch as the symbol *a* originally meant the sound of *ah*. It is worth notice, on the other hand, that the sound of the *a* in *name* is so far from being always represented by the symbol *a*, that it can be represented in *twenty* different ways. Examples are : *fate, pain, pay, dahlia, vein, they great, eh, gaol, gauge, champagne, campaign, straight, feign, eight, played, obeyed, weighed, trait, halfpenny.*

APPENDIX VI.—BILINGUALISM ; DOUBLETS.

Bilingual Character of English. — One of the most notable peculiarities of English is the bilingual or double character of its vocabulary ; § 398. Thus Romanic and Teutonic words of the same, or of almost the same, meaning frequently go in pairs ; nouns of Teutonic origin are provided with adjectives of Romanic origin ; or the same noun has two adjectives, one Teutonic and the other Romanic. A few examples will now be given in illustration of this point :—

(i) *Words in pairs.*

Teut.	Rom.	Teut.	Rom.
Abode	domicile	Brow	front
Answer	reply, respond	Build	construct
Ask	inquire	Building	edifice
Begin	commence	Burial	funeral
Belief	faith	Bury	inter
Bemoan	deplore	Buy	purchase
Bent	curved	Calling	vocation
Blunder	error	Clasp	embrace
Boldness	fortitude	Clothes	vestments
Bright	radiant	Cold	frigid

(ii) *Romanic Adjectives to Teutonic Nouns.*

Teut.	Rom.	Lat. word.	Teut.	Rom.	Lat. word.
Cat	feline	*felis*	Eye	ocular	*oculus*
Church(Gr.)	ecclesiastical	*ecclesia*(Gr.)	Foe	hostile	*hostis*
Cow	vaccine	*vacca*	Fox	vulpine	*vulpis*
Dog	canine	*canis*	Gospel	evangelical	*evangelium*
Ear	auricular	*auris*	Head	capital	*capit-is*
Egg	oval	*ovum*	Hearing	audible	*audi-o*

Teut.	Rom.	Lat. word.	Teut.	Rom.	Lat. word.
Horse	equine	*equus*	Sight	visible	*vis-um*
Husband	marital	*maritus*	Son ⎫	filial	⎧ *fili-us*
Island	insular	*insula*	Daughter ⎭		⎩ *fili-a*
Light	lucid	*luc-is*	Sun	solar	*sol-is*
Lip	labial	*labium*	Spring	vernal	*ver-is*
Mankind	human	*homo*	Stream	fluvial	*fluvi-us*
Moon	lunar	*luna*	Tongue	lingual	*lingua*
Mouth	oral	*or-is*	Tooth	dental	*dent-is*
Name	nominal	*nomin-is*	Tree	arboreal	*arbor-is*
Nose	nasal	*nas-us*	Wheel	rotatory	*rotat-um*
Ox	bovine	*bov-is*	Wife ⎫	conjugal	*conjug-is*
Sea	marine	*mar-e*	Husband ⎭		
Sheep	ovine	*ov-is*	Womb	uterine	*uter-us*
Side	lateral	*later-is*			

(iii) *Two Adjectives to the same Noun.*

Teut. noun.	Teut. adj.	Rom. adj.	Lat. noun.
Blood	bloody	sanguinary	*sanguin-is*
Body	bodily	corporeal	*corpor-is*
Brother	brotherly	fraternal	*frater*
Burden	burdensome	onerous	*oner-is*
Child	childish	puerile	*puer*
Cloud	cloudy	nebular	*nebula*
Day	daily	diurnal	*dies*
Earth	earthly	terrestrial	*terra*
Father	fatherly	paternal	*pater*
Fear	fearful	timorous	*timor*
Fire	fiery	igneous	*ignis*
Flesh	fleshly	carnal	*carn-is*
Friend	friendly	amicable	*amic-us*
Frost	frosty	glacial	*glacies*
God	godlike	divine	*div-us*
Hand	handy	manual	*man-us*
Heart	hearty	cordial	*cord-is*
Heaven	heavenly	celestial	*cæl-um*
Home	homely	domestic	*domus*
Kind	kindly	generic	*gener-is*
King	kingly	regal	*reg-is*
Knight	knightly	equestrian	*eques*
Life	lively	vital	*vita*
Milk	milky	lacteal	*lact-is*
Mother	motherly	maternal	*mater*
Night	nightly	nocturnal	*noct-is*
Room	roomy	spacious	*spatium*
Skin	skinny	cutaneous	*cutis*
War	warlike	bellicose	*bellum*
Water	watery	aqueous	*aqua*
Will	wilful	voluntary	*voluntas*
Woman	⎧ womanly	feminine ⎫	*femina*
	⎩ womanish	effeminate ⎭	
World	worldly	mundane	*mundus*

(iv) *Verbs in pairs.*

Back up (support) a claim.
Bear out (substantiate) a charge.
Beat off (repel) an attack.
Block up (obstruct) a passage.
Blot out (obliterate) a word.
Blow out (extinguish) a candle.
Break up (dissolve) a meeting.
Breathe out (exhale).
Bring under (reduce) a fever.
  ,,   forth (produce) fruit.
  ,,   out (elicit) facts.
  ,,   out (publish) a book.
  ,,   in (introduce) a custom.
  ,,   to (resuscitate) a patient.

Bring on (cause) a debate.
  ,,   up (educate) a child.
  ,,   forward (produce) facts.
Buy back (redeem).
Call over (recite) the names.
  ,,   off (divert) attention.
  ,,   in (summon) a doctor.
  ,,   up (recollect) a matter.
  ,,   forth (evoke) applause.
Cast out (expel) from society.
  ,,   down (dejected) with grief.
  ,,   off (discarded) clothes.
  ,,   aside (reject) facts.
Clothe (dress).

DOUBLETS.

Doublet defined.—Words derived from the same original elements, but differing in form and generally differing in meaning, are called *doublets*.

Origin of Doublets.—Doublets have arisen from various causes :—

(*a*) Our semi-vowel *w* was seldom sounded in French; so it was usually changed to a *g* or *gu* :—

Wile, guile ; ward, guard ; wise (manner), guise.

(*b*) Words of Romanic or Greek origin frequently appear in two different forms, one " Popular " and the other " Learned ":—

Abridge, abbreviate ; aggrieve, aggravate ; allow, allocate ; amiable, amicable ; antic, antique ; appraise, appreciate ; benison, benediction ; chance, cadence ; challenge, calumny, etc.

(*c*) Substitution of one letter for another :—

Fabric, forge ; boss, botch ; locust, lobster ; deck, thatch ; aptitude, attitude ; cask, casque ; prune, plum ; servant, serjeant ; ant, emmet ; sect, sept ; wrap, lap ; porridge, pottage, etc.

(*d*) *Metathesis*, or change of place among consonants :—

Granary, garner ; wight, whit ; scarp, scrap ; task, tax ; ask, ax (vulgar) ; thrill, thirl ; gabble, jabber (here *r* is substituted for *l*).

(*e*) Palatalisation, or the substitution of a palatal consonant for a guttural :—

Bank, bench ; dike, ditch ; kirk, church ; trickery, treachery ; gaud, joy ; gabble, jabber ; gig, jig ; lurk, lurch ; disc, dish, desk, dais ; etc.

(*f*) A change of inner vowel :—

Brown, bruin ; shock, shake ; these, those ; dune, down ; grove, groove ; hale, whole ; load, lade ; lust, list ; truth, troth ; cavalry, chivalry ; clause, close ; custom, costume ; one, an ; assay, essay.

(*g*) Excision of an initial letter or syllable :—

Adamant, diamond ; engine, gin ; defence, fence ; appeal, peal ; history, story ; affray, fray ; etiquette, ticket ; ensample, sample ; estrange, strange, etc.

(*h*) Interchange of words from cognate roots :—

Name, noun ; barb, beard ; beaker, pitcher ; knot, node ; foam, spume ; corn, horn ; eatable, edible ; brother, friar, etc.

APPENDIX VII.—WORD-BUILDING : COMPOUNDS AND DERIVATIVES.

COMPOUNDS.

1. Simple words.—A word that is not combined with any other word or syllable is called a Simple or Primary word ; such as *buy, walk, come* (verbs) ; *bench, fire, name* (nouns) ; *hot, cold, stiff* (adjectives).

2. Compounds, Derivatives.—Most of our words, however, are not Simple, but either Compounds or Derivatives.

When one *word* is added to another, the combination is called a **Compound** ; as *man-kind*.

When a *particle* (*i.e.* a syllable which does not make a complete word, or is not *now* used as one) is added to a word, the combination is called a **Derivative** ; as *man-ly*.

If one Simple word is formed from another by means of some internal change, as *graze* from *grass*, *bleed* from *blood*, *raise* from *rise*, this is called a **Primary** Derivative ; but a Derivative formed by adding a particle to the beginning or end of a word, as " man-*ly*," " *un*-man-*ly*," is called **Secondary**.

3. Compounds.—Such words fall into four main classes :—

(1) *Noun Compounds.*

(1) *Adjective + Noun :* blue-bell, mid-day, sweet-heart, noble-man.
(2) *Noun + Noun :* noon-tide, plough-man, sports-man, rail-road.
(3) *Pronoun + Noun :* he-goat, she-goat, she-ass.
(4) *Verb + Noun :* tell-tale, dare-devil, pick-pocket, break-fast.
(5) *Verb + Adverb :* keep-sake, break-down, stand-still, draw-back.
(6) *Adverb + Verb :* out-come, off-spring, out-lay, in-come.
(7) *Adverb + Noun :* by-path, after-life, up-land, in-land, over-coat.

(2) *Adjective Compounds.*

(1) *Noun + Adject.* : sky-blue, blood-red, foot-sore, air-tight.
(2) *Adject. + Adject.* : red-hot, high-born, blue-green, ready-made.
(3) *Prep. + Noun* : over-land, under-hand, over-hand.

(3) *Verb Compounds.*

(1) *Noun + Verb* : back-bite, way-lay, hen-peck, brow-beat.
(2) *Adject. + Verb* : white-wash, rough-hew, safe-guard, rough-shoe (chiefly seen in the participial form "rough-shod").
(3) *Adverb + Verb* : back-slide, over-awe, up-set, with-hold.
(4) *Verb + Adverb* : doff (do off), don (do on), turn out, put on.

(4) *Adverb Compounds.*

(1) *Adject. + Noun* : mean-time, other-wise, mid-way, yester-day.
(2) *Adverb + Prep.* : here-in, forth-with, there-for(e), here-upon.
(3) *Noun + Noun* : length-ways, side-ways.

DERIVATIVES.

4. Root, Stem, Prefixes, Suffixes.—A word reduced to its simplest etymological form, is called a **Root**.

A **Stem** is the change of form (if any) assumed by the root, before a suffix is added to it. Thus in the word "fals-i-ty" the root is *fals* (Lat. *fals*-us) ; the stem is *falsi ;* and the suffix is *ty.* The stem and the root, however, often coincide ; as in *man* (root or stem) + *ly* (suffix).

Particles added to the *end* of a stem are called **Suffixes**. Those added to the *beginning* are called **Prefixes**. The name "Affix" stands for either, though more commonly used for Suffix.

As a general rule Prefixes alter the meanings of words, while Suffixes show to what Part of Speech they belong. Thus there is a very radical difference of meaning between "*pre*-scribe," to order, and "*pro*-scribe," to prohibit. Again "dark-*ness*" is a noun, "dark-*ly*" is an adverb, "dark-*en*" is a verb.

5. Sources of Prefixes and Suffixes.—The three sources from which our Prefixes and Suffixes have come are :—

I. Teutonic (Anglo-Saxon, with a few Norse and Dutch). These are sometimes, but wrongly, called "English."

II. Romanic (Latin or French, with a few Spanish and Italian).

III. **Greek** (borrowed either directly or through French).

6. Hybrids.—The name "hybrid" (which means "of mixed origin") is applied to any Compound or Derivative word, whose parts have come from different sources, *i.e.* are neither purely Teutonic, nor purely Romanic, nor purely Greek. Hybrids are very common in our language.

Thus in *en-dear* the prefix is Romanic, the stem is Teutonic. In *starv-ation* the stem is Teutonic, the suffix is Romanic. In *be-siege* the stem is Romanic, the prefix is Teutonic. In *false-hood* the stem is Teutonic, the suffix is Teutonic. In *bi-cycle* the stem is Greek, the prefix is Romanic. In *art-ist* the stem is Romanic, the suffix is Greek.

SECTION 1.—SUFFIXES: TEUTONIC, ROMANIC, GREEK.

7. Noun-forming.—We may classify the principal suffixes under the following headings :—

(*a*) Denoting agent, doer, or one appointed to act :—

Teutonic :—

-er, -ar, -or (modern forms of A.S. *-ere*) : bak-*er*, do-*er*, li-*ar*, tail-*or*, London-*er*, law-y-*er*, saw-y-*er*.

-ther, -der (A.S. *-ther, -der*) : fa-*ther*, bro-*ther*, daugh-*ter*, spi(n)-*der*.

Romanic :—

-or, -eur (Latin *-or, -ator*, French *-eur*) : aggress-*or*, doct-*or*, amat-*eur*, emper-*or*, cens-*or*, specul-*ator*.

-ary, -aire, -ar, -eer, -ier (Latin *-arius, -aris*) : secret-*ary*, million-*aire*, schol-*ar*, volunt-*eer*, cash-*ier*, brigad-*ier*.

-an, -ain, -en, -ian, -on (Latin *-anus*) : public-*an*, capt-*ain*, citiz-*en*, guard-*ian*, sext-*on*.

-ant, -ent (Latin *-antem, -entem*) : merch-*ant*, tru-*ant*, ten-*ant*, combat-*ant ;* stud-*ent*, rod-*ent*, cli-*ent*.

-ate (Latin *-atus, -atem*) : candid-*ate*, magistr-*ate*, prim-*ate*.

-ee, -ey, -y (French *-é*, from Latin *-atus*) : deput-*y*, jur-*y*, attorn-*ey*, grand-*ee*, employ-*é*.

-ive, -iff (Latin *-ivus*, Fr. *-if*) : fugit-*ive*, mot-*ive ;* plaint-*iff*, bail-*iff*.

Greek :—

-ist, -ast (Greek *-ist-es, -ast-es*) : soph-*ist*, art-*ist*, psalm-*ist*, botan-*ist*, nihil-*ist ;* enthusi-*ast*.

-ot (Greek *-ot-es*) : patri-*ot*, zeal-*ot*, idi-*ot*, Iscari-*ot*.

-ite, -it (Greek *-it-es*) : Israel-*ite*, erem-*ite*, herm-*it*, Jesu-*it*.

(*b*) Marking the Feminine gender :—

Teutonic :—

-ster (A.S. *-es-tre*), **-en** (A.S. *-en*): spin-*ster*, vix-*en* (Fem. of "fox").

Romanic :—

-ess (Latin *-ix*, French *-esse*) : testatr-*ix*, shepherd-*ess*.

Note.—"Sultan-*a*," "donn-*a*." Here the *a* is Italian.

Greek :—

-ine (Greek *in-e*, French *-ine*) : hero-*ine*, czar-*ina*.

(c) Diminutives (denoting smallness, endearment, contempt) :—

Teutonic :—

-en (A.S. *-en*) : maid-*en*, chick-*en*.

-ing, -ling (A.S. *-ing*, *-el*+*ing*) ; farth-*ing*, tith-*ing* ; hire-*ling*, duck-*ling*.

-kin (Dutch *-ken*) : fir-*kin*, nap-*kin*.

-ock, -k (A.S. *-uc*, *-c*) : bull-*ock*, hill-*ock*, stir-*k* (little steer).

-y, -ey, -ie (A.S. *-ig*) : bab-*y*, Tomm-*y*, Charl-*ey*, bird-*ie*, lass-*ie*.

-el, -le, -l (A.S. *-el*) : hov-*el*, bund-*le*, freck-*le*, gir-*l*.

-erel, -rel (A.S. *-er*+*el*) : cock-*erel*, mong-*rel*, dogg-*erel* (?).

-ster (A.S. *es-tre*) : trick-*ster*, pun-*ster*, young-*ster*, rhyme-*ster*.

Romanic : —

-aster (Lat. *-aster*, cf. A.S. *-estre*) : ole-*aster*, pil-*aster*, poet-*aster*.

-ule, -le (Lat. *-ulus*) : pill-*ule*, sched-*ule* ; circ-*le* (hence circ-*ul*-ar).

-cule, -cle (Lat. *-cu-lus*, Fr. *-cle*) : animal-*cule*, pinna-*cle*.

-el, -le, -l, -elle (Lat. *-ellus*) : dams-*el*, cast-*le*, vea-*l*, bagat-*elle*, vermi-c-*elli*, umbr-*ella*, violon-c-*ello* (Ital.).

-et, -ot, -ette (Fr. *-et*, fem. *-ette* ; Ital. *-etto*) : lock-*et*, lanc-*et* ; ball-*ot* ; brun-*ette*, cigar-*ette* ; stil-*etto*.

-let (Double suffix, *-el*+*et*) : brook-*let*, rivu-*let*, ham-*let*, cut-*let*.

-ito (Span. *-ito*) : negr-*ito*, mosqu-*ito*.

Greek :—

-isk (Gr. *-iscos*) : aster-*isk*, obel-*isk*.

(d) Augmentatives (denoting greatness, or excess to a fault) :—

Romanic :—

-ard, -art (Low Lat. *-ardus*) : drunk-*ard*, wiz-*ard*, bragg-*art*.

-oon, -on, -one (Fr. *-on*, Ital. *-one*) : ball-*oon*, flag-*on*, tromb-*one*.

(e) Abstract suffixes (denoting act, state, quality, etc.) :—

Teutonic :—

-dom (A.S. *dóm*) : free-*dom*, martyr-*dom*, earl-*dom*.

-hood, -head (A.S. *hád*) : man-*hood*, priest-*hood*, maiden-*head*.

-lock, -ledge (A.S. *lác*) : wed-*lock*, know-*ledge*.

-red (A.S. *réd*) : hat-*red*, kind-*red*.

-ric (A.S. *rice*) : bishop-*ric*.

-ness (A.S. *-nis*, *-nes*) : dark-*ness*, aloof-*ness*, holi-*ness*.

-ship (A.S. *scipe*) : friend-*ship*, wor-*ship*, owner-*ship*.

-t, -th (A.S. *-ith*) : leng-*th*, tru-*th*, heigh-*t*, ligh-*t*, sigh-*t*.

-ter, -der (A.S. *-ther*, *-der*) : slaugh-*ter*, laugh-*ter*, mur-*der*.

Romanic : —

-age (Fr. *-age*) : cour-*age*, hom-*age*, umbr-*age*, bond-*age*.

-al (Fr. *-aille*) : refus-*al*, tri-*al*, surviv-*al*, bestow-*al*.

-ance, -ence, -ancy, -ency (Lat. *-antia*, *-entia*) : dist-*ance*, prud-*ence*, guid-*ance*, const-*ancy*, urg-*ency*.

-cy, -acy (Lat. *-tia*) : cur-*acy*, prel-*acy*, secre(t)-*cy*, idio(t)-*cy*.

-ice, -ise, -ess (Lat. *-itia*, Fr. *-esse*) : serv-*ice*, exerc-*ise*, prow-*ess*.

-ion (Lat. *-ionem*) : relig-*ion*, fash-*ion*, suspic-*ion*, relat-*ion*.

-ment (Lat. *-mentum*) : enjoy-*ment*, fer-*ment*, attach-*ment*.

I 2

-**mony** (Lat. *-monia*, or *-monium*) : parsi-*mony*, matri-*mony*.
-**or**, -**our**, -**eur** (Lat. *-or*, Fr. *-eur*) : err-*or*, fav-*our*, grand-*eur*.
-**ry**, -**ery** (Fr. *-rie*, *-erie*) : slave-*ry*, trick-*ery*, brave-*ry*.
-**tude** (Lat. *-tudo*) : forti-*tude*, longi-*tude*, magni-*tude*.
-**ty** (Lat. *-tas*, Fr. *-té*) : cruel-*ty*, certain-*ty*, frail-*ty*.
-**ure** (Lat. *-ura*) : seiz-*ure*, cult-*ure*, capt-*ure*, us-*ury*.
-**y** (Lat. *-ia*, *-ium*) : infam-*y*, stud-*y*, perjur-*y*.

Greek :—

-**ism**, -**asm** (Gr. *-ismos*, *-asmos*) : optim-*ism*, enthusi-*asm*.
-**y** (Gr. *-ia*) : monarch-*y*, energ-*y*, sympath-*y*.

(*f*) Collective (denoting a collection, or the place of one) :—

Romanic :—

ade (Fr. *-ade*) : arc-*ade*, colonn-*ade*, balustr-*ade*.
-**age** (Fr. *-age*) : foli-*age*, plum-*age*, vill-*age*, cott-*age*.
-**ry**, -**ery** (Fr. *-rie*, *-erie*) : tenant-*ry*, rook-*ery*, gent-*ry*.
-**ory** (Lat. *-orium*) : dormit-*ory*, fact-*ory*, invent-*ory*.
-**ary** (Lat. *-arium*) : gran-*ary*, libr-*ary*, gloss-*ary*.

(*g*) Miscellaneous suffixes, not included in the above :—

Teutonic :—

-**m**, -**om** (A.S. *-m*, *-ma*) : bloo-*m* (from *blow*), doo-*m* (from *do*), bes-*om*.
-**nd**, -**and** (A.S. Pres. Part. ending) : frie-*nd*, wi-*nd*, husba-*nd*.
-**ow**, -**w** (A.S. *-u*, *-we*) : mead-*ow*, shad-*ow*, stra-*w*, de-*w*.

Romanic :—

-**ace** (Lat. *-atio*, *-atium ;* Fr. *-ace*) : popul-*ace*, terr-*ace*, pal-*ace*.
-**ine**, -**in** (Lat. *-inus*) : libert-*ine*, cous-*in* (Lat. consobr-*inus*).
-**me**, -**m** (Lat. *-men*) : cri-*me*, char-*m*, real-*m* (Lat. regali-*men*).
o (Lat. *-us*, *-um ;* Span. *-o*) : studi-*o*, grott-*o*, incognit-*o*.
-**cre**, -**chre** (Lat. *-crum*) : sepul-*chre*, lu-*cre*.

Greek :—

-**on** (Gr. *-on*) : criteri-*on*, skelet-*on*, col-*on*, phenomen-*on*.
-**ic**, -**ics** (Gr. *-ikos*, *-ika*) : log-*ic*, mus-*ic*, phys-*ics*, eth-*ics*.

8. II. **Adjective-forming** :—

(*a*) Possessing a quality of any kind :—

Teutonic :—

-**ed** (A.S. *-d*) : wretch-*ed*, gift-*ed*, fabl-*ed*, money-*ed*.
-**en** (A.S. *-en*) : wheat-*en*, gold-*en*, heath-*en*, op-*en*.
-**ly** (A.S. *-líc*) : god-*ly*, woman-*ly*, man-*ly*.
-**some** (A.S. *-sum*) : toil-*some*, hand-*some*, whole-*some*, bux-*om*.
-**y**, -**ey** (A.S. *-ig*) : might-*y*, wood-*y*, clay-*ey*, drear-*y*, an-*y*.

Romanic :—

-**al** (Lat. *-alis*) : vit-*al*, parti-*al*, mort-*al*, comic-*al*.
-**an**, -**ane**, -**ain** (Lat. *-anus*) : pag-*an*, hum-*an*, hum-*ane*, cert-*ain*.
ant, -**ent** (Lat. *-antem*, *-entem*) : dist-*ant*, abs-*ent*, pres-*ent*.

-ar, -ary, -arious (Lat. -aris, -arius) : lun-ar, contr-ary, vic-arious.
-esque (Lat. -iscus, Fr. -esque) : pictur-esque, grot-esque.
-ile, -il, -eel, -le, -el (Lat. -ilis) : frag-ile, fra-il, gent-eel, gent-le, hum(b)-le, cru-el.
-ic, -ique (Lat. -icus, -iquus) : rust-ic, com-ic, un-ique, obl-ique.
ine (Lat. -inus) : div-ine, clandest-ine, infant-ine.
-lent (Lat. -lentem) : pesti-lent, corpu-lent, vio-lent.

(b) Possessing a quality in a high degree :—

Teutonic :—
-ful (A.S. -ful, Eng. -full) : plenti-ful, beauti-ful, master-ful.

Romanic :—
-ous, -ose (Lat. -osus) : numer-ous, fam-ous, verb-ose.

(c) Possessing a quality in a slight degree ; hence sometimes used in a depreciative sense :—

Teutonic :—
-ish (A.S. -isc) : pal-ish, redd-ish, woman-ish (fit for a woman, but not fit for a man), snapp-ish, upp-ish, slav-ish, baby-ish.

Note.—The prefix *sub-* (Latin) sometimes means "slightly" ; as, sub-acid, sub-tropical (not quite tropical).

(d) Conveying an Active sense :—

Romanic :—
-ive (Lat. -ivus) : recept-ive, act-ive: (capt-ive is exceptional).
-ory, -orious (Lat. -orius) : illus-ory, cens-orious.
-fic (Lat. -ficus) : terri-fic, honori-fic, beati-fic.

(e) Conveying a Passive sense :—

Romanic :—
-able, -ible (Lat. -bilis) : laugh-able, eat-able, ed-ible.

(f) Describing nation, sect, creed, etc. :—

Teutonic :—
-ish, ch (A.S. -isc) : Engl-ish, Ir-ish, Span-ish, Fren-ch.

Romanic :—
-an (Lat. -anus) : Rom-an, Austri-an, Belgi-an, Christi-an.
-ese (Lat. -ensis) : Chin-ese, Siam-ese, Portugu-ese.

Greek :—
-ite (Gr. -it-es) : Israel-ite, Irving-ite, Carmel-ite.

(g) Miscellaneous suffixes, not included in the above :—

Teutonic :—
-teen, -ty (A.S. -tén, tig, ten) : thir-teen (3+10), thir-ty (3 × 10).
-ern (A.S. irn-an, to turn) : north-ern, north-er(n)-ly.
-ther (A.S. ther, Comp. degree) : o-ther, fur-ther, whe-ther, ne-ther

Romanic :—

ior (Lat. comp. degree): exter-*ior*, pr-*ior*, super-*ior*.
-monious (Lat. -*monius*): cere-*monious*, sancti-*monious*.
-ple, -ble (Lat. -*plex*, Fr. -*ple*, fold): tri-*ple*, tre-*ble*.
Greek :—
-astic, -istic (Gr. -*astikos*, -*istikos*): dr-*astic*, art-*istic*.

9. III. Verb-forming :—

(*a*) Causative; hence forming Transitive verbs :—
Teutonic :—
-en (A.S. -*en* or -*n*): dark-*en*, sweet-*en*, length-*en*, height-*en*
Romanic :—
-fy (Lat. *facio*): magni-*fy*, terri-*fy*, stupe-*fy*.
Greek :—
-ise (through French -*iser*): galvan-*ise*, brutal-*ise*, fertil-*ise*.

Note.—Some Prefixes are also used for the same purpose :— *Teutonic* **be-**, as *be*-friend, *be*-calm, *be*-numb; *Romanic* **im-, en-,** as *im*-peril, *en*-dear.

(*b*) Frequentative, denoting frequency or continuance :—
Teutonic :—
-el, -le, -l : cack-*le*, jost-*le*, sniv-*el* (sniff), draw-*l* (draw).
-er, -r : batt-*er* (beat), sputt-*er* (spout), glimm-*er* (gleam).
-k : har-*k* (hear), hear-*k*-en, lur-*k*, tal-*k* (tell).

(*c*) Other verb-forming suffixes :—
Romanic :—
-ate (Lat. -*atum*): captiv-*ate*, gradu-*ate*, filtr-*ate*.
-ish (Lat. -*isc*, Fr. -*iss*): pun-*ish* (pun-*ch*), per-*ish*, flour-*ish*.
-esce (Lat. -*esco*, inceptive): coal-*esce*, acqui-*esce*.

10. IV. Adverb-forming :—

Teutonic :—
-ly (A.S. *líc-e*, in a like way): on-*ly*, bad-*ly*, dark-*ly*, open-*ly*.
-ling, -long (A.S. *linga*): head-*long*, dark-*ling*, side-*long*.
-meal (A.S. *mǽl*, a time): piece-*meal*, inch-*meal* (Shakspeare).
-ward, -wards (A.S. *weard*, direction): back-*ward*, back-*wards*.
-wise (A.S. *wís-e*, manner): like-*wise*, other-*wise*.
-way, -ways (A.S. *weg*, way): straight-*way*, al-*ways*.
-s, -ce (sign of Possessive): need-*s*, twi-*ce*, back-ward-*s*, some-time-*s*.
-n : whe-*n*, the-*n*, the-*n*-*ce*. (The *n* in *often* is an intruder.)
-re : whe-*re*, the-*re*.
-om (old Dative ending; cf. who-*m*, the-*m*, hi-*m*): whil-*om*, seld-*om*.
-ther (direction) : whit-*ther*, hi-*ther*, hi-*ther*-to.

Note.—We have no Romanic or Greek suffixes for forming Adverbs.

SECTION 2.—PREFIXES : TEUTONIC, ROMANIC, GREEK.

11. Teutonic Prefixes.—These have been distinguished into (*a*) Separable, and (*b*) Inseparable :—

(a) *Separable; i.e.* capable of being used as separate words; such as *after-*life, *by-*path, *fore-*cast, *forth-*coming, *off-*shoot, *on-*set, *out-*let, *through-*ticket, *up-*start, *wel-*fare. Such words might be called Compounds (§ 141). These do not require further explanation. The few mentioned below are somewhat peculiar.

Out-.—This gives certain verbs the sense of surpassing; as *out-*live (to live beyond), *out-*vote (to defeat by votes), *out-*run, *out-*shine.

Over-.—This denotes excess; as *over-*eat (eat too much), *over-*sleep (sleep too long), *over-*worked (worked too much).

Under-.—This denotes deficiency, too little; as *under-*fed, *under-*paid, *under-*valued, *under-*cooked.

With-.—This denotes "back," "against"; as *with-*stand, *with-*hold, *with-*draw. ("Drawing-room" means "with-drawing-room.")

(b) *Inseparable; i.e.* not used as separate words :—

A- (*on, in*) : *a-*bed, *a-*shore, *a-*jar, *a-*stir, *a-*sleep, etc.

A- (*of, from*) : *a-*down (off a down or hill), *a-*fresh, *a-*kin, *a-*new.

A- (Intensive) : *a-*rise, *a-*waken, *a*(f)-fright, *a*(c)-cursed.

Al- (*all*) : *al-*one, *l-*one, *al-*most, *al-*ready, *al-*together.

Be- (*by*) : (1) Transitive force ; as *be-*calm. (2) Intensive force ; as *be-*smear. (3) Forming adverbs or prepositions ; as *be-*sides, *be-*fore. (4) Privative force in *be-*head.

For- (not the prep. "for") : (1) Intensive ; as *for-*bear, *for-*lorn. (2) Privative; as *for-*bid, *for-*get, *for-*swear, *for-*go (not *fore-*go, which means *precede*. The prefix *fore* is quite distinct from *for*).

Gain (A.S. *gegn*, against) : *gain-*say, *gain-*strive (out of use).

N- (Indef. article "a," the *n* being wrongly detached) : *n-*ewt (for *an ewt*), *n-*ugget (for *an ingot*), *n-*ickname (for *an eke-name*).

N- (Negative prefix) : *n-*or, *n-*either, *n-*ay.

Mis- (*miss*) : *mis-*take, *mis-*hap, *mis-*deed, *mis-*trust.

Twi- (A.S. *twi*, double) : *twi-*light, *twi-*n, *twi-*ce, *twi-*st.

Un- (A.S. *un-*) : (1) Negative : *un-*wise. (2) Reversal : *un-*twist. (In "*un-*loose" the *un-* is merely Intensive.)

12. Romanic Prefixes.—The following are of frequent occurrence :—

A-, ab-, abs- (*from*) : *a-*vert, *ab-*use, *ab-*normal, *abs-*tain.

Ad- (*to*) : *ad-*vice, *ab-*breviate, *ac-*cent, *af-*fable, *ag-*gressor, *al-*lude, *an-*nex, *ap-*pear, *ar-*rears, *as-*sert, *at-*tain.

Ambi- (*on both sides, around*) : *amb-*iguous, *amb-*ition.

Ante-, anti-, ant- (*before*) : *ante-*cedent, *anti-*cipate, *ant-*ique.

Bene- (*well*) : *bene-*fit, *bene-*volent, *ben-*ison.

Bis-, bi-, bin- (*twice*) : *bis-*cuit, *bi-*ped, *bi-*cycle, *bin-*ocular.

Circum-, circu- (*around*) : *circum-*stance, *circu-*it, *circum-*ference.

Cis- (*on this side*) : *cis-*Alpine, on this side of the Alps.

Con- (*with*), **coun-** (Fr.) : *con-*tend, *col-*lege, *com-*pete, *cor-*rect, *coun-*sel, *con-*temporary.

Contra- (*against*), **counter** (Fr.) : *contra-*dict, *contra-*st, *counter-*act.

De- (*down, from, astray*) : *de-*grade, *de-*part, *de-*viate.

  „ (Reversal) : merit, *de-*merit ; *en-*camp, *de-*camp.

  „ (Intensive) : *de-*liver, *de-*clare, *de-*file, *de-*fraud.

Dis-, di- (*asunder*): *dis*-tract, *dis*-miss, *dis*-member, *di*-vulge.
,, (Intensive): *dis*-sever, *dis*-annul, *di*-minish.
,, (Reversal): en-chant, *dis*-enchant ; illusion, *dis*-illusion.
,, (Negative): ease, *dis*-ease ; honour, *dis*-honour ; *dif*-ficult.
Ex-, e-, extra- (*out*): *ex*-ample, *e*-lapse, *extra*-vagant.
,, (*loss of office*): *ex*-king, *ex*-empress.
In-, en-, em- (*in*): *in*-ject, *im*-pute, *ir*-ritate, *en*-close, *em*-ploy.
In- (*not*): *in*-firm, *il*-literate, *im*-pious, *ir*-regular, *i*-gnorance.
Inter-, enter- (*among*): *inter*-est, *intel*-lect, *enter*-prise.
Intro-, intra- (*within*): *intro*-duce, *intra*-tropical, *intr*-insic.
Male-, mal- (*badly*): *male*-volent, *male*-factor, *mal*-ady.
Mis- (Lat. *minus*, badly): *mis*-chance, *mis*-chief, *mis*-nomer.
Non-, ne-, neg- (*not*): *non*-sense, *ne*-uter, *neg*-lect.
Ob- (*against*): *ob*-ject, *oc*-cur, *of*-fer, *op*-press, *os*-tensible, *o*-mit.
Pen- (Latin *pæne*, *almost*): *pen*-insula, *pen*-ultimate.
Per- (*through*): *per*-form, *per*-haps, *pel*-lucid.
,, (*wrong direction*): *per*-vert, *per*-jury, *per*-fidy, *per*-ish.
Post- (*after*): *post*-script, *post*-pone, *post*-ern.
Pre- (Latin *præ, in front, before*): *pre*-occupy, *pre*-tend, *pre*-dict.
Preter- (Latin *præter, beyond*): *preter*-natural, *preter*-ite.
Pro-, por-, pur- (Latin *pro, for, before*): *pro*-fess, *por*-tray, *por*-trait, *pur*-pose.
Re-, red- (*back*): *re*-fer, *re*-new, *red*-eem, *red*-undant.
Retro- (*backwards*): *retro*-cession, *retro*-grade.
Se-, sed- (*apart*): *se*-cret, *se*-cure, *se*-parate, *sed*-ition.
Semi-, demi- (*half*): *semi*-circle, *demi*-god.
Sub- (*under*): *sub*-ject, *suc*-cour, *suf*-fice, *sug*-gest, *sum*-mon, *sup*-pose, *sur*-render, *sus*-pend, *sub*-marine, "under the sea."
,, (*slightly*): *sub*-acid, *sub*-tropical.
,, (*of lower rank*): *sub*-judge, *sub*-committee, *sub*-division.
Subter- (*under, secretly*): *subter*-fuge.
Super-, sur- (*above*): *super*-fluous, *sur*-face, *sur*-vive.
Trans-, tra- (*across*): *trans*-mit, *trans*-gress, *tra*-duce, *tra*-ffic.
Tri-, tre- (*three, thrice*): *tri*-angle, *tri*-nity, *tri*-vial, *tre*-ble.
Ultra- (*beyond, excess*): *ultra*-marine, *ultra*-radical.
Vice-, vis- (*instead of*): *vice*-roy, *vis*-count.

13. Greek Prefixes :—

Amphi- (*on both sides*): *amphi*-bious, *amphi*-theatre.
An-, a- (*not*): *an*-archy, *an*-ecdote, *a*-pathy, *a*-theism.
Ana- (*again, back*): *ana*-logy, *ana*-lyse, *ana*-tomy.
Anti-, ant- (*against*): *anti*-podes, *anti*-pathy, *ant*-agonist.
Apo-, aph- (*from*): *apo*-logy, *apo*-state, *apo*-stie, *aph*-orism.
Archi-, arch- (*chief*): *archi*-tect, *arch*-bishop.
Auto- (*self*): *auto*-mobile, *auto*-graph, *auth*-entic.
Cata-, cath- (*down*): *cata*-ract, *cath*-edral, *cat*-echism.
Dia- (*through*): *dia*-logue, *dia*-meter, *dia*-gnosis.
Dis-, di- (*in two*): *dis*-syllable, *di*-phthong, *di*-lemma.
Dys- (*ill, badly*): *dys*-entery, *dys*-pepsia.
Ek-, ex- (*out*): *ec*-stasy, *ex*-odus.
En- (*in*): *en*-thusiasm, *em*-phasis, *el*-lipsis.
Eu-, ev- (*well*): *eu*-phony, *eu*-logy, *ev*-angelist.

Epi-, eph- (*on*) : *epi*-taph, *ep*-och, *eph*-emeral, *ep*-isode.
Hemi- (*half*) : *hemi*-sphere.
Hyper- (*above, beyond*) : *hyper*-critical, *hyper*-bole.
Hypo-, hyph- (*under*) : *hypo*-crite, *hypo*-thesis, *hyph*-en.
Meta-, meth-, met- (*after*) : *meta*-phor, *meth*-od, *met*-eor.
Mono-, mon- (*single*) : *mono*-poly, *mon*-arch, *mon*-k.
Pan-, panto- (*all*) : *pan*-orama, *panto*-mime.
Para-, par- (*beside*) : *para*-ble, *para*-graph, *par*-allel.
Peri- (*around*) : *peri*-od, *peri*-phrasis, *peri*-meter.
Pro- (*before*) : *pro*-gramme, *pro*-phet, *pro*-blem.
Syn- (*with*) : *syn*-od, *syl*-lable, *sym*-bol, *sym*-pathy, *sy*-stem.
Tri- (*thrice*) : *tri*-pod, *tri*-syllable.

14. General results, regarding the uses of Prefixes :—

(*a*) Prefixes denoting the **undoing** of something done :—

Teutonic :—
un- : *un*-bolt, *un*-tie, *un*-lock, *un*-fold.

Romanic :—
dis- : *dis*-mount, *dis*-arm, *dis*-appear, *dis*-close.
de- : *de*-odorise, *de*-plete, *de*-camp, *de*-throne.

(*b*) Prefixes denoting a **Negative**, with one Suffix :—

Teutonic :—
un- : *un*-happy, *un*-safe, *un*-ready, *un*-certain.
-less : hap-*less*, law-*less*, hope-*less*, spot-*less*.
n- : *n*-one, *n*-ever, *n*-or, *n*-either.

Romanic :—
ne-, neg-, non- : *ne*-uter, *neg*-lect, *non*-sense.
dis-, di- : *dis*-contented, *dif*-ficult, *dif*-fident.
in- : *in*-human, *ir*-rational, *im*-moral, *ig*-noble, *il*-legible.
ab- : *ab*-normal.

Greek :—
a-, an- : *a*-pathy, *an*-archy.

(*c*) Prefixes indicating something **good** :—

Teutonic :—
well- : *wel*-fare, *wel*-come, *well*-bred.

Romanic :—
bene- : *bene*-volent, *bene*-fit, *ben*-ignant, *ben*-ison.

Greek :—
eu-, ev- : *eu*-phony, *ev*-angelist.

(*d*) Prefixes indicating something **bad** :—

Teutonic :—
mis- (from *miss*) : *mis*-deed, *mis*-take, *mis*-hap.

Romanic :—
mis- (from *minus*) : *mis*-carry, *mis*-use, *mis*-fortune.
male-, mal- : *male*-factor, *mal*-ignant, *mal*-treat.

Greek :—
dys- : *dys*-entery, *dys*-pepsia.

I. *Exercise on Word-building.*

(*a*) 1. Supply the feminine forms of *sultan, hero, testator, shepherd, spinner, fox.* 2. Break up *mistrustfully, unwholesomeness* into syllables, and show how each syllable contributes to the meaning of the words. 3. What are the suffixes in the following words :—*farthing, foremost, kingdom, fatten, English, thirsty.* 4. Reverse the meaning of each of the following words by adding a prefix :—*happy, possible, rational, contented, valid, noble, sense.* 5. Give four examples of diminutive forms in English nouns. 6. Form adjectives from *disaster, two, wheat,* and adverbs from *gay, holy, other, south, week.* 7. How are verbs formed (*a*) from nouns ; (*b*) from adjectives ; (*c*) from other verbs. Give two examples of each, and show the exact force of the change of the word. 8. By the use of a suffix, change each of the following nouns into an adjective, and give the force of each suffix :— *sister, fame, quarrel, slave, silver.* 9. What is meant by saying that the word *bicycle* is a hybrid ? 10. Write words (one in each case) containing the following prefixes and suffixes :—*ante-, anti-, auto-, vice-, -ess, -ness, -ry, -kin.* (*Oxford and Cambridge, Junior and Senior.*)

(*b*) 1. How are Compound verbs formed ? Write down ten Compound verbs with different prefixes, giving the meaning of these. 2. Give the diminutive forms of *stream, hill, duck, lass ;* and the meaning of the prefix in each of the following words :—*mischance, importunate, retrospect, subterfuge, constant.* 3. Why is *co*-temporary an incorrect form ? What different forms do *cum, in, ad, inter, per* assume in composition ? 4. Write down suffixes employed to denote (1) the agent, (2) diminution, (3) gender. 5. Give with examples three affixes (suffixes) of Latin origin, by which Abstract nouns in English are formed. 6. Give the exact force of the following prefixes and affixes (suffixes) :—man*hood*, spin*ster*, tire*some,* sparkl*e ; mis*give, *for*get, *be*troth, *in*nocent. 7. What is the force of the prefixes in the words *impossible, except.* From what languages are they respectively taken ? Write down three other examples of the use of each of these prefixes. 8. Explain the meaning of the following prefixes, and write words formed by means of them :—*un-, ante-, bi-, circum-, inter-.* 9. Give (i.) three prefixes of Latin origin, and (ii.) three noun suffixes ; and by examples show what effect they have upon words in which they are introduced. (*Preceptors', Second and Third Classes.*)

(*c*) 1. Give the different ways of forming adverbs in English. 2. Explain the force of the syllables in *Italics* in the following words :— spin*ster*, head*long*, twen*ty*, *im*proper, hillo*ck*, elde*st*, king*dom*, *be*-sprinkle. 3. In the following words what is the force of the parts printed in *Italics?*—*a*round, numer*ous*, *a*loud, governe*sses*, *re*cite, Eng*lish*, Itali*an.* 4. Mention *two* ways in which *abstract* nouns can be formed from *common* nouns, and give *two* examples of each. 5. What is meant by *diminutives* and *augmentatives.* Illustrate by examples the suffixes used in the formation of such words. 6. What are *compound* adjectives ? Give *three* examples. 7. Give the meanings of the following Latin Prefixes, and illustrate each by *two* English words :— *ab-, bis-, con-, non-, pro-, se-.* 8. Give the meanings of the following *prefixes*, and *two* instances of the use of each :—*in-, per-, dis-, re-*. (*Preceptors', Second and Third Classes.*)

(*d*) 1. Say what you know about the Feminine endings in *vixen, spinster, duchess, baxter, margravine, infanta*, and *testatrix*. 2. Mention six English Inseparable prefixes ; and give two examples of words formed with each of them. 3. What is the force of the prefix in *undismayed, mislay, behind, forgive, withstand, prefix, extravagant, postpone, superscription, anarchy, epitaph, perimeter* ? 4. Give the meaning and function of the following prefixes (with *two* examples in each case), and state whether they are English or Latin :—*be-, con-, for-, gain-, in-, pro-, re-, with-*. 5. Give the derivation and meaning of each of the following suffixes, with two examples of each :—*-ard* or *-art, -fy, -kin, -ock, -ous, -some, -ster, -tude*. 6. Give the meaning and function of the following suffixes ; and state whether they are added to nouns, or verbs, or adjectives :—*-ing, -lock, -m, -red, -ther, -s, -ward*. 7. Give examples of the following suffixes, and state their derivation and their meaning :—*-ster, -kin, -ly, -tude, -let, -ous, -fy, -ise*. 8. Explain with examples the force of the following prefixes and suffixes :—*be-, for-, with-, cata-, intro-, -der, -nd, -ship, -eer, -le, -ment*. 9. Give the origin and meaning of the prefix in each of the following words :—*advent, contradict, forlorn, hypercritical, interpose, mistake, reopen, transmarine, unkind, withstand*. 10. Give the meaning and derivation of the suffixes (distinctly specifying these) of the following words :—*wisdom, bounty, slavish, clayey, worship, blackness, longitude, sepulchre, strengthen, gamble*. 11. Explain the force of the terminations in any five of the following :—*oxen, vixen, maiden, holden, wooden, open, often*. 12. With what different suffixes, and derived from what sources, do we form Abstract nouns ? Give one or two examples of each. 13. Point out the force of the prefix in each of the following, explaining the words themselves :—*hypercritical, antechamber, cisalpine, synchronous, percolate, cataract*. (*Preceptors', First Class.*)

II. *Write short sentences illustrating the difference of meaning in each of the following pairs of Abstract nouns formed with different suffixes :—*

(*a*) *Teutonic suffixes :—*

Dearth, dearness.	Sloth, slowness.
Drought, dryness.	Truth, trueness.
Hardness, hardihood.	Witness, wisdom.
Sleight, slyness.	

(*b*) *Romanic suffixes :—*

Acquitt-ance, acquitt-al.	Creat-ure, creat-ion.
Appar-it-ion, appear-ance.	Degener-at-ion, degener-ac-y.
Benefact-ion, benefic-ence.	Depart-ment, depart-ure.
Committ-al, commiss-ion.	Destin-y, destin-at-ion.
Compos-ure, compos-it-ion.	Dispos-al, dispos-it-ion.
Content-ment, content-ion.	Eject-ment, eject-ion.
Continu-ance, continu-at-ion.	Expos-ure, expos-it-ion.

Fixt-ure, fix-ity.

Fract-ure, fract-ion, frag-ment.

Impost-ure, impos-it-ion.

Impress-ment, impress-ion.

Intim-at-ion, intim-ac-y.

Luxury, luxuri-ance.

Observ-ance, observ-at-ion.

Post-ure, posit-ion.

Propos-al, propos-it-ion.

Protest-er, protest-ant.

Serv-i-tude, serv-ice.

Signific-ance, signific-at-ion.

Stat-ure, stat-ion.

Tempera-ment, tempera-ture.

Vac-ancy, vac-at-ion.

(c) Romanic and Teutonic suffixes :—

Appropriate-ness, appropriat-ion.

Apt-ness, apt-i-tude.

Close-ness, clos-ure.

Complete-ness, complet-ion.

Direct-ion, direct-ness.

Distinct-ness, distinct-ion.

Exact-ness, exact-ion.

False-hood, fals-ity, false-ness.

Human-ity, humane-ness.

Ingenu-ity, ingenu-ous-ness.

Just-ness, just-ice.

Lax-ity, lax-ness.

Pall-or, pale-ness.

Proced-ure, proceed-ing.

Quiet-ude, quiet-ness.

Remiss-ness, remiss-ion.

Secure-ness, secur-ity.

Till-age, til-th.

(d) Greek and Romanic suffixes :—

Barbar-ism, barbar-ity.

Commun-ism, commun-ity.

Fatal-ism, fatal-ity.

Formal-ism, formal-ity.

Vulgar-ism, vulgar-ity.

III. *Show by an example the difference of meaning, if any, in each of the following pairs of adjectives formed with different suffixes :—*

Beneficial, beneficent.

Ceremonious, ceremonial.

Childlike, childish.

Comic, comical.

Comprehensive, comprehensible.

Congenial, congenital.

Contemptible, contemptuous.

Continual, continuous.

Corporate, corporal.

Credible, creditable.

Definite, definitive.

Dramatic, dramatical.

Elemental, elementary.

Exceptional, exceptionable.

Expedient, expeditious.

Godlike, godly.

Illusive, illusory.

Imaginary, imaginative.

Imperial, imperious.

Industrial, industrious.

Ingenious, ingenuous.

Innocent, innocuous.

Judicial, judicious.

Luxurious, luxuriant.

Masterly, masterful.

Momentary, momentous.

Notable, notorious.

Official, officious.

Ordinal, ordinary.

Permissive, permissible.

Politic, political.

Popular, populous.

Respective, respectful.

Reverend, reverent.

Sanatory, sanitary.

Sensitive, sensible.

Sensual, sensuous.

Silvery, silvern.

Spirituous, spiritual.

Temporal, temporary.

Tragic, tragical.

Transit-ory, transit-ional.

Verbal, verbose.

Virtual, virtuous.

IV. *Substitute a single word (an adjective) for the words printed below in italics :—*

(a) This writing is *such as cannot be read.*
(b) The plan you mention *cannot be put into practice.*
(c) He is *one who cannot according to the rules be elected.*
(d) That herb is *fit to be eaten.*
(e) The colour is *beyond my perception.*
(f) You are *liable to be called to account* for your actions.
(g) The plan you propose is *open to objections.*
(h) That word is *no longer in use.*
(i) This is a bird *of passage.*
(j) Your office is *one for which no salary is paid.*
(k) His motive was merely *to get some money.*
(l) His position was *beyond all hope of improvement.*
(m) His manners are *more like those of a woman than of a man.*
(n) He is *one who takes no trouble* about his work.
(o) His style is *too full of words.*
(p) He is *inclined to find fault.*
(q) A wolf is an animal *that cannot be tamed.*
(r) That problem is *one which is never likely to be solved.*
(s) His character *has an evil reputation.*
(t) The use of opium is *likely to do much injury.*
(u) That impression is *too vivid ever to be effaced.*
(v) He is *unable to pay his debts.*

V. *To each of the verbs, nouns, or adjectives given below, add some Abstract suffix or suffixes :—*

Serve, coward, right, grand, err, miser, apt, victor, acrid, just, merchant, trick, pass, seize, try, judge, compel, admit, patron, repent, regent, bankrupt, accurate, poor, rely, captive, fragile, facile, felon, sole, assist, scarce, secret, defy, father, real.

VI. *Form Diminutive nouns out of the following by adding to each of them its appropriate Diminutive suffix :—*

Animal, code, pouch, brook, poet, cigar, vase, lance, globe, mode, pill, bill, car, cellar, statue, part, song, sign, table, home, wagon, hump, park, maid, cut, lamb, hill, change, bird, lad, scythe, corn.

VII. *Point out the six different senses of the suffix* "age" *as exemplified in the following words :—*

Herbage, hermitage, courage, postage, breakage, personage.

VIII. *Describe the uses of the suffix* "-en" *as exemplified in the following words :—*

Maiden, flaxen, vixen, fatten, drunken, kitten, alien, rotten, golden, oxen, haven.

IX. *In the following sentences the meaning of the word to which* "re-" *has been prefixed depends upon whether a hyphen has or has not been placed between the prefix and the verbal root. Substitute some other verb or phrase in each sentence :—*

(1) { I have never remarked this before.
{ The box must be re-marked.

(2) { My losses were soon recovered.
{ The chairs must be re-covered.

(3) { He has rejoined his post.
{ He has re-joined the two planks.

(4) { Their wrongs were soon redressed.
{ The doll must be re-dressed.

(5) { His character was reformed.
{ The classes were re-formed.

(6) { I cannot recollect this.
{ You must re-collect all the coins that have been lost.

(7) { I will not recount my sorrows.
{ You had better re-count all these coins.

(8) { You must return that book.
{ Having turned the verse into prose, he re-turned the prose into verse.

(9) { This has been reserved for future use.
{ The summons, which he could not then receive, must be re-served upon him.

(10) { A. went out of office and was replaced by B.
{ A. has been re-placed in his appointment.

X. *Define and distinguish the three meanings of the prefix* " **sub-** " *in the following words :—*

(*a*) Sub-terranean, sub-montane ; (*b*) sub-acid, sub-tropical ; (*c*) sub-judge, sub-deputy.

XI. *Show the difference of meaning implied in the following words by the prefix* " **non-** " *and the prefix* " **in-** " *or* " **un-** " :—

(*a*) Non-active, inactive ; (*b*) non-effective, ineffective ; (*c*) non-Christian, unchristian ; (*d*) non-famous, infamous ; (*e*) non-professional, unprofessional ; (*f*) non-judicial, unjudicial.

XII. *Form sentences showing the difference of meaning between—*

Confidant, confident ; dependant, dependent ; pendant, pendent ; plaintive, plaintiff.

XIII. *Show what prefixes are disguised in the following words :—*

Cost, essay (trial), spend, pilgrim, sudden, sovereign, outrage, trespass, sojourn, umpire, entrails, deluge, ancestor, balance, anoint, sombre, provost, runagate, puny.

XIV. *Distinguish the suffixes in each of the following pairs :—*

Hatred, hundred ; hemlock, wedlock ; learning, farthing ; freckle, spindle ; seedling, darkling ; friend, reverend.

XV. *Distinguish the suffix* " **-ther** " *in each of the following :—*

Other, father, hither.

XVI. *Distinguish the prefix " a " in each of the following :—*

Aspect, apathy, avert, afresh, afloat, arise, ado, amend.

XVII. *Separate the stem from the affixes (prefixes or suffixes) of the following words, and the affixes from each other :—*

Undenominationalism, valetudinarian, unsophisticated, renegade, instrumentality, disproportionate, talkativeness, protestantism, absenteeism, accidentally, miscreant, indentures, intoxicate, interest, intellectual, demonetise, telephone, introspection, captivate, insignificant, homogeneous, inaccessible, procedure, likelihood.

I. INDEX OF SUBJECTS.

The references are to pages.

II. INDEX OF SELECTED WORDS AND PHRASES

The references are to pages.

THE END

PRINTED BY R. & R. CLARK, LTD., EDINBURGH

CLASSIFIED LIST OF TEXT=BOOKS

FOR THE

STUDY AND COMPOSITION OF ENGLISH

By J. C. NESFIELD, M.A.

Series I.—ON ENGLISH GRAMMAR

ENGLISH GRAMMAR FOR ELEMENTARY SCHOOLS. Globe 8vo.

BOOK I. Uses of the Parts of Speech as shown by Examples.

BOOK II. Modifications of Subject, Predicate, and Object, by Words, Phrases, and Easy Sentences.

BOOK III. Parsing and Easy Analysis.

BOOK IV. Analysis and Word-Forming by Prefixes and Suffixes.

OUTLINE OF ENGLISH GRAMMAR. Globe 8vo.

This book sets forth in some detail the principles of Accidence, Parsing, and Syntax, and the Analysis and Conversion of sentences. Pages 178 to the end, dealing with derivation, phonetics, and some elements of historical English, are more difficult, and can be passed over for later study if the teacher thinks fit.

Key to Outline of English Grammar.

PREPARATORY ENGLISH GRAMMAR. Adapted from "Outline of English Grammar," by Ashley Sampson. Crown 8vo.

MACMILLAN AND CO. LTD., LONDON

ENGLISH GRAMMAR PAST AND PRESENT.
Globe 8vo.

This is a much more advanced book than the preceding. Parts I and II deal mainly with the grammar and idiom of modern English ; Part III with those of Anglo-Saxon or Early English, and with the history of the English language from the beginning down to modern times.

Key to English Grammar Past and Present.

ENGLISH GRAMMAR SERIES.   Crown 8vo.

Book I. Modern Edition.
Book II.

Book III.
Book IV.

MODERN ENGLISH GRAMMAR WITH CHAPTERS ON IDIOM AND CONSTRUCTION.   Globe 8vo.

This book is a reprint of Parts I and II of " English Grammar Past and Present."

Key to Modern English Grammar.

ORAL EXERCISES IN ENGLISH COMPOSITION.   Globe 8vo.

This book could be taught, if the teacher thinks fit, in conjunction with the " Outline of English Grammar " described before in Series I.

MACMILLAN AND CO. LTD., LONDON

JUNIOR COURSE OF ENGLISH COMPOSITION.
Globe 8vo.

This book leads the student by degrees to the composition of short narratives or essays. The last chapter deals with letter-writing—private, commercial, and official.

SENIOR COURSE OF ENGLISH COMPOSITION.
Globe 8vo.

This book is in continuation of the preceding. After dealing with the Structure of Sentences and Paragraphs, it gives a series of lessons and exercises in narration, description, reflection, exposition, and argumentation.

Key to Senior Course of English Composition.

ERRORS IN ENGLISH COMPOSITION. Globe 8vo.

The errors dealt with in this book are of five different kinds—errors in Grammar, in Construction, in the Order of words, in Prepositions, and in Conjunctions. Part II contains a solution of the examples given in Part I, which the student may consult after he has tried his own hand at correction.

Series III.—ON GRAMMAR AND COMPOSITION COMBINED

ELEMENTARY LESSONS IN ENGLISH COMPOSITION, ORAL AND WRITTEN. Globe 8vo.

Book I (Stages I and II).   For the lower classes in
Book II (Stages III and IV).   Secondary Schools.
Book III (Stages V, VI, and   For the middle classes in
VII).   Secondary Schools.

In each of these books composition is taught on the basis of Grammar. Some of the lessons are intended to be oral, others written.

MACMILLAN AND CO. LTD., LONDON

MANUAL OF ENGLISH GRAMMAR AND COMPOSITION. Globe 8vo.

This book contains a fairly complete account of Accidence, Parsing, and Analysis, the enlargement of the vocabulary by metaphor and metonymy, and the use of prefixes and suffixes. Under the heading of Composition it deals with the order of words, the structure of sentences, emphasis, purity of diction, propriety, perspicuity, simplicity, brevity, and elegance.

AIDS TO THE STUDY AND COMPOSITION OF ENGLISH. Globe 8vo.

This book is not only more complete, but it represents a higher standard than any of those preceding it. The aim of this book, stated in the fewest words, is to help the student in the study of English language, in the practice of English composition, and in the study of English literature.

MATRICULATION ENGLISH COURSE. Globe 8vo.

This book is called "Matriculation English Course," because it is mainly adapted to the Matriculation Standard of the London and Provincial Universities ; but it also covers the ground of the Oxford Senior Local, the Cambridge Senior Local, the College of Preceptors First Class, the Central Welsh Board, and the School Leaving Certificates of Scotland and elsewhere.

MACMILLAN AND CO. LTD., LONDON